AMERICA IN
1876

BY LALLY WEYMOUTH/DESIGNED BY MILTON GLASER

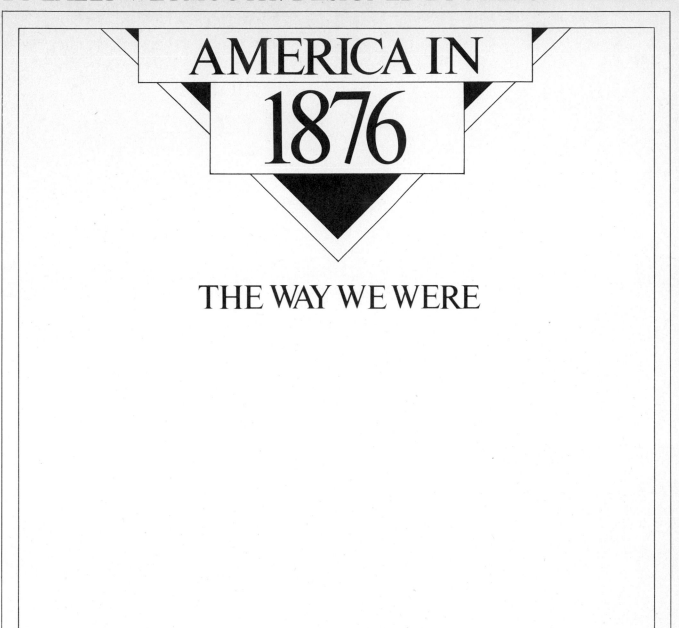

AMERICA IN
1876

THE WAY WE WERE

RANDOM HOUSE
NEW YORK

Copyright © 1976 by Lally Weymouth and Milton Glaser
All rights reserved under International and Pan-American Copyright Conventions.
Published in the United States by Random House, Inc., New York,
and simultaneously in Canada by Random House of Canada Limited, Toronto.

Library of Congress Cataloging in Publication Data

Weymouth, Lally.
America in 1876.
Bibliography: p.
1. United States—History—1865-1898.
I. Glaser, Milton, joint author: II. Title.
E661.W47   1976b   973.8'2   75-40547
ISBN 0-394-40247-2

Manufactured in the United States of America
First Edition   2   4   6   8   9   7   5   3

AMERICA IN
1876

CONTENTS

ACKNOWLEDGMENTS

We would like to thank a few of the people who helped us with this book: Mr. Weston Naef for the use of his magnificent collection of stereo cards and for large amounts of his time; Mr. John Winthrop Aldrich for the use of the Rokeby picture collection; Mrs. Vincent Astor, Mr. John Richardson, Mr. and Mrs. R. Thornton Wilson, Mr. Harry Lunn, Mr. Chauncey Stillman, Mr. W. Averell Harriman, Mr. Louis Auchincloss, Mr. Clendenin Ryan, Mr. Paul Mellon and J. & W. Seligman and Co. for generously lending pictures; Mr. Silvio Bedini for his help and for making the pictures of the Smithsonian Institution available.

We would also like to thank Peter Mollman, David Rivchin, Susan Child, Barbara Willson, Charlotte Staub, Ellen Vanook, Freddie Templeton, Linda Gemmell, Carol Anderson and Adrienne Dolgin of Random House, and Sheldon Lewis, Prudence Carlson, Marion Lister, Louise Mayo, Irene Javors, Diane Hamilton and Katherine Kreusi for their work.

Arthur Schlesinger, Jr., Walker Cowen and Sheldon Hackney were extremely kind. Thanks to: Sam and Ken Schatten for making their research on the election of 1876 available to us and to Timothy Dickinson for suggestions and for reading the manuscript. We are especially grateful to George Trow for suggestions, encouragement and endless help.

Thanks also to Diana Vreeland, Ashton Hawkins, Annette Reed, Preston Brown, Katharine Weymouth, Pamela Weymouth, Katharine Graham, Donald Graham, Stephen Graham, Paula Schmid and Isabel Pamplona.

Special thanks to both Ferle Bramson, who typed most of the manuscript and put the most incredible effort into this project, and to Sheila Selden, who worked so hard on the layout.

And last but not least, thanks to our editor, Jason Epstein.

Lally Weymouth and Milton Glaser

INTRODUCTION

The United States in 1876 had come a long way since its foundation. Its population had grown from 2.5 million to 46 million. By 1876 there were thirty-eight states, stretching from the Atlantic to the Pacific. There were 35,000 miles of railroad track, and passengers and freight traveled regularly from California to New York. By 1876 America was well on its way to becoming an industrial power. Behind it lay a Civil War in which over half a million people had died, and behind, too, lay the era of Reconstruction and the moral crusades for social equality for black Americans. Ahead lay the era of trusts and the robber barons.

The Centennial year was itself crowded with great incidents. It was the year that Sitting Bull and his Sioux followers slaughtered General Custer and his troops at the Battle of Little Big Horn—a brief victory for the Indians but in the long term merely an episode in the conquest of the West by white Americans. 1876 was also the year of the disputed presidential election between Democratic Governor Samuel J. Tilden of New York and Republican Governor Rutherford B. Hayes of Ohio. Tilden won a majority of the popular vote, but after four months of intricate political maneuvers and fraud, Hayes entered the White House, triumphant by one electoral vote, in a bargain that spelled the final end to Reconstruction. The Greenback party had a strong candidate in the election of 1876: Peter Cooper. He received 80,000 votes from citizens who were suffering from the severe depression which had begun in 1873 and still had not ended three years later.

Despite the depression, the industrial explosion was creating vast new fortunes. The Astors were the undisputed leaders of New York society; they had already accumulated a vast fortune from urban real estate and were just starting to spend it with an extravagance never seen before in this country. The reverse side of the industrial adventure was the violence and exploitation symbolized by the Molly Maguires, Irish immigrant laborers in the anthracite coal fields of Pennsylvania. In 1876 a Pennsylvania judge ordered the execution of twenty Molly Maguires, who were accused of murdering their bosses. The corruption of the Grant Administration produced a more widespread bitterness, a feeling that the Republic was already contaminated—that it now belonged to the rich and powerful. An opposing feeling of nostalgia for the days of innocence no doubt helped to speed the enormous popularity of *The Adventures of Tom Sawyer*—Mark Twain's elegy to American boyhood and pre–Civil War rural life, which was published in 1876.

And 1876 was the year of the great Centennial Exhibition at Fairmount Park in Philadelphia. Millions of Americans traveled there to see for the first time Alexander Graham Bell's telephone, and gallery after gallery crammed with American and foreign artifacts and commodities: everything from Iowa soil, displayed in glass tubes, to one arm of the Statue of Liberty—

given by France in that year—to plows, jewelry, industrial machinery, domestic appliances and even a white hearse and a display of artificial teeth.

Most popular of all the exhibits was the 1,500-horsepower Corliss engine, dominating Machinery Hall. William Dean Howells viewed it along with millions of his fellow Americans and wrote exaltedly: "The Corliss engine does not lend itself to description; its personal acquaintance must be sought by those who would understand its vast and almost silent grandeur..."

The Corliss engine was the most potent symbol of the Centennial Exhibition; it represented the new technology and industrial might which would produce America's wealth.

Wealth was the obsession of the age. In New York the rich began to plan fine new mansions, copied from European castles and palaces. All across the country older immigrants, editorialists and politicians raised the alarm about how this wealth was being amassed: on the backs of cheap labor, wretchedly poor immigrants pouring in from the Old World and—fewer but more despised—from China.

I have tried to show what America was like in 1876 through the writings, photographs and paintings of the period. It was impossible to keep strictly within the framework of those twelve months. Edith Wharton, for example, observed as a child the life of rich New Yorkers in the mid-1870's and only recorded her impressions many years later. And it was also much later that Mrs. Custer recorded her emotions upon hearing the news of her husband's death at the Battle of Little Big Horn. I have used whatever source seemed most useful or interesting to illustrate and explain what was going on in the 1870's and in the Centennial year itself.

My hope had been that one hundred years later, Americans will be interested to see what their forefathers thought they had accomplished and what their expectations were; what was wrong with America and what was right. We are nearer to them in historical affinity than they were to their ancestors who had founded the Republic. By 1876 Americans were embarked on the industrial era, proclaiming infinite possibilities for each worthy individual. A hundred years later we can understand such ecstasies if no longer believe in them with such fervor.

Lally Weymouth

"...the problem of the future of America is in certain respects as dark as it is vast.
Pride, competition, segregation, vicious wilfulness, and license beyond example brood already upon us.
Unwieldy and immense, who shall hold in behemoth? who bridle leviathan?
Flaunt it as we choose, athwart and over the roads of our progress loom huge uncertainty,
and dreadful threatening gloom. It is useless to deny it:
Democracy grows rankly up the thickest, noxious, deadliest plants and fruits of all
—brings worse and worse invaders
—needs newer, larger, stronger, keener compensations and compellers."

Walt Whitman, Democratic Vistas

PHOTO CREDITS

I   THE EXHIBITION OF 1876

Bird's Eye View of the Centennial Buildings, pp. 12-13, Courtesy of the Library of Congress.

Centennial Opening–The Orators, p. 16. Collection of the Free Library of Philadelphia.

Ulysses S. Grant, p. 17, Courtesy of the Library of Congress.

W.D. Howells, from a painting by E.P. Vinton, p. 22. Courtesy of the New York Public Library, Astor, Lenox and Tilden Foundations.

Centennial Encampment, p. 22. Courtesy of the Mary and Weston Naef Collection of Stereographs.

The Centennial Exposition–The Art Gallery, p. 23. Courtesy of the Mary and Weston Naef Collection of Stereographs.

Interior–Art Gallery, p. 24. Courtesy of the Mary and Weston Naef Collection of Stereographs.

Portrait of Professor Gross, by Thomas Eakins, p. 25. Courtesy of Jefferson Medical College, Thomas Jefferson University.

Interior of Machinery Hall, p. 26. Collection of the Free Library of Philadelphia.

Alexander Graham Bell, p. 28. Courtesy of the Library of Congress.

The Main Building, p. 29. Collection of the Free Library of Philadelphia.

Centennial Bock Bier, by Currier & Ives, p. 34. Courtesy of the Library of Congress.

Café do Brazil, p. 34. Collection of the Free Library of Philadelphia.

Kindergarten Building, p. 36. Courtesy of the Mary and Weston Naef Collection of Stereographs.

Dreaming Iolante, p. 37. Courtesy of the Mary and Weston Naef Collection of Stereographs.

Interior of Agricultural Hall, p. 39. Courtesy of the Mary and Weston Naef Collection of Stereographs.

Old Mammoth Grape Vine, p. 39. Courtesy of the Mary and Weston Naef Collection of Stereographs.

Temperance Fountain, p. 42. Collection of the Free Library of Philadelphia.

One Hundred Years Old, pp. 46-47. Courtesy of the Library of Congress.

II   THE WESTERN EMPIRE

Thomas Moran, Chasm of the Colorado, pp. 48-49. Department of Interior.

General George Armstrong Custer, p. 51. Courtesy of the Library of Congress.

George A. Custer with Scout Bloody, Private Noonan and Capt. Ludlow, p. 52. Courtesy of the Library of Congress.

Custer's Last Charge–Currier & Ives, p. 53. Courtesy of the Library of Congress.

Sitting Bull, p. 55. Courtesy of the Library of Congress.

General and Mrs. Custer and Tom Custer, the General's Brother, p. 56. Courtesy of the Library of Congress.

Scene of Custer's Last Stand, p. 60. U.S. Army Signal Corps No. 111-sc-28966, The National Archives.

Battle of Little Big Horn, p. 62. Courtesy of the Library of Congress.

H. Steinegger, General Custer's Death Struggle, p. 63. Courtesy of the Library of Congress.

John Mulvany, Custer's Last Rally, p. 62. Courtesy of Memphis Pink Palace Museum.

Sioux Drawing of the Battle of Little Big Horn, p. 63. Smithsonian Institution, National Anthropological Archives.

Custer's Last Charge, by Feodor Fuchs, pp. 64-65. Courtesy of the Library of Congress.

Monument at Custer's Last Stand, p. 66. The National Archives.

Life Among the Navajos in New Mexico. p. 66. Princeton Collections of Western Americans, Princeton University Library.

Crow Indian Burial Ground, by F.J. Haynes, p. 67. Courtesy of the Mary and Weston Naef Collection of Stereographs.

Sitting Bull's Deserted Tepee, by F.J. Haynes, p. 67. Courtesy of the Mary and Weston Naef Collection of Stereographs.

Young Apache Warrior and His Squaw, Near Camp Apache, Arizona, p. 68. Courtesy of the Mary and Weston Naef Collection of Stereographs.

Lost River Murderers, by L. Heller, p. 68. Courtesy of the Mary and Weston Naef Collection of Stereographs.

Interior of a Pueblo Indian Home, p. 69. Princeton Collections of Western Americans, Princeton University Library.

Apache Squaw and Papoose, by T.H. O'Sullivan, p. 69. Courtesy of the Mary and Weston Naef Collection of Stereographs.

Apache Braves Ready for the Trail, Arizona, by T.H. O'Sullivan, p. 70. Courtesy of the Mary and Weston Naef Collection of Stereographs.

Los Pueblos de Taos, by W.H. Jackson, p. 71. Courtesy of the Mary and Weston Naef Collection of Stereographs.

Railroad Tracks, by W.H. Jackson, p. 72. Courtesy of Mary and Weston Naef Collection of Stereographs.

East Meets West: The Joining of the Union Pacific and Central Pacific Transcontinental Railroad, p. 73. Courtesy of the Library of Congress.

Train Station, Western Pacific Railroad, p. 74. Courtesy of the Mary and Weston Naef Collection of Stereographs.

Luxurious Dinner Party on Board the Pullman Palace Car "Cosmopolitan," Western Pacific Railroad, wood engraving, p. 75. Courtesy of the Mary and Weston Naef Collection.

An Interior View of the Silver Palace Car, Central Pacific Railroad, p. 75. Courtesy of the Mary and Weston Naef Collection of Stereographs.

The Savage Mine, by T.H. O'Sullivan, pp. 76-77. Courtesy of the Mary and Weston Naef Collection.

U.S. Geological Survey Team en Route, by W.H. Jackson, p. 78. The National Archives.

Valley of the Yosemite, by Eadweard Muybridge, p. 79. Courtesy of the Mary and Weston Naef Collection.

The Windmill at Laramie, by A.J. Russell, p. 79. Courtesy of the Print Department, Boston Public Library.

Horse and Rider in Motion, by Eadweard Muybridge, pp. 80-81. The Metropolitan Museum of Art, Harris Brisbane Dick Fund, 1946.

Green River, Colorado, by T.H. O'Sullivan, p. 80. Courtesy of the Library of Congress.

Ancient Ruins in the Canyon de Chelle, New Mexico, by T.H. O'Sullivan, p. 81. Courtesy of the Library of Congress.

The Flying Studio, by Eadweard Muybridge, p. 82. Courtesy of The Bancroft Library.

Salt Lake City, by C.E. Watkins, p. 82. Courtesy of the Utah State Historical Society.

"Taking Breath," p. 82. Rare Book Division, The New York Public Library (Astor, Lenox and Tilden Foundations).

Cactus, by T.H. O'Sullivan, p. 83. Courtesy of the Mary and Weston Naef Collection.

A Mormon Family, Great Salt Lake, by A.J. Russell, pp. 84-85. Courtesy of the Print Department, Boston Public Library.

III   WASHINGTON

The Senate Chamber, p. 92. Courtesy of the Library of Congress.

Section through Dome of U.S. Capitol, p. 93. Courtesy of the Library of Congress.

Arlington House, Arlington, Va., p. 94. Courtesy of the Mary and Weston Naef Collection of Stereographs.

James Russell Lowell, p. 95. The Metropolitan Museum of Art, Bequest of Charles A. Munn, 1924.

Sir Edward Thornton, p. 96. The Metropolitan Museum of Art, David Hunter McAlpin Fund, 1966.

Roscoe Conkling as Senator from New York, p. 96. Courtesy of the New-York Historical Society.

James G. Blaine, p. 96. Courtesy of the New-York Historical Society.

The Blue Room in the President's House, p. 97. Courtesy of the Mary and Weston Naef Collection of Stereographs.

The Green Room in the President's House, p. 97. Courtesy of the Mary and Weston Naef Collection of Stereographs.

The East Room in the President's House, p. 97. Courtesy of the Mary and Weston Naef Collection of Stereographs.

Reception at the White House, p. 100. Smithsonian Institution.

President Rutherford B. Hayes, p. 107. Courtesy of the Library of Congress.

Mrs. Rutherford B. Hayes, p. 109. Courtesy of the Library of Congress.

Nast Cartoon: Mulligan Letters, p. 111. Courtesy of the Library of Congress.

Patent Office, p. 112. Courtesy of Lunn Gallery/Graphics International Ltd., Washington, D.C.

Conservatory–Agricultural Department, p. 114. Courtesy of Lunn Gallery/Graphics International Ltd., Washington, D.C.

Smithsonian Institution, p. 114. Courtesy of Lunn Gallery/Graphics International Ltd., Washington, D.C.

Agricultural Department, p. 114. Courtesy of Lunn Gallery/Graphics International Ltd., Washington, D.C.

State Department, p. 115. Courtesy of Lunn Gallery/Graphics International Ltd., Washington, D.C.

Treasury, p. 115. Courtesy of Lunn Gallery/Graphics International Ltd., Washington, D.C.

IV   THE STOLEN ELECTION OF 1876

Grand National Republican Banner, Currier & Ives, 1876, p. 116. Courtesy of the Library of Congress.

National Democratic Chart, 1876, p. 117. Courtesy of the Library of Congress.

Republican National Convention Ticket, p. 119. Smithsonian Institution.

Samuel J. Tilden, p. 120. Courtesy of the Library of Congress.

Woman's Suffrage, January 2, 1877, p. 121. Courtesy of the Library of Congress.

Elizabeth Cady Stanton and Susan B. Anthony, p. 122. Smithsonian Institution.

General Sickles, p. 123. Courtesy of the Library of Congress.

Tilden and Hendricks Have Been Elected and Shall Be Inaugurated, Badge, p. 124. Ralph E. Becker Collection, Smithsonian Institution.

Hayes Lantern, p. 126. Ralph E. Becker Collection, Smithsonian Institution.

Tilden and Hendricks Lantern, p. 127. Ralph E. Becker Collection, Smithsonian Institution.

Wade Hampton, p. 129. Courtesy of the Library of Congress.

New York City–a Characteristic Election Scene, p. 130. Courtesy of the Library of Congress.

South Carolina–a Rustic Election Scene, p. 130. Courtesy of the Library of Congress.

General Lew Wallace, p. 131. Picture Collection, The Branch Libraries, The New York Public Library.

Judge David Davis, p. 135. Picture Collection, The Branch Libraries, The New York Public Library.

The Electoral Commission in Session, p. 136. Courtesy of the Library of Congress, Collection of the Architect of the Capitol.

Judge Joseph P. Bradley, p. 136. Picture Collection, The Branch Libraries, The New York Public Library.

Abram S. Hewitt, p. 137. Picture Collection, The Branch Libraries, The New York Public Library.

Tilden and Hendricks Reform Songs for the Centennial Campaign of 1876, p. 137. Ralph E. Becker Collection, Smithsonian Institution.

The Ten White Men and Two Negroes Who Defrauded the American People Out of Their Choice for President in 1876, p. 139. Courtesy of the Library of Congress.

"Governor Tilden Is Our Man," song sheet, p. 139. Ralph E. Becker Collection, Smithsonian Institution.

Inauguration of Rutherford B. Hayes, by Mathew Brady, pp. 140-141. Courtesy of the Library of Congress.

Colonel Thomas A. Scott, p. 141. Picture Collection, The Branch Libraries, The New York Public Library.

Rutherford B. Hayes, p. 142. Courtesy of the Library of Congress.

V   THE PLIGHT OF THE POOR

In the Land of Promise: Castle Garden, by Charles Ulrich, pp. 144-145. In the Collection of the Corcoran Gallery of Art.

Emigrants on Shipboard, p. 150. Courtesy of the Library of Congress.

Between Decks in an Emigrant Ship–Feeding Time, p. 151. The Metropolitan Museum of Art, Harris Brisbane Dick Fund, 1928.

And We Open Our Arms to Them, p. 152. Courtesy of the Library of Congress.

New York City–Health Officers Vaccinating Russian and Polish Emigrants, p. 153. Courtesy of the Library of Congress.

Castle Garden: In the Old Erie Emigrant Days–a Scene Now Gone Forever, p. 156. Courtesy of The New York Public Library, Astor, Lenox and Tilden Foundations.

The Future Site of the Statue of Liberty, Lies Beyond Castle Garden, p. 157. Courtesy of The New York Public Library, Astor, Lenox and Tilden Foundations.

Emigrants Departing for the West, p. 157. Courtesy of the Library of Congress.

Chinese Children in California, ca. 1876, p. 160. Courtesy of the Mary and Weston Naef Collection of Stereographs.

The Chinese Agitation in San Francisco, a Meeting of the Workingmen's Party on the Sand Lots, p. 161. Courtesy of the Library of Congress.

Mark Twain, p. 162. Courtesy of the Library of Congress.

Chinese Sleeping Accommodations, p. 163. Courtesy of the Library of Congress.

Chinese Meat Market–San Francisco, California, by J.J. Reilly, p. 164. Courtesy of the Mary and Weston Naef Collection of Stereographs.

Interior, Chinese Restaurant, San Francisco, by Watkins, p. 164. Courtesy of the Mary and Weston Naef Collection of Stereographs.

Dennis Kearney, p. 167. Courtesy of the Library of Congress.

War Episodes: The Contraband, by Thomas Waterman

Wood, p. 170. The Metropolitan Museum of Art, Gift of Charles Stewart Smith, 1884.

Albion W. Tourgee, p. 171. Courtesy of the Library of Congress.

Robert Smalls, p. 173. Courtesy of the Library of Congress.

Sorting Cotton—St. Helena's Island, S.C., p. 174. Courtesy of the Mary and Weston Naef Collection of Stereographs.

Cotton Is King—A Plantation Scene, Georgia, p. 175. Courtesy of the Mary and Weston Naef Collection of Stereographs.

A Black School, p. 175. Courtesy of the Mary and Weston Naef Collection of Stereographs.

The New South, Family Circle, p. 178. Courtesy of the Mary and Weston Naef Collection of Stereographs.

Two Negro Boys, p. 178. Courtesy of the Mary and Weston Naef Collection of Stereogrpahs.

Visit of the Ku Klux Klan, p. 178. Courtesy of the Library of Congress.

Cotton Culture, p. 179. Courtesy of the Library of Congress.

The Carnival, by Winslow Homer, pp. 176-177. The Metropolitan Museum of Art, Lazarus Fund, 1922.

Down among "de Cotton," p. 179. Courtesy of the Mary and Weston Naef Collection of Stereographs.

Frederick Douglass, p. 180. Courtesy of the Library of Congress.

The First Colored Senator and Representatives, p. 180. Courtesy of the Library of Congress.

Heroes of the Colored Race, lithograph by J. Hoover, 1881, p. 181. Courtesy of the Library of Congress.

Hon. B.K. Bruce from Mississippi, p. 181. The Meserve Collection.

Booker T. Washington, p. 183. Courtesy of the Library of Congress.

Hampton Institute—the New Building, p. 182. Courtesy of the Library of Congress.

Primary School for Freedmen, in Charge of Mrs. Green, at Vicksburg, Miss., p. 184. Courtesy of the Library of Congress.

Five Points, ca. 1876, p.185. Courtesy of the Mary and Weston Naef Collection of Stereographs.

The Streets of New York—Running the Gauntlet of Horrors, p. 185. Courtesy of the Library of Congress.

New York City Police, ca. 1870, p. 188. Courtesy of the Museum of the City of New York.

Albany Orphan Asylum—Children, p. 190. Courtesy of the Mary and Weston Naef Collection of Stereographs.

Albany Orphan Asylum—Dining Room, p. 190. Courtesy of the Mary and Weston Naef Collection of Stereographs.

New York City Life—The Brutal Slave Punishing the Little Slave for Not Earning 75 Cents during the Day with the Violin, pp. 190-191. Courtesy of the Library of Congress.

Albany Orphan Asylum—Schoolroom, p. 191. Courtesy of the Mary and Weston Naef Collection of Stereographs.

Albany Orphan Asylum—Dormitory, p. 191. Courtesy of the Mary and Weston Naef Collection of Stereographs.

Cells and Passage in House of Correction, p. 194. Courtesy of the Mary and Weston Naef Collection of Stereographs.

Interior of the Tombs, p. 194. Courtesy of the Mary and Weston Naef Collection of Stereographs.

Forging the Shaft: A Welding Heat, by John F. Weir, p. 195. The Metropolitan Museum of Art, Gift of Lyman L. Bloomingdale, 1901.

Hat Manufactory, late 1870's, p. 196. Courtesy of the Mary and Weston Naef Collection of Stereographs.

Putnam Machine Company's Shop, p. 196. Courtesy of the Mary and Weston Naef Collection of Stereographs.

Interior of Factory, p. 196, Courtesy of the Mary and Weston Naef Collection of Stereographs.

National Eight-Hour Law, lithograph by J.J. Rey, 1870, p. 197. Courtesy of the Library of Congress.

Removing Bodies of Victims from the Mine, p. 203. Courtesy of the Library of Congress.

Samuel Gompers, p. 204. Courtesy of the Library of Congress.

The Great Strike—Burning at the Road-House at Pittsburgh, p. 205. Courtesy of the Library of Congress.

Baltimore & Ohio Railroad Strike, p. 206. Courtesy of the Library of Congress.

Terence Powderly, p. 207. Courtesy of the Library of Congress.

VI   THE GREAT AMERICAN FORTUNES

The William Astor Family, by Lucius Rossi, 1878, pp. 208-209. Courtesy of Mrs. Vincent Astor.

A.T. Stewart, p. 210. Picture Collection, The Branch Libraries, The New York Public Library.

Cornelius Vanderbilt, p. 210. Courtesy of the Library of Congress.

William B. Astor, by Eastman Johnson, p. 211. Collection of The New York Public Library, Astor, Lenox and Tilden Foundations.

John Jacob Astor, p. 211. Picture Collection, The Branch Libraries, The New York Public Library.

Rokeby, Front View, p. 212. Rokeby Collection, Courtesy of Richard Aldrich and Others, Barrytown, N.Y.

A.T. Stewart's Marble Mansion, N.W. 34th St. and 5th Ave.—1876, p. 215. Courtesy of Brown Brothers.

Commodore Cornelius Vanderbilt, 1876, p. 218. Picture Collection, The Branch Libraries, The New York Public Library.

Ruined—from Harper's Weekly Woodcut, p. 221. Courtesy of Mrs. Mildred Bright Minnigerode. Reprinted from Certain Rich Men, by Meade Minnigerode (G.P. Putnam's, 1927).

The New York Stock Exchange, p. 223. Courtesy of J. & W. Seligman & Co.

The Great Race for the Western Stakes, by Currier & Ives, p. 224. The Metropolitan Museum of Art, Bequest of Adele S. Colgate, 1963.

Colonel Jim Fisk, by Thomas Nast, 1866, p. 225. Courtesy of the Library of Congress.

Jay Gould, p. 228. Courtesy of J. & W. Seligman & Co.

American Railroad Scene, by Currier & Ives, p. 231. Courtesy of J. & W. Seligman & Co.

Wall Street, ca. 1876, p. 232. Courtesy of the Mary and Weston Naef Collection of Stereographs.

Jay Cooke, about 1879, p. 232. Picture Collection, The Branch Libraries, The New York Public Library.

August Belmont, p. 232. Picture Collection, The Branch Libraries, The New York Public Library.

Mrs. August Belmont, p. 233. Picture Collection, The Branch Libraries, The New York Public Library.

Joseph Seligman, p. 233. Courtesy of J. & W. Seligman & Co.

Jesse Seligman, p. 233. Courtesy of J. & W. Seligman & Co.

The Hatch Family, by Eastman Johnson, 1871, p. 234. The Metropolitan Museum of Art, Gift of Frederick H. Hatch.

J.P. Morgan in 1876, p. 234. Picture Collection, The Branch Libraries, The New York Public Library.

J.P. Morgan in Egypt, p. 235. Reprinted from J. Pierpont Morgan: An Intimate Portrait, by Herbert L. Satterlee (Macmillan, 1939). By permission.

James Stillman, p. 235. Courtesy of Mr. Chauncey Stillman.

Andrew W. Mellon, p. 235. Courtesy of Mr. Paul Mellon.

Jacob Schiff, p. 235. Courtesy of the American Jewish Archives.

E.H. Harriman, p. 236. Courtesy of Mr. W. Averell Harriman.

Henry Clay Frick at the Age of Twenty-five, p. 236. From Henry Clay Frick—The Man, by George Harvey (Scribner's, 1928).

The Frick Dollar Bill, p. 236. From Henry Clay Frick—The Man, by George Harvey (Scribner's, 1928).

Thomas Fortune Ryan, p. 236. Courtesy of Mr. Clendenin J. Ryan.

John D. Rockefeller as a Young Man, p. 237. Courtesy of the Rockefeller Family Archives.

John D. Rockefeller's House in Cleveland, p. 237. Courtesy of the Rockefeller Family Archives.

The Pennsylvania Oil Fields, p. 237. Courtesy of the Mary and Weston Naef Collection of Stereographs.

The Pennsylvania Oil Fields, p. 237. Courtesy of the Mary and Weston Naef Collection of Stereographs.

Andrew Carnegie, ca. 1878, p. 237. From The Autobiography of Andrew Carnegie. Copyright 1920, renewed 1948 by Margaret Carnegie Miller. Reprinted by permission of Houghton Mifflin Company.

Edgar Thomson Steel Works, p. 238. Carnegie Library of Pittsburgh.

Chicago after the Fire, July 1874, p. 238. Courtesy of J. & W. Seligman & Co.

Potter Palmer, p. 239. Courtesy of the Chicago Sun-Times.

Palmer House after the Fire, p. 239. Picture Collection, The Branch Libraries, The New York Public Library.

Mrs. Potter Palmer, p. 239. Courtesy of the Chicago Historical Society.

Marshall Field, p. 240. Courtesy of the Chicago Historical Society.

Marshall Field's Chicago Mansion, p. 240. Courtesy of the Chicago Historical Society.

Levi Leiter, p. 240. Courtesy of the Chicago Historical Society.

George Pullman, p. 240. Picture Collection, The Branch Libraries, The New York Public Library.

Philip Danforth Armour, p. 241. Courtesy of the Chicago Historical Society.

The McCormick Harvester & Wirebinder of 1876, p. 241. International Harvester Archives—Chicago.

Cyrus Hall McCormick, p. 241. International Harvester Archives—Chicago.

James G. Fair, p. 242. Courtesy of the Library of Congress.

John W. Mackay, p. 242. Picture Collection, The Branch Libraries, The New York Public Library.

Adolph H. Sutro, p. 242. Courtesy of J. & W. Seligman & Co.

The Palace Hotel, San Francisco, p. 243. Courtesy of the Mary and Weston Naef Collection of Stereographs.

The Interior of the Palace Hotel, San Francisco, p. 243. Courtesy of the Mary and Weston Naef Collection of Stereographs.

Three Gentlemen Relaxing in the Palace Hotel, p. 243. Courtesy of the Mary and Weston Naef Collection of Stereographs.

Darius Ogden Mills, p. 243. Courtesy of the Library of Congress.

William A. Clark: The Copper King, p. 244. Courtesy of the Library of Congress.

George Hearst, p. 244. Courtesy of the Library of Congress.

Collis P. Huntington, p. 244. Courtesy of the Library of Congress.

Mark Hopkins Residence, p. 244. Courtesy of the Mary and Weston Naef Collection of Stereographs.

Leland Stanford, p. 244. Courtesy of the Library of Congress.

Residence of Gov. Leland Stanford, p. 245. Courtesy of the Mary and Weston Naef Collection of Stereographs.

Stanford's Painting Purchases, p. 245. Courtesy of M. Knoedler & Co., Inc.

Residence of Charles Crocker, p. 245. Courtesy of the Mary and Weston Naef Collection of Stereographs.

Mr. and Mrs. Charles Crocker, 1876, p. 245. Picture Collection, The Branch Libraries, The New York Public Library.

James J. Hill, p. 246. Courtesy of the James J. Hill Reference Library—St. Paul Minn.

James B. Duke, p. 247. Courtesy of The Duke Endowment.

Edith Wharton, p. 248. From Edith Wharton, A Biography, by R.W. B. Lewis. (Harper & Row Publishers) Copyright © 1975 by William R. Tyler. Reprinted by permission of A. Watkins, Inc.

Caroline Astor, photo by Mora, p. 249. Courtesy of the New-York Historical Society.

Ward McAllister, p. 250. Courtesy of Brown Brothers.

Portrait of Caroline Astor, by Carolus Duran, p. 251. Courtesy of Mr. R. Thornton Wilson, Jr.

William Astor, ca. 1876, p. 251. Rokeby Collection, Courtesy of Richard Aldrich and Others, Barrytown, N.Y.

Home of Mr. and Mrs. William Astor, 350 Fifth Avenue, p. 251. Courtesy of Mr. R. Thornton Wilson, Jr.

Mr. John Jacob Astor III, p. 252. Rokeby Collection, Courtesy of Richard Aldrich and Others, Barrytown, N.Y.

Mrs. John Jacob Astor III, p. 252. Rokeby Collection, Courtesy of Richard Aldrich and Others, Barrytown, N.Y.

The Rules of Conduct That Govern Good Society, p. 252. Courtesy of the Library of Congress.

At the Opera. 1874, p. 253. Courtesy of Brown Brothers.

Ward McAllister, by Thomas Nast, p. 255. Courtesy of the Library of Congress.

Mrs. Wm. Astor in Ball-Dress, ca. 1875, p. 255. Rokeby Collection, Courtesy of Richard Aldrich and Others, Barrytown, N.Y.

Delmonico's—1876—26th St. and 5th Ave., p. 256. Courtesy of Brown Brothers.

Lorenzo Delmonico, p. 257. Courtesy of Brown Brothers.

The Metropolitan Museum of Art Before Its Move Uptown, 128 West 14th St. ca. 1874-1879, p. 258. The Metropolitan Museum of Art.

The Metropolitan Museum of Art—5th Ave. at 82nd St., p. 259. The Metropolitan Museum of Art.

First Dinner of the Coaching Club, p. 260. Courtesy of The Coaching Club.

Lawn Tennis, p. 260. Reprinted from J. Pierpont Morgan: An Intimate Portrait, by Herbert L. Satterlee (Macmillan, 1939). By permission.

The Music Lesson, by John George Brown, 1870, p. 260. The Metropolitan Museum of Art. Gift of Col. Charles A. Fowler, 1921.

Col. DeLancey Kane's Schedule for his New York–New Rochelle Trip, p. 261. Courtesy of The Coaching Club.

Original Members of the Coaching Club, Gordon Bennett, p. 262. Courtesy of The Coaching Club.

Original Members of The Coaching Club, Frederic Bronson, p. 262. Courtesy of The Coaching Club.

Original members of The Coaching Club, William P. Douglas, p. 262. Courtesy of The Coaching Club.

Leaving the Brunswick Hotel, Col. DeLancey Kane, Coachman, p. 262. Courtesy of The Coaching Club.

Col. DeLancey Kane's Coach, "Tally-Ho." p. 263. Courtesy of The Coaching Club.

Original Members of The Coaching Club, William Jay, p.

(continued on page 320)

THE EXHIBITION OF 1876

"The Centennial Exhibition will be a grand event in our national history, and in every way worthy of the people whose progress in the arts, sciences, and industries will be shown in the various departments," boasted one of *Harper's Weekly*'s correspondents.

On May 10, 1876, President Grant opened the Centennial Exhibition in Philadelphia. For seven months it was visited, amid expressions of extraordinary enthusiasm, by literally millions of people. In the single month of October, just over two and a half million people poured through the turnstiles. By November 10, the day the Exhibition closed, over eight million visitors had come and paid fifty cents each. Almost another two million had enjoyed free admission.

Transports of wonderment and applause filled magazines and newspapers of the time. "It is impossible to describe it," wrote a correspondent of *The Cultivator and Country Gentleman.* "Nothing but seeing it

Bird's-eye View, Centennial Buildings
To pay for the almost two hundred buildings that were built for the exhibition and to pay for the cost of the event itself, a Centennial Board of Finance was created on June 1, 1872. The board was given the power "to raise a capital stock, which was fixed at $10,000,000, one quarter of which was readily taken up in subscription shares of $50, mostly by the citizens of Philadelphia," according to *Harper's Weekly*. "Besides the private subscriptions, appropriations of $500,000 in 1875 and $1,500,000, in the following session were made by Congress as an advance loan, while the city of Philadelphia appropriated $1,500,000, the State of Pennsylvania, $1,000,000, and other States and Territories various lesser amounts."

Arm of the Statue of Liberty
The arm of the future Statue of Liberty was
given to America by France in 1876 and put
on display at the Centennial. The future
statue was supposedly to have three arms,
each holding a light.

with your own eyes can give you any conception of its
magnitude. Suffice it to say that everything that was grand,
beautiful, useful and ludicrous is there, not only from our
own beloved land, but from every nation I ever heard of
and some I have not heard of."

Over thirty foreign countries sent contributions to
the Exhibition, and potentates of nations as far afield as
Brazil traveled to Philadelphia. All observers saw the
Exhibition as a triumphant benchmark of American
progress. President Grant himself summed it up when he
said, "One hundred years ago our country was new and
but partially settled. Our necessities have compelled us to
chiefly expend our means and time in felling forests,
subduing prairies, building dwellings, factories, ships,
docks...roads, canals, machinery, etc.... Burdened by
these great primal works of necessity which could not be
delayed, we have yet done what this exhibition will
show in rivalling older and more advanced nations in
law, medicine and theology, in science, literature and the
fine arts." Grant might have added that the Exhibition
was also a proclamation of America's rapidly growing
industrial might. The centerpiece of Machinery Hall and
the most popular exhibit was the Corliss engine. William
Dean Howells reserved his most eloquent prose for a
description of it, rising "loftily in the center of the huge
structure, an athlete of steel and iron with not a super-
fluous ounce of metal on it; the mighty walking-beams
plunge their pistons downward, the enormous fly-wheel
revolves with a hoarded power that makes all tremble,
the hundred life-like details do their office with unerring
intelligence."

If the Exhibition was an expression of America's
potential and of its industrial dreams, it was also, more
crudely, a shot in the arm for a nation still in the midst of a
depression. Referring to the Exhibition, James D. McCabe
noted in his *Illustrated History of the Centennial Exhibition,* published in 1876, that "An immediate gain·is the
modification of the rigors of the prevalent hard times.
Undoubtedly the setting in motion of millions of people,
each with money to spend, has had an effect in breaking
the lethargy that has stifled enterprise in the business
world and in causing the hopeful beginnings of a revival of
trade..."

Exhibitions and trade fairs have become, in the latter

half of the twentieth century, no great occasions of surprise and astonishment. In 1876 things were very different. The Exhibition was at once a festival and an assertion of national pride and purpose. One reviewer rose to heights of exaltation in his analysis of what the Exhibition accomplished. He foresaw, throughout the country a "substitution...of useful and entertaining conversation about things for the thoughtless scandal about people that is so prevalent in many social circles." Beyond that he saw America's international reputation vastly enhanced and, for each visitor, a transcending of "the narrow limits of his surroundings, so that his horizon stretched out to embrace the whole human race."

Map of Exhibition Grounds in Fairmount Park, Philadelphia

There were 450 acres of exhibits; 42 acres were devoted to agricultural machinery. *Harper's Weekly* said: "Let us give a word of advice to visitors. Before entering the grounds let them provide themselves with a good map... [so] one can find his way through the grounds without any difficulty, and with entire independence of guides and policemen."

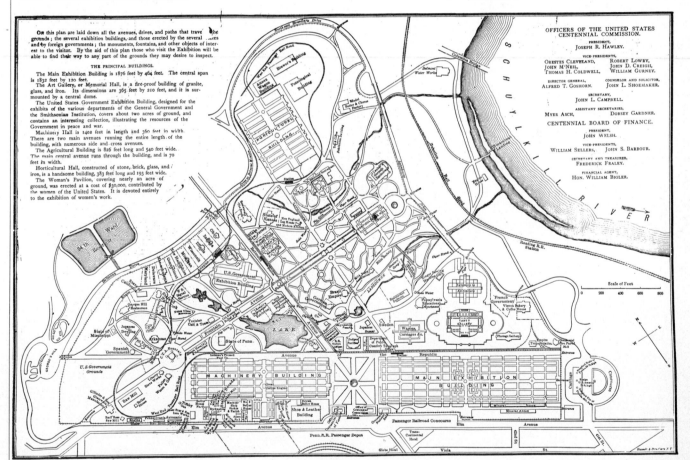

Program for the Opening Ceremonies, May 10, 1876

1. 10.15 A.M.—National Airs by the Orchestra.
2. 10.30—Arrival of the President of the United States.
3. Centennial Inauguration March, by Richard Wagner.
4. Prayer, by the Right Reverend Bishop Simpson.
5. Hymn, by John Greenleaf Whittier. Music, by John K. Paine, of Massachusetts. Organ and Orchestral accompaniment.
6. Presentation of the Buildings to the Commission by the President of the Centennial Board of Finance.
7. Cantata, by Sidney Lanier, of Georgia. Music, by Dudley Buck, of Connecticut.
8. Presentation of the Exhibition to the President of the United States by the President of the Centennial Commission.
9. Address by the President of the United States.
10. Unfurling of the flag, Hallelujah Chorus, Salutes of Artillery and Ringing of the Chimes.
11. Procession through the Main Building and Machinery Hall.
12. Reception by the President of the United States in the Judges' Pavilion.

Whittier's Centennial Hymn

The following hymn, written by John Greenleaf Whittier, was sung at the opening of the exhibition:

"Our fathers' God! from out whose hand
The centuries fall like grains of sand,
We meet to-day, united, free,
And loyal to our land and Thee,
To thank Thee for the era done,
And trust Thee for the opening one....

Be with us while the New World greets
The Old World, thronging all its streets,
Unveiling all the triumphs won
By art or toil beneath the sun;
And unto common good ordain
This rivalship of hand and brain....

For art and labor met in truce,
For beauty made the bride of use,
We thank Thee, while withal we crave
The austere virtues strong to save,
The honor proof to place or gold,
The manhood never bought or sold!

O! make Thou us, through centuries long,
In peace secure, and justice strong;
Around our gift of freedom draw
The safeguards of Thy righteous law,
And, cast in some diviner mould,
Let the new cycle shame the old!"

That Whittier was not present on May 10 to hear his hymn sung was no accident. He was not enthusiastic about the Exposition:
"The very thought of that Ezekial's vision of machinery and the nightmare confusion of the world's curiosity shop appalls me, and I shall not venture myself amidst it."

THE OPENING CEREMONY: MAY 10, 1876

Harper's Weekly reported that:

The International Exhibition of Arts, Manufactures, and Products of the Soil and Mine, to which the citizens of the United States had been looking forward with eager anticipation, was opened in Fairmount Park, Philadelphia, on the 10th of May, 1876.

The Fair...the sixth of the great World's Fairs and the first one held in this country, was also an anniversary exhibition of the country's progress in the hundredth year of its national existence.

The opening...was a grand and inspiring pageant, which every American may look back upon with patriotic pride and exultation. Philadelphia was crowded with strangers from all parts of the world...

The weather was propitious...At an early hour all the avenues leading to the Centennial grounds were crowded by thousands of eager people, and when the gates were opened, at nine o'clock, a dense but orderly mass of humanity was waiting at each of the entrances. The inflow at once began, but it was some time before any decrease was perceptible in the crowds outside...Every square foot of the room between the Main Building and Memorial Hall, except the parts marked for specified occupation, was covered by half past nine o'clock.

At a quarter past ten o'clock the ceremonies began with music...The police, assisted by the military, were scarcely able to keep the mass of people from crushing through the lines into the space reserved for invited guests. The unhappy spectators in the front row had a hard time of it between the police, who were pushing them back, and those behind them pushing forward. Over the vast sea of heads rose the two granite pedestals in front of Memorial Hall, upon each of which as many persons were standing as could find a foot-hold there; and several daring boys had climbed, in defiance of threatening policemen, upon the very backs of the winged horses that surmount the pedestals.

Meanwhile the invited guests, several thousand in number, were pouring in a constant stream through the Main Building into the reserved space. There was a picturesque commingling of nationalities and costumes never before witnessed in this country—Japanese and Chinese side by side with Europeans and Americans, French and Spanish officers in full uniform, Norwegians, Swedes, Germans, Congressmen, Senators, broadbrimmed Quakers, and fashionably attired ladies...Enthusiastic cheering greeted the appearance of famous personages as they were recognized by the waiting crowd....

President Grant made his appearance, and was received with hearty cheers. The President and the Emperor of Brazil conversed for a short time, and when...all had taken their seats, the orchestra played Wagner's "Centennial March"—a grand composition, worthy of the master and of the occasion. Bishop Simpson then invoked the Divine blessing, and on the conclusion of the prayer, Whittier's hymn was sung by a strong chorus, with organ and orchestral accompaniment. Enthusiastic cheering greeted the rendering of this noble hymn.

The cantata composed for the occasion, the words by Mr. Sidney Lanier, and the music by Mr. Dudley Buck, was then rendered with fine effect.

PRESIDENT GRANT SPOKE

"My Countrymen,—It has been thought appropriate, upon this Centennial occasion, to bring together in Philadelphia, for popular inspection, specimens of our attainments in the industrial and fine arts, and in literature, science, and philosophy, as well as in the great business of agriculture and of commerce.

"That we may the more thoroughly appreciate the excellences and deficiencies of our achievements, and also give emphatic expression to our earnest desire to cultivate the friendship of our fellow-members of this great family of nations, the enlightened agricultural, commercial, and manufacturing people of the world have been invited to send hither corresponding specimens of their skill to exhibit on equal terms in friendly competition with our own. To this invitation they have generously responded: for so doing we render them our hearty thanks.

"The beauty and utility of the contributions will this day be submitted to your inspection by the managers of this Exhibition. We are glad to know that a view of specimens of the skill of all nations will afford to you unalloyed pleasure, as well as yield to you a valuable practical knowledge of so many of the remarkable results of the wonderful skill existing in enlightened communities...While proud of what we have done, we regret that we have not done more...

"And now, fellow-citizens, I hope a careful examination of what is about to be exhibited to you will not only inspire you with a profound respect for the skill and taste of our friends from other nations, but also satisfy you with the attainments made by our own people during the past one hundred years...

"I declare the International Exhibition now open."

President Ulysses Simpson Grant
President Grant spoke at the opening ceremonies of the Centennial Exhibition on May 10, 1876.

The Crush on Opening Day

Mr. Fukui, Japanese commissioner to the exhibition, described the May 10 opening ceremony: "The first day crowds come like sheep, run here, run there, run everywhere, one man start, one thousand follow. Nobody can see anything, nobody can do anything. All rush, push, tear, shout, make plenty noise, say damn great many times, get very tired, and go home."

Dom Pedro, Emperor of Brazil

Dom Pedro, born in 1825, became Emperor of Brazil in July 1841 at the age of sixteen. "The emperor desires to travel as a private gentleman, and would prefer to lay aside altogether his official rank; but he will find it rather difficult to go about the country as plain Mr. Alcantara, when everybody knows him to be the ruler of a great nation," reported *Harper's Weekly*. Dom Pedro, "a close and intelligent observer, always seeks to make his travels of use for the improvement of his own country. His reign has been an era of uninterrupted prosperity for a land previously distracted by factions and petty civil wars and revolutions. Since his accession to the throne the Brazilians have made great advances in civilization and social and material development."

Dom Pedro was described as ruler of "elevated character," whose "enlightened views of government are so well known that popular demonstrations of respect can scarcely be avoided."

PRESIDENT GRANT AND DOM PEDRO STARTED THE CORLISS ENGINE

The Corliss engine was the most popular exhibit at the Exhibition. The 1,500-horsepower engine provided the power to operate all of the machinery in Machinery Hall. A reporter in *Harper's Weekly* vividly described Dom Pedro, the Emperor of Brazil, and President Grant starting the giant engine on the opening day of the exhibition:

Marching up one of the avenues, escorted by the City Guard of Philadelphia, the two "observed of all observers" reached the steps leading to the platform of the great Corliss engine, where Mr. Corliss stood bareheaded awaiting them. The President and...the Emperor ascended the steps and cordially greeted the hero of the day. Mr. Corliss...stationed the President at the left throttle-valve and the Emperor at the right. It does not happen often in a man's existence to station two rulers of such nations at their posts to await his word of command.

"Are you both ready? Then your Majesty will turn that handle." A sound of a rush of steam; the great walking-beam is seen to move. "Now, Mr. President, yours." The sound of steam is multiplied, and the other engine joins in the work. Soon...the engine takes its regular rate. The sounds of planing, stamping, turning, and the whir of wheels make a chorus to the murmur of the bevel-gear of the underground shafting—and the opening ceremonies are complete.

President Grant and Dom Pedro Starting the Corliss Engine at the Opening of the Exhibition, May 10, 1876

Harper's Weekly *reported that "The Emperor of Brazil is in the ascendant so far as having made the best Centennial joke is concerned. On learning the number of revolutions per minute of the great Corliss engine at the Philadelphia Exposition, he said, 'That beats our South American republics.'"*

William Dean Howells

"Nobody writes a finer and purer English than Motley, Howells, Hawthorne, and Holmes," wrote Mark Twain.

Makeshift Lodgings for Exhibition Guests

On May 4, 1876, the Centennial Commission assured citizens that there was room for all in Philadelphia: "The city hotels can entertain about 15,000 guests above the present occupancy; the Centennial Lodginghouse Agency, 20,000; accommodations by relatives and friends, 40,000; boarding-houses, 13,000; Patrons of Husbandry (for Grangers), 5,000; Camp Scott (for military organizations), 5,000; camp in Fairmount Park (for military), 5,000; suburban hotels, 20,000.

"...Philadelphia and her citizens have spent millions in preparing for the reception and care of guests. There is no disposition or evidence of extortion. Increased business at usual rates is considered sufficient compensation for the vast amount of capital and labor expended. Living is as cheap, if not cheaper, than in any large city in America. Accommodations are unsurpassed. All grades of society can be accommodated..."

J. R. Hawley, President, the United States Centennial Commission

ONE VISITOR'S VIEW OF THE EXHIBITION

In 1876 thirty-nine-year-old William Dean Howells was the editor of the *Atlantic Monthly*. He had already published a book of poems, a campaign biography of Lincoln, and several novels. When he died in 1920, he had written over a hundred novels, including probably his most famous work, *The Rise of Silas Lapham*. In the *Atlantic Monthly* in July 1876, Howells wrote "A Sennight of the Centennial"—an account of his seven-day visit to the Centennial Exhibition. In the article Howells compared America's achievements to those of other countries. He especially admired American machinery, although he warned his readers of its potential dangers.

A SENNIGHT OF THE CENTENNIAL, BY WILLIAM DEAN HOWELLS

The Centennial is what every one calls the great fair now open at Philadelphia. "Have you been at the Centennial?" "How do you like the Centennial?" The English...called the first international exhibition the World's Fair. But this simple and noble name does not quite serve for us, since our World's Fair means the commemoration of our hundredth national anniversary; and so, Centennial is the best name....

We may...suppose that one's acquaintance with the Centennial is to be most fortunately formed upon a dull, drizzling day, somewhat cold and thoroughly unpleasant, like the 17th of May, for example. On that day, a week after the opening of the show, the first impression was certainly that of disorder and incompleteness, and the Centennial had nothing to do but to grow upon the visitor's liking. The paths were broken and unfinished, and the tough, red mud of the roads was tracked over the soft asphalt into all the buildings. Carts employed in the construction came and went everywhere, on easy terms alike with the trains of the circular railway whose engines hissed and hooted at points above the confusion, and with the wheel-chairs in which ladies, huddling their skirts under their umbrellas, were trundled back and forth among the freight cars of the Pennsylvania Railroad. At many points laborers were digging over the slopes of the grounds and vigorously slapping the sides of the claying embankments with the flat of their spades; and ironical sign-boards in all directions ordered you to keep off the grass on spaces apparently dedicated to the ceramic arts forever. Even if these grassless spots had been covered with tender herbage, there seemed not enough people present to justify the vigilance that guarded them; but I think this was an illusion, to which the vastness of the whole area and its irregular shape and surface contributed. There were probably fifteen thousand visitors that day, but many thousands more dispersed over the grounds...would have given nowhere the impression of a crowd....

From day to day the crowd sensibly increased, but it never struck one as a crowd, and it hardly ever incommoded one, except perhaps in the narrow corridors of the Art Hall, and the like passages of the Annex to that building; these were at times really thronged.

If we had been the most methodical of sight-seers we could hardly have systematized our observations on a first day...We wandered quite aimlessly about from one building to another, and, if we ever had anything definite in view, gave ourselves the agreeable surprise of arriving at something altogether different. Nevertheless from these desultory adventures some distinct impressions remained,—such, namely, as that of a great deal of beauty in the architecture. The Agricultural Hall we did not see till next day, and we therefore did not see what I believe is considered the best of the temporary structures; but the Main Building has a lightness, in spite of its huge extent, which is as near grace as it might hope to come; and the Machinery Hall has the beauty of a most admirable fitness for its purpose.

THE ART HALL

The show of sculpture within seems to have been almost entirely left to the countrymen of Michelangelo, who are here reposing, for the most part, upon his laurels. One of them has posted in the most conspicuous place in the rotunda his conception of Washington,—Washington perched on an eagle much too small for him. The group is in plaster; the eagle life-size and the Washington some six feet high from the middle up; having no occasion for legs in the attitude chosen, Washington thriftily dispenses with them. The poor man who made this thing is so besotted with it as to have placarded his other works, "By the sculptor of the Washington." This is not his fault, perhaps, and I am not so sure after all that his Washington is as bad as the bronze statue of Emancipation, a most offensively Frenchy negro, who has broken his

The Rush for Rooms at the Philadelphia Hotels

The Art Building
The Art Building, designed "in the modern Renaissance style," was intended as a permanent monument and gallery of art, and it is today the Philadelphia Museum of Fine Arts.

A Centennial Shine
"'A Centennial Shine' will appeal to the feelings of everyone who has tramped for an hour or two over the avenues of the Exhibition grounds... A Philadelphia contemporary admits that, 'The walks show spots that, like the celebrated blood stains upon Lady Macbeth's hand, persistently appear, in spite of all efforts to clean them. They seem to have been constructed solely in the interest of bootblacks.'"
Harper's Weekly, *1876*

chain, and spreading both his arms and legs abroad is rioting in a declamation of something from Victor Hugo; one longs to clap him back into hopeless bondage.

After the objects I have mentioned, I think the room devoted to the German paintings is most disagreeable. The pictures are indifferent, good and bad; the taste, the gross and boastful vanity, the exultant snobbishness of the show is intolerable...There is one picture, the Surrender of Sedan, which ought not to have been admitted except for extraordinary artistic merits; and these it has not. On the brow of a hill stand Wilhelm, Bismarck, and the other Chiefs of Police, swollen with prodigious majesty and self-satisfaction, while a poor little Frenchman, with his hat in one hand and a paper in the other, comes creeping abjectly up the slope, half bowed to the earth and not daring to lift his eyes to the imperial presence. It is a picture to make any Frenchman "bound" with rage, if he happens not to laugh, and I do not see how we are to escape our share of the outrage offered in it, by the singularly offensive despotism from which it comes, to our ancient friend and sister republic. When I think of it, I am ready to justify the enormous charges at the restaurant of the Trois Frères Provençaux (so called because each of the Brothers makes out his bill of Three Prices, and you pay the sum total), as a proper reprisal upon us...

THE ART ANNEX

The rooms devoted to the English pictures were most delightful. There were many works of their masters; they had sent us of their best, and not of their second-best, as the French had done, and there was a kindliness of intent and a manifest good feeling toward our fair, if not toward our nation, to which every generous American must at once respond. Not only had they sent us of their best, but their pictures are for our pleasure and not their profit; they are owned by Englishmen who risk everything that may happen to their treasures in the voyage over-seas, and gain nothing but the satisfaction of doing a gracious and graceful thing. To courtesy of which we cannot be too sensible we owe the sight not only of famous Gainsboroughs, Reynoldses, Wests, and Lawrences, but also the works of the great modern painters, Landseer, Leighton, Millais, Alma Tadema, and the rest. I may be wrong in stating that no other nation has done anything like this, but I certainly recollect nothing else of the kind...By all odds theirs is the most satisfactory department of the Art Hall; and they have not only done us a great pleasure, but have done themselves great honor...These great Englishmen have not merely painted well, but they have painted about something; their pictures tell stories, and suggest stories when they do not tell them. I...speak as one of the confessedly unlearned in art, when I say that their pictures interested me far beyond any others. We had certainly no cause, considering all things, to be ashamed of the show of American paintings in comparison even with many of the English, and still less with those of other nations. There were not many positively poor, and there were many strikingly good, especially landscapes painted with sympathy, and portraits painted with character; but they showed a distracting variety of influences, and they did not detain you and call you back again and again to tell you something more, and to add yet this suggestion and that. Some did so, but most did not; a perception of their merely artistic qualities exhausted them—the point at which the English pictures began more deeply to delight. They were too often unstoried like our scenery, without our scenery's excuse. You

Inside the Art Hall

Statue of George Washington Perched on an Eagle

"They decided to separate. Mr. Peterkin and Agamemnon would take the little boys to the Agricultural Building, and to the American Restaurant for lunch, while Elizabeth Eliza and Solomon John planned the Art Gallery..."

Elizabeth Eliza and Solomon John "were so crushed in the Art Gallery by the mass of people, that Elizabeth Eliza could not even lift her note-book, or examine her catalogue. She believed they had been into every room in the Art Gallery and in the Annex, but she could only look at the upper pictures, and could not stop at any. She was sure there must be more United States pictures than from any other country. The only work of art which she could remember enough to describe was the large bust of Washington, sitting on the eagle. They wondered why the eagle was not crushed."

Lucretia P. Hale, *The Peterkin Papers*

Thomas Eakins: The Gross Clinic
Eakins painted this picture especially for the Centennial Exhibition. He chose the subject because of his studies with Dr. Samuel David Gross, the famed surgeon of the Jefferson Medical College. Eakins is in the painting at the left sketching, while Dr. Gross operates. The painting was considered shocking because of the explicit medical detail and was denied installation at the Centennial.

felt that American art had made vast advances on the technical side, but that it lacked what English art has got from its intimate association with literature; that it was not poetical; that generally its subjects were seen, not deeply felt and thought; it wanted charm....

Comparatively few of the [French] pictures were yet in position, and the display had nothing of the strongly distinctive quality of the English. Whole rooms devoted to the French were barred against the public, but enough was visible to emphasize the national taste for the nude. When one caught sight of this in paintings just unpacked and standing against the wall, it was as if the subjects had been surprised before they had time to dress for the Centennial, so strongly is the habit of being clothed expressed in the modern face....

Italy had sent no pictures that commended themselves to special remembrance. Her strength—or her weakness—was her sculpture, which had at its best the character of illustration. England alone of all

Centennial Award Medal
About twelve thousand of these medals were presented for exhibits which were considered outstanding.

"The method of awards adopted by the American Centennial Commission differs from the preceding systems. It dispenses with the international jury, and substitutes a body of judges, one-half foreign, chosen individually for their high qualifications," wrote James D. McCabe in 1876. He added, "The medals awarded by the Commission were of bronze, round in shape, four inches in diameter, very chaste in appearance, and the largest of the kind ever struck in the United States. The stamps were engraved by Henry Mitchell, of Boston, and the medals were struck at the United States Mint at Philadelphia. In the centre of the face is a female figure, representing America, seated on an elevation, and holding a crown of laurels over the emblems of industry that lie at her feet. At equal distances apart on the outside zone of the face are four other female figures in bas-relief, which with appropriate symbols represent America, Europe, Asia, and Africa, respectively. The reverse side has in the centre the words: 'Awarded by the United States Centennial Commission,' and, on the outside zone: 'International Exhibition at Philadelphia. MDCCCLXXVI.' "

Interior of Machinery Hall

Inside Horticultural Hall

A visitor to the Centennial described Horticultural Hall: "The main floor is occupied by a spacious conservatory, with a high glass roof, and a light gallery from which visitors may look down upon the wealth of tropical beauty which glows below. In the centre of the floor stands a fountain of beautiful and appropriate design, from which radiating walks divide the space into beds filled with plants from the luxuriant South. Here are palms; here are orange and lemon trees laden with their golden fruit; here may be seen the banana, with its heavily laden branch, the guava, the India-rubber tree, and hundreds of other growths—some beautiful for shape or color, some interesting for their uses or rarity— unknown in our hard Northern climate. One seems to breathe the very air of the balmy South in this palace of enchantment."

Lyall's Positive Motion Loom

the foreign countries had sent of her best art to the Centennial. At almost any sale of French pictures in Boston you see the work of more famous painters; here there was not one first-rate name; and this was true of the Continent generally. The show impressed one as that of pictures that had not succeeded at home.

HORTICULTURAL HALL

The Horticultural Hall is one of the buildings which are to remain, and its lovely architecture, in which the light arabesque forms express themselves in material of charming colors, merits permanence. It is extremely pleasing, and is chiefly pleasing as architecture; for the show of plants is not very striking to the unbotanized observer, who soon wearies of palms and cactuses and unattainable bananas, and who may not have an abiding joy in an organ played by electricity, with a full orchestral accompaniment similarly operated.

MACHINERY HALL

We went next to the Machinery Hall, through the far extent of which we walked, looking merely to the right and left as we passed down the great aisle. Of that first impression the majesty of the great Corliss engine, which drives the infinitely varied machinery, remains most distinct. After that is the sense of too many sewing-machines. The Corliss engine does not lend itself to description; its personal acquaintance must be sought by those who would understand its vast and almost silent grandeur...In the midst of this ineffably strong mechanism is a chair where the engineer sits reading his newspaper, as in a peaceful bower. Now and then he lays down his paper and clambers up one of the stairways that cover the framework, and touches some irritated spot on the giant's body with a drop of oil, and goes down again and takes up his newspaper; he is like some potent enchanter there, and this prodigious Afreet is his slave who could crush

Lyall's Positive Motion Loom

"Shortly after the Main Building was completed, someone asked a noted carpet manufacturer what the cost would be of covering the immense floor space with the finest quality of carpeting. The manufacturer went through a brief calculation, and replied that he would not take a contract to supply the material for less than two dollars per square foot. As this would aggregate a sum actually more than the entire superstructure itself cost, the fact was widely published... It so happened that the present writer had occasion to repeat this story to a well-known inventor and manufacturer of textile machinery, who listened quietly, and then, with a twinkle in his eye...remarked, 'Well, to cover the Main Building would require a big carpet; but if occasion required it, I could weave that carpet in a single loom and in a single piece of a width equal to the length of the building.'

"Now the Main Building is some 1876 feet in length, and to offer to weave a carpet of that width was something well calculated to provoke considerable astonishment....

"The statements were not exaggerations, and further, of this every visitor to the Centennial might easily assure himself. True, the immense machine capable of the remarkable work cited was not on exhibition, nor has it ever been built, but others were displayed which embodied the principle which might be applied not only to looms of a width limited only by the exigencies of mechanical construction. As an indication of this possibility, the inventor contented himself with building the largest loom in the world, and placing it in his display in Machinery Hall; and there it has worked, weaving a fabric twenty-four feet in width at the rate of forty yards per ten hours, or completing 320 square yards per day, from the opening to the close of the vast fair.

"The inventor of the 'positive motion loom' is Mr. James Lyall...of New York City... That the invention we have described is rapidly revolutionizing the textile art, the statistics of the weaving industry in this country clearly show."

Harper's Weekly, 1876

Wallpaper Printing Press

The wallpaper printing machine was exhibited in Machinery Hall. It was just one of many machines that were changing the lives of Americans in 1876.

"The application of machinery in this country to the printing of wallpaper-hangings," explained a reporter in *Harper's Weekly*, "has so cheapened the cost of production that American papers compete in foreign markets with those of European manufacture in design, quality, and price. ... Judging from the improvements already introduced or in progress... America must take the lead over all other countries in this important branch of industry...."

Alexander Graham Bell Exhibiting His Telephone

Although the telephone was exhibited at the Centennial, it was the Corliss engine, not the telephone, that drew the biggest crowds. On November 4, 1876, the New York Tribune *reported:*

"The Centennial Exhibition has afforded the opportunity to bring into public view many inventions and improvements which otherwise would only have been known to the smaller circles....The telephone is a curious device that might fairly find place in the magic of Arabian Tales. Of what use is such an invention? Well, there may be occasions of state when it is necessary for officials who are far apart to talk with each other without the interference of an operator. Or some lover might wish to pop the question directly into the ear of a lady and hear for himself her reply, though miles away; it is not for us to guess how courtships will be carried on in the Twentieth Century...."

him past all semblance of humanity with his lightest touch. It is alas! what the Afreet has done to humanity too often, where his strength has superseded men's industry; but of such things the Machinery Hall is no place to speak, and to be honest, one never thinks of such things there. One thinks only of the glorious triumphs of skill and invention; and wherever else the national bird is mute in one's breast, here he cannot fail to utter his pride and content. It would be a barren place without the American machinery. All that Great Britain and Germany have sent is insignificant in amount when compared with our own contributions; the superior elegance, aptness, and ingenuity of our machinery is observable at a glance. Yes, it is still in these things of iron and steel that the national genius most freely speaks; by and by the inspired marbles, the breathing canvases, the great literature; for the present America is voluble in the strong metals and their infinite uses. I have hinted already that I think she talks too much in sewing-machines, but I dare say that each of these patents has its reason for being, and that the world would go mostly unclad without it. Nevertheless, a whole half-mile of sewing-machines seems a good deal; and *is* there so very much difference between them?...In the midst, the Corliss engine set an example of unwearying application to business...Innumerable spindles began to whirr and shuttles to clack...

Exterior of the Main Building

THE MAIN BUILDING

The Main Building is provided with many fountains of the soda sort, and one large fountain for the unsophisticated element, all of which were pretty, and contributed to that brightness of effect which was so largely owing to the handsomeness of the show-cases and pavilions. The finest of these were American. We were thought to have sometimes dimmed the lustre of our jewels by the brilliancy of the casket, but the general display gained by this error. In the middle of the building a band played many hours every day...

Our first general impressions of the different buildings were little changed by close acquaintance. What we found interesting in the beginning, that we found interesting at the end, and this is an advantage to those whose time is short at the Centennial. This is peculiarly the case in the Main Building, where the contrasts are sharpest, and the better and worse most obvious.

Our second day at the Centennial began in the Main Building, where...we found ourselves presently amid the delicate silver-work, the rich furs, the precious and useful metals: the artistic representations of national life in Norway. It was by far the completest department in the building, and for that little country, winterbound in paralyzing cold and dark for so great a part of the year, the display of tasteful and industrial results was amazing.

The Viking race is not extinct, but the huge energies are refined and directed by the modern spirit to the production of things that may take the mighty West and the delicate South equally by surprise....The most interesting things in this and the Swedish departments were, of course, the life-size figures illustrative of present costumes and usages...It was like reading one of Björnson's charming stories, to look at these vividly characteristic groups, all of which were full of curious instruction. In one place an old peasant and his wife sit reading in a cottage room; in another a bereaved family surround the cradle of a

Bentwood Furniture—Austrian Section

The bentwood display was arranged by a Moravian firm which, thanks to the "modern" production techniques of 1876, was making half a million pieces of furniture of all kinds annually. Bentwood furniture was invented by Michael Thonet. In 1876 the Thonet Brothers had five factories in Moravia and Hungary and branches in Vienna, Berlin, Hamburg, Amsterdam, Paris and New York, among other cities. They were producing two thousand pieces of furniture a day.

The Main Building

The Main Building was an astounding 21½ acres in area. That building alone was larger than the entire Crystal Palace Exhibition held in London in 1851. About one fourth of the Main Building was occupied by United States exhibits.

James D. McCabe called the Main Building "the most imposing structure of the Exhibition...It is superb in its massiveness...[and] constitutes an object which long holds the gazer's eye and elicits his warmest praise."

Ice Cream Soda Fountain at the Philadelphia Exhibition

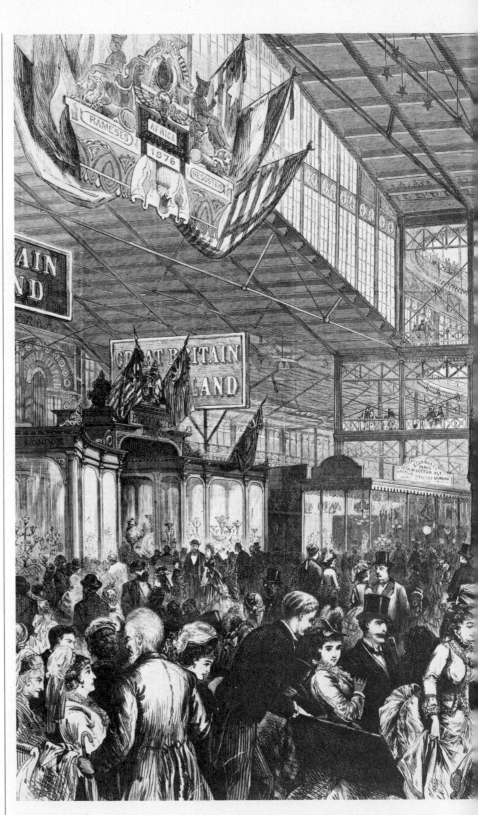

dead child;...yonder are a Norwegian bride and groom in their wedding-gear, the bride wearing a crown and ornaments of barbaric gold,—which in this case were actual heirlooms descended from mother to daughter in one peasant family through three hundred years. All was for sale. "We will even separate husband and wife, and sell the bride away from the groom," laughingly explained the

Furniture

A writer in *Harper's Weekly* ecstatically described the display of furniture. He singled out one particular fireplace for comment:

"One of the most beautiful displays of furniture is that of Messrs. Howard & Sons, of London.... So costly and so delicate are the articles exhibited that the display has been guarded from intrusion by ropes, to prevent injury by careless handling.

"The work surrounding the fire-place is of oak, beautifully inlaid with black-walnut in gracefully artistic designs. The inlaying is done by a new process, patented by Messrs. Howard & Sons, which will soon be introduced into this country. It is not only capable of the highest artistic treatment, but so marvelously cheap that it will bring the means of a beautiful style of household decoration within the reach of persons of modest incomes. The chair opposite the one in which a lady is reclining was made expressly for the Duke of Edinburgh...."

New industrial processes would enable the masses to have what only the wealthy had been able to afford.

commissioner. The very pavilion itself, built of Norse pines, and ornamented in the forms of the old Norse architecture, was to be sold...The Norwegians had not merely contributed their wares, but had done us an honor and a pleasure by the thoroughly artistic character of their exhibition. So had the Swedes.

The Danish and Egyptian Departments

A row of pavilions offered the American tourist views of products from foreign lands. The *New York Times* said in January 1876 that the most important effect of the Centennial would be "the added knowledge... gained by various sections of our own people, as to the industries and productions of this and other countries." In the Danish department the visitor could behold skins and furs, and a Danish country house prepared for the winter. In the Egyptian department, visitors were struck, according to *Harper's*, "by the splendor, richness, and strangeness of the display that meets the eye on passing under the temple gateway of the pavilion. One seems to have suddenly entered the world of the *Arabian Nights*. One of the first objects that arrests attention is the magnificent collection of saddles and the attendant trappings.... After examining this gorgeous array, the visitor will not fail to notice the massive round covers for coffee trays, gold and silver flowers worked by hand on a velvet foundation. These are very showy and very costly, each being valued at $2,000. In the same case may be seen two hanging lamps of glass, with colored decorations worked in them. These are very ancient, and the art of making them is lost. Costly stuffs woven of silk and gold and silver thread hang near by."

THE DANISH PAVILION

The Danes showed some interesting figures illustrative of the Danish military service, actual and historic, and a display of exquisite pottery, shaped and colored in the most delicate spirit of antique art, Greek and Egyptian, was certainly one of the most charming features of the fair.

THE EGYPTIAN PAVILION

The Khedive of Egypt, whose section was in perfect order, has superbly commanded, it is said, that nothing shall be returned to him and nothing shall be sold, but that all his contributions shall be appropriately given away in this country...[Howells was not uncritically impressed by:] despotic splendor that one could more admire if one did not know that the Khedive's march of improvement has been through the blood and tears of his subjects, and that his prosperity is in reality the pomp of a successful slave-driver.

THE ITALIAN, BRAZILIAN AND FRENCH DEPARTMENTS

The Italian department, to anyone who knows what Italy's wealth in objects of art is, seems—with some signal exceptions—a rather poverty-stricken effort of bric-a-bracishness. It presents a huddled, confused appearance; it is a shop where the prices asked are worthy of the Trois Frères themselves. The spirit of the Brazilian exhibition is in pleasant contrast. The things shown are sincere evidences of the national industry and illustrative of the national civilization; moreover, they are displayed in a Saracenic pavilion that pleases the eye, and are tastefully and intelligibly ordered.

It was not posssible, when we saw it, to judge the French department as a whole, and I ought not perhaps to speak of it at all, since so much of it was incompletely arranged. Yet, with all the richness and infinite variety of material the general effect was one of shoddiness.

THE ENGLISH AND AMERICAN EXHIBITS

The British show...represented...that wide and beautiful expression of the artistic feeling in household decoration in which England is now leading the world. We Americans could long ago show machinery whose ingenuity and perfection surpassed anything the insular brain had conceived, and now we show in the utilitarian application of the metals, as in tools, and the like, an easy equality, but we cannot yet approach the English in the subjection of material to the higher purposes of both use and pleasure. Their show of tiles, of brasses, of artistically wrought steel and iron, of pottery, of painted glass, was wonderful. We ought, however, to take credit where it is due; in artificial teeth and all the amiable apparatus of dentistry, nothing could approach us. And I must except from a sweeping confession of inferiority the style and workmanship of several large American displays of gas-fixtures: as the most gas-burning people in the world, we were here fitly first. We were first too, I thought, in the working of silver. The shapes and ornamentations by the different great silver-working houses did justice to the nation which owns the Nevada mines; it proved our capacity for rising equal to an advantage. In glass, however, after the rich colors and manifold lovely forms of the foreign exhibits, we were cold and gray, and in all manufactured stuffs dull and uninteresting; we may have been honest, but we looked poor. I say nothing of our supremacy in a thousand merely ingenious applications and adaptations: that goes without saying; and I say nothing of the display of the publishing houses: books were the last things I cared to

A View in the American Department—Main Building

Jewelry

The diamond necklace was one of the most popular exhibits. A writer in Harper's *said: "The diamond necklace...a part of the Tiffany collection of jewels in the Main Building probably attracted more observation than any other object at the Centennial if we exempt, perhaps, the great Corliss engine. It is formed of twenty-seven rare Golconda diamonds of matchless beauty and purity, and the mere mention of its money value ($80,000 in gold) tells at once that it far surpasses in costliness any jewel ever worn in America. ...The number of people who at the Centennial saw diamonds at all for the first time might be counted by hundreds of thousands...."*

Advertisement for German Beer

Present Aspects of the Food Question at the Exhibition

Harper's Weekly, May 13, 1876.

Centennial Visitors Enjoy Brazilian Coffee

see at the Centennial. But I heard from persons less disdainful of literature that the show of book-making did us great honor.

RESTAURANTS

We thought it well during our week at the Centennial to lunch as variously as possible, and I can speak by the card concerning the German Restaurant, the two French Restaurants, and the Vienna Bakery; the native art in cooking we did not test. The German Restaurant and the Lafayette Restaurant are very reasonable in their charges, less expensive, indeed, than most first-class city restaurants. The Trois Frères Provençaux is impudently extortionate. Not that dishes cooked with so much more sentiment than any you can find elsewhere are not worth more, but that there are absurd charges for what Americans ordinarily pay nothing for: bread, butter, and service at double and quadruple the Parisian rates. But it is even worse at the Vienna Bakery, where they have twenty-five cents for a cup of coffee, and not good coffee at that—not at all the coffee of Vienna. Happily, no one is obliged to go to these places for sustenance. There are a hundred others within the grounds where you may lunch cheaply and well, or cheaply and ill, which most of our nation like better. There is, for instance, a large pavilion where one may surcharge the stomach with pie and milk at a very low price. There is an American Restaurant, there is a Southern Restaurant (served by lustrous citizens of color), there is no end to them; and I am very glad to say of them, and of all other American enterprises for the public comfort that their opportunity has not been improved to the public ruin. The extortion seems to be all by the foreigners.

Our Artist's Dream of the Centennial Restaurants

A *Harper's Weekly* cartoon.

French Restaurant: Aux Trois Frères Provençaux
The Trois Frères restaurant, known by Centennial visitors for its high prices, could accommodate about one thousand guests. It was named after a famous restaurant in Paris.

The Kindergarten

"Close by the Women's Pavilion, and forming, as it were, an annex of that building, is a little cottage, where are shown, under the auspices of the Women's department, actual methods of education in use in the infant school system of Froebel, termed the 'Kindergarten.' Here the system is developed, and can be seen on certain days of the week, illustrating its working with eighteen little children from three to six years of age.... Friedrich Froebel introduced this new method of teaching into his native country of Germany in 1837, giving it the name of 'Kindergarten' (children's garden)... The idea involves a large, well-ventilated, well-lighted and pleasant room, opening upon a garden where should be combined a playground for general enjoyment, a large garden-plot, and smaller plots for each child old enough to cultivate one. Here the little ones should be taught to plant and cultivate flowers, useful vegetables, and even trees...

"Froebel's system did not contemplate corporal punishment, exclusion from a game or from the garden being considered sufficiently severe treatment.

"Froebel died in 1852. During his life more than fifty Kindergartens were established in Germany, Belgium, and Switzerland.

"Although no government has yet introduced the system in the public schools in the United States, these schools have become quite numerous in New York, Washington, Philadelphia and Boston... It is likely that the exhibition of the Kindergarten at the Centennial will introduce the system into many cities where it is at present unknown."

Leslie's Magazine, 1876

THE STATE BUILDINGS

In the afternoon we made the tour of the State buildings, of which, generally speaking, it is hard to detect at once the beauty or occasion...The most picturesque building is that of New Jersey; that of Massachusetts was comfortable and complete...The Ohio building has some meaning in being of Ohio Stones, and it is substantially and gracefully designed; but really the most interesting...is the Mississippi house, which is wholly built of Mississippi woods, the rough bark logs showing without, and the gables and porch decked with gray streamers of Spanish mosses. A typical Mississippian, young in years but venerable in alligator-like calm, sits on this porch (or did there sit on the afternoon of our visit), with his boots on the railing and his hat drawn over his eyes and sheltering his slowly moving jaws as they ruminate the Virginian weed. He had probably been over-questioned, for he answered all queries without looking up or betraying the smallest curiousity as to the age, sex, or condition of the questioner. Being tormented (I will not name the sex of his tormentress), concerning the uses of a little hole or pouch (it was for letters, really) in the wall near the door, he said that it was to receive contributions for a poor orphan. "I," he added, "am the orphan;" and then at last he looked up, with a faint gleam in his lazy eye which instantly won the heart. This Mississippian was white; another, black, showed us civilly and intelligently through the house, which was very creditable in every way to the State, and told us that it was built of seventy different kinds of Mississippi wood. We came away applauding the taste and sense shown in the only State building that seemed to have anything characteristic to say for itself. But in a country where for the most part every State is only more unrepresentative in its architecture than another, it is very difficult for the building to be representative.

THE WOMEN'S PAVILION

The women of the United States contributed $30,000 to build their own pavilion at Philadelphia. In the pavilion were displays of labor-saving devices such as a machine for washing blankets and a dish-washing machine. There were also photographs of various charitable institutions established or conducted by women such as the Shelter for Colored Orphans at West Philadelphia. And in the middle of the building was a small printing office where women set type for *The New Century for Women,* a journal published entirely by women and distributed from the pavilion. Howells wrote:

It was not till our third day that we went to the Women's Pavilion. Those accustomed to think of women as the wives, mothers, and sisters of men will be puzzled to know why the ladies wished to separate their work from that of the rest of the human race, and those who imagine an antagonism between the sexes must regret, in the interest of what is called the cause of woman, that the Pavilion is so inadequately representative of her distinctive achievement. The show is chiefly saved to the visitor's respect by the carved wood-work done by ladies of the Cincinnati Art School. Even this, compared with great wood-carving,

Inside the Kindergarten

lacks richness of effect; it is rather the ornamentation of the surface of wood in the lowest relief; but is very good of its kind, full of charming sentiment; it is well intentioned, and executed with signal delicacy and refined skill. It is a thing that one may be glad of as American art, and then, if one cares, as women's work, though there seems no more reason why it should be considered more characteristic of the sex than the less successful features of the exhibition. We did not test the cuisine of the School of Cooking attached to the Women's Pavilion. If it had been a Man's Pavilion, I should have thought it the dustiest building on the grounds. It seems not yet the moment for the better half of our species to take their stand apart from the worse upon any distinct performance in art or industry; even when they have a building of their own, some organizing force to get their best work into it is lacking; many of those pictures and pincushions were no better than if men had made them; but some paintings by women in the Art Hall, where they belonged, suffered nothing by comparison with the work of their brothers. Woman's skill was better represented in the Machinery Hall than in her own Pavilion; there she was everywhere seen in the operation and superintendence of the most complicated mechanisms, and showed herself in the character of a worker of unsurpassed intelligence.

Dreaming Iolanthe in Butter
This product of a butter press was displayed in the Women's Pavilion.

Fishes of the Sea

These casts of some four hundred and thirty fish were on display in the Government Building.

Costumes of the United States Army Since 1800

War, too, was changed by technological advances and as war changed, so did army uniforms. "Military uniforms are not, as a rule, so gorgeous nowadays as they were before war became a matter of science and engineering, and show and display were sacrificed to utility," said a reporter in *Harper's*. "The modern soldier is by no means the gorgeous creature that made the paradegrounds of a hundred years ago so brilliant. He has become a machine, and is dressed for work instead of show."

THE UNITED STATES GOVERNMENT BUILDING

Monday was hot and abated our zeal for the Philadelphian spring by giving us a foretaste of what the Philadelphian summer must be....In the United States Building we should not have lost patience with the heat if it had not been for the luxurious indifference of that glass case full of frozen fishes which as they reposed in their comfortable boxes of snow with their thermometer at 30° did certainly appeal to some of the most vindictive passions of our nature; and I say that during the hot months it will be cruelty to let them remain. There are persons who would go down from Massachusetts to join a mob in smashing that case on the 4th of July, and tearing those fish to pieces. There are also people of culture in this region who would sign a petition asking the government to change the language of the placard on the clothes of the Father of his Country, which now reads, "Coat, Vest, and Pants of George Washington," whereas it is his honored waistcoat which is meant, and his buckskin breeches: pantaloons were then unknown, and "pants" were undreamt-of by a generation which had time to be decent and comely in its speech. This placard is a real drawback to one's enjoyment of the clothes, which are so familiar that one is startled not to find Washington's face looking out of the coat-collar. The government had been well advised in putting on view these and other personal relics, like his camp-bed, his table furniture, his sword, his pistols, and so forth. There are also similar relics of other heroes, and in the satisfaction of thus drawing nearer to the past in the realization of those historic lives, one's passion for heroic wardrobes mounts so that it stays at nothing....We were mortified to think of no modern worthy thus to hand down a coat and hat to the admiration of posterity....

I have to leave in despair all details of the government show of army and navy equipments, the varied ingenuity and beautiful murderousness of the weapons of all kinds, the torpedoes with which alone one could pass hours of satisfaction, fancifully attaching them to the ships of enemies and defending our coasts in the most effectual manner; the exquisite models of marine architecture; the figures of soldiers of all arms—not nearly so good as the Danish, but dearer, being our own....There was manufacture of Centennial stamped envelopes, which constantly drew a large crowd, and there were a thousand and one other things which every one must view with advantage to himself and with applause of the government for making this impressive display in the eyes of other nations.

AGRICULTURAL HALL

I sometimes fancied that the Agricultural Hall might reclaim the long sojourning visitor rather oftener than any other building, if he were of a very patriotic mind. It seems the most exclusively American, and it is absorbingly interesting in traits of its display. There are almost as many attractive show-cases and pavilions as in the Main Building, and they are somehow seen to better advantage. Then there is obviously a freer expression of individual tastes and whims. It was delightful,for example, to walk down the long avenue of mowing and reaping machines, and see those imperfectly surviving forms of "dragons of the prime," resplendent in varnished fine woods and burnished steel, and reposing upon spaces of Brussels carpeting, attended by agents each more firmly zealous than another in the dissemination of advertisements and in the faith that his machine was the last triumph of invention. Their fond pride in their machines was admirable; you

Inside Agricultural Hall

Old Mammoth Grapevine
This grapevine was moved all the way from Santa Barbara, California, to Philadelphia for the Exhibition. It was described as "the largest and most celebrated vine in the world." It produced six tons of grapes every year; its diameter was over 18 inches and it covered an area of 12,000 square feet.

An Old-Fashioned Windmill
The windmill was a display that served to remind Americans of their amazing industrial progress: "This mill is built in exact imitation of those used a hundred years ago in flat countries where there was no available water-power.... The windmill with us, like many other things picturesque and attractive in their original state, has become the victim of modern progress. It is now built on highly scientific principles, and is about as unsightly as science can make it. Doubtless it does better service; but unfortunately it seems always to be the mission of inventions to develop the useful at the expense of the aesthetic...."
Harper's Weekly, 1876

could not but sympathize with it....We came to our favorite case of sugar-cured hams: a glass case in which hung three or four hams richly canvased, not in the ordinary yellow linen, but in silk of crimson, white, and gold. These were of course from Cincinnati, and the same pork-packer had...shown a humorous fancy in the management of material which does not lend itself readily to the plastic arts in their serious tempers.

The most artistic use of any material was undoubtedly made by some Louisville tobacco dealers, who had arranged the varieties and colors of their product with an eye to agreeable effect which I never saw surpassed in any Italian market, and who had added a final touch by showing different sorts of tobacco growing in pots....

There were fanciful and effective arrangements of farm implements; exhibitions of farm products both foreign and domestic; shows of the manufactured and raw material—literally without number. To remember one was to forget a thousand, and yet each was worthy to be seen. I remember the cotton from India with its satisfying Hindoo names; the pavilion of Brazilian cotton, and the whole array of Brazilian products; the pavilions of American wines and the bacchanal show of Rhine wines, where the vine in leaf and cluster wreathed pillar and cornice, and a little maid sat making more vine-leaves out of paper. But there were many cases and many pavilions which were tasteful and original in high degree: and when one looked about on the work of preparation still going forward over the whole territory of the building,—as large, almost, as a German principality,—one felt that the tale was but half told.

Among many other things...they had in the Agricultural Building the famous war-eagle, Old Abe, whom a Wisconsin regiment [had] carried through the war....The next morning we made haste to see him. We found him in charge of one of the sergeants who had borne him through thirty battles, and who had once been shot down with the eagle on his perch, and left for dead on the field. The sergeant was a slim young fellow, with gray eyes enough like the eagle's to make them brothers and he softly turned his tobacco from one cheek to the other while he discoursed upon the bird—his honors from the State government of Wisconsin, which keeps him and a man to care for him at the public charge; his preference for a diet of live chicken; his objection to new acquaintance, which he had shown a few days before by plunging his beak into the cheek of a gentleman who had offered him some endearments. We could not see that Old Abe looked different from other bald eagles (which we had seen in pictures); he had a striking repose of manner, and his pale, fierce eye had that uninterested, remote regard said to characterize all sovereign personages. The sergeant tossed him up and down on his standard, and the eagle threw open his great vans; but otherwise he had no entertainment to offer except the record of his public services,—which we bought for fifty cents.

Vastly and more simply impressive was a wholly different exhibition from Iowa, to some of whose citizens the happy thought of showing the depth and quality of the soil in several counties of the State had occurred. Accordingly there it was in huge glass cylinders, in which it rose to a height of four, five, and six feet—a boast of inexhaustible fertility which New England eyes could hardly credit. This was one of the inspirations which gave a shock of agreeable astonishment, and revived the beholder even after a day of sightseeing.

The Wines of the Rhine, Agricultural Hall
There were seventy-two exhibitors of German wines at the Centennial.

The Soils of Iowa
The rich soil from different counties was displayed in glass cylinders.

Temperance Fountain
This ice water fountain was built by the Sons of Temperance of the State of Pennsylvania.

Railway Station
Most of the nine million Americans who visited the Centennial arrived here at the Pennsylvania Railroad Centennial Depot.

THE RAILROAD

We took our first ride on the narrow-gauge railroad, of which the locomotive with its train of gay open cars coughs and writhes about the grounds in every direction, with a station at each of the great buildings....The fare is five cents for the whole tour or from any one point to another; the ride is luxuriously refreshing, and commands a hundred charming prospects. To be sure, the cars go too fast, but that saves time; and I am not certain that the flagmen at the crossings are sufficiently vigilant to avert the accidents whose possibility forms a greater objection to the railroad than mere taste can urge against it.

THE CARRIAGE HALL

I have left the Carriage Hall to the last, though it was one of the first things we saw. I am not a connoisseur of wheeled vehicles, and I dare say I admired not too wisely. The American shapes seemed to me the most elegant; there was a queerness, a grotesqueness, an eccentricity, about the English, when they were not too heavy. But what most seizes the spectator is some one's ghastly fancy of a white hearse. It shows that

An Italian and an American Carriage
Carriages were an important mode of transportation, and over a hundred different varieties of them were on display at the Centennial Exhibition. There were pleasure carriages, family, park and seaside coaches, children's carriages and even a hearse.

a black hearse is not the most repulsive thing that can be. There are some exquisite specimens of car-architecture for a Brazilian railroad; a buggy from Indiana is kept—I do not know why—in a glass case; and there is a very resplendent Pullman car through which we walked, for no reason that I can give—probably the mere overmastering habit of sightseeing.

HOWELLS CONCLUDES HIS VISIT

The grounds of the Centennial are open twelve hours every day, and your payment of fifty cents admits you for all that time to everything there. No account, however close, however graphic, can give a just conception of the variety and interest of the things to be seen. The whole season would not exhaust them; a week or a month enables you to study a point here and there. Yet if you have but a single day to spend, it is well to go. You can never spend a day with richer return.

A very pleasant thing about the Exhibition is your perfect freedom there. There are innumerable officials to direct you, to help you, to care for you, but none of them bothers you. If you will keep off those clay slopes and expanses which are placarded Grass, there will be no interference with any caprice of your personal liberty. This is the right American management of a public pleasure....

It is curious to see the great new hotels of solid and flimsy construction near the grounds, and the strange city which has sprung up in answer to the necessities of the World's Fair. From every front and top stream the innumerable flags, with which during a day in town we found all Philadelphia also decked. Yet it is an honest and well-behaved liveliness. There is no disorder of any sort. Nowhere in or about the Centennial did I see anyone who had overdrunk the health of his country.

Not the least prodigious of the outside appurtenances of the Centennial is that space allotted on a neighboring ground to the empty boxes and packing cases of the goods sent to the fair. Their multitude is

Kiosk of stuffed birds exhibited in the Main Building

Exhibit of Adam Exton's Crackers, in Agricultural Hall

The Evening Rush for the Cars
"No one who can make the visit and remain several days in studying the wonders of the Exhibition will ever regret the expenditure of time and money. Even one day wisely devoted to a general survey of the buildings and grounds will be an event to be remembered during a lifetime," said an enthusiastic reporter in Harper's Weekly.

truly astonishing, and they have a wild desolation amidst which I should think the gentlemen of the Centennial Commission, in case of a very disastrous failure of the enterprise, would find it convenient to come and rend their garments. But no one expects failure now. Every day of our week there saw an increase of visitors, and the reader of the newspapers knows how the concourse has grown since. The undertaking merits all possible prosperity, and whatever were the various minds in regard to celebrating the Centennial by an international fair, no one can now see the fair without a thrill of patriotic pride.

OTHER ADMIRERS OF THE EXHIBITION

Mosaic Rug in the Russian Exhibit, in the Main Building

Other writers in 1876 joined Howells in praising the Exhibition. One *Harper's Weekly* reporter observed:

Wherever one is traveling this fall, whether on cars or steamboats, the universal topic of conversation is "the Centennial." Parties are returning from Philadelphia to their homes in all parts of the country, and it is noticeable that among the uneducated, as well as among the more cultivated classes, the senseless chit-chat and injurious gossip so often indulged in have given place to conversation of a higher tone, arising from the curious, beautiful, and useful, as seen at the Exhibition. To have visited the Centennial is a sort of basis for an informal acquaintance among many who chance to be thrown together in traveling....Conversation soon drifts into a comparison of experiences in reviewing the great show. Thousands who have seldom left their quiet country homes have this year taken an unaccustomed journey. Their thoughts have been turned from old, worn channels, their feelings quickened and freshened, and the wholesome effect will be as wide-spread as the entire country. For months to come there will be something for the farmer to talk about besides his crops; the views of the machinist and mechanic have been widened; the quiet country mother, no less than her fashionable city sister, can give her children some fresh entertainment of a winter evening; the merchant has had a thought of something different from banks and creditors tucked into his brain; and thousands of young people have had their minds enriched as by a visit to foreign countries....

Artificial Teeth

James D. McCabe in his *Illustrated History of the Centennial Exhibition* wrote of his hope that America's material progress would be hastened by the Exhibition:

Apart from [the] general and cosmopolitan culture in which all participated, each found valuable fruits of knowledge adapted to his own need. The farmer saw new machines, seeds and processes; the mechanic, ingenious inventions and tools, and products of the finest workmanship; the teacher, the educational aids and systems of the world; the man of science, the wonders of nature and the results of the investigations of the best brains of all lands. Thus each returned to his home with a store of information available in his own special trade or profession.

The material benefits accruing from the Exhibition are manifold, and will be realized for years to come as well as in the near future....Many improvements in manufactures and the introduction of new branches of industry will soon follow as the result of the study by

Old Abe

"Mr. Peterkin and his party were wild with enthusiasm. They had been through Agricultural Hall, and had seen 'Old Abe,' looking so much like a stuffed eagle, that they were astonished when he moved his head."

Lucretia P. Hale, *The Peterkin Papers*

inventors, skilled mechanics, and men of enterprise of the products of the globe. They have discovered that many articles which we have been buying from other countries can be profitably made here, and that many which we already make can be improved in quality or in the element of taste, or produced at lower cost, so as to command new markets, and the result will be a still wider development of our national industries.

In the eyes of the nations of the world we have attained a rank never accorded to us before, and this will prove of great material as well as moral benefit...We were regarded as a smart half-cultured people, of immense energy and remarkable ingenuity, but deficient in the higher graces and achievements of civilization, and depending upon the Old World for all finer grades of manufactures. The reports of foreign commissioners, jurors, journalists, and travellers, all concurring in

One Hundred Years Old

Brother Jonathan (The Uncle Sam of his day) delivers his address of welcome to John Bull and representatives of Germany, France, Spain, and other nations: "You see that we have grown a good deal in a century but just think how big we will be when you visit us again in 1976. Don't forget to come, and bring all of your neighbors along!"

Harper's Weekly, 1876

expressions of surprise and admiration at the excellence of our manufactures, our schools, our railroads, our newspapers, and the soundness of our social life, have greatly modified public opinion abroad, and gone far towards introducing more just views of us. Those who mingled much in foreign circles at the Exhibition know that the astonishment and wonder of our visitors from abroad at our resources and accomplishments was great and universal.

The importance of the Exhibition to the Americans of 1876 was summed up by the Chicago *Tribune*, which urged: "Come at all events, if you have to live six months on bread and water to make up for the expense."

AMERICA IN
1876

THE WESTERN EMPIRE
GENERAL CUSTER AND THE BATTLE OF LITTLE BIG HORN

"The 'Great American Desert,' which we school boys a quarter of a century ago saw on the map of North America, has disappeared at the snort of the iron horse; coal and iron are found to abound on the plains...the very desert becomes fruitful, and in the midst of the sage-brush and alkali country, you will see corn, wheat, potatoes, and fruits of different kinds growing luxuriantly, with the help of culture and irrigation; proving that this vast tract, long supposed to be worthless, needs only skillful treatment to become valuable.

One can not help but speculate upon what kind of men we Americans shall be when all these now desolate plains are filled; when cities shall be found where now only the lonely depot or the infrequent cabin stands; when the iron and coal of these regions shall have become, as they soon must, the foundation of great manufacturing populations; and when, perhaps, the whole continent will be covered by our Stars and Stripes."

Charles Nordhoff
California: A Book for Travellers and Settlers

The Chasm of the Colorado, by Thomas Moran

Moran, the renowned painter of American western landscape, finished this painting in 1876. It was purchased by Congress and hung in the Senate wing of the Capitol. The inspiration for this painting came from Moran's trip in 1873 to Utah and Arizona when he accompanied Major John W. Powell's surveying party. On this trip, he made his first sketches of the Grand Canyon.

Describing his own paintings, Moran explained: "I place no value upon literal transcripts from Nature. My general scope is not realistic; but my tendencies are toward idealization."

These reflections of Charles Nordhoff were published in 1873. By the middle of the 1870's the settling of what he called the Great American Desert was well under way. One prime obstacle remained: the Indians. For the West to be properly settled, the Indians had to be removed. Clearance of Indians from the southwestern part of the Great Plains had in fact been successfully engineered by 1876, notably after General George Custer's triumph at the battle of Washita.

But to the north the Sioux Indians still posed a serious problem. In 1868 the U.S. government had signed a treaty recognizing the Sioux's rights to the Black Hills of Dakota. Six years later Custer led an expedition to the Black Hills; gold was discovered. Over the next two years miners poured into the area, breaching the treaty.

In 1876 the government mounted an expedition to round up the "hostiles"—the Sioux and Cheyenne Indians. Custer was part of the expedition, but overall leadership was denied him because he had incurred the disfavor of President Grant by testifying against William Belknap, the corrupt Secretary of War. Custer was given command only of his own regiment;General Alfred Terry was in charge of the whole expedition.

Custer and his regiment moved out of Fort Lincoln on May 26, 1876. A month later Custer and his regiment of 655 men arrived in the vicinity of Little Big Horn. In a series of maneuvers which have excited dispute ever since, Custer divided his forces into three parts and advanced to attack a force of approximately 2,500 to 4,000 Indians. Custer and every one of his men were killed by the Sioux.

The news of the defeat at the Little Big Horn came as an enormous shock to the American public, unaccustomed to such conspicuous routs of its forces. But by the fall, revenge was well under way. The leader of the Sioux, Sitting Bull, escaped to Canada; many of the other chiefs were either seized and thrown in jail or made their own accommodations with the white man. The sacred Black Hills were finally signed away by Red Cloud. Sitting Bull surrendered at Fort Buford in 1881, to be rescued later from life imprisonment by Buffalo Bill Cody, who placed him as a prime attraction in his Wild West Show. As Sitting Bull toured the United States in this troupe, the Great Plains continued sedately along the road of domestication dreamed of a decade before by Nordhoff.

GENERAL GEORGE ARMSTRONG CUSTER

General George Armstrong Custer
A contemporary wrote of Custer: "At the head of the horsemen rode Custer of the golden locks, his broad sombrero turned up from his hard, bronzed face, the ends of his crimson cravat floating over his shoulder, gold galore spangling his jacket sleeves, a pistol in his boots, jangling spurs on his heels, and a ponderous claymore swinging at his side. A wild, dare-devil of a General and a prince of advance guards."

Custer first distinguished himself during the Civil War. Known for his daring, he was controversial during his entire army career. After his death at the age of thirty-seven at the battle of Little Big Horn, the *New York Times* described him as:

...one of the bravest and most widely known officers in the United States Army. He has for the past fifteen years been known to the country and to his comrades as a man who feared no danger, as a soldier in the truest sense of the word...daring to a fault...At the ever-memorable battle of Cedar Creek his division was on the right, and not engaged in the rout of the morning, so that when Sheridan arrived on the field, after the twenty-mile ride, he found at least one command ready for service. His immediate order was "Go in, Custer!" The brave young General only waited for the word, he went in and never came out until the enemy was driven several miles beyond the battle field...For this service Custer was made a Brevet Major General of Volunteers. Sheridan, as a further mark of approbation, detailed him to carry the news of the victory and the captured battle flag to Washington. From this time on his fortune was made, and he continued steadily to advance in the esteem of his superiors and of the American people...He was appointed Lieutenant Colonel of the Seventh United States Cavalry (in 1866) and since that time has been almost constantly engaged in duty upon the frontier.

The "daredevil" general took time off from fighting to write an account of the struggles with the Indians in the Southwest.

Custer on Hunting Party
General George Custer with a grizzly bear which he killed on his famous 1874 expedition into the Black Hills of Dakota. It was on this expedition that Custer discovered gold; he reported "gold at the roots of the grass" in the Black Hills. Custer's discovery led miners to rush into the Black Hills, which according to an 1868 treaty belonged to the Sioux Indians.

by W.H. Illingworth

"MY LIFE ON THE PLAINS," BY G. A. CUSTER

If the character given to the Indian by Cooper and other novelists, as well as by well-meaning but mistaken philanthropists of a later day, were the true one; if the Indian were the innocent, simple-minded being he is represented, more the creature of romance than reality, imbued only with a deep veneration for the works of nature, freed from the passions and vices which must accompany a savage nature; if, in other words, he possessed all the virtues which his admirers and works of fiction ascribe to him, and were free from all the vices which those best qualified to judge assign to him, he would be just the character to complete the picture...

It is to be regretted that the character of the Indian as described in Cooper's interesting novels is not the true one. But as, in emerging from childhood into the years of a maturer age, we are often compelled to cast aside many of our earlier illusions and replace them by beliefs less inviting but more real, so we, as a people, with opportunities enlarged and facilities for obtaining knowledge increased, have been forced by a multiplicity of causes to study and endeavor to comprehend thoroughly the character of the red man. So intimately has he become associated with the Government as ward of the nation, and so prominent a place among the questions of national policy does the much mooted "Indian question" occupy, that it behooves us no longer to study this problem from works of fiction, but to deal with it as it exists in reality. Stripped of the beautiful romance with which we have been so long willing to envelop him, transferred from the inviting pages of the novelist to the localities where we are compelled to meet with him, in his native village, on the war path, and when raiding upon our frontier settlements and lines of travel, the Indian forfeits his claim to the appellation of the "*noble* red man." We see him as he is, and, so far as all knowledge goes, as he ever has been, a *savage* in every sense of the word; not worse, perhaps, than his white brother would be, similarly born and bred, but one whose cruel and ferocious nature far exceeds that of any wild beast of the desert. That this is true no one who has been brought into intimate contact with the wild tribes will deny...But the Indian, while he can seldom be accused of indulging in a great variety of wardrobe, can be said to have a character capable of adapting itself to almost every occasion. He has one character, perhaps his most serviceable one, which he preserves carefully, and only airs it when making his appeal to the Government or its agents for arms, ammunition, and license to employ them. This character is invariably paraded, and often with telling effect, when the motive is a peaceful one. Prominent chiefs invited to visit Washington invariably don this character, and in their "talks" with the "Great Father" and other less prominent personages they successfully contrive to exhibit but this one phase. Seeing them under these or similar circumstances only, it is not surprising that by many the Indian is looked upon as a simple-minded "son of nature," desiring nothing beyond the privilege of roaming and hunting over the vast unsettled wilds of the West, inheriting and asserting but few native rights, and never trespassing upon the rights of others. This view is equally erroneous with that which regards the Indian as a creature possessing the human form but divested of all other attributes of humanity, and whose traits of character, habits, modes of life, disposition, and savage customs disqualify him from the exercise of all rights and privileges, even those pertaining to life itself. Taking him as we find him, at peace or at war, at home or abroad, waiving all prejudices and laying aside all partiality, we will discover...a race incapable of being judged by the rules or laws applicable to any other known race of men; one between which and civilization there seems to have existed from time immemorial a determined and unceasing warfare—a hostility so deep-seated and inbred with the Indian character, that in the exceptional circumstances where the modes and habits of civilization have been reluctantly adopted, it has been at the sacrifice of power and influence as a tribe, and the more serious loss of health, vigor, and courage as individuals.

In studying the Indian character, while shocked and disgusted by many of his traits and customs, I find much to be admired, and still more of deep and unvarying interest. To me Indian life, with its attendant ceremonies, mysteries, and forms, is a book of unceasing interest. Grant that some of its pages are frightful, and, if possible, to be avoided, yet the attraction is none the weaker. Study him, fight him, civilize him if you can, he remains still the object of your curiosity, a type of man peculiar and undefined, subjecting himself to no known law of civilization, contending determinedly against all efforts to win him from his chosen mode of life. He stands in the group of nations solitary and reserved, seeking alliance with none, mistrusting and opposing the advances of all. Civilization may and should do much for him, but it can never civilize him.

Custer's Last Charge
An 1876 Currier & Ives lithograph.

CUSTER OPPOSES GRANT'S INDIAN POLICY

Custer outlined his opposition to Grant's Indian policies in his memoirs. In 1876 he openly voiced his criticism in testimony before a congressional committee alleging that Grant's Secretary of War, William Belknap, was selling post-traderships. "General Custer testified...that he had called Belknap's attention to abuses, but with no result," reported the New York *Herald* on March 30, 1876. "The sale of post-traderships was a peculiarly mean piece of robbery, for all the money that was got out of such bargains...was forced out of the pockets of poor soldiers." Belknap was impeached. Custer explained:

I believe the reasons why the Indians should be controlled by the Department of War, the department which must assume the reins of power when any real control is exercised, are convincing. This I believe to be the true solution of our difficulties with the Indians at the present day. It seems almost incredible that a policy which is claimed and represented to be based on sympathy for the red man and a desire to secure to him his rights, is shaped in reality and manipulated behind the scenes with the distinct and sole object of reaping a rich harvest by plundering both the Government and the Indians. To do away with the vast army of agents, traders, and civilian employees which is a necessary appendage of the civilian policy, would be to deprive members of Congress of a vast deal of patronage which they now enjoy.

On July 29, 1876, *Harper's Weekly* published these drawings, said to be executed by Sitting Bull. *Harper's* explained that the collection of drawings "was brought into Fort Buford by a Yanktonnais Sioux, and sold for a dollar and fifty cents worth of provisions. When cross-questioned regarding the ownership of the book, the Indian shuffled and prevaricated so as to confirm the belief that he had stolen it from SITTING BULL himself...The series consists of fifty-five designs,....clearly outlined with a pen and a brown ink resembling sepia....Of all the objects presented by the artist, the figure of the buffalo bull is elaborated with the most intelligent and loving minuteness."

His First Adventure

Without Regard To Number Or Sex

Kills A Crow Indian

Counts Coup On An Irishman

There are few, if any, more comfortable or desirable places of disposing of a friend who has rendered valuable political service or electioneering aid, than to secure for him the appointment of Indian agent. The salary of an agent is comparatively small. Men without means, however, eagerly accept the position; and in a few years, at furthest, they almost invariably retire in wealth. Who ever heard of a retired Indian agent or trader in limited circumstances? How do they realize fortunes upon so small a salary? In the disposition of the annuities provided for the Indians by the Government, the agent is usually the distributing medium. Between himself and the Indian there is no system of accountability, no vouchers given or received, no books kept, in fact no record except the statement which the agent chooses to forward to his superintendent...The trader is usually present at the distribution of annuities. If the agent, instead of distributing to the Indians all of the goods intended for them by the Government, only distributed one half and retains the other half, who is to the wiser? Not the Indian, defrauded though he may be, for he is ignorant of how much is coming to him. The word of the agent is his only guide."

THE BATTLE OF WASHITA

At the battle of Washita (in what is now Oklahoma), on November 27, 1868, Custer defeated Black Kettle's Cheyennes. The battle marked the culmination of the campaign against the Indians of the southern Great Plains. Custer wrote:

From and after the Washita campaign the frontiers of Kansas have enjoyed comparative peace and immunity from Indian depredations. No general Indian war has prevailed in that part of the country, nor is it probable that anything more serious in this way than occasional acts of horse-stealing will occur hereafter.

SITTING BULL

Sitting Bull, who directed the annihilation of Custer's column at the Little Big Horn, was well known and much feared before the battle made his name famous forever. In the 1870's, the Cheyenne, Arapaho and Sioux Indians who inhabited the northern Great Plains rallied around Sitting Bull. Edward P. Smith, the Commissioner of Indian Affairs, warned in his report in 1875 that it would "probably be found necessary to compel the northern non-treaty Sioux, under the leadership of Sitting Bull, who have never in any way recognized the United States Government except by snatching rations occasionally at an agency...to cease marauding and settle down...This may occasion conflict between this band of Indians and the soldiers." So many myths grew up about Sitting Bull that it is difficult to distinguish fact from fiction. Some said that there were two Sitting Bulls; others credited him with

Steals A Drove Of Horses

(Copyrighted, 1884, by PALMQUIST & JURGENS.)

Sitting Bull, the Chief of the Unkpapa Sioux

A nineteenth-century biographer described the life of the famous chief: "In early life he was somewhat noted both as a hunter and warrior, and in early middle age gained prestige as a medicine man (the Sioux order of priesthood) and counselor. Although destitute of hereditary claims to chieftainship, by shrewdness, diplomacy and force of character he gained both influence and followers, while by his pronounced and bitter hostility to the whites he earned notoriety throughout the United States. When Custer was killed on the Little Big Horn, in June, 1876, Sitting Bull was the consulting head of five thousand warriors. After that massacre, the huge camp was broken up, and Sitting Bull with a thousand or more retreated into the British territory whence until 1881, he made frequent raids upon American soil. His band constantly suffered depletion until, in the summer of 1881, he had but one hundred and sixty followers remaining. These he surrendered to Lieut. Col. Brotherton at Fort Buford, and with them was sent as a prisoner to Fort Randall, Dakota: Here he remained until May, 1883, when he was released and sent to his present home, among his kindred, at Standing Rock Agency, seventy miles south of Bismarck, on the Missouri River. He has had four wives and seven children."

Kills A Frontiers-man

Storms A Crow Encampment And Takes Thirty Scalps

A Regular Duel

Bags A Bearer Of Dispatches

General & Mrs. Custer and Tom Custer, the General's Brother

The two brothers were almost inseparable and they died together in the battle of Little Big Horn. Three days before his terrible death, George Custer wrote to his wife: "I have but a few moments to write, as we move at twelve...do not be anxious about me. You would be surprised to know how closely I obey your instructions about keeping with the column. I hope to have a good report to send you by the next mail..." There was, of course, no next report.

Mrs. Custer, who accompanied her husband in the field for twelve years, vividly described in her diary the life of a woman on the frontier: "My danger in connection with the Indians was twofold. I was in peril from death or capture by the savages, and liable to be killed by my own friends to prevent my capture. During the five years I had been with the regiment in Kansas I had marched many hundred miles. Sometimes I had to join my husband going across a dangerous country, and the exposure from Indians all those years had been constant. I had been a subject of conversation among the officers, being the only woman who, as a rule, followed the regiment;...A woman on the frontier is so cherished and appreciated, because she has the courage to live out there, that there is nothing that is not done for her if she be gracious and courteous. In twenty little ways the officers spoiled us; they never allowed us to wait on ourselves, to open or shut a door, to draw up our own chair, or to do any little service that they could perform for us."

writing poems in French and Latin. In July 1876, *Harper's Weekly* published a series of drawings attributed to Sitting Bull showing some of the Indian chief's adventures. An article accompanying the drawings described him:

Sitting Bull—the *nom de guerre* of this notorious personage—is a chief of the Unkpapa tribe of the Sioux nation, inhabiting the country about the Yellowstone and Powder rivers. He first gained renown in border history by his exploits near Fort Buford, and ranging up and down the Missouri River for several hundred miles above and below the post. At the head of sixty or seventy warriors, from 1866 to 1870 he was the terror of mail-carriers, wood-choppers, scouts, and small parties that trusted themselves outside the fort in any direction. During that period he captured and destroyed the United States Mail several times, besides killing and scalping Yankees enough to entitle him to a seat in Congress. It is also computed that he captured over two hundred head of cattle, to say nothing of horses, mules and Indians of the neighboring tribes.

ELIZABETH B. CUSTER

Elizabeth Custer accompanied her husband in the field for twelve years. In her diary she described every aspect of the life of a woman on the plains. She lived for over fifty years after Custer's death and she devoted much of that time to writing articles and books in defense of her husband's actions in the battle of Little Big Horn. Her description of receiving the news of her husband's death is especially poignant. She was at a fort in the Dakota territory when the battle took place.

BOOTS AND SADDLES, BY ELIZABETH B. CUSTER

Our women's hearts fell when the fiat went forth that there was to be a summer campaign, with probably actual fighting with Indians. Sitting Bull refused to make a treaty with the government and would not come in to live on a reservation. Besides, his constant attacks on the white settlers, driving back even the most adventurous, he was incessantly invading and stealing from the land assigned to the peaccable Crows. They appealed for help to the government that had promised to shield them.

The preparations for the expedition were completed before my husband returned from the East, whither he had been ordered. [Custer had been away in the East testifying about Belknap. Mrs. Custer does not discuss either her husband's testimony or Grant's displeasure with Custer which led to General Terry being placed in charge of the expedition against the Sioux instead of Custer.]

The morning for the start came only too soon. My husband was to take Sister Margaret and me out for the first day's march, so I rode beside him out of camp. The column that followed seemed unending. The grass was not then suitable for grazing, and as the route of travel was through a barren country, immense quantities of forage had to be transported. The wagons themselves seemed to stretch out interminably. There were pack mules, the ponies already laden, and cavalry, artillery, and infantry followed, the cavalry being in advance of all. The number of men, citizens, employees, Indian scouts, and soldiers was about twelve hundred. There were nearly seventeen hundred animals in all.

As we rode at the head of the column, we were the first to enter the confines of the garrison. About the Indian quarters, which we were obliged to pass, stood the squaws, the old men, and the children, singing, or rather moaning, a minor tune that has been uttered on the going out of Indian warriors since time immemorial. Some of the squaws crouched on the ground, too burdened with their troubles to hold up their heads; others restrained the restless children who, discerning their fathers, sought to follow them.

The Indian scouts themselves beat their drums and kept up their peculiar monotonous tune, which is weird and melancholy beyond

The New Alliance—We Stand for Retrenchment and Reducing the Army of the United States

In this drawing, Thomas Nast, the famed Republican cartoonist, implies that the Democrats, by cutting back the army, were perhaps to blame for the Little Big Horn massacre.

"Bill Passed Providing for Two New Military Posts" by the Generous Democratic House

Another Nast cartoon ridiculing the soft policy of the Democrats toward the Indians.

description. Their war song is misnamed when called music. It is more of a lament or a dirge than an inspiration to activity. This intoning they kept up for miles along the road. After we had passed the Indian quarters we came near Laundress Row, and there my heart entirely failed me. The wives and children of the soldiers lined the road. Mothers, with streaming eyes, held their little ones out at arm's length for one last look at their departing fathers. The toddlers among the children, unnoticed by their elders, had made a mimic column of their own. With their handkerchiefs tied to sticks in lieu of flags, and beating old tin pans for drums, they strode lustily back and forth in imitation of the advancing soldiers. They were fortunately too young to realize why the mothers wailed out their farewells....

When our band struck up "The Girl I Left Behind Me," the most despairing hour seemed to have come. All the sad-faced wives of the officers who had forced themselves to their doors to try to wave a courageous farewell and smile bravely to keep the ones they loved from knowing the anguish of their breaking hearts gave up the struggle at the sound of the music.

...From the hour of breaking camp, before the sun was up, a mist had enveloped everything. Soon the bright sun began to penetrate this veil and dispel the haze, and a scene of wonder and beauty appeared. The cavalry and infantry in the order named, the scouts, pack mules, and artillery, all behind the long line of white-covered wagons, made a column altogether some two miles in length. As the sun broke through the mist a mirage appeared, which took up about half of the line of cavalry, and thenceforth for a little distance it marched, equally plain to the sight on the earth and in the sky.

The future of the heroic band, whose days were even then numbered, seemed to be revealed, and already there seemed a premonition in the supernatural translation as their forms were reflected from the opaque mist of the early dawn.

...The general could scarcely restrain his recurring joy at being detained on other duty. His spirits at the prospect of the activity of field life that he so loved made him like a boy. He was sanguine that but a few weeks would elapse before we would be reunited and used this argument to animate me with courage to meet our separation.

As usual we rode a little in advance and selected camp, and watched the approach of the regiment with real pride. They were so accustomed to the march the line hardly diverged from the trail. There was a unity of movement about them that made the column at a distance seem like a broad dark ribbon stretched smoothly over the plains.

We made our camp the first night on a small river a few miles beyond the post. There the paymaster made his disbursements, in order that the debts of the soldiers might be liquidated with the sutler.

In the morning the farewell was said, and the paymaster took sister and me back to the post.

With my husband's departure my last happy days in garrison were ended, as a premonition of disaster that I had never known before weighed me down.

A picture of one day of our life in those disconsolate times is fixed indelibly in my memory.

On Sunday afternoon, June 25, our little group of saddened women, borne down with one common weight of anxiety, sought solace in gathering together in our house. We tried to find some slight surcease from trouble in the old hymns; some of them dated back to our childhood days, when our mothers rocked us to sleep to their soothing strains. I remember the grief with which one fair young wife threw herself on the carpet and pillowed her head in the lap of a tender friend. Another sat dejected at the piano and struck soft chords that melted into the notes of the voices. All were absorbed in the same thoughts, and their eyes were filled with faraway visions and longings. Indescribable yearning for the absent, and untold terror for their safety, engrossed each heart.

At that very hour the fears that our tortured minds had portrayed in imagination were realities, and the souls of those we thought upon were ascending to meet their Maker.

On July 5—it took that time for the news to come—the sun rose on a beautiful world, but with its earliest beams came the first knell of disaster. A steamer came down the river bearing the wounded from the battle of the Little Big Horn, of Sunday, June 25. This battle wrecked the lives of twenty-six women at Fort Lincoln, and orphaned children of officers and soldiers joined the cry to that of their bereaved mothers.

From that time the life went out of the hearts of the "women who weep," and God asked them to walk on alone and in the shadow.

The Gold Regions of the Black Hills, Showing the Scene of the Massacre of General Custer's Troops, and the Indian Reservations and Military Posts in the Western Portion of the United States.

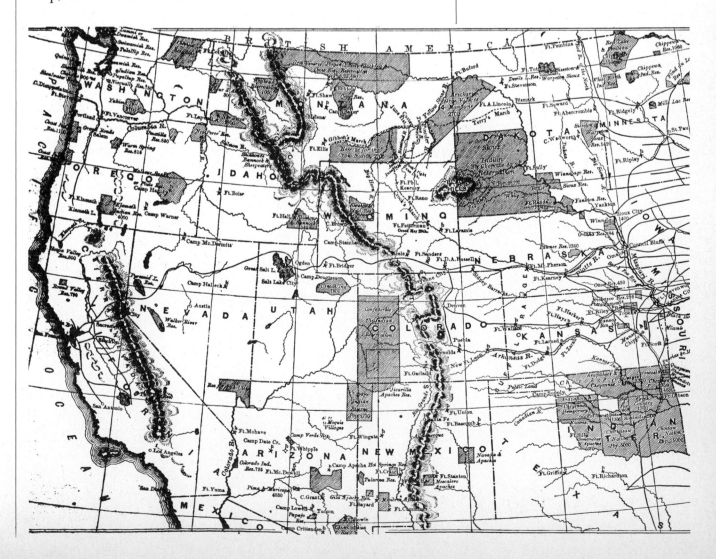

One year later: Scene of Custer's Last Stand—a pile of bones is all that remains.

THE BATTLE OF LITTLE BIG HORN

Not until July 6, 1876, did news of the Little Big Horn massacre reach the East Coast. The *New York Times* headlined:

> GEN. CUSTER AND SEVENTEEN COMMIS-SIONED OFFICERS BUTCHERED IN A BAT-TLE OF THE LITTLE HORN—ATTACK ON AN OVERWHELMINGLY LARGE CAMP OF SAV-AGES—THREE HUNDRED AND FIFTEEN MEN KILLED AND THIRTY-ONE WOUNDED—THE BATTLE-FIELD LIKE A SLAUGHTER PEN.

A FULLER REPORT FROM THE SCENE— GENERAL TERRY ARRIVES AT THE SITE

They met a sight to appall the stoutest heart...General Custer had evidently attempted to attack the village...the trail was found to lead back up to the bluffs and to the northward, as if he had been repulsed and compelled to retreat...The bluffs are separated by enormous ravines and all along these slopes and ridges, and in the ravines lay the dead, lying in the order of battle as they had fought. Line held, till at last few were left to fight, and then, huddled in a narrow compass, horses and men were piled promiscuously. At the highest point of the ridge lay Custer, surrounded by his chosen band. Here were his two brothers, and his nephew, all lying within a circle of a few yards, their horses beside them. Here the last stand had been made, and here one after another of these last survivors of Custer's five companies had met their death...Not a man had escaped to tell the tale, but it was inscribed on the surface of these barren hills in a language more eloquent than words.

...It is obvious that the troops were completely surrounded by a force of ten times their number...

...Information derived from Army sources...leads to the conclusion that 2,500 or 3,000 Indians composed the fighting force arrayed against Custer and his 600.

By July 7 the debate over the battle and its causes had begun. Much of the debate focused on Custer. Many felt the general had behaved impetuously, seeking glory for himself and willfully risking the lives of his men by attacking the Sioux without an adequate force or adequate arms. Army officers seemed united in blaming Custer for the disaster:

It is the opinion of Army officers in Chicago, Washington, and Philadelphia, including Gens. Sherman and Sheridan, that Gen. Custer was rashly imprudent to attack such a large number of Indians. Sitting Bull's force being 4,000 strong. Gen. Sherman thinks that the accounts of the disaster are exaggerated...

...In reply to an inquiry as to whether the attack was made by Gen. Custer of his own accord, or under orders from the department, an answer was given that Custer made the charge of his own volition...

GENERAL TERRY EXONERATES HIMSELF– ACCUSES CUSTER OF DISOBEYING ORDERS

We calculated it would take Gibbons' column until the 26th to reach the mouth of the Little Big Horn, and that the wide sweep I had prepared Custer should make would require so much time that Gibbon would be able to co-operate with him in attacking any Indians that might be found on the stream. I asked Custer how long his marches would be. He said they would be at the rate of about thirty miles a day. Measurements were made and calculations based on that rate of progress. I talked with him about his strength and at one time suggested that perhaps it would be well for me to take Gibbon and go with him. To the latter suggestion he replied that he would prefer his own regiment alone...I learned that on the 22nd the cavalry marched twelve miles; on the 23rd, twenty-five miles, from 5 A.M. till 8 P.M. of the 24th, forty-five miles, and then after night ten miles further, resting, but without unsaddling, twenty-three miles, to the battle-field...I do not tell you this to cast any reflections upon Custer, for whatever errors he may have committed Custer's action is unexplainable...

CAUSES OF THE DISASTER

Army officers were interested in the tactics of the battle. Others tried to look beyond the battle itself to find the underlying causes of the disaster. "The remote cause," as the *New York Times* pointed out on July 7, 1876, was Custer's discovery of gold in the Black Hills in 1874 which had led to an invasion of the Sioux territory by miners:

The campaign against the wild Sioux was undertaken under disadvantageous circumstances owing to the refusal of Congress to appropriate money for the establishment of military posts on the upper Yellowstone River...which in case of anticipated troubles would give the troops a base of supplies about four hundred miles nearer the hostile country than they could otherwise have...This is regarded as the immediate cause of the disaster. The remote cause was undoubtedly the expedition into the Black Hills two years ago in violation of laws and treaties, authorized by Secretary Belknap and led by Gen. Custer..The feeling was common today that the campaign is a failure, and that there must follow a general Indian war, promising to be costly in men and money. The Sioux are a distinct race of men from the so-called Indians of the Southwest, among whom the army found much easy work two or three years ago...This difference between the foes in the North and the Southwest seems not to have been well counted upon, nor provided for, and formed as it might, prudently, no restraint upon the...fatal charge of the 300. If the tale told by the courier Taylor is true, the charge has scarce a parallel in the history of civilized or savage warfare...The reasons for an expedition against the Indians this Summer is not well understood, nor has any satisfactory explanation been published. The wild Sioux had never been willing to live upon the reservations marked out for them and the understanding has been that they were to be whipped into submission...The question of the policy and right of the war will now be renewed and discussed, and indeed is discussed today. Those who believe in the policy of the

George Catlin

This drawing appeared in the 1876 edition of George Catlin's *Customs of the North American Indians*.

In 1876 George Catlin had been dead for four years, but many Americans were familiar with the six hundred or more paintings he had done of the Indians.

Catlin had sympathized with the plight of the Indian: "He who will sit and contemplate that vast Frontier, where...one hundred and twenty thousand of these poor people...have been removed several hundred miles to the West...will assuredly pity them...I have closely studied the Indian character in its native state. I have seen it in every phase...yet the greater part of those who have lingered along the Frontiers, and been kicked like dogs, by white men, and beaten into a sort of civilization, are very far from being what I would be...proud to call them, civilized...

"Standing on the soil which they have occupied from their childhood, and inherited from their fathers; with the dread of 'pale faces,'...the deadly prejudices that have been reared in their breasts against them, for the destructive influences which they have introduced into their country, which have thrown the greater part of their friends and connections into the grave, and are now promising the remainder of them no better prospect than the dreary one of living a few years longer, and then to sink into the ground themselves; surrendering their lands and their fair hunting grounds to the enjoyment of their enemies, and their bones to be dug up and strewed about the fields, or to be labelled in our Museums...

...for the Nation, there is an unrequitted account of sin and injustice that sooner or later will call for *national retribution*..."

1. Battle of the Big Horn, by Kurz and Allison, 1889

The *New York Times,* on July 7, 1876, said: "Sitting Bull's band of Sioux left their reservation with hostile intent. They refused negotiations for peace. They defied the power and authority of the United States. They invited war. A force was sent against them. This force became divided, and General Custer, with five companies, coming up to the main body of the Sioux, attacked them impetuously, without waiting for the support of the remainder of the column. The result was that the entire body of men...fell into a death-trap..."

2. General Custer's Death Struggle

This lithograph by H. Steinegger after a drawing done by S. H. Redman in 1878 shows Custer fighting off the Indians on all sides. The New York *Herald* quoted Sitting Bull as saying of Custer: "When the last stand was made, the Long Hair stood like a sheaf of corn with all the ears fallen around him."

1

3. Custer's Last Rally, by John Mulvany

Finished in 1881, this is one of the best-known paintings of the battle of Little Big Horn. Note the saber in Custer's left hand, which was an invention of the artist. There were no sabers or swords used in the fight, and Custer wore a buckskin coat, not the full-dress uniform in which he was painted by Mulvany.

4. Sioux Drawing of the Battle of Little Big Horn, by Red Horse of the Cheyenne River Agency

3

2

4

Custer's Last Charge
Lithograph after the drawing by Feodor Fuchs, 1876.

On July 10, 1876, Walt Whitman published in the New York *Tribune* "A Death-Sonnet for Custer":

...Thou of the sunny, flowing hair, in battle,
I erewhile now, with erect head, pressing
  ever in front, bearing a bright sword
  in thy hand,
Now ending well the splendid favor of thy
  deeds, (I bring no dirge for it or thee—
  I bring a glad, triumphal sonnet;)
There in the far northwest, in struggle,
  charge, and saber-smite,
Desperate and glorious—aye in defeat
  most desperate, most glorious,
After thy many battles, in which, never
  yielding up a gun or a color,
Leaving behind thee a memory sweet to
  soldiers
Thou yieldest up thyself.

The monument erected on the summit of the ridge overlooking the valley of the Little Big Horn River in Montana. The names of the fallen are inscribed on the monument.

Photo by F. J. Haynes

Life Among the Navajos in New Mexico, c. 1873

By 1876 few Indian tribes were untouched by civilization. The peaceful Navajos were among the last to be affected by the white man's culture. Here textiles are being woven on a primitive loom.

extermination of the Indians, and think the speedier the better its accomplishment, look upon the condition of war as inevitable, and are for pouring thousands of troops into the Indian country and giving them a terrible punishment. This class is small, even in the Army, where the policy of extermination is not popular save with a few high and restless officers. The invasion of the Black Hills has been condemned over and over again by the peace party, and there are very many who can truthfully say, "I told you so." From that unwarranted invasion the present difficulties have gradually sprung up, so that an expedition that originally cost a hundred thousand dollars perhaps, must lead to an expenditure of millions, which will advance civilization in no way, except by the destruction of the uncivilized.

THE SENATE ASKS SOME QUESTIONS

...On motion of Mr. Ingalls, the Senate today adopted a resolution requesting the President to inform the Senate whether the Sioux Indians made any hostile demonstrations prior to the invasion of their treaty reservation by the gold hunters, whether the present military operations are conducted for the purpose of protecting said Indians in their rights under the treaty of 1868, or of punishing them for resisting the violation of that treaty...

The Secretary of War, J. D. Cameron, wrote a letter to President Grant on July 8 providing Grant with answers to the Senate's questions. Cameron explained:

...The Sioux, or Dakota nation of Indians,...have long been known as the most brave and war-like savages of this continent. They have for centuries been pushed westward by the advancing tide of civilization, till in 1868 an arrangement or treaty was made with them by special commission named by Congress, whereby for certain payment or stipulations they agreed to surrender their claims to all of that vast region which lies west of the Missouri River and north of the Platte, to live at peace with their neighbors, to restrict themselves to a territory bounded east by the Missouri River, south by Nebraska, west by the one hundred and fourth meridian, and north by the forty-sixth parallel of latitude, a territory as large as the State of Michigan. The terms of this treaty have been liberally performed on the part of the United States, and have also been complied with by the great mass of the Sioux Indians. Some of these Indians, however, have never recognized the binding force of this treaty, but have always treated it with contempt, have continued to rove at pleasure, attacking scattered settlements in Nebraska, Wyoming, Montana, and Dakota, stealing horses and cattle and murdering peaceful inhabitants and travelers. [Cameron explained that the Secretary of the Interior had on December 3, 1875] directed the Commissioner of Indian Affairs to notify...Sitting Bull and others outside their reservation that they must remove to the reservation before the 31st day of January, 1876; that if they neglected or refused to move, that they will be reported to the War Department as hostile Indians, and that a military force will be sent to compel them to obey the order of the Indian officer.

On the 1st day of February the Secretary of the Interior...notified the Secretary of War, the time given...Sitting Bull in which to return to an agency having expired,...the said Indians are hereby turned over to the War Department for such action on the part of the Army as you may deem proper...

CAMERON DENIES LUST FOR GOLD AS MOTIVE

The accidental discovery of gold on the western border of the Sioux reservation and the intrusion of our people thereon have not caused this war...The object of these military expeditions was in the interest of the peaceful parts of the Sioux nations supposed to embrace at least nine-tenths of the whole, and not one of these peaceful treaty Indians has been molested by the military authorities.

CONSEQUENCES: THE GOVERNMENT DETERMINED TO CHASTISE THE INDIANS

After Custer's defeat there was a general cry for revenge against the Indians. General Sheridan wrote to General Sherman that "There is nothing to be regretted but poor Custer's death...There is no cause for uneasiness and we will soon give the Indians another turn."

And the *New York Times* reported on July 8:

It is agreed on all hands that there must now be an Indian war till the hostile Indians of the Northwest have been chastised and subjugated. The cause and the responsibility of the Little Big Horn massacre are matters of small moment in deciding what shall be done. Western men freely predict that unless extraordinary efforts at defense are immediately made the miners in the Black Hills and the principal settlements in Montana will be harassed and many of them destroyed. The regular Army is not believed to be sufficiently strong to protect them, and a resort to raising volunteers is thought by many to be necessary.

GRANT, SHERMAN AND CAMERON DISCUSS PLANS FOR REVENGE

Gen. Sherman returned today from Philadelphia and, together with Secretary Cameron, spent the evening with the President, discussing the disaster to Gen. Custer and his command. A vigorous campaign will be immediately organized against the hostile Sioux under the personal directions of Gen. Sheridan...An impression is also felt in the highest quarters that the troops now in the West near the scene of the present operations against the Indians are numerically, as well as in every other respect, able to enforce the demands of the Government upon the hostile tribes and to inflict proper chastisement upon them.

RETALIATION SUCCESSFUL: SIOUX AND CHEYENNES BROUGHT UNDER CONTROL

In September, General Crook, the well-known Indian-fighter, struck the first successful blow against a camp of Oglala, Brule and Minneconjou Indians at Slim Buttes, Dakota Territory. In the camp of the defeated Indians, "Gray Fox Crook" found three horses that had belonged to the Seventh Cavalry and other evidence that those

This photograph by F. Jay Haynes shows a Crow Indian burial ground. This stereo card was part of Haynes's series published circa 1876 "comprising scenes along the entire line of the Northern Pacific Railroad from St. Paul and Lake Superior to Portland and Puget Sound." In 1876 Haynes became the official photographer of Yellowstone National Park. Haynes was part of a group of landscape photographers who were more interested in what the tourist wanted to buy than in the quality of the photograph.

Sitting Bull's Deserted Tepee, by F. Jay Haynes, c. 1876

The Indian outside of this tepee, which ostensibly belonged to Sitting Bull, was definitely posed by the photographer. Sitting Bull, who escaped into Canada after the battle of Little Big Horn, was said to have asked, "What have we done that the white people want us to stop? We have been running up and down this country, but they follow us from one place to another."

Young Apache Warrior and His Squaw, Near Camp Apache, Arizona, by T. H. O'Sullivan

In his memoirs, General George A. Custer described admiringly the Indian method of marriage and divorce: "According to Indian customs the consent of the bride to a proposed marriage is not deemed essential. All that is considered absolutely essential is, that the bridegroom shall be acceptable to the father of the bride, and shall transfer to the possession of the latter ponies or other articles of barter, in sufficient number and value to be considered a fair equivalent for the hand of the daughter..." Describing one particular Indian marriage with which he was familiar, Custer wrote: "...When it is stated that from two to four ponies are considered as the price of the average squaw, and that the price for the hand of Mo-nah-se-tah, as finally arranged, was eleven ponies, some idea can be formed of the high opinion entertained of her...all the formalities were duly executed which, by Indian law and custom, were necessary to constitute Mo-nah-se-tah the wife of a young brave. She was forced to take up her abode in his lodge, but refused to acknowledge him as her husband, or to render him that obedience and menial service which the Indian husband exacts from his wife...Here was a clear case of 'incompatibility of disposition'; and within the jurisdiction of some of our State laws a divorce would have been granted... When her husband, or rather the husband who had been assigned to her, attempted to establish by force an authority which she had persistently refused to recognize, she reminded him that she was the daughter of a great chief, and rather than submit to the indignities which he was thus attempting to heap upon her, she would resist even to the taking of life; and suiting the action to the word, she levelled a small pistol which she had carried concealed beneath her blanket and fired, wounding him in the knee and disabling him for life." Mo-nah-se-tah's father learned of her action and "finding upon investigation that his daughter had not been to blame, concluded to cancel the marriage—to grant a divorce—which was accomplished simply by returning to the unfortunate husband the eleven ponies which had been paid for the hand of Mo-nah-se-tah. What an improvement upon the method prescribed in the civilized world! No lawyer's fees, no publicity nor scandal; all tedious delays are avoided, and the result is as nearly satisfactory to all parties as is possible."

Indians had been at the Little Big Horn. Colonel Ronald McKenzie struck the next blow, this time at the Cheyennes at Willow Creek in Montana. Kill Eagle, Sioux chief, was put in jail. And Red Cloud, chief of the Oglala Sioux, sold out his people by signing over the Black Hills to the government. Helen Hunt Jackson, a novelist who sympathized with the plight of the Indian, described the terms of the settlement with Red Cloud:

In the months of September and October, 1876, the various Sioux agencies were visited by a commission appointed under the Act of Congress, August 15th of that year, to negotiate with the Sioux for an agreement to surrender that portion of the Sioux Reservation which included the Black Hills, and certain hunting privileges outside that reserve, guaranteed by the treaty of 1868; to grant a right of way across their reserve; and to provide for the removal of the Red Cloud and Spotted Tail bands to new agencies on the Missouri River. The commission were successful in all the negotiations with which they were charged, and the Indians made every concession that was desired by the Government.

Lost River Murderers, by L. Heller

These three so-called murderers were Modoc Indians, who came from Lost River, Oregon, and fought a war against one thousand U.S. Army troops between November of 1872 and June of 1873. The Indians did not want to retreat to the government reservation designed for them in Oregon. They were defeated in 1873.

Eadweard J. Muybridge photographed the war and admired the courage of the Modoc fighters: "....the few Indians with the bravery at least of the classic three hundred, defied and fought the army of the Union..."

This war was one of many battles between the Indians and whites which culminated in the Battle of Little Big Horn.

Helen Hunt Jackson, probably the most prolific woman writer of the day, attempted to awaken the nation from its self-righteous slumber to what she considered to be the shocking plight of the Indian: "If I can do one-hundredth part for the Indians as Mrs. Stowe did for the Negro, I will be thankful." Her book, *A Century of Dishonor,* published in 1881, shocked the nation:

A CENTURY OF DISHONOR, BY HELEN HUNT JACKSON

Interior of a Pueblo Indian Home, c. 1875
The Pueblo Indians inhabited New Mexico.

There is not among these three hundred bands of Indians one which has not suffered cruelly at the hands either of the Government or of white settlers. The poorer, the more insignificant, the more helpless the band, the more certain the cruelty and outrage to which they have been subjected. These Indians found themselves all of a sudden surrounded by and caught up in the great influx of gold-seeking settlers....There was not time for the Government to make treaties; not even time for communities to make laws....Colorado is as greedy and unjust in 1880 as was Georgia in 1830, and Ohio in 1795; and the United States Government breaks promises now as deftly as then and with the added ingenuity from long practice. One of its strongest supports in so doing is the wide-spread sentiment among the people of dislike of the Indian, of impatience with his presence as a "barrier to civilization," and distrust of it as a possible danger.

However great perplexity and difficulty there may be in the details of any and every plan possible for doing at this late day anything like justice to the Indian, however hard it may be for good statesmen and good men to agree upon the things that ought to be done, there certainly is, or ought to be, no perplexity whatever, no difficulty whatever, in agreeing upon certain things that ought not to be done, and which must cease to be done before the first steps can be taken toward righting the wrongs, curing the ills, and wiping out the disgrace to us of the present condition of our Indians.

Apache Squaw and Papoose, by T. H. O'Sullivan
The child, securely lashed in the wicker basket which was attached to the back of the mother, was often carried all day in this manner.

Cheating, robbing, breaking promises—these three are clearly things which must cease to be done. One more thing, also, and that is the refusal of the protection of the law to the Indian's rights of property, "of life, liberty, and the pursuit of happiness."

Till these four things have ceased to be done, statesmanship and philanthropy alike must work in vain, and even Christianity can reap but small harvest.

It has come to be such an accepted thing in the history and fate of the Indian that he is always pushed on, always in advance of what is called the march of civilization...Such uprooting, such perplexity , such loss, such confusion and uncertainty, inflicted once on any community of white people anywhere in our land, would be considered quite enough to destroy its energies and blight its prospects for years. It may very well be questioned whether any of our small communities would have recovered from such successive shocks, changes, and forced migrations, as soon and as well as have many of these Indian tribes. It is very certain that they would not have submitted to them as patiently...

Apache Braves, Ready for the Trail, Arizona, by T. H. O'Sullivan

The total number of hostile Indians in the Northwest and Southwest was officially estimated by Francis A. Walker, the Commissioner of Indian Affairs in 1872, at seven thousand. They were, said Walker, "mainly Kiowas, Comanches, and Apaches raiding from Arizona and from the Indian Territory through Texas into Mexico." According to the *New York Times* on July 23, 1876: "In 1874-5 the majority of these came in and gave themselves up, and the worst characters, or those reputed to be the worst, were sent off to Florida and imprisoned. The operations of the Government within the last three years...have reduced the number of hostiles among the Sioux in the Northwest and the Apaches in Arizona to less than a thousand warriors....In other words, all the actively hostile Kiowas, Comanches, Apaches, Utes, and Sioux...number today less than twenty-five hundred....If, as the late official dispatches from Red Cloud and Spotted Tail Agencies in Dakota represent, no Sioux have left those agencies to join the northern band of non-treaty Sioux, against whom Gen. Crook is planning a campaign, there cannot be now over three or four hundred actually hostile Sioux in all that Northwest region....These original occupants of the Black Hills, have a foolish notion that they ought to receive some sort of an equivalent for the country surrendered, besides whisky and disease which our frontier civilization offers them."

In contrast to Mrs. Jackson, Commissioner Smith in his report shows no concern or feeling for the Indian. He was adamant that the Indians must learn to live like white men, that they must abandon their idea of tribal ownership and become individual landowners. It was his view that would triumph, not that of Helen Hunt Jackson, for it sanctioned the white man's appropriation of the West.

REPORT OF COMMISSIONER OF INDIAN AFFAIRS J. Q. SMITH, OCTOBER 30, 1876

From the first settlement of the country by white men until a comparatively recent period, the Indians have been constantly driven westward from the Atlantic. A zigzag, ever-varying line...has been known as the "frontier" or "border." Along this border has been an almost incessant struggle, the Indians to retain and the whites to get possession; the war being broken by periods of occasional and temporary peace, which usually followed treaties whereby the Indians agreed to surrender large tracts of their lands. This peace would continue until the lands surrendered had been occupied by whites, when the pressure of emigration would again break over the border and the Indian, by force or treaty, be compelled to surrender another portion of his cherished hunting grounds.

...Toward the close of the first half of this century the tide of emigration and adventure swept even the frontier away and rushed across the continent. Throughout the vast regions of the West the adventurous, grasping Anglo-Saxon race is dominant and in possession of the fairest and richest portion of the land...No new hunting-grounds remain, and the civilization or the utter destruction of the Indians is inevitable. The next twenty-five years are to determine the fate of a race. If they cannot be taught, and taught very soon, to accept the necessities of their situation and begin in earnest to provide for their own wants by labor in civilized pursuits, they are destined to speedy extinction.

From the fact that for so long a period Indian civilization has been retarded, it must not be concluded that some inherent characteristic in the race disqualifies it for civilized life. It may well be doubted whether this be true of any race of men. Surely it cannot be true of a race, a portion of which has made the actual progress realized by some of our Indians. They can and do learn to labor; they can and do learn to read. Many thousands to-day are engaged in civilized occupations...The welfare and progress of the Indians require the adoption of three principles of policy:

First: Concentration of All Indians on a Few Reservations

...Wherever an Indian reservation has on it good land, or timber, or minerals, the cupidity of the white man is excited, and a constant struggle is inaugurated to dispossess the Indian, in which the avarice and determination of the white man usually prevails.

...By the concentration of Indians on a few reservations, it is obvious that much of the difficulty now surrounding the Indian question will vanish. The aggregate boundary-lines between the reservations and country occupied by white people would be greatly reduced, and the danger of violence, bloodshed, and mutual wrong materially lessened.

Second: Allotment to Them of Lands in Severalty

...It is doubtful whether any high degree of civilization is possible without individual ownership of land. The records of the past and the experience of the present testify that the soil should be made secure to the individual by all the guarantees which law can devise, and that nothing less will induce men to put forth their best exertions...It seems to me a matter of great moment that provision should be made not only permitting, but requiring, the head of each Indian family to accept the allotment of a reasonable amount of land, to be the property of himself and his lawful heirs, in lieu of any interest in any common tribal possession.

Third: Extension over Them of United States Law and the Jurisdiction of United States Courts

My predecessors have frequently called attention to the startling fact that we have within our midst 275,000 people, the least intelligent portion of our population, for whom we provide no law, either for their protection or for the punishment of crime committed among themselves.

...Our Indians are remitted by a great civilized government to the control, if control it can be called, of the rude regulations of petty, ignorant tribes. Year after year we expend millions of dollars for these people in the faint hope that, without law, we can civilize them.

...I believe it to be the duty of Congress at once to extend over Indian reservations the jurisdiction of United States courts, and to declare that each Indian in the United States shall occupy the same relation to law that a white man does...I regard this suggestion as by far the most important which I have to make in this report.

Since our Government was organized two questions, or rather two classes of questions, have transcended all others in importance and difficulty, viz, the relations of the Government and the white people to the negroes and to the Indians. The negro question has doubtless absorbed more of public attention, aroused more intense feeling, and cost our people more blood and treasure than any other question, if not all others combined. That question, it is to be hoped, is settled forever in the only way in which its settlement was possible—by the full admission of the negro to all the rights and privileges of citizenship. Next in importance comes the Indian question, and there can be no doubt that our Indian wars have cost us more than all the foreign wars in which our Government has been engaged. It is time that some solution of this whole Indian problem, decisive, satisfactory, just, and final, should be found. In my judgment it can be reached only by a process similar to that pursued with the negroes.

For a hundred years the United States has been wrestling with the "Indian question," but has never had an Indian policy...Surely it is time that a policy should be determined on...We cannot afford to allow this race to perish without making an honest effort to save it. We cannot afford to keep them in our midst as vagabonds and paupers.

This stereo card had a photograph by W. H. Jackson of a town built by the Taos Indians in northern New Mexico. The card provided the buyer with the following information on "Los Pueblos de Taos": "The Pueblo or town of the Taos Indians is situated in Northern New Mexico....There are 19 Pueblos in New Mexico, inhabited by about 10,000 Indians. These, in a measure, preserve their old tribal distinctions....These Indians all support themselves by agriculture and stock raising. Their houses are peculiar; they are built almost entirely of adobe and a distinguishable feature is their many storied pyramidal form, the roofs of the lower stories forming a platform for those above them....The Taos Pueblo consists of two large buildings many stories in height, surrounded by quite a number of smaller houses, the whole enclosed by an adobe wall, arranged somewhat as a pentagon and embracing some 10 or 12 acres of ground. A clear and cold mountain stream divides the town in about two equal parts. Within these walls are four of their Estufas, or secret council chambers, and outside three more. These are circular subterranean rooms in which are held their councils and in which they perform the peculiar rites of their native religion. It is said that in one of them is preserved the ever burning fire, which must not be extinguished until the second coming of Montezuma. The Pueblo now number about 400 souls. They elect a governor each year by ballot, who in turn appoints deputies for the management of the Pueblo. The people are divided into clans, each of which has its chief, and in authority above all is the Cacique, a sort of chief justice, a hereditary position, and held for life..."

The Tracks Stevenson Followed, by W. H. Jackson

Robert Louis Stevenson described the train that traveled these tracks from New York to California: "I suppose the reader has some notion of an American railroad-car, that long, narrow wooden box, like a flat-roofed Noah's ark, with a stove and a convenience, one at either end, a passage down the middle, and transverse benches upon either hand. Those destined for emigrants on the Union Pacific are only remarkable for their extreme plainness, nothing but wood entering in any part into their constitution, and for the usual inefficacy of the lamps, which often went out and shed but a dying glimmer even while they burned. The benches are too short for anything but a young child. Where there is scarce elbow-room for two to sit, there will not be space enough for one to lie..."

While others were debating the future of the Indians, Robert Louis Stevenson was riding throught the West on the newly completed transcontinental railroad. He was going from New York to California to find Mrs. Fanny Osbourne, whom he had met and fallen in love with in France in 1876. The novelty of the American western landscape was particularly striking to Stevenson, perhaps because it was so very different from his native Scotland.

FROM SCOTLAND TO SILVERADO, BY ROBERT LOUIS STEVENSON

To one hurrying through by steam there was a certain exhilaration in the spacious vacancy, this greatness of the air, this discovery of the whole arch of heaven, this straight, unbroken, prison-line of the horizon. Yet one could not but reflect upon the weariness of those who passed by there in old days, at the foot's pace of oxen, painfully urging their teams, and with no landmark but that unattainable evening sun for which they steered, and which daily fled them by an equal stride. They had nothing, it would seem, to overtake; nothing by which to reckon their advance; no sight for repose or for encouragement; but stage after stage, only the dead green waste under foot, and the mocking, fugitive horizon...It is the settlers, after all, at whom we have a right to marvel. Our consciousness, by which we live, is itself but the creature of variety. Upon what food does it subsist in such a land? What livelihood can repay a human creature for a life spent in this huge sameness? He is cut off from books, from news, from company, from all that can relieve existence but the prosecution of his affairs. A sky full of stars is the most varied spectacle that he can hope for. He may walk five miles and see nothing; ten, and it is as though he had not moved; twenty, and still he is in the midst of the same great level, and has approached no nearer to the one object within view, the flat horizon which keeps pace with his advance.

...Down the long, sterile cañons, the train shot hooting, and awoke the resting echo. That train was the one piece of life in all the deadly land; it was the one actor, the one spectacle fit to be observed in this paralysis of man and nature. And when I think how the railroad has been pushed through this unwatered wilderness and haunt of savage tribes, and now will bear an emigrant for some twelve pounds from the Atlantic to the Golden Gates; how at each stage of the construction, roaring, impromptu cities, full of gold and lust and death, sprang up and then died away again, and are now but wayside stations in the desert; how in these uncouth places pig-tailed Chinese pirates worked side by side with border ruffians and broken men from Europe, talking together in a mixed dialect, mostly oaths, gambling, drinking, quarrelling, and murdering like wolves;...and then when I go on to remember that all this epical turmoil was conducted by gentlemen in frock-coats, and with a view to nothing more extraordinary than a fortune and subsequent visit to Paris, it seems to me, I own, as if this railway were the one typical achievement of the age in which we live, as if it brought together into one plot all the ends of the world and all degrees of social rank, and offered to some great writer the busiest, the most extended, and the most varied subject for an enduring literary work. If it be romance, if it be contrast, if it be heroism that we require, what was Troy town to this? But, alas! it is not these things that are necessary—it is only Homer.

Another race shared among my fellow-passengers in the disfavor of the Chinese; and that, it is hardly necessary to say, was the noble red man of old story—he over whose own hereditary continent we had been steaming all these days. I saw no wild or independent Indian; indeed, I hear that such avoid the neighbourhood of the train; but now and again at way-stations, a husband and wife and a few children, disgracefully dressed out with the sweeping of civilization, came forth and stared upon the emigrants. The silent stoicism of their conduct, and the pathetic degradation of their appearance, would have touched any thinking creature, but my fellow-passengers danced and jested round them with a truly Cockney baseness. I was ashamed for the thing we call civilization. We should carry upon our consciences so much, at least, of our forefathers' misconduct as we continue to profit by ourselves.

If oppression drives a wise man bad, what should be raging in the hearts of these poor tribes, who have been driven back and back, step after step, their promised reservations torn from them one after another as the States extended westwards, until at length they are shut up into these hideous mountain deserts of the centre—and even there find themselves invaded, insulted, and hunted out by ruffianly diggers? The eviction of the Cherokees (to name but an instance), the extortion

East Meets West: The Joining of the Union Pacific and Central Pacific Railroads on May 10, 1869 at Promontory, Utah, by A. J. Russell

This event changed life in America. Coast-to-coast travel was possible for the first time.

Charles Nordhoff wrote: "...west of Chicago men live on the cars. In the East a railroad journey is an interruption to our lives. We submit to it, because no one has yet been ingenious enough to contrive a flying-machine, and the telegraph wires do not carry passengers by lightning; but we submit to it reluctantly, we travel by night in order to escape the tedium of the journey and no one thinks of amusing himself on the cars. When you leave Chicago you take up your residence on the train.

The cars are no longer a ferry to carry you across a short distance: you are to live in them for days and nights; and no Eastern man knows the comfort or pleasure of traveling by rail until he crosses the Plains..."

An Emigrant Train

Robert Louis Stevenson traveled west in a train like this one. He described the beginning of his voyage in New York: "It was about two in the afternoon of Friday that I found myself in front of the Emigrant House, with more than a hundred others, to be sorted and boxed for the journey. A white-haired official, with a stick under one arm, and a list in the other hand, stood apart in front of us, and called name after name in the tone of a command. At each name you would see a family gather up its brats and bundles and run for the hindmost of the three cars that stood awaiting us, and I soon concluded that this was to be set apart for the women and children. The second or central car, it turned out, was devoted to men travelling alone, and the third to the Chinese..."

Train Station, Western Pacific Railroad

Emigrants, like Stevenson, lived in fear of being left behind at the station: "Equality, though conceived very largely in America, does not extend so low down as to an emigrant. Thus in all other trains a warning cry of 'All aboard!' recalls the passengers to take their seats; but as soon as I was alone with emigrants, and from the Transfer all the way to San Francisco, I found this ceremony was pretermitted; the train stole from the station without note of warning, and you had to keep an eye upon it even while you ate. The annoyance is considerable, and the disrespect both wanton and petty."

of Indian agents, the outrages of the wicked, the ill-faith of all, nay, down to the ridicule of such poor beings as were here with me upon the train, make up a chapter of injustice and indignity such as man must be in some ways base if his heart will suffer him to pardon or forget.

When I awoke next morning, I was puzzled for a while to know if it were day or night, for the illumination was unusual. I sat up at last, and found we were grading slowly downward through a long snowshed; and suddenly we shot into an open; and before we were swallowed into the next length of wooden tunnel, I had one glimpse of a huge pine-forested ravine upon my left, a foaming river, and a sky already coloured with the fires of dawn. I am usually very calm over the displays of nature; but you will scarce believe how my heart leaped at this. It was like meeting one's wife. I had come home again—home from

A Luxurious Dinner Party On Board the Pullman Palace Car "Cosmopolitan," Western Pacific Railroad

An Interior View of Silver Palace Car, Central Pacific Railroad

Railroad fares were:
Chicago to San Francisco $118
Return 118
To this add, for sleeping cars, about $3 per night.

unsightly deserts to the green and habitable corners of the earth. Every spire of pine along the hill-top, every trouty pool along that mountain river, was more dear to me than a blood-relation. And thenceforward down by Blue Canon, Alta, Dutch Flat, and all the old mining camps, through a sea of mountain forces, dropping thousands of feet toward the far sea-level as we went, not I only, but all the passengers on board, threw off their sense of dirt and heat and weariness, and bawled like schoolboys, and thronged with shining eyes upon the platform, and became new creatures within and without. The sun no longer oppressed us with heat, it only shone laughingly along the mountain-side, until we were fain to laugh ourselves for glee. For this was indeed our destination; this was "the good country" we had been going to so long.

The Savage Mine, Nevada, by T. H. O'Sullivan

Robert Louis Stevenson traveled west to find the woman he loved. But others traveled the same route in search of gold and silver. The white man's lust for gold and land led him into battle with the Indian, as we have seen in the Black Hills. While the rest of the country was plunged into a terrible financial panic in 1873, Virginia City, Nevada, was reaping the benefits of the Big Bonanza, the biggest silver strike in the history of American mining. The silver came from Nevada's famed Comstock Lode. The largest yields from the Big Bonanza came in the years 1876 through 1878; some $36,000,000 in silver ore were extracted annually during that period.

In 1876 George Wheeler's survey team visited the Comstock Lode: "The Washoe district, celebrated for its Comstock Lode, is...in the immediate vicinity of Virginia City...It is connected by rail with Reno, on the Central Pacific Railroad....The principal ores are chloride of silver, or cerargyrite, brittle silver, or stephanite...free gold, native silver...and iron and copper pyrite... Gold occurs in all of the silver ores, and forms an important share of their values...Only two mines, the Belcher and the Imperial Empire were visited...Since work began on the Belcher in 1860, silver and gold bullion to the value of $28,000,000 has been extracted. The yield for...1875 was $200,000 per month."

In the fall of 1876 Dan de Quille's history of the Big Bonanza was published. "If miners knew the exact spot in which the rich deposits are located," wrote De Quille, "it would be an easy matter to sink a shaft or to run a drift to tap them. Thus it happened that it was fourteen years after the discovery of silver and the Comstock Lode before what is now known as the 'Big Bonanza'—the chief of all bonanzas—was found. For fourteen years men daily and hourly walked over the ground under which lay the greatest mass of wealth that the world has ever seen in the shape of silver ore, yet nobody suspected its presence."

In the late 1870's there were no new discoveries and production from the old ones diminished. Virginia City, which sprang up in a flush, fell upon leaner days, but De Quille, like so many others, kept hoping for another strike and stayed on.

U.S. Geological Survey Team En Route, by W. H. Jackson, 1871

W. H. Jackson and Thomas Moran accompanied Dr. Ferdinand V. Hayden, former professor of geology, on his survey of the Yellowstone region in 1871. Jackson's photographs along with Moran's paintings helped convince Congress to pass a bill on March 1, 1872, establishing Yellowstone National Park, the first park of its kind in the world.

THE RISE OF LANDSCAPE PHOTOGRAPHY

Robert Louis Stevenson observed the West through a train window. Many others did not have the same chance. The photographs of Timothy O'Sullivan, A. J. Russell, William H. Jackson, Carleton E. Watkins and Eadweard J. Muybridge offered to those who could not travel a chance to see the magnificent western landscape. These photographers accompanied expeditions which the government sent out to conduct systematic surveys of the western lands. O'Sullivan, known for his Civil War photographs, went with the U.S. Geological Exploration of the fortieth parallel, under the direction of Clarence King, the noted geologist. William Henry Jackson, using a camera with 20 x 40 plates, went with the survey under the command of F. V. Hayden. Photographers had to carry a darkroom with them; Jackson had a tent for a darkroom lined with orange calico. Jackson's photographs of the Yellowstone region taken in 1872 helped persuade Congress to turn the region into a national park.

The great photographers in 1876 were the ones who were using the American wilderness as their subject. From the photographs that follow one gains both a sense of the development of the art of photography in the thirty-seven years that had passed since the daguerreotype was first invented and a sense of the magnificence of the West in 1876.

Valley of the Yosemite, by Eadweard J. Muybridge, 1873

Charles Nordhoff wrote of the Yosemite Valley: "In its present condition the Valley will not remain. It must either be made more beautiful, as I have suggested, or it will become a wreck, denuded of fine trees, combered with enterprising toll-takers, and made nauseous by the taint of selfish and sordid speculation. California will do wisely for her own glory, if she will engage Mr. Olmsted, or some other competent person, to take general charge of the improvement of the Yosemite, and allow a company under his eye...to make it into a truly national park and pleasure-ground..."

The Windmill at Laramie, Wyoming, by A. J. Russell

Russell, a famous Civil War photographer, became the official photographer of the Union Pacific Railroad.

Horse and Rider in Motion, by Eadweard J. Muybridge, 1878

Eadweard J. Muybridge, who was forty-six years old in 1876, had reached a transition point in his career. Already well known for his photographs of Yosemite, San Francisco, the Modoc War and Central America, he was just beginning the photographs that are always associated with his name—his studies of animals and men in motion. In 1872 Muybridge began photographing Governor Leland Stanford's horse, Occident; the governor had bet a friend that a galloping horse had all four feet off the ground at the same time, and he wanted to prove that his contention was correct. But in 1875 Muybridge had to interrupt his work and go to Central America because of the widely publicized trial in which he was acquitted for having "justifiably" murdered his wife's lover in 1874. By 1877 Muybridge had resumed his study of motion. And the next year he discovered how to use twelve cameras to photograph every phase of a horse's stride. By 1879 Muybridge had expanded his studies to include photographs of men in motion. Muybridge's photographs, such as the ones we see below, of Governor Stanford's horses, have been called the precursors of the motion picture.

Green River, Colorado, by T. H. O'Sullivan, 1872
This is one of a series of photographs made by O'Sullivan of the Green River in Colorado. The series was an attempt to document the passage of time.

Ancient Ruins in the Canyon de Chelle, New Mexico, 1873 by T. H. O'Sullivan
In 1873 O'Sullivan led a surveying expedition which visited the Zuni and Magia pueblos and the Canyon de Chelle. During the next two years O'Sullivan spent most of his time in the Southwest photographing Indians. In his photographs, he tried to capture the Indian in his true environment. After the 1875 Wheeler survey, O'Sullivan returned to the East forever.

The Flying Studio
Eadweard J. Muybridge developed his photographs of the Wild West in this tent, which served as a traveling darkroom.

Salt Lake City, by C. E. Watkins, c. 1876
"Salt Lake need not hold any mere pleasure traveler more than a day," said Charles Nordhoff. "You can drive all over it in two hours; and when you have seen the Tabernacle—an admirably-arranged and very ugly building... the Menagerie, within Brigham Young's inclosure, which contains several bears, some lynxes and wild-cats—natives of these mountains—and a small but interesting collection of minerals and Indian remains; and enjoyed the magnificent view which is seen from the back of the city of the valley and the snow-capped peaks which lie on the other side—a view which you carry with you all over the place—you have done Salt Lake City...."

Clarence King, by A. J. Russell
Clarence King, noted geologist, mining engineer and friend of Henry Adams, conducted a government survey between 1867 and 1877 in an area between eastern Colorado and the California border. In his famous work Mountaineering in the Sierra Nevada, *published in 1872, but still widely read in 1876, King said: "That brave spirit of Westward Ho! which has been the pillar of fire and cloud leading on the weary march of progress over stretches of desert, lining the way with graves of strong men; of new-born lives; of sad, patient mothers, whose pathetic longing for the new home died with them; of the thousand old and young whose last agony came to them as they marched with eyes strained on after the sunken sun, and whose shallow barrows scarcely lift over the drifting dust of the desert: that restless spirit which has dared to uproot the old and plant the new, kindling the grand energy of California, laying foundations for a State to be, that is admirable, is poetic, is to fill an immortal page in the story of America; but when, instead of urging on to wresting from new lands something better than old can give, it degenerates into mere weak-minded restlessness, killing the power of growth, the ideal of the home, the faculty of repose, it results in that race of perpetual emigrants who roam as dreary waifs over the West, losing possessions, love of life, love of God, slowly dragging from valley to valley, till they fall by the wayside, happy if some chance stranger performs for them the last rites,—often less fortunate, as blanched bones and fluttering rags upon too many hillsides plainly tell."*

Cactus, by T. H. O'Sullivan, c. 1876

A Mormon Family, Great Salt Lake, by A. J. Russell

Nordhoff thought that because of the Mormons' belief in polygamy they were subject to undue hardship: ''...considering what an immense quantity of good land there is in these United States, I should say that Brigham Young made what they call in the West 'a mighty poor land speculation' for his people. 'If we should stop irrigation for ninety days, not a tree, shrub, or vine would remain alive in our country,' said a Mormon to me as I walked through his garden...

''Moses led his people through the wilderness, but he landed them in Canaan, flowing with milk and honey. Brigham was a very poor sort of Moses.

''But, said a Mormon to whom I gave these impressions, 'President Young's object was to isolate the people from the world, and this he accomplished.' ''

AMERICA IN
1876

WASHINGTON

Not until 1921 was it finally confirmed that *Democracy* was actually written by Henry Adams, great-grandson of one President and grandson of another. At the time of its publication in 1880, the authorship was kept a deep secret, for *Democracy* was a harsh and unforgiving satire of political life in Washington in 1876.

Adams pilloried some of the most important politicians of the day—not only Presidents Hayes and Grant but also Senator James G. Blaine (named Senator Silas P. Ratcliffe in the novel), who was one of the leading Republicans of his time, finally brought low by his complicity in a railroad scandal. But Adams' aim in *Democracy* was to do more than write a sharp political *roman à clef*. He sought to portray the political corruption of a city and of an age.

The corruption evident in political life in post-Civil War America has become a common theme of almost all histories of the period. The New York

Bird's-eye View of Washington, D.C.

" 'Tis the times' plague, when madmen lead the blind."—Shakespeare

Thomas Nast's vision of America in 1876. Nast, a Republican, was a regular contributor to *Harper's Weekly*. With his pen he had helped bring down Boss Tweed in New York. Abraham Lincoln had appreciated the power of Nast's cartoons and called Nast "our best recruiting sergeant" for his pro-Union cartoons during the Civil War.

Legislature was auctioned off to the highest bidder as Cornelius Vanderbilt and Daniel Drew fought for control of the Erie Railroad. Grant's Secretary of War, William Belknap, was impeached for selling post-traderships in the West. The Whiskey Ring defrauded the government of millions of dollars in taxes, and Grant's own private secretary, Orville Babcock, was indicted for conspiring with the Ring.

Looking back on that time, christened by Mark Twain, "The Gilded Age," Theodore Roosevelt said that it was "a riot of individualistic materialism, under which complete freedom for the individual...turned out in practice to mean perfect freedom for the strong to wrong the weak..."

This was the atmosphere in which Adams set *Democracy*, and the repugnance he felt for it burns throughout the book, parts of which are presented in this chapter. "I declare to you," Adams makes the cynical Baron Jacobi say, "that in all my experience I have found no society which has had elements of corruption like the United States. The children in the street are corrupt, and know how to cheat me. The cities are all corrupt, and also the towns and the counties and the States' legislatures and the judges. Everywhere men betray trusts both public and private, steal money, run away with public funds....I do much regret that I have not yet one hundred years to live...The United States will then be more corrupt than Rome under Caligula; more corrupt than the Church under Leo X; more corrupt than France under the Regent!"

The baron's sense of the future was acute, and Adam's pessimism accurate. After all, had the baron returned to Washington in time for the Bicentennial, he would have found a scene to gladden his world-weary heart: a disgraced President, corruption in government and in business. Adams' great satire was as much a signpost as an epitaph.

HENRY ADAMS

Henry Adams, age thirty-eight, was an assistant professor at Harvard in 1876. One year later, he moved to Washington and lived and observed Washington life from a house on Lafayette Square, as did the heroine of *Democracy*, Mrs. Lightfoot Lee. He published *Democracy* in 1880.

DEMOCRACY, BY HENRY ADAMS

For reasons which many persons thought ridiculous, Mrs. Lightfoot Lee decided to pass the winter in Washington. Since her husband's death, five years before, she had lost her taste for New York society... Was it ambition—real ambition—or was it mere restlessness that made Mrs. Lightfoot Lee so bitter against New York and Philadelphia, Baltimore and Boston, American life in general and all life in particular? What did she want? Not social position, for she herself was an eminently respectable Philadelphian by birth...Though not brighter than her neighbors, the world persisted in classing her among clever women; she had wealth, or at least enough of it to give her all that money can give by way of pleasure to a sensible woman in an American city; she had her house and her carriage; she dressed well; her table was good, and her furniture was never allowed to fall behind the latest standard of decorative art. She had travelled in Europe, and after several visits, covering some years of time, had returned home, carrying in one hand, as it were, a green-gray landscape, a remarkably pleasing specimen of Corot, and in the other some bales of Persian and Syrian rugs and embroideries, Japanese bronzes and porcelain. With this she declared Europe to be exhausted, and she frankly avowed that she was American to the tips of her fingers; she neither knew nor greatly cared whether America or Europe were best to live in; she had no violent love for either, and she had no objection to abusing both; but she meant to get all that American life had to offer, good or bad, and to drink it down to the dregs, fully determined that whatever there was in it she would have, and that whatever could be made out of it she would manufacture....

Here, then, was the explanation of her restlessness, discontent, ambition,—call it what you will. It was the feeling of a passenger on an ocean steamer whose mind will not give him rest until he has been in the engine-room and talked with the engineer....She was bent upon getting to the heart of the great American mystery of democracy and government...She meant to see what amusement there might be in politics. Her friends asked what kind of amusement she expected to find among the illiterate swarm of ordinary people who in Washington represented constituencies so dreary that in comparison New York was a New Jerusalem, and Broad Street a grove of Academe. She replied that if Washington society were so bad as this, she should have gained all she wanted, for it would be a pleasure to return,—precisely the feeling she longed for....What she wished to see...was the clash of interests, the interests of forty millions of people and a whole continent, centering at Washington; guided, restrained, controlled, or unrestrained and uncontrollable, by men of ordinary mould; the tremendous forces of government, and the machinery of society, at work. What she wanted was *power*.

Perhaps the force of the engine was a little confused in her mind with that of the engineer, the power with the men who wielded it. Perhaps the human interest of politics was after all what really attracted her, and, however strongly she might deny it, the passion for exercising power, for its own sake, might dazzle and mislead a woman who had exhausted all the ordinary feminine resources. But why speculate

Mrs. Lee probably dressed much like this fashionable lady who was on the front page of *Harper's Bazar* in 1876. Mrs. Lee "was woman enough to assume that all the graces were well enough employed in decorating her, and it was enough if the other sex felt her superiority. Men were valuable only in proportion to their strength and their appreciation of women."

In 1876 the population of Washington was 131,700; the city covered an area of sixty square miles. In a guidebook written in 1869, John B. Ellis described postwar Washington: "The first glimpses of the Federal City are not pleasant. The train passes through a succession of old fields, over which are widely scattered a few dirty, dingy frame houses. Some of these aspire to the dignity of paint, but the majority are ornamented with whitewash. The fields are full of stagnant pools, and the geese, pigs, and children swarming about them appear to be on a footing of perfect equality. The denizens of this section are both white and black, and both classes seem to be very poor. They have a decided 'hard-times' look, and evidently have to struggle desperately with poverty. During the war these fields had a busy appearance, which makes them now seem doubly dilapidated. Then they were covered with long rows of cars, wagons, carts, tents, and shanties, and alive with soldiers and laborers connected with the Quartermaster and Commissary Departments. Then the inhabitants of this section drove a thriving trade in newspapers, cheap books, pies, cakes, apples, tobacco, and contraband liquids. The war was a God-send to them, and it is not improbable that some of the most enterprising and thrifty will, if they have not already done so, date their rise to fortune from the 'start' which this trade gave them."

A Few Moments of Leisure

In 1876 approximately one third of Washington's population was black. President Hayes appointed Frederick Douglass marshal of the District of Columbia in 1877. Douglass, a former slave, had organized black troops during the Civil War and worked continually for justice for his race.

about her motives? The stage was before her, the curtain was rising, the actors were ready to enter; she had only to go quietly on among the supernumeraries and see how the play was acted and the stage effects were produced....On the first of December, Mrs. Lee took the train for Washington, and before five o'clock that evening she was entering her newly hired house on Lafayette Square.

MRS. LEE AND HER SISTER ENTER WASHINGTON SOCIETY

Adams' character Mrs. Lee was modeled on Mrs. Bigelow Lawrence, a society lady who was a neighbor of Adams' during the summers he and his wife spent at Beverly Farms, Massachusetts. Mrs. Lee was also somewhat based upon Adams himself. They both observed Washington life from a house on Lafayette Square, and shared an equal fascination and horror for political life in the Gilded Age. Mrs. Lee's sister, Sybil Ross, was based upon Mrs. Lawrence's sister, Fanny Chapman.

Sybil—Miss Sybil Ross—was Madeleine Lee's sister. The keenest psychologist could not have detected a single feature or quality which they had in common, and for that reason they were devoted friends. Madeleine was thirty, Sybil twenty-four. Madeleine was indescribable; Sybil was transparent. Madeleine was of medium height with a graceful figure, a well-set head, and enough golden-brown hair to frame a face full of varying expression. People who envied her smile said that she cultivated a sense of humor in order to show her teeth. Perhaps they were right; but there was no doubt that her habit of talking with gesticulation would never have grown upon her unless she had known that her hands were not only beautiful but expressive. She dressed as skillfully as New York women do, but in growing older she began to show symptoms of dangerous unconventionality....The secret was that Mrs. Lee had artistic tendencies, and unless they were checked in time, there was no knowing what might be the consequences. But as yet they had done no harm; indeed, they rather helped to give her that sort of atmosphere which belongs only to certain women; as indescribable as the after-glow; as impalpable as an Indian summer mist; and non-existent except to people who feel rather than reason. Sybil had none of it. The imagination gave up all attempts to soar where she came. A more straightforward, downright, gay, sympathetic, shallow warm-hearted, sternly practical young woman has rarely touched this planet. Her mind had room for neither gravestones nor guide-books; she could not have lived in the past or the future if she had spent her days in churches and her nights in tombs. "She was not clever, like Madeleine, thank Heaven."

Madeleine was sober in her tastes. She wasted no money. She made no display. She walked rather than drove, and wore neither diamonds nor brocades. But the general impression she made was nevertheless one of luxury. On the other hand, her sister had her dresses from Paris, and wore them and her ornaments according to all the formulas; she was good-naturedly correct, and bent her round white shoulders to whatever burden the Parisian autocrat chose to put upon them. Madeleine never interfered, and always paid the bills. Before

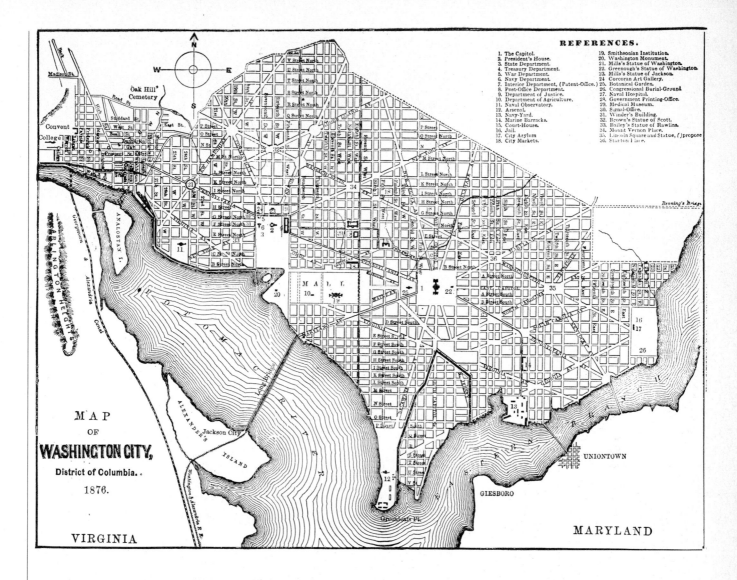

REFERENCES.

1. The Capitol.
2. President's House.
3. State Department.
4. Treasury Department.
5. War Department.
6. Navy Department.
7. Interior Department, (Patent-Office.)
8. Post-Office Department.
9. Department of Justice.
10. Department of Agriculture.
11. Naval Observatory.
12. Arsenal.
13. Navy-Yard.
14. Marine Barracks.
15. Court-House.
16. Jail.
17. City Asylum.
18. City Markets.
19. Smithsonian Institution.
20. Washington Monument.
21. Mills's Statue of Washington.
22. Greenough's Statue of Washington.
23. Mills's Statue of Jackson.
24. Corcoran Art Gallery.
25. Botanical Garden.
26. Congressional Burial-Ground
27. Naval Hospital.
28. Government Printing-Office.
29. Medical Museum.
30. Signal-Office.
31. Winder's Building.
32. Brown's Statue of Scott.
33. Bailey's Statue of Rawlins.
34. Mount Vernon Place.
35. Lincoln Square and Statue, ( )propose
36. Stanton Place.

MAP
OF
WASHINGTON CITY,
District of Columbia.
1876.

Map of Washington City, District of Columbia, 1876

they had been ten days in Washington, they fell gently into their place. Society was kind; there was no reason for it being otherwise. Mrs. Lee and her sister had no enemies, held no offices, and did their best to make themselves popular. Sybil had not passed summers at Newport and winters in New York in vain; and neither her face nor her figure, her voice nor her dancing, needed apology. Politics were not her strong point....

Her sister was more patient and bolder. She went to the Capitol nearly every day for at least two weeks. At the end of that time her interest began to flag, and she thought it better to read the debates every morning in the *Congressional Record*....Nevertheless she still had energy to visit the Senate gallery occasionally when she was told that a splendid orator was about to speak on a question of deep interest to his country. She listened...and, whenever she could, she did admire. She said nothing, but she listened sharply. She wanted to learn how the machinery of government worked, and what was the quality of the men who controlled it. One by one, she passed them through her crucibles, and tested them by acids and by fire. A few survived her tests and came out alive, though more or less disfigured, where she had found impurities.

The Ladies' Reception Room Inside the Capitol

"On the House side of the Capitol building is a reception room, which has been denominated by newspaper correspondents as the 'Cattery.' This name was selected because it was believed to possess a significance peculiarly appropriate to designate those who made it a resort. At any hour during congressional sitting this room is fairly filled with females, some of whom are honest women who have legitimate business with congressmen; but a very large majority of these waiters are fair appearing concubines or professional bawds."

J. W. Buel, *Mysteries and Miseries of America's Great Cities*

The Senate Chamber
In 1876 there were seventy-six senators. Mary Clemmer Ames, a resident of Washington, described the Senate Chamber in 1877: "It can not boast of the ampler proportions of the Hall of Representatives. Its golden walls and emerald doors can not rescue it from insignificance."

It was to the visiting gallery surrounding the chamber that Mrs. Lee went to hear Senator Ratcliffe's speeches.

At this point in the novel, there appears John Carrington, a Southerner and a Washington lawyer who was modeled on Adams' good friend John Lowndes. Carrington serves as a reminder that the destruction wrought by the Civil War was still very much in evidence in the mid-seventies.

JOHN CARRINGTON

In these early visits to Congress, Mrs. Lee sometimes had the company of John Carrington, a Washington lawyer about forty years old...a Virginian. Carrington was a man whom she liked, and he was one whom life had treated hardly. He was of the unfortunate generation in the south which began existence with civil war, and he was perhaps the more unfortunate because, like most educated Virginians of the old Washington school, he had seen from the first that, whatever issue the war took, Virginia and he must be ruined. At twenty-two he had gone into the rebel army as a private and carried his musket modestly through a campaign or two, after which he slowly rose to the rank of senior captain in his regiment, and closed his services on the staff of a major-general, always doing scrupulously enough what he conceived to be his duty, and never doing it with enthusiasm. When the rebel armies surrendered, he rode away to his family plantation—not a difficult thing to do, for it was only a few miles from Appomattox—and at once began to study law...[Carrington told Mrs. Lee about] the ruin which the war had brought on him and his family; how, of his two brothers, one had survived the war only to die at home, a mere wreck of

The Rotunda of the Capitol

In 1793 George Washington laid the corner-
stone for the Capitol. Dr. William Thornton
had been chosen to design the building.
Thomas Jefferson wrote: "Thornton's plan
has captivated the eyes and the judgment of
all. It is simple, noble, beautiful, excellently
arranged and moderate in size." The Capitol
has undergone many changes and additions
supervised by different architects since
Thornton's day.

This fresco covered the canopy which
stretched over the Rotunda of the Capitol. In
the middle of the fresco is George Washington with Freedom on his right and Victory on
his left. The thirteen female figures in the
center represent the thirteen original states.
(By 1876 there were thirty-eight states.) The
six groups on the outer edge of the circle
represent Agriculture, Mechanics, Commerce, Marine, and Arts and Sciences. The
fresco, which measured some sixty-five feet
in diameter, was ordered by Congress in
1864 and was executed by Constantino Bru-
midi. It cost $50,000.

Section Through Dome of U.S. Capitol
Here we see a section of the dome of the Capitol, which was completed in 1865. The
painting in the dome is suspended from a cast-iron frame. On top of the dome sits the
statue of Freedom.

Arlington House

This was Robert E. Lee's house before the Civil War. On the eve of the outbreak of the war, Lee is said to have paced up and down on the porch gazing across the Potomac River at Washington, trying to decide whether his loyalties should lie with the Union or the Confederacy.

Sybil and Carrington rode to Arlington; "they crept through the great metropolis of Georgetown" and came upon "the bridge which crosses the noble river just where its bold banks open out to clasp the city of Washington in their easy embrace...Reaching the Virginia side they cantered gaily up the laurel-margined road...Sybil was startled as she rode through the gate and found herself suddenly met by the long white ranks of head-stones, stretching up and down the hillsides by thousands, in order of battle; as though Cadmus had reversed his myth and had sown living men, to come up as dragons' teeth. '...The Lees were old family friends of mine,' said Carrington. 'I used to stay here when I was a boy...The last time I sat here it was with them. We were wild about disunion and talked about nothing else..We never thought there would be a war...I was a Union man and did not want the State to go out. But though I felt sure that Virginia must suffer, I never thought we could be beaten. Yet now I am sitting here a pardoned rebel, and the poor Lees are driven away and their place is a graveyard.'"

disease, privation, and wounds; the other had been shot by his side, and bled slowly to death in his arms during the awful carnage in the Wilderness; how his mother and two sisters were struggling for a bare subsistence on a wretched Virginian farm, and how all his exertions barely kept them from beggary.

"You have no conception of the poverty to which our southern women are reduced since the war," said he; "they are many of them literally without clothes or bread."

Adams' character Nathan Gore, a man of letters, was largely modeled on the poet James Russell Lowell, today famous for his satirical *Bigelow Papers*. Lowell was appointed U.S. Minister to Spain in 1877 by Hayes; in *Democracy*, Gore had been Minister to Spain for four years and wished to be appointed again. Some of Gore's characteristics are also traceable to John Lothrop Motley, author of the well-known *Rise of the Dutch Republic* and *History of the United Netherlands*. Appointed Minister to Great Britain in 1869 by President Grant, Motley was dismissed in 1870. One of the reasons for Motley's dismissal cited by Secretary of State Hamilton Fish was that he parted his hair in the middle, which the President considered a sign of sissified Anglophilia; Gore's reappointment in *Democracy* is refused for the same reason. Both Lowell and Motley, like Gore, came from Massachusetts:

A much higher type of character was Mr. Nathan Gore, of Massachusetts,...in his youth a successful poet whose satires made a noise in their day, and are still remembered for the pungency and wit of a few verses; then a deep student in Europe for many years, until his famous "History of Spain in America" placed him instantly at the head of American historians, and made him minister at Madrid, where he remained four years to his entire satisfaction, this being the nearest approach to a patent of nobility and a government pension which the American citizen can attain. A change of administration had reduced him to private life again, and after some years of retirement he was now in Washington, willing to be restored to his old mission. Every President thinks it respectable to have at least one literary man in his pay, and Mr. Gore's prospects were fair for obtaining his object, as he had the active support of a majority of the Massachusetts delegation.

BARON JACOBI

Adams now introduces Baron Jacobi, the "Bulgarian Minister" to Washington, who was modeled on the Turkish Minister to Washington, Aristarchi Bey. Bey is the representative of the Old World.

Old Baron Jacobi, the Bulgarian minister, fell madly in love with both sisters, as he commonly did with every pretty face.... He was a witty, cynical, broken-down Parisian roué, kept in Washington for years past by his debts and his salary; always grumbling because there was no opera, and mysteriously disappearing on visits to New York; a voracious devourer of French and German literature, especially of novels; a man who seemed to have met every noted or notorious personage of the century, and whose mind was a magazine of amusing information.

MR. C. C. FRENCH

Mr. C. C. French was drawn from William Walter Phelps, a Republican congressman from New Jersey between 1873 and 1875, and later Minister to Austria-Hungary:

A different visitor was Mr. C. C. French, a young member of Congress from Connecticut, who aspired to act the part of the educated gentleman in politics, and to purify the public tone. He had reform principles and an unfortunately conceited manner; he was rather wealthy, rather clever, rather well-educated, rather honest, and rather vulgar.

Seventh Street, Northwest, c. 1876
Twain described Washington as "a wide stretch of cheap little brick houses, with here and there a noble architectural pile lifting itself out of the midst—government buildings, these....You will wonder at the shortsightedness of the city fathers, when you come to inspect the streets, in that they do not dilute the mud a little more and use them for canals."

James Russell Lowell
James Russell Lowell, who was represented in Democracy *as Gore, was fifty-seven years old in 1876. A well-known poet and former abolitionist, Lowell was a professor of French and Spanish languages and literature at Harvard. A delegate to the 1876 Republican National Convention, Lowell was a Hayes supporter. Hayes repaid his support in 1877 by appointing him Minister to Spain.*

Matthew Brady's photograph of
Sir Edward Thornton, England's Minister to
the United States, who is depicted as Lord
Skye in *Democracy*.

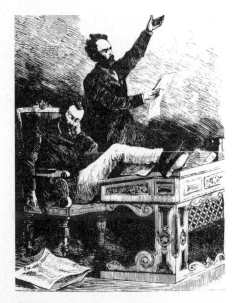

Congressional Buncombe

"Speechmaking is a weakness of Congressmen...The Congress of the United
States...does not, as a whole, represent the
intelligence or the eloquence of the nation."

John B. Ellis, *The Sights and Secrets of the
National Capital.*

*Senator Silas P. Ratcliffe was a mixture of Senator Roscoe Conkling of New York (left)
and Senator James G. Blaine of Maine (right). In 1876 these two men were powerful
leaders of rival factions of the Republican party. Both were strong candidates for the
Republican presidential nomination. Conkling was known as a firm supporter of the
spoils system and a successful machine politician. Blaine would probably have been
nominated in 1876 if his involvement in a railroad swindle had not been exposed. The two
men loathed each other. During a debate in the House of Representatives in 1866,
Conkling said of Blaine, "If the member from Maine had the least idea how profoundly
indifferent I am to his opinion on the subject which he has been discussing, or upon any
other subject personal to me, I think he would hardly have troubled to rise here and
express his opinion." To which Blaine replied, "The contempt of that large-minded
gentleman is so wilting, his haughty disdain, his grandiloquent swell, his majestic,
supereminent, turkey-gobbler strut has been so crushing to myself and all the members of
the House, that I know it was an act of temerity for me to venture upon a controversy
with him."*

*Blaine was eventually nominated as the Republican candidate for President in 1884.
Asked to campaign for Blaine, Conkling replied, "No thank you, I don't engage in
criminal practice."*

SENATOR RATCLIFFE

Senator Ratcliffe combined some of characteristics of
Senator Roscoe Conkling of New York and Senator James
G. Blaine of Maine. Conkling, an archopponent of Civil
Service reform, supported Grant but was a bitter personal
enemy of Blaine. Blaine headed one faction of the
Republican party known as the Half-Breeds; Conkling
headed another faction known as the Stalwarts.

One morning in December, Carrington entered Mrs. Lee's parlor
towards noon, and asked if she cared to visit the Capitol.

"You will have a chance of hearing today what may be the last
great speech of our greatest statesman,...the Prairie Giant of Peonia,
the Favorite Son of Illinois, the man who came within three votes of
getting the party nomination for the Presidency last spring,...the
Honorable Silas P. Ratcliffe, Senator from Illinois. He will run for the
Presidency yet...He is the stumbling-block of the new President, who is
to be allowed no peace unless he makes terms with Ratcliffe; and so
everyone thinks that the Prairie Giant of Peonia will have the choice of

A Holiday Reception at the White House—Arrival and Departure of Guests

*"Beyond the Treasury is a fine large white barn, with wide unhandsome grounds about it,"
wrote Twain describing the White House. "The President lives there. It is ugly enough
outside, but that is nothing to what it is inside. Dreariness, flimsiness, bad taste reduced to
mathematical completeness is what the inside offers to the eye." The White House, the
oldest federal structure standing, was begun in 1792. President John Adams and his wife,
Abigail, were the first occupants of the White House. During the War of 1812, British
troops invaded Washington and set fire to the White House; Dolly Madison fled with
Gilbert Stuart's portrait of George Washington under her arm. The White House was
rebuilt after the war and numerous additions have been made since then.*

the State or Treasury Department. If he takes either it will be the
Treasury, for he is a desperate political manager, and will want the
patronage for the next national convention."

DINNER IN WASHINGTON

Mrs. Lee dashed at her Peonia Giant, who was then consuming his fish,
and wishing he understood why the British Minister had worn no
gloves, while he himself had sacrificed his convictions by wearing the
largest and whitest pair of French kids that could be bought for money
on Pennsylvania Avenue. There was a little touch of mortification in the
idea that he was not quite at home among fashionable people, and at
this instant he felt that true happiness was only to be found among the
simple and honest sons and daughters of toil. A certain secret jealousy
of the British Minister is always lurking in the breast of every American
Senator, if he is truly democratic; for democracy, rightly understood, is
the government of the people, by the people, for the benefit of senators,
and there is always a clear danger that the British Minister may not
understand this political principle as he should....

In ten minutes Mrs. Lee had this devoted statesman at her feet.
She had not studied the Senate without a purpose. She had read with
unerring instinct one general characteristic of all Senators, a boundless
and guileless thirst for flattery, engendered by daily droughts from
political friends or dependents, then becoming a necessity like a dram,
and swallowed with a heavy smile of ineffable content....

"My judgment may not be worth much, Mr. Senator, but it does
seem to me that...the passage in your speech of yesterday which began
with, 'Our strength lies in this twisted and tangled mass of isolated

The Blue Room in the President's House

The Green Room in the President's House

The East Room c. 1876
According to a contemporary description,
the East Room, seventy-eight feet long by
forty feet wide, was furnished very elaborately with carpets, chairs, sofas, mirrors,
chandeliers, vases, bronzed ornaments and
portraits of Presidents. It was the chief
reception room for daily visitors.

How Two Dashing Members of Congress Represented Their Constituents

"The chances are that a man cannot get into Congress now without resorting to arts and means that should render him unfit to go there; of course there are exceptions....Why, it is telegraphed all over the country and commented on as something wonderful if a congressman votes honestly and unselfishly and refuses to take advantage of his position to steal from the government....In a free country like ours, where any man can run for Congress and anybody can vote for him, you can't expect immortal purity all the time—it ain't in nature.—Sixty or eighty or a hundred and fifty people are bound to get in who are not angels in disguise....Even in these days, when people growl so much and the newspapers are so out of patience, there is still a very respectable minority of honest men in Congress."

Mark Twain, *The Gilded Age*

The Female Lobbyist Plying Her Seductive Arts

"This woman has the senator in her grasp... Two years ago she was an adventuress among Wall Street nabobs....A coast million-aire, with visions of transcontinental railways in his head...made her a tempting and acceptable offer, after which he had a bill drafted appropriating millions of public lands to a construction company of which he was the soul, body and members, to assist in the building of a railroad....

"This woman is a professional lobbyist now, and if she succeeds in having the bill passed, $50,000 will be her reward."

J. W. Buel, *Mysteries and Miseries of America's Great Cities*

principles, the hair of the half-sleeping giant of Party,' is both for language and imagery quite equal to anything of Webster's."

The Senator from Illinois rose to this gaudy fly like a huge, two-hundred-pound salmon; his white waistcoat gave out a mild silver reflection as he slowly came to the surface and gorged the hook. He made not even a plunge, not one perceptible effort to tear out the barbed weapon, but floating gently to his feet, allowed himself to be landed as though it were a pleasure. Only miserable casuists will ask whether this was fair play on Madeleine's part; whether flattery so gross cost her conscience no twinge, and whether any woman can without self-abasement be guilty of such shameless falsehood....But she could not deny that she had wilfully allowed the Senator to draw conclusions very different from any she actually held....

To her eyes he was the high-priest of American·politics; he was charged with the meaning of the mysteries, the clue to political hieroglyphics. Through him she hoped to sound the depths of statesmanship and to bring up from its oozy bed that pearl of which she was in search; the mysterious gem which must lie hidden somewhere in politics. She wanted to understand this man; to turn him inside out; to experiment on him and use him as young physiologists use frogs and kittens. If there was good or bad in him, she meant to find its meaning....What equality was there between these two combatants? what hope for him? what risk for her? And yet Madeleine Lee had fully her match in Mr. Silas P. Ratcliffe.

CORRUPTION IN GOVERNMENT

Mrs. Lee, with much earnestness of manner, still pressed her question: "Surely something can be done to check corruption. Are we forever to be at the mercy of thieves and ruffians? Is a respectable government impossible in a democracy?"

"My reply," said Ratcliffe, "is that no representative government can long be much better or much worse than the society it represents. Purify society and you purify the government."

"A very statesmanlike reply," said Baron Jacobi, with a formal bow, but his tone had a shade of mockery. Carrington, who had listened with a darkening face, turned to the baron and asked him what conclusion he drew from the reply.

"Ah!" exclaimed the baron, with his wickedest leer, "what for is my conclusion good? You Americans believe yourselves to be excepted from the operation of general laws. You care not for experience. I have lived seventy-five years, and all that time in the midst of corruption. I am corrupt myself, only I do have courage to proclaim it, and you others have it not. Rome, Paris, Vienna, Petersburg, London, are all corrupt; only Washington is pure!... And you gentlemen in the Senate very well declare that your great United States, which is the head of the civilized world, can never learn anything from the example of corrupt Europe. You are right—quite right! The great United States needs not an example. I do much regret that I have not yet one hundred years to live. If I could then come back to this city, I should find myself very content—much more than now. I am always content where there is much corruption, and ma parole d'honneur!" broke out the old man with fire and gesture, "the United States will then be more corrupt than Rome under Caligula; more corrupt than the Church under Leo X; more corrupt than France under the Regent!"...

"I wish you would explain why," replied Mrs. Lee; "tell me, Mr.

**The Political Problem:
The Law-Maker and Law-Breaker,
One and Inseparable, by Thomas Nast,
1876**

Mark Twain's words could easily have
accompanied Nast's cartoon, since both
shared the same view of the men who made
the laws in 1876. In *The Gilded Age,* Twain
set forth the plan of one robber baron: "Mr.
Bigler's plan...was the building of the Tunk-
hannock, Rattlesnake and Youngwomans-
town Railroad, which would not only be a
great highway to the west, but would open
to market inexhaustible coal-fields and
untold millions of lumber....'We'll buy the
lands,' explained he, 'on long time, backed
by the notes of good men; and then mortgage them for money enough to get the
road well on. Then get the towns on the line
to issue their bonds for stock, and sell their
bonds for enough to complete the road and
partly stock it, especially if we mortgage
each section as we complete it. We can then
sell the rest of the stock on the prospect of
the business of the road through an
improved country, and also sell the lands at
a big advance, on the strength of the road.
All we want is a few thousand dollars to start
the surveys and arrange things in the legislature!' Mr. Bigler, the 'public benefactor,' went
on to complain that the legislature consisted
of 'an uncommon poor lot this year....Con-
sequently, an expensive lot. The fact is...that
the price is raised so high on United States
Senators now, that it affects the whole market; you can't get any public improvement
through on reasonable terms.'...Mr. Bigler
went on and gave some very interesting
details of the intimate connection between
railroads and politics..."

Gore—you who represent cultivation and literary taste hereabouts—
please tell me what to think about Baron Jacobi's speech."

Gore was too experienced in politics to be caught in such a trap as
this. He evaded the question. "Mr. Ratcliffe has a practical piece of
work to do; his business is to make laws and advise the President; he
does it extremely well. We have no other equally good practical
politician; it is unfair to require him to be a crusader besides."

"No!" interposed Carrington, curtly; "but he need not obstruct
crusades. He need not talk virtue and oppose the punishment of vice."

"He is a shrewd practical politician," replied Gore, "and he feels
first the weak side of any proposed political tactics."

With a sigh of despair Madeleine went on: "Who, then, is right?
How *can* we all be right? Half of our wise men declare that the world is
going straight to perdition; the other half that it is fast becoming
perfect. Both cannot be right. There is only one thing in life," she went
on, laughing, "that I must and will have before I die. I must know
whether America is right or wrong. Just now this question is a very
practical one, for I really want to know whether to believe in Mr.
Ratcliffe. If I throw him overboard, everything must go, for he is only a
specimen."

RATCLIFFE: PARTY LOYALTY

"Believing as I do that great results can only be accomplished by
great parties, I have uniformly yielded my own personal opinions
where they have failed to obtain general assent. I shall continue to
follow this course, and the President may with perfect confidence count

Reception at the White House

"Receptions were attended by more women than men, and those interested in the problem might have studied the costumes of the ladies present, in view of this fact, to discover whether women dress more for the eyes of women or for effect upon men. It is a very important problem, and has been a good deal discussed, and its solution would form one fixed, philosophical basis, upon which to estimate woman's character. We are inclined to take a medium ground, and aver that woman dresses to please herself, and in obedience to a law of her own nature."

Mark Twain, *The Gilded Age*

upon my disinterested support of all party measures, even though I may not be consulted in originating them."

Madeleine thoughtfully inquired: "Is nothing more powerful than party allegiance?"

"Nothing, except national allegiance," replied Ratcliffe.

AMBITION

Ratcliffe told her frankly that the pleasure of politics lay in the possession of power. He agreed that the country would do very well without him. "But here I am," said he, "and here I mean to stay." He had very little sympathy for thin moralizing, and a statesmanlike contempt for philosophical politics. He loved power, and he meant to be President. That was enough.

THE WHITE HOUSE

When Mrs. Lee visited the White House, she was horrified at what she felt was a "droll aping of monarchial forms." In a time when most Americans were concentrating on the extraordinary opportunities available, Adams foresaw "the end of American society; its realization and dream at once."

One evening, Mrs. Lee went to the President's first evening reception.... Mrs. Lee accepted Mr. French for an escort, and walked across the Square with him to join the throng that was pouring into the doors of the White House. They took their places in the line of citizens and were at last able to enter the reception-room. There Madeleine found herself before two seemingly mechanical figures, which might be wood or wax, for any sign they showed of life. These two figures were the President and his wife; they stood stiff and awkward by the door, both their faces stripped of every sign of intelligence, while the right hands of both extended themselves to the column of visitors with the mechanical action of toy dolls. Mrs. Lee for a moment began to laugh, but the laugh died on her lips. To the President and his wife this was clearly no laughing matter. There they stood, automata, representatives of the society which streamed past them. Madeleine seized Mr. French by the arm.

"Take me somewhere at once," said she, "Where I can look at it. Here! In the corner. I had no conception how shocking it was!"

Mr. French supposed she was thinking of the queer-looking men and women who were swarming through the rooms. Mrs. Lee... stopped him short:—

"There, Mr. French! Now go away and leave me. I want to be alone for half an hour." And there she stood, with her eyes fixed on the President and his wife, while the endless stream of humanity passed them, shaking hands.

What a strange and solemn spectacle it was, and how the deadly fascination of it burned the image in upon her mind! What a horrid warning to ambition! And in all that crowd there was no one besides herself who felt the mockery of this exhibition. To all the others this task was a regular part of the President's duty, and there was nothing ridiculous about it. They thought it a democratic institution, this droll aping of monarchial forms....To her it had the effect of a nightmare, or

of an opium-eater's vision. She felt a sudden conviction that this was to be the end of American society; its realization and dream at once. She groaned in spirit.

"Yes! At last I have reached the end! We shall grow to be wax images, and our talk will be the squeaking of toy dolls. We shall all wander round and round the earth and shake hands. No one will have any object in this world, and there will be no other. It is worse than anything in the 'Inferno.' What an awful vision of eternity!"...

Mrs. Lee did not repeat the experiment of visiting the White House...To Senator Ratcliffe she expressed her opinions strongly. The Senator tried in vain to argue that the people had a right to call upon their chief magistrate, and that he was bound to receive them;..."Who gave the people any such right?" asked Mrs. Lee...."You know better, Mr. Ratcliffe! Our chief magistrate is a citizen like any one else. What puts it into his foolish head to cease being a citizen and to ape royalty? Our governors never make themselves ridiculous. Why cannot the wretched being content himself with living like the rest of us, and minding his own business? Does he know what a figure of fun he is?" And Mrs. Lee went so far as to declare that she would like to be the President's wife only to put an end to this folly; nothing should ever induce *her* to go through such a performance; and if the public did not approve of this, Congress might impeach her, and remove her from office; all she demanded was the right to be heard before the Senate in her own defense....

Nevertheless, there was a very general impression in Washington that Mrs. Lee would like nothing better than to be in the White House...True it is, beyond peradventure, that all residents of Washington may be assumed to be in office or candidates for office....To the

A State Dinner at the White House

In *The Gilded Age,* Twain has Colonel Sellers describe a meal at the White House: "The President's table is well enough...for a man on a salary, but God bless my soul, I should like him to see a little old-fashioned hospitality—open house, you know....The President has variety enough, but the quality. Vegetables of course you can't expect here.... But I *am* surprised about the wines. I should think they were manufactured in the New York Customs House. I must send the President some from my cellar."

Scene at the Pennsylvania Avenue Entrance to the Capitol Grounds at Washington on the Daily Adjournment of Congress.

In *The Gilded Age,* Mark Twain described Washington:

"It seemed...a feverish, unhealthy atmosphere in which lunacy would be easily developed....Everybody attached to himself an exaggerated importance, from the fact of being at the national capital, the center of political influence, the fountain of patronage, preferment, jobs and opportunities.

"People were introduced to each other as from this or that state, not from cities or towns, and this gave a largeness to their representative feeling. All the women talked politics as naturally and glibly as they talk fashion or literature elsewhere. There was always some exciting topic at the Capitol, or some huge slander was rising up like a miasmatic exhalation from the Potomac, threatening to settle no one knew exactly where. Every other person was an aspirant for a place, or, if he had one, for a better place, or more pay; almost every other one had some claim or interest or remedy to urge; even the women were all advocates for the advancement of some person, and they violently espoused or denounced this or that measure as it would affect some relative, acquaintance or friend.

"Love, travel, even death itself, waited on the chances of the dies daily thrown in the two Houses, and the committee rooms there. If the measure went through, love could afford to ripen into marriage, and longing for foreign travel would have fruition; and it must have been only eternal hope springing in the breast that kept alive numerous old claimants who for years and years had besieged the doors of Congress, and who looked as if they needed not so much an appropriation of money as six feet of ground."

In August 1876 Congress voted funds to complete the half-finished Washington Monument. The monument, originally designed by Robert Mills, a neoclassical architect from South Carolina, was begun in 1848. But work stopped in 1854 due to lack of funds. In 1879, thanks to the new appropriation, work on it was resumed. In 1886 the public was admitted to the 555-foot monument. Above is one architect's scheme for the monument.

Washingtonians it was a matter of course that Mrs. Lee should marry Silas P. Ratcliffe. That he should be glad to get a fashionable and intelligent wife, with twenty or thirty thousand dollars a year, was not surprising. That she should accept the first public man of the day, with a flattering chance for the Presidency—a man still comparatively young and not without good looks—was perfectly natural, and in her undertaking she had the sympathy of all well-regulated Washington women who were not possible rivals; for to them the President's wife is of more consequence than the President; and, indeed, if America only knew it, they are not very far from the truth.

RATCLIFFE FIXES ELECTION RETURNS

Senator Ratcliffe's story of fixing the election returns in a state election was perhaps a reminder of the national election of 1876, when fraud was quite reasonably suspected in the returns of three states, Florida, South Carolina and Louisiana. The changed votes in these three states gave the election to Governor Rutherford B. Hayes of Ohio, by one electoral vote, instead of to the winner of the popular vote, Governor Samuel Tilden of New York.

"The story is this, Mrs. Lee; and it is well-known to every man, woman, and child in the state of Illinois, so that I have no reason for softening it. In the worst days of the war there was almost a certainty that my state would be carried by the peace party, by fraud, as we thought....Had Illinois been lost then, we should certainly have lost the Presidential election, and with it probably the Union....I believed the fate of the war to depend on the result. I was then Governor, and upon me the responsibility rested. We had entire control of the northern counties and of their returns. We ordered the returning officers in a certain number of northern counties to make no returns until they heard from us, and when we had received the votes of all the southern counties and learned the precise number of votes we needed to give us a majority, we telegraphed to our northern returning officers to make the vote of their districts such and such, thereby overbalancing the adverse returns and giving the State to us....I am not proud of the transaction, but I would do it again, and worse than that, if I thought it would save this country from disunion..."

The man who has committed a murder for his country is a patriot and not an assassin, even when he receives a seat in the Senate as his share of the plunder. Women cannot be expected to go behind the motives of that patriot who saves his country and his election in times of revolution.

CHANGE IN ADMINISTRATION

In February, the weather became warmer and summer-like. In such a world there should be no guile—but there is a great deal of it notwithstanding. Indeed, at no other season is there so much. This is the moment when the two whited sepulchres at either end of the Avenue reek with the thick atmosphere of bargain and sale. The old is going; the new is coming. Wealth, office, power are at auction. Who bids highest? who hates with most venom? who intrigues with most skill? who has done the dirtiest, the meanest, the darkest, and the most political work? He shall have his reward.

Senator Ratcliffe was absorbed and ill at ease. A swarm of applicants for office dogged his steps and beleaguered his rooms in quest of his endorsement of their paper characters. The new President was to arrive on Monday. Intrigues and combinations, of which the Senator was the soul, were all alive, awaiting this arrival.

GEORGE WASHINGTON: SYMBOL OF LOST PURITY

"Washington was no politician at all, as we understand the word," replied Ratcliffe abruptly. "He stood outside of politics. The thing couldn't be done today. The people don't like that sort of royal airs."

"I don't understand!" said Mrs. Lee. "Why could you not do it now?"

"Because I should make a fool of myself," replied Ratcliffe, pleased to think that Mrs. Lee should put him on a level with Washington....

"Mr. Ratcliffe means that Washington was too respectable for our time," interposed Carrington.

This was deliberately meant to irritate Ratcliffe, and it did so all the more because Mrs. Lee turned to Carrington, and said, with some bitterness: "Was he then the only honest public man we ever had?"

"Oh no!" replied Carrington cheerfully; "there have been one or two others...."

Ratcliffe was exasperated at Carrington's habit of drawing discussion to this point. He felt the remark as a personal insult, and he knew it to be intended. "Public men," he broke out, "cannot be dressing themselves today in Washington's old clothes. If Washington were President now, he would have to learn our ways or lose the next election. Only fools and theorists imagine that our society can be handled with gloves or long poles. One must make one's self a part of it. If virtue won't answer our purpose, we must use vice, or our opponents will put us out of office, and this was as true in Washington's day as it is now, and always will be."

Mrs. Lee began to wonder if she was becoming part of the corrupt world around her:

Was she, unknown to herself gradually becoming tainted with the life about her? Or was Ratcliffe right in accepting the good and the bad together, and in being of his time since he was in it? Why was it, she said bitterly to herself, that everything Washington touched, he purified, even down to the associations of his house; and why is it that everything we touch seems soiled? In spite of Mr. Ratcliffe, is it not better to be a child and to cry for the moon and stars?

RATCLIFFE VS. THE PRESIDENT

Ratcliffe's success in his contest with the new President depended on the amount of "pressure" he could employ. To keep himself in the background, and to fling over the head of the raw Chief Magistrate a web of intertwined influences, any one of which alone would be useless, but which taken together were not to be broken through...this was Ratcliffe's intention and towards this he had been directing all his manipulation for weeks past. How much bargaining and how many promises he found it necessary to make was known to himself alone...

The Washington Monument as it looked in 1876. Mark Twain sardonically observed: "The Monument to the Father of his Country towers out of the mud—It has the aspect of a factory chimney with the top broken off. The skeleton of a decaying scaffolding lingers about its summit, and tradition says that the spirit of Washington often comes down and sits on those rafters to enjoy this tribute of respect which the nation has reared as the symbol of its unappeasable gratitude. The Monument is to be finished, some day, and at that time our Washington will have risen still higher in the nation's veneration, and will be known as the Great-Great-Grandfather of his Country."

This statue of George Washington by Horatio Greenough was ordered by Congress in 1832. The enormous statue of the half-draped Washington, cut out of a block of Carrara marble, weighed twelve tons, was twelve feet high, and cost $44,000. It was too heavy for the Capitol floor and was therefore placed outside where it became the talk of the town, not all of the talk being favorable. Mary Clemmer Ames described the uproar over the statue:

"This is the grandest and most criticised work of art about the Capitol. The form being nude to the waist and the right arm out-stretched, it is a current vulgar joke that he is reaching out his hand for his clothes which are on exhibition in a case at the Patent Office. It is true that a sense of personal dis-comfort seems to emanate from the drap-ery—or lack of it....This statue is designed in imitation of the antique statue of Jupiter Tonans. The ancients made their statues of Jupiter naked above and draped below as being visible to the gods but invisible to men. But the average American citizen, being accustomed to seeing the Father of his country decently attired in small clothes, nat-urally receives a shock at first beholding him in next to no clothes at all. It is impossible for him to reconcile a Jupiter in sandals with the stately George Washington in knee-breeches and buckled shoes. The spirit of the statue, which is ideal, militates against the spirit of the land which is utilitarian if not commonplace. Nevertheless, in poetry of feeling, in grandeur of conception, in exqui-site fineness of detail and in execution, Horatio Greenough's statue of George Washington is transcendently the greatest work in marble yet wrought at the command of the government for the Capitol."

Ratcliffe was a great statesman. The smoothness of his manipulation was marvelous. No other man in politics, indeed no other man who had ever been in politics in this country, could—his admirers said—have brought together so many hostile interests and made so fantastic a combination. The beauty of his work consisted in the skill with which he evaded questions of principle. As he wisely said, the issue now involved was not one of principle but of power. The fate of that noble party to which they all belonged...depended on their letting principle alone. Their principle must be the want of principles.

A NEW PRESIDENT

The President in *Democracy* was a mixture of President Rutherford B. Hayes, who was elected in 1876, and President Ulysses Grant, who had served two corruption-ridden terms before Hayes. Adams calls the President "Old Granite," an obvious reference to Grant.

On Monday afternoon the President-elect arrived in Washington, and the comedy began. The new President was...an unknown quantity in political mathematics. In the national convention of the party, nine months before, after some dozens of fruitless ballots in which Ratcliffe wanted but three votes of a majority, his opponents had done what he was now doing: they had laid aside their principles and set up for their candidate a plain Indiana farmer, whose political experience was limited to stump-speaking in his native State, and to one term as Governor. They had pitched upon him, not because they thought him

The Civil Service As It Is.
Hon. Member of Congress presenting a few of his constituents for office.

competent, but because they hoped by doing so to detach Indiana from Ratcliffe's following, and they were so successful that within fifteen minutes Ratcliffe's friends were routed, and the Presidency had fallen upon this new political Buddha....

That he was honest, all admitted; that is to say, all who voted for him. This is a general characteristic of all new presidents. He himself took great pride in his homespun honesty, which is a quality peculiar to nature's noblemen. Owing nothing, as he conceived, to politicians...he affirmed it to be his first duty to protect the people from those vultures, as he called them, those wolves in sheep's clothing, those harpies, those hyenas, the politicians; epithets which, as generally interpreted, meant Ratcliffe and Ratcliffe's friends. His cardinal principle in politics was hostility to Ratcliffe....He came to Washington determined to be the Father of his country; to gain a proud immortality—and a re-election.

RATCLIFFE MEETS THE PRESIDENT

The President received Ratcliffe awkwardly....It had seemed a mere flea-bite, as he expressed it, to brush Ratcliffe aside, but in Washington the thing was somehow different. Even his own Indiana friends looked grave when he talked of it, and shook their heads. They advised him to be cautious and gain time; to lead Ratcliffe on, and if possible to throw on him the responsibility of a quarrel.

A PROFFER OF OFFICE

The President had undertaken...either to force him (Ratcliffe) into a hostile and treacherous Cabinet, or to throw on him the blame of a refusal and a quarrel....He (Ratcliffe) meant to accept the Treasury and he was ready to back himself with a heavy wager to get the government entirely into his own hands within six weeks.

RATCLIFFE TELLS MRS. LEE OF HIS STRUGGLE WITH THE PRESIDENT

Busy as he was, the Senator made his appearance the next evening at Mrs. Lee's, and finding her alone...Ratcliffe told Madeleine the story of his week's experience...He told her how matters stood at the moment, and how the President had laid a trap for him which he could not escape....This half revelation of the meanness which distorted politics; this one-sided view of human nature in its naked deformity playing pranks with the interests of forty million people, disgusted and depressed Madeleine's mind. Ratcliffe spared her nothing except the exposure of his own moral sores. He carefully called her attention to every leprous taint upon his neighbors' persons, to every rag in their foul clothing, to every slimy and fetid pool that lay beside their path. It was his way of bringing his own qualities into relief.

A PLEA FOR GUIDANCE

"And what *is* most for the public good?" [asked Ratcliffe].

Madeleine half opened her mouth to reply, then hesitated, and stared silently into the fire before her. What was indeed most for the public good? Where did the public good enter at all into this maze of personal intrigue, this wilderness of stunted natures where no straight road was to be found, but only the tortuous and aimless tracks of beasts and things that crawl? Where was she to look for a principle to guide, an ideal to set up and to point at?

For the first time, Mrs. Lee began to feel his power. He was simple,

President Rutherford B. Hayes

A Private Wine and Gambling Room

"It is commonly supposed throughout the country that Washington City is the most immoral place in the land. That there is a frightful amount of immorality prevalent in the city is true, but it is not fair to charge it to the *citizens*....There is, in addition to the citizens proper, an average floating population during the sessions of Congress, of from ten to twenty-five thousand persons....These persons represent all classes of society, and have a vast amount of leisure time on their hands....Undoubtedly the Washingtonians are guilty of a fair share of it, but the sum total would not be so great were not the city so much over run with idlers from other parts of the country."

John B. Ellis, *The Sights and Secrets of the National Capital.*

The Style of Drama Most Popular in Washington

"Washington is generally regarded as a theatrical graveyard, and very few Thespian artists appear there....The noticeable lack of public amusement is compensated for by numerous private theatricals and ministerial balls....Balls and receptions become monotonous by such frequent repetition, so that it is necessary to devise other means for amusement through the long, cold winter evenings. As every lady and most gentlemen, too, arrogate to themselves the possession of some dramatic genius, private theatricals have become decidedly fashionable with the ultra-aesthetic society people of Washington....Those who engage in these performances include none but the *crème de la crème* of society, and not infrequently the plays are the product of Washington authors, who generally draw their characters from actual persons, thereby adding greatly to the excitement of the play."

J. W. Buel, *Mysteries and Miseries of America's Cities*

straightforward, earnest. His words moved her. How should she imagine that he was playing upon her sensitive nature precisely as he played upon the President's coarse one, and that this heavy western politician had the instincts of a wild Indian in their sharpness and quickness of perception; that he divined her character and read it as he read the faces and tones of thousands from day to day? ...What woman of thirty, with aspirations for the infinite, could resist an attack like this? What woman with a soul could see before her the most powerful public man of her time, appealing—with a face furrowed by anxieties, and a voice vibrating with only half-suppressed affection—to her for counsel and sympathy, without yielding some response?... Ratcliffe, too, had a curious instinct for human weaknesses. No magnetic needle was ever truer than his finger when he touched the vulnerable spot in an opponent's mind. Mrs. Lee was not to be reached by an appeal to religious sentiment, to ambition, or to affection. Any such appeal would have fallen flat on her ears and destroyed its own hopes. But she was a woman to the very last drop of her blood. She could not be induced to love Ratcliffe, but she might be deluded into sacrificing herself for him. She atoned for want of devotion to God, by devotion to man. She had a woman's natural tendency towards asceticism, self-extinction, self-abnegation.

THE INAUGURATION

Madeleine and Sybil went to the Capitol and had the best places to see and hear the Inauguration, as well as a cold March wind would allow. Mrs. Lee found fault with the ceremony; it was of the earth, earthy, she said. An elderly western farmer, with silver spectacles, new and glossy evening clothes, bony features, and stiff, thin, grey hair, trying to address a large crowd of people under the drawbacks of a piercing wind and a cold in his head, was not a hero.

MRS. LEE CALLS ON THE FIRST LADY

The First Lady in the *roman à clef* was Lucy Webb Hayes, known as "Lemonade Lucy," who banned alcohol and low-cut dresses from the White House.

The lady, who was somewhat stout and coarse-featured, and whom Mrs. Lee declared she wouldn't engage as a cook, showed qualities which, seen under that fierce light which beats upon a throne, seemed ungracious. Her antipathy to Ratcliffe was more violent than her husband's, and was even more openly expressed...She extended her hostility to everyone who could be supposed to be Ratcliffe's friend, and the newspapers, as well as private gossip, had marked out Mrs. Lee as one who, by an alliance with Ratcliffe, was aiming at supplanting her own rule over the White House. Hence, when Mrs. Lightfoot Lee was announced, and the two sisters were ushered into the presidential parlor, she put on a coldly patronizing air, and in reply to Madeleine's hope that she found Washington agreeable, she intimated that there was much in Washington which struck her as awful wicked, especially the women; and, looking at Sybil, she spoke of the style of dress in this city which she said she meant to do what she could to put a stop to. She'd heard tell that people sent to Paris for their gowns, just as though America wasn't good enough to make one's clothes! Jacob (all Presidents' wives speak of their husbands by their first names) had promised her to get a law passed against it. In her town in Indiana, a young woman who was seen on the street in such clothes wouldn't be spoken to. At these remarks, made with an air and in a temper quite unmistakable, Madeleine became exasperated beyond measure, and said that "Washington would be pleased to see the President do something in regard to dress-reform—or any other reform"; and with this allusion to the President's ante-election reform speeches, Mrs. Lee turned her back and left the room.

This drawing was titled "Washington Belles Practicing the Chivalrous Art of Fencing." Mr. J. W. Buel explained: "Another fashionable amusement has lately attained importance among the ladies, viz.: fencing matches. This is regarded with special favor by Southern belles sojourning at the Capital, because it has some elements of chivalry and French *passe temps,* besides affording great opportunity for display of personal grace. There is much divertissement in an exhibition of skill with foils between ladies who are in dress, or, rather, undress; arms, busts and limbs, show to much advantage, which enriches beauty and heroizes the participants before a delighted audience."

Lucy Webb Hayes in 1877
President Hayes called his wife "large, but not unwieldly...As she grows older [she] preserves her beauty...The only drawback is her frequent attacks of sick headache. Perhaps twice a month she suffers for a day or two."

"School of Scandal," by Thomas Nast

This Nast cartoon had a caption reading, "February 22, 1876 Chorus of rising patriots (?) 'We cannot tell a lie! We did not do it!'" But there is not much left of the tree of truth that the students in the 1876 "School of Scandal" have chopped down with the axes they are hiding behind their backs.

MRS. LEE LOSES HER STANDARDS

She reconciled herself to accepting the Ratcliffian morals, for she could see no choice. She herself had approved every step she had seen him take. She could not deny that there must be something wrong in a double standard of morality, but where was it? Mr. Ratcliffe seemed to her to be doing good work with as pure means as he had at hand. He ought to be encouraged, not reviled....

Mr. Gore...said [to Mrs. Lee], "Are you satisfied with what you have seen?"

"I have got so far as to lose the distinction between right and wrong. Isn't that the first step in politics?" she asked.

MR. CARRINGTON ON MR. RATCLIFFE

"You and I," said Carrington [to Mrs. Lee], "are wide apart in our estimates of Mr. Ratcliffe. To you, of course, he shows his best side. He is on his good behavior, and knows that any false step will ruin him. I see in him only a coarse, selfish, unprincipled politician, who would either drag you down to his level, or, what is more likely, would very soon disgust you and make your life a wretched self-immolation before his vulgar ambition, or compel you to leave him. In either case you would be the victim."

CARRINGTON LEAVES D.C.; HE LEAVES LETTER EXPOSING RATCLIFFE WITH MRS. LEE'S SISTER, SYBIL

Carrington was the executor of the estate of the lobbyist, Samuel Baker. In this capacity he had access to all of Baker's papers which included a letter implicating Ratcliffe in a scandal involving a steamship company. Adams based his plot on the Mulligan letters which exposed Senator James G. Blaine's involvement in a railroad scandal and helped finish his hopes for the presidential nomination in 1876.

SYBIL IN LOVE WITH CARRINGTON

For the first time in her life, Sybil had found a man who gave some play to her imagination; one who had been a rebel, and had grown used to the shocks of fate, so as to walk with calmness into the face of death and to command or obey with equal indifference. She felt that he would tell her what to do when the earthquake came, and would be at hand to consult, which is in a woman's eyes the great object of men's existence, when trouble comes...One thing and one thing only was clear: if Sybil loved Carrington, she should have him. How Madeleine expected to bring about this change of heart in Carrington was known only to herself. She regarded men as creatures made for women to dispose of, and capable of being transferred like checks, or baggage-labels, from one woman to another, as desired....Mrs. Lee never doubted that she could make Carrington fall in love with Sybil provided she could place herself beyond his reach. At all events, come what might, even though she had to accept the desperate alternative offered by Mr. Ratcliffe, nothing should be allowed to interfere with Sybil's happiness.

RATCLIFFE PROPOSES

"I am not one of those who are happy in political life. I am a politician because I cannot help myself; it is the trade I am fittest for....In politics we cannot keep our hands clean. I have done many things in my political career that are not defensible. To act with entire honesty and self-respect, one should always live in a pure atmosphere, and the atmosphere of politics is impure. Domestic life is the salvation of many public men, but I have for many years been deprived of it. I have now come to that point where increasing responsibilities and temptations make me require help. I must have it. You alone can give it to me. You are kind, thoughtful, conscientious, highminded, cultivated, fitted better than any woman I ever saw for public duties. Your place is there. You belong among those who exercise an influence beyond their time. I only ask you to take the place which is yours...."

In all the offers of marriage she had ever heard, this was the most unsentimental and businesslike. As for his appeal to her ambition, it fell quite dead upon her ear, but a woman must be more than a heroine who can listen to flattery so evidently sincere, from a man who is pre-eminent among men, without being affected by it. To her, however, the great and overpowering fact was that she found herself unable to retreat or escape...The offer was made. What should she do with it?

RATCLIFFE EXPOSED

"You have really made up your mind, then? Nothing I can say will change it?"

Mrs. Lee...shook her head slowly and decidedly.

"Then," said Sybil, "there is only one thing more I can do. You must read this!" and she drew out Carrington's letter, which she held before Madeleine's face.

"The Haunted House; or, the 'Murdered' Rag Baby Will Not Be Still"

Nast's cartoon about inflation which he pictured as a "rag baby." He blamed inflation on the Democrats and considered it one of the scandals of the time.

The Mulligan Letters

Nast's cartoon refers to the so-called "Mulligan Scandal," which badly tarnished James G. Blaine's reputation. In the sixties and early seventies Blaine had written a series of letters to a Mr. Warren Fisher, Jr., the holder of a contract to build the Little Rock & Fort Smith Railroad in Arkansas. The letters got into the hands of Fisher's bookkeeper, James Mulligan, who on May 31, 1876, revealed his possession of them while testifying before a congressional committee which was investigating the sale of Little Rock & Fort Smith bonds to the Union Pacific Railroad Company. Blaine got the letters, refused to disclose them, and on June 5, 1876, read them aloud on the floor of the House, claiming that he was not guilty of any wrongdoing. But Blaine never managed to totally clear his name. As Speaker of the House in 1869, Blaine had presided over a debate on a land grant for that particular railroad and had helped its promoters to keep the measure from defeat. One of Mulligan's letters showed that Blaine had written to Fisher asking to be a part of his undertaking and implying that he might be useful to Fisher. Blaine's opponents used the Mulligan letters to help defeat his bid for the presidential nomination in both 1876 and 1880. Not until 1884 was he nominated as the Republican candidate for President.

Patent Office

In 1877 Mary Clemmer Ames called the Patent Office "next to the Capitol...the most august building in Washington." The Patent Board was created in 1790 to "promote the progress of science and the useful arts." This building was erected, starting in 1836, to house both the Board and a vast display of objects to which patents had been granted. The Model Room stretched some 274 feet in length; models were arranged in glass cases. There were models of clocks, telegraphs, burglar and fire alarms, musical instruments, lighthouses, streetcars, stoves, sewing machines, corsets and hundreds of other inventions. Mrs. Ames felt that the most remarkable inventions were "a machine to force a hen to lay eggs, and a silver worm hook, invented to fish worms out of the human stomach."

The Model Room, Patent Office

CARRINGTON'S LETTER

Washington, 2nd April.

My Dear Mrs. Lee,

This letter will only come into your hands in case there should be a necessity for your knowing its contents....

You asked me the other day whether I knew anything against Mr. Ratcliffe which the world did not know, to account for my low opinion of his character. I evaded your question then....

I do know facts in regard to Mr. Ratcliffe, which have seemed to me to warrant a very low opinion of his character, and to mark him as unfit to be, I will not say your husband, but even your acquaintance....

Just eight years ago, the great "Inter-Oceanic Mail Steamship Company," wished to extend its service round the world, and, in order to do so, it applied to Congress for a heavy subsidy. The management of this affair was put into the hands of Mr. Baker, and all his private letters to the President of the Company...as well as the President's replies, came into my possession....

It appeared from this correspondence that the bill was carried successfully through the House, and, on reaching the Senate, was referred to the appropriate Committee. Its...passage was very doubtful; the end of the session was close at hand; the Senate was...evenly divided, and the Chairman of the Committee was decidedly hostile. The Chairman of that Committee was Senator Ratcliffe....

At last Mr. Baker wrote that Senator had put the bill in his pocket, and unless some means could be found of overcoming his opposition, there would be no report, and the bill would never come to a vote....In this exigency Baker suggested that the Company should give him authority to see what money would do....Two days later he wrote that the bill was reported, and would pass the Senate within forty-eight hours; and he congratulated the Company on the fact that he had used only one hundred thousand dollars....

The bill was actually reported, passed, and became law as he foretold and the Company has enjoyed its subsidy ever since. Mrs. Baker also informed me that to her knowledge her husband gave the sum mentioned, in United States Coupon Bonds, to Senator Ratcliffe.

This transaction...explains the distrust I have always expressed for him. You will, however, understand that all these papers have been destroyed....

In trusting this secret to you, I rely firmly upon your mentioning it to no one else....You are at liberty, if you wish, to show this letter to one person only—to Mr. Ratcliffe himself. That done, you will, I beg, burn it immediately.

Ever most truly yours,

John Carrington

Against the sentiment of all her friends she had insisted upon believing in this man; she had wrought herself up to the point of accepting him for her husband; a man who, if law were the same thing as justice, ought to be in a felon's cell; a man who could take money to betray his trust. Her anger at first swept away all bounds....How had this happened? How had she got into so foul a complication? When she left New York, she had meant to be a mere spectator in Washington....She had, with her eyes open, walked into the quagmire of politics, in spite of remonstrance, in spite of conscience.

RATCLIFFE REJECTED

She grew more and more angry with herself, and as her self-reproach increased, her anger against Ratcliffe faded away. She had no right to be angry with Ratcliffe....He had always openly enough avowed that he knew no code of morals in politics; that if virtue did not answer his purpose, he used vice. How could she blame him for acts which he had repeatedly defended in her presence and with her tacit assent...?

The worst was that this discovery had come on her as a blow, not as a reprieve from execution....She had not known the recesses of her own heart. She had honestly supposed that Sybil's interests and Sybil's happiness were forcing her to an act of self-sacrifice; and now she saw that in the depths of her soul very different motives had been at work: ambition, thirst for power, restless eagerness to meddle in what did not concern her, blind longing to escape from the torture of watching other women with full lives and satisfied instincts, while her own life was hungry and sad. For a time she had actually, unconscious as she was of the delusion, hugged a hope that a new field of usefulness was open to her...and that here at last was an object for which there would be almost a pleasure in squandering the rest of existence even if she knew in advance that the experiment would fail. Life was emptier than ever now that this dream was over. Yet the worst was not in that disappointment, but in the discovery of her own weakness and self-deception.

She had at first the keen mortification of reflecting how easily she had been led by mere vanity into imagining that she could be of use in the world. The ease with which Ratcliffe alone had twisted her about his finger, now that she saw it, made her writhe, and the thought of what he might have done, had she married him, and of the endless succession of moral somersaults she would have had to turn, chilled her with mortal terror....Then as she grew calmer, Ratcliffe's sins took on a milder hue; life, after all, had not been entirely blackened by his arts; there was even some good in her experience, sharp though it were....The antics of Presidents and Senators had been amusing—so amusing that she had nearly been persuaded to take part in them. She had saved herself in time. She had got to the bottom of this business of democratic government, and found out that it was nothing more than government of any other kind. She might have known it by her own common sense, but now that experience had proved it, she was glad to quit the masquerade....As for Mr. Ratcliffe, she felt no difficulty in dealing with him. Let Mr. Ratcliffe, and his brother giants, wander on their own political prairie, and hunt for offices, or other profitable game, as they would. Their objects were not her objects, and to join their company was not her ambition....

Mrs. Lee was alone in her parlor and rose rather gravely as he entered, but welcomed him as cordially as she could. She wanted to put an end to his hopes at once and to do it decisively, but without hurting his feelings.

"Mr. Ratcliffe," said she, when he was seated, "I am sure you will be better pleased by my speaking instantly and frankly....What you wish is impossible. I would rather not even discuss it. Let us leave it here and return to our old relations."

His first sensation was only one of anger that his projects had miscarried...yet he did not despair, for it was his theory that Mrs. Lee, in the depths of her soul, wanted to be at the head of the White House as much as he wanted to be there himself, and that her apparent coyness was mere feminine indecision in the face of temptation.

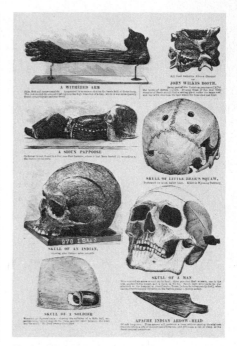

Curiosities
From the Army Medical Museum, Washington

The Main Hall of the Army Medical Museum

Conservatory, Agricultural Department, c. 1876

Smithsonian Institution, c. 1876

Agricultural Department
Thé Bureau of Agriculture moved its seventy-two employees into this building in 1868.

RATCLIFFE'S ANSWER TO THE LETTER

Next Adams involved Ratcliffe in a second stolen election, this time on the national level. The reference to a "violent contest and a very close vote" cannot fail to remind the reader of the Hayes-Tilden election. Continually Adams reminds us that Ratcliffe has one moral code, the code of the age, and that Mrs. Lee operates by another code.

'I meant to have told you of that affair myself...."
"Then it is true!" said Mrs. Lee....
"True in its leading facts; untrue in some of its details, and in the impression it creates. During the Presidential election which took place eight years ago last autumn, there was...a violent contest and a very close vote. We believed...that the result of that election would be almost as important to the nation as the result of the war itself. Our defeat meant that the government must pass into the bloodstained hands of rebels, men whose designs were more than doubtful....In consequence we strained every nerve. Money was freely spent...in excess of our resources....A large sum had been borrowed...and must be repaid....The end was that towards the close of the session the head of the committee, accompanied by two senators, came to me and told me that I must abandon my opposition to the Steamship Subsidy. They made no open avowal of the reasons, and I did not press for one. Their declaration...that certain action on my part was essential to the interests of the party, satisfied me. I accordingly reported the bill, and voted for it....At the time this affair occurred, I was a Senator of the United States. I was also a trusted member of a great political party which I looked upon as identical with the nation. In both capacities I owed duties to my constituents, to the government, to the people. I might interpret these duties narrowly or broadly. I might say: Perish the government, perish the Union, perish this people, rather than that I should soil my hands! Or I might say, as I did, and as I would say again: Be my fate what it may, this glorious Union, the last hope of suffering humanity, shall be preserved....

"Did I not here, on this very spot, when challenged once before by this same Carrington, take credit for an act less defensible than this? Did I not tell you then that I had even violated the sanctity of a great popular election and reversed its result? That was my sole act! In comparison with it, this is a trifle! Who is injured by a steamship company subscribing one or ten hundred thousand dollars to a campaign fund? Whose rights are affected by it? Perhaps its stockholders receive one dollar a share in dividends less than they otherwise would. If they do not complain, who else can do so? But in that election I deprived a million people of rights which belonged to them as absolutely as their houses!...Not a word of blame or criticism have you ever uttered to me on that account....Why are you now so severe upon the smaller crime?"

A DOOMED PERSISTENCE

Ratcliffe grew more and more somber as he became aware that defeat was staring him in the face. He was tenacious of purpose, and he had never in his life abandoned an object which he had so much at heart as this. For the moment, so completely had the fascination of Mrs. Lee got the control of him, he would rather have abandoned the Presidency itself than her. He really loved her as earnestly as it was in his nature to love anything. To her obstinacy he would oppose an obstinacy greater still....Was it not possible to change his ground; to offer inducements that would appeal even more strongly to feminine ambition and love of display than the Presidency itself? He began again:

"Is there no form of pledge I can give you? No sacrifice I can make? You dislike politics. Shall I leave political life? I will do anything rather than lose you. I can probably control the appointment of Minster to England...."

She was exasperated by this obstinate disregard of her forbearance, this gross attempt to bribe her with office, this flagrant abandonment of even a pretense of public virtue; the mere thought of his touch on her person was more repulsive than a loathsome disease. Bent upon teaching him a lesson he would never forget, she spoke out abruptly, and with evident signs of contempt in her voice and manner:

"Mr. Ratcliffe, I am not to be bought. No rank, no dignity, no consideration, no conceivable expedient would induce me to change my mind. Let us have no more of this!...

"Mr. Ratcliffe! I have listened to you with a great deal more patience and respect than you deserve. For one long hour I have degraded myself by discussing with you the question whether I should marry a man who by his own confession has betrayed the highest trusts that could be placed in him, who has taken money for his votes as a Senator, and who is now in public office by means of a successful fraud of his own, when in justice he should be in a State's prison. I will have no more of this. Understand, once for all, that there is an impassable gulf between your life and mine. I do not doubt that you will make yourself President, but whatever or wherever you are, never speak to me or recognize me again!"

MRS. LEE ESCAPES

"Sybil, dearest, will you go abroad with me again?"

"Of course I will," said Sybil; "I will go to the end of the world with you."

"I want to go to Egypt," said Madeleine, still smiling faintly. "Democracy has shaken my nerves to pieces. Oh, what rest it would be to live in the Great Pyramid and look out forever at the polar star!"

SYBIL TO CARRINGTON

May 1st, New York

My Dear Mr. Carrington,

I promised to write you, and so, to keep my promise, and also because my sister wishes me to tell you about our plans, I send this letter. We have left Washington—forever, I am afraid—and are going to Europe next month....Madeleine is going to add a postscript.... Hoping to hear from you soon.

Sincerely yours,

Sybil Ross

Mrs. Lee's P.S. was very short:

The bitterest part of all this horrid story is that nine out of ten of our countrymen would say I had made a mistake.

State, War, and Navy Building

In 1876 work was still in progress on the State, War, and Navy Building, today known as the Executive Office Building. In 1875 the south wing had been completed for the State Department. Designed by Alfred B. Mullett in the French Renaissance style, the structure was often attacked for its non-Greek appearance. In 1877 Mary Clemmer Ames looked forward to the completion of "the magnificent structure now going up, for the combined use of the State, War and Navy Departments." But not until 1888 was the building finally completed.

The Treasury

Of the Treasury Building, Mark Twain observed: "You wrench your gaze loose and you look down in front of you and see the broad Pennsylvania Avenue stretching straight ahead for a mile or more till it brings up against the iron fence in front of a pillared granite pile, the Treasury building—an edifice that would command respect in any capital."

THE STOLEN ELECTION

Despite much confusion about the presidential election of 1876, there is agreement about the central fact: the Democratic candidate, Governor Samuel J. Tilden of New York, won the election by a large majority, but Governor Rutherford B. Hayes, the Republican candidate, ended up as President.

Between Election Day on November 7, 1876, and Inauguration Day on March 5, 1877, Americans did not know who would be their next leader. Amid the uncertainty, there was even the threat of another civil war. Historians still disagree about how the disputed election was actually settled. One faction argues that Southern congressmen, wearied with the failure of Reconstruction, made a deal in which they exchanged Southern electoral votes for Northern investment capital. Others say that a single man fixed the election: Dan Sickles, the general who had overextended the Union lines at Gettysburg, and who on election night saw

LIBERTY AND UNION

GOV. RUTHERFORD B. HAYES,

HON. WM. A. WHEELER

FOR PRESIDENT.

FOR VICE-PRESIDENT.

Copyright 1876, by Currier & Ives, N.Y.

GRAND NATIONAL REPUBLICAN BANNER.

The Ultimate Victor: Governor Rutherford B. Hayes (Republican) of Ohio

The Winner of the Popular Vote: Governor Samuel J. Tilden (Democrat) of New York

that by swinging the electoral votes of Louisiana, South Carolina and Florida to Hayes, he could take the election away from the Democrat, Tilden. There is, in short, more than one detective story about the election of 1876. One can only—as in this chapter—examine all the clues. At least the solution is known: after five months of haggling over the results of the election, the country inaugurated Hayes and got on with what most men at the time considered far more important than politics—making money.

THE DIARY OF RUTHERFORD B. HAYES

Rutherford B. Hayes was one of three Presidents we know of who kept a diary, the other two being John Quincy Adams and James K. Polk. On October 12, 1875, when Hayes was re-elected to a third term as Governor of Ohio, he knew that he would be considered as a presidential candidate. In his diary he wrote:

12th October, 1875—Election Day...I am as nearly indifferent, on personal grounds, to the result of this day as it is possible to be. I prefer success. But I anticipate defeat with very great equanimity. If victorious I am likely to be pushed for the Republican nomination for President...Defeat in the next Presidential Election is almost a certainty...

17th October, 1875—Elected—a pleasant serenade from my neighbors—a day of doubt and anxiety as to the result.

Tuesday, 15th February, 1876—Since I came to Columbus six weeks ago, there has been no day in which I have not had letters and visits on the subject of my nomination for the Presidency.

HAYES CONSIDERS HIS QUALIFICATIONS AND CHANCES FOR THE PRESIDENCY

I feel less diffidence in thinking of this subject than perhaps I ought. It seems to me that good purposes, and the judgment, experience and firmness I possess would enable me to execute the duties of the office well. I do not feel the least fear that I should fail! This all looks egotistical, but it is sincere. On the other hand I do not desire the place with any strong or uneasy feeling.

WIDESPREAD FEAR THAT GRANT WILL RUN FOR A THIRD TERM

Hayes was opposed to Grant's seeking a third term:

I am opposed to the course of Gen. Grant on the 3rd term, the Civil Service, and the appointment of unfit men on partisan or personal grounds.

Grant's chances for a third term were badly hurt by the exposure in 1875 of the Whiskey Ring in which his own personal secretary, among others, was involved in taking payoffs in return for helping St. Louis distillers avoid

"Rutherford B. Hayes, the Republican candidate for President...was born in Delaware, Ohio, October 4, 1822. His parents were natives of Vermont, and emigrated to Ohio in 1817. Young Hayes graduated at Kenyon College in 1842, and three years afterward he graduated at the Law School, was admitted to the bar...and began the practice of his profession at Fremont, Ohio...In 1849 he removed to Cincinnati, and nine years later he was elected City Solicitor. This office he held until the breaking out of the Southern rebellion, when...he raised a regiment for the Union service....Lieutenant-Colonel Hayes was severely wounded in the arm, but remained with his regiment throughout the action. In 1864 he was nominated to represent the Second Congressional District of Ohio, and...in 1866 he was re-elected. Before his congressional term expired, in 1867, he was elected Governor of the State, and was re-elected in 1869....In 1874 he was unanimously nominated for the third term as Governor."

Harper's Weekly, July 1876

taxes. And then in the spring of 1876 the scandal-ridden Grant Administration was rocked by yet another revelation: Secretary of War William Belknap was exposed for selling post-traderships in the West. These scandals helped to make sure that the 1875 resolution of the House of Representatives prevailed, which said that a third term would be:

...unwise, unpatriotic and fraught with peril to our free institutions.

HAYES'S RIVALS FOR THE 1876 REPUBLICAN NOMINATION FOR THE PRESIDENCY

In 1876 the Republican party was split in several directions. The reformers in the party favored Benjamin Bristow of Kentucky, appointed Secretary of the Treasury by Grant in 1874. Much of Bristow's following consisted of men who had been part of the Liberal party, which in 1872 had supported Horace Greeley, editor of the New York *Tribune*, against Grant. Bristow, who favored Civil Service reform, had earned the admiration of reformers for prosecuting the men involved in the Whiskey Ring fraud.

Other Republicans supported Senator Roscoe Conkling of New York, who represented everything that Bristow and his followers wanted to abolish; Conkling's New York machine was based on patronage, bestowing federal Civil Service jobs on the loyal rather than the deserving.

Another candidate was Conkling's archrival, Senator James G. Blaine of Maine. But Blaine's otherwise very good chances for the nomination were much diminished by the revelation of his involvement in a railroad scandal through the famous Mulligan letters.

In his diary on May 17, 1876, Hayes reflected on Conkling's chances:

I have never doubted that Conkling would be the final machine candidate, and very strong for that reason. But he would be so distasteful to all but the regulation Republicans that I can not but hope even his supporters will see it...They are making great efforts to unite the N.Y. press upon him. But New England is strong against him.

And two days later Hayes wrote of his rival Blaine:

I still think Blaine is so far ahead in the number of delegates he has secured and is securing that his nomination is not improbable.

REPUBLICAN NATIONAL CONVENTION, IN CINCINNATI, NOMINATES RUTHERFORD B. HAYES ON JUNE 16, 1876

Hayes was nominated on the seventh ballot on June 16

Ticket of Admission to the Republican Convention of 1876
The Atlanta *Constitution* was very pleased with the outcome of the Republican Convention at Cincinnati. On June 17 the paper reported:

"We return our thanks to our radical crew at Cincinnati for burying the hyena Blaine in the center of political refuse. There let him satisfy himself to his heart's content. This man for president would indeed have been a cruel insult and experience for the southern people. He pandered to the basest passions of bad men and stooped to the dirtiest revilings of better men than himself only to subserve a mad personal ambition. He has his reward, and that from the hands of his party. Let him enjoy the sweet pill."

with 384 votes; Blaine was second with 351 votes. On June 17, the day after Hayes's nomination, the Louisville *Courier-Journal* wrote:

The agony at Cincinnati is over, and it is not Mr. Blaine. It is not Mr. Blaine nor Mr. Conkling nor Mr. Bristow....It is Mr. Hayes. The dark horse from Ohio came in at an easy canter on the homestretch, beating the favorite of the field by a full length and a half. Our telegraphic reports, special and otherwise, tell the exciting story; how the bold rider from Kennebec and Penobscot, prancing defiantly about the track, lost his position in the start; how after the first dash of a mile, he was caught in a pocket made for him by the...Kentucky and New York horses respectively, and how finally he was passed at the critical moment by the Ohio colt.

Rutherford B. Hayes is the Great Unknown. The ex-speaker [Blaine] prophesied aright. He was not afraid of Bristow, or Conkling....He dreaded the Great Unknown, and by the Great Unknown he has been overcome and vanquished...The rejection of Mr. Bristow will cause a wider reach of disappointment, and a disappointment of a sincerer kind, than the defeat of any of the other candidates except Mr. Blaine. The small vote cast for Mr. Bristow and the large vote cast for Mr. Blaine show that administrative reform is not a prevailing idea with the Republicans.

The San Francisco *Chronicle* of June 17 enthusiastically assessed Hayes's qualifications for the Presidency:

His position on all the important issues now before the people is clearly defined. He is uncompromising as a champion of a sound currency...He was a General on the Union side during the rebellion, and made a creditable war record. His character and career constitute a platform in themselves. He has not been touched by the breath of scandal.

THE DEMOCRATIC NATIONAL CONVENTION IN ST. LOUIS NOMINATES SAMUEL J. TILDEN FOR PRESIDENT

The panic of 1873 helped to usher in the revival of the Democratic party, which had been largely destroyed by the Civil War. In 1874, for the first time since the end of that war, the Democrats held a majority in the House of Representatives. The year 1874 also brought New York State a new Democratic governor, Samuel J. Tilden. Tilden had become wealthy from a lucrative law practice involving many railroad financing deals. "Tilden and Reform" was his campaign slogan, which was supposed to remind voters of the part that Tilden as Governor of New York had played in disbanding the Tweed ring. Although Tilden himself favored hard money, many members of his party did not, and the currency issue was an important one in the campaign of 1876. Democrats in sections of the

"Governor Tilden was born at New Lebanon in the...state of New York, in the year 1814....

"The governor's father, a farmer and merchant...was a man of notable judgment and practical sense and the accepted oracle of the county upon all matters of public concern, while his opinion was eagerly sought by all his neighbors, but by none more than by the late President Van Buren....

"Young Tilden entered college in...the fall of 1832...Mr. Tilden had not been long at Yale College before his health gave way, and obliged him to leave...After some rest he was enabled to resume his studies, and in 1833 entered the university of New York, where he completed his academic education. He then entered the law office of John W. Edmunds, in the city of New York....In 1844 he was sent to the assembly from the city of New York, and while a member of that body was elected to the convention for the remodelling of the constitution of the state.... In both of these bodies Mr. Tilden was a conspicuous authority....He inherited no fortune, but depended upon his own exertions for a livelihood....With an assidulty and a concentration of energy which have characterized all the transactions of his life, Mr. Tilden now gave himself up to his profession. It was not many years before he became well known at the bar....He...became one of the greatest corporation lawyers of the American bar.... With the peace [the end of the Civil War] came to Mr. Tilden the most important political labor of his life....He assailed and overthrew the combined republican and democratic ring which ruled and ruined New York....The result was overwhelming and not only changed the city representation in the legislative bodies of the state, but in its moral effect crushed the 'Ring.'...

"Mr. Tilden gave his chief attention during the session of the legislature to the promotion of those objects for which he consented to go there, the reform of the judiciary and the impeachment of the creatures who had acquired the control of it under the Tweed dynasty."

—The *Daily Constitution*, Atlanta, 1876

country that were suffering from the depression advocated easy money.

The Atlanta *Constitution* endorsed Tilden's candidacy, explaining that:

There is no question of the fact, that the strength of the Cincinnati nominees renders it all the more necessary that our strongest men should be placed in the front. It was certain before the Cincinnati convention that without two or three northern states the democratic party could not possibly win. It is now doubly certain that without the great state of New York success is impossible, and there is now greater danger of the loss of that state than ever. The very first requisite then, in the democratic nominee, is his ability to carry the state of New York. A second requisite is that he be a man of reform, who has fought the corruptions and corrupt men of the times, and who will purify the government...A third requisite is that he should be a democrat against whom no sectional prejudices at the north could be arrayed, and who will therefore have free access to the hearts and judgments of the people, probably enabling him to carry a number of northern and eastern states on the principles of public honesty and governmental reform. We believe there is but one such man, that is, one who unites all these requisites of successful leadership and that man is Sam. J. Tilden, the present democratic governor of New York.

The Atlanta *Constitution*'s fondest wish was granted. Samuel J. Tilden was nominated as the Democratic candidate for President. Hayes wrote of Tilden's nomination:

The nomination of Tilden makes doubtful the States of N.Y., N.J., and Ct. [Connecticut]. Our adversaries reckon on a united South. This is their hope. We must meet them on this.

CAMPAIGN ISSUES

In their platform, Republicans also chanted the refrain of reform, promising "speedy, thorough, and unsparing" prosecution of any and all corrupt men holding public office. Rutherford B. Hayes wrote in his diary that he thought he should remind the country of the progress made under Republican rule:

When the Republican party came into power—and what it [the country] is now, a solid Nation, free, debt paid—&c &c all people united and harmonious, to celebrate the 100th anniversary of our Independence—...all which was accomplished in opposition to the great body of our adversaries—And now the past secure, we approach the questions of the present & future....In the midst of the tremendous events of the last sixteen years there have been mistakes and errors in Civil and Military affairs. But the Rep[ublican] party in dealing with the questions of the time did not make the great mistake on the debt, of opposing its honest payment, nor the mistake in reconstruction of opposing equal rights civil and political to all Citizens of the Republic—nor the mistake of opposing the measures of Lincoln which

Lobbyist Sara Spencer pleaded with Republicans for recognition of women's right to vote: "In 1872...the Republican party declared that it had emancipated 4,000,000 human beings and established universal suffrage...Where were the 10,000,000 women citizens of this Republic? When will you make this high-sounding declaration true?

"We ask you for a plank that will place that mighty emblem of power, the ballot, in the hands of 10,000,000 American citizens—the wives and daughters of this fair Republic...."

A Suffragette, c. 1871
The Republican platform of 1876 called for "respectful consideration" of the demands for women's suffrage. That much recognition women had managed to achieve. Furthermore, in 1869, Wyoming, then a territory, had given women the right to vote within the territory, and Utah had allowed women the same right in 1870. But not until the passage of the Nineteenth Amendment in 1920 would all American women be granted the right to vote.

Elizabeth Cady Stanton and Susan B. Anthony

On July 4, 1876, while the nation was celebrating one hundred years of progress, Susan B. Anthony and some other fighters for women's rights attended the celebration of the nation's birth in Philadelphia and presented the "Declaration of Rights of the Women of the United States." Miss Anthony read the "Declaration," which demanded the vote for women: "While the Nation is buoyant with patriotism, and all hearts are attuned to praise, it is with sorrow we come to strike the one discordant note, on this hundredth anniversary of our country's birth. When subjects of Kings, Emperors, and Czars, from the Old World, join in our National Jubilee, shall the women of the Republic refuse to lay their hands with benedictions on the nation's head?...Yet, we cannot forget, even in this glad hour, that while all men of every race and clime, and condition, have been invested with the full rights of citizenship, under our hospitable flag, all women still suffer the degradation of disenfranchisement.

"The history of our country the past hundred years, has been a series of assumptions and usurpations of power over woman, in direct opposition to the principles of just government, acknowledged by the United States at its foundation which are:
First. The natural rights of each individual.
Second. The exact equality of these rights.
Third. That these rights, when not delegated by the individual, are retained by the individual.
Fourth. That no person can exercise the rights of others without delegated authority.
Fifth. That the non-use of these rights does not destroy them.

"And for the violation of these fundamental principles of our Government, we arraign our rulers on this 4th day of July, 1876."

destroyed Slavery—nor the mistake of opposing the Measures wh[ich] saved the Union and made of this people one Nation.

And now the new questions:
1. How to deal with Corruption in office and especially in Legislative bodies
2. How to secure a sound currency

ELECTION DAY, NOVEMBER 7, 1876

About eight and a half million votes were cast; 4,284,265 for Tilden and 4,033,295 for Hayes, giving Tilden a plurality of 250,970.

ELECTION NIGHT

On election night, as the returns poured in, most Republicans gave up hope for Hayes's election and abandoned the Republican National Committee headquarters in the Fifth Avenue Hotel in New York. But General Dan Sickles did not abandon hope so easily; he went to headquarters around midnight and by sending telegrams to the governors of South Carolina, Louisiana, Florida and Oregon, very possibly changed the outcome of the election.

Sickles, who had been a Democratic congressman, had become a major-general in the Civil War, and owing to a wound inflicted at Gettysburg, had lost his leg. He then served his country as Minister to Spain. Speculation on Sickles' role in the election is based on accounts of other Republicans and on a memorandum he wrote himself in 1902.

THE SICKLES MEMORANDUM

I had known Tilden from boyhood and always cherished a warm personal regard for him, but his political attitude from the begin[n]ing to the end of the war for the Union was so offensive to my convictions of patriotic duty that I became his political adversary....

On the night of the election [of 1876], I went to the theatre with a party of friends, with whom I took supper afterwards. Returning home about midnight, I stopped at the Republican headquarters to hear the news. The rooms were deserted....The chief clerk told me that Tilden was elected; that his friends at the Everett House, on Union Square, were celebrating his triumph; that the *New York Tribune* in its extra edition admitted the defeat of Hayes. I asked him to show me the returns received at headquarters.

"You will find them," he replied, "on the desk of Mr. Chandler, the chairman. He retired an hour ago, saying he didn't want to see anybody..."

Sitting down at the Chairman's desk, I looked over the telegrams containing the returns from different parts of the country and after a careful scrutiny reached the conclusion that the contest was really very close and doubtful, but by no means hopeless. According to my figures, based on fair probabilities, Hayes was elected by at least one majority

in the Electoral College. This estimate assumed that Hayes would receive the votes of South Carolina, Louisiana, Florida and Oregon.

I immediately drafted several telegrams, one to Gov. Chamberlain of South Carolina, one to Gov. Kellogg of Louisiana, one to Gov. Osborn of Florida [Sickles made a mistake: Marcellus L. Stearns was Governor of Florida–Thomas Osborne was an important Florida Republican] and one to the Chairman of the Republican State Committee of Oregon, the Governor of that state being a Democrat. I said in each of these telegrams, "With your state sure for Hayes, he is elected. Hold your state."

Calling the chief clerk to my side and showing him the telegrams, I asked him if he felt authorized to sign the name of the chairman of the Republican National Committee to the dispatches I had written. At that moment I heard the voice of General Chester A. Arthur, afterwards President, in the hallway; going to the door I asked the General to come to the Committee room for a moment, on a matter of importance...Arthur came into the Committe[e] rooms; I showed him my figures and the telegrams I had drafted, adding:

"General, if you advise it, I have no doubt the chief will feel authorized to send off these telegrams with the signature of the Chairman."

Arthur replied, "Let them be sent off at once. It seems to me your forecast of the result is accurate...."

The telegrams were sent...I took my seat at Chairman Chandler's desk and remained in sole charge, during the night, of the Republican National Headquarters.

It was a long and weary wait before any replies were received to the telegrams sent out....About three o'clock in the morning a reply was

General Dan Sickles (in center): His Telegrams Helped Give the Election to Hayes
One contemporary described Sickles, saying:

"Here is a man still in his prime...whose career has been as diversified and romantic as if he had filled out a full century of endless action...Few characters in our country, or in our history, have passed through so many ordeals."

George Templeton Strong was less enthusiastic about Sickles; he wrote:

"One might as well try to spoil a rotten egg as to damage Dan's character."

Democratic Campaign Badge

received from Gov. Chamberlain of Columbia, South Carolina, saying,

"All right. South Carolina is for Hayes. Need more troops. Communication with interior cut off by mobs...."

About six o'clock in the morning, an answer was received from Oregon, which was encouraging as to the vote of that state.

Further telegrams were sent at once to all four states, informing them that the enemy claimed each of them and enjoining vigilance and diligence.

Early in the morning, the secretary, Wm. E. Chandler, arrived from Concord. I communicated to him all that had transpired during the night and turned over the business to his hands. It was too early to make a report to Chairman Zachariah [Zachariah Chandler], and I withdrew, resigning my function as chairman *ad interim* of the Republican National Committee.

MORE TELEGRAMS, MORE FRAUD

Although Sickles sent his telegrams around midnight, credit has usually been given to John C. Reid, an editor of the Republican *New York Times,* and to William E. Chandler, a lobbyist and an important figure in the Republican party, for sending the telegrams to the governors of the three Southern states and perhaps changing the outcome of the election. Chandler and Reid did send a set of telegrams several hours after Sickles claimed to have sent similar messages. To Governor Daniel Chamberlain of South Carolina, Reid and Chandler wired, "Hayes is elected if we have carried South Carolina, Florida, and Louisiana. Can you hold your State? Answer immediately." They also wired Florida, Louisiana, Oregon and California. Chandler wrote to Governor Hayes on November 9, two days after the election:

Yesterday A.M. at daylight I arrived at 5th Avenue Hotel...and found all had gone to bed...convinced of Tilden's election. Just then in rushed J.C. Reid,...editor [of the] Times, with news up to 6 A.M.—he had Florida reported for us and Oregon also by Asso. Press Dispatches. I immediately telegraphed to Florida, Louisiana, S. Car., Nevada and Oregon that all depended on them and that with them we were safe, to look out for Demo. frauds and to telegraph us when sure....Very soon I began to get answers and when our people came around in this morning it seemed as if the dead had been raised.

Reid later claimed credit for doing more than Chandler in the election-night swindle. The tale of election night at Republican headquarters becomes even more confused by William Chandler's subsequent admission that he saw Sickles' telegrams before sending out his own, although he denied seeing Sickles as Sickles claimed in his memo. William Chandler later recalled:

Looking over the table of Mr. Zachariah Chandler, the chairman, I found and read many dispatches. Among these in your [Sickles'] handwriting were several dispatches to the southern states advising them of the possibility of the election of Hayes and warning them to beware of democratic violence and fraud. Apparently these dispatches...had been sent...some two or three hours before.

If Sickles is to be believed, Chandler's telegrams were only of secondary importance, a follow-up on the earlier ones. The details will probably never be totally clear, but the fact remains that whoever gets the credit, either Sickles or Chandler or Reid concluded that if he could swing to Hayes the electoral votes of Louisiana, South Carolina, Florida and Oregon, the Republicans could turn around what appeared to be a Democratic victory. The telegrams are but one clue in attempting to understand how Hayes became President of the United States.

THE DAY AFTER THE ELECTION

The day after the election, newspapers across the country declared Tilden the victor. The Atlanta *Constitution* called for "Three Cheers for the Little Man of Albany," declaring "Samuel J. Tilden will be inaugurated on the fifth day of next March, that much is settled by the dispatches that appear everywhere from about thirty states." The New York *World*, a Democratic paper, also declared a big Tilden victory. The newspaper did not even hint at a problem with the election returns; the headlines read:

> TILDEN TRIUMPHANT
> THE DOMINATION OF THE REPUBLICAN PARTY
> OVERTHROWN. GREAT DEMOCRATIC VICTORIES.
> THE SOUTH CALMLY PUTS ASIDE THE RULE OF
> ITS CARPETBAGGERS.

On the day after the election, the *World* gave 206 votes to Tilden and 133 to Hayes. Tilden, who believed he had won, told the *World*:

My election was due...to the issues...I received a great number of Republican votes...The election was decided in part on my record as Governor...The closeness of the contest shows...the opposition I had to overcome...I did not expect a large majority in the Electoral College.

But the Republican *Times* refused to concede victory to Tilden. The first edition of the *Times* on November 8 called the election "doubtful" and put Hayes ahead of Tilden. In a later edition the paper conceded that Tilden was ahead with 184 electoral votes, one short of the

The day after the election the Louisville *Courier-Journal* called Tilden the winner.

Twain supports Hayes

Although Tilden tried to link his name with reform, some, like Mark Twain, actively supported Hayes on the grounds that Hayes would bring about the much needed reform of the Civil Service. When he became President, Hayes was not in fact able to achieve the reform that Twain had hoped for. On September 30, 1876, Twain addressed a Republican rally at Hartford, Connecticut:

"Some one asked me the other day why it was that nearly all the people who write books and magazines had lately come to the front and proclaimed their political preference, since such a thing had probably never occurred before in America, and why it was that almost all of this strange, new band of volunteers, marched under the banner of Hayes and Wheeler. I think these people have come to the front mainly because they think they see at last a chance to make this Government a good Government, because they think they see a chance to institute an honest and sensible system of civil service which shall so amply prove its worth and worthiness that no succeeding President can ever venture to put his foot upon it. Our present...system, born of Gen. Jackson and the Democratic Party, is so idiotic, so contemptible, so grotesque, that it would make the very savages of Dahomey jeer and the very gods of solemnity laugh. We will not hire a blacksmith who never lifted a sledge...We will not have a man about us in our business life, in any walk of it, low or

(continued on following page)

---

majority needed to win. The headlines of the later edition of the *Times* read:

RESULTS STILL UNCERTAIN
A SOLID SOUTH EXCEPT FOR LOUISIANA, FLORIDA, AND
SOUTH CAROLINA FOR THE DEMOCRACY
—TILDEN CARRIES HIS OWN STATE,
CONNECTICUT, AND INDIANA—THE NORTH DIVIDED

The *Times* was correct—Tilden was one vote short of victory and he would have trouble in South Carolina, Florida and Louisiana.

The *Times* headline also underlined a new and important development—the creation of the solid South. Contrary to popular belief, the South had not always voted as a unit and before the Civil War had in fact split down two-party lines—Whigs vs. Democrats.

REPUBLICANS TAKE HOPE

By the night of November 8, Republicans had taken new hope. Having received replies from the telegrams sent by Sickles and Chandler, Republican headquarters declared:

Dispatches received at these headquarters report that Louisiana, Florida, South Carolina, Wisconsin, Oregon, Nevada and California have given Republican majorities. There is no reason to doubt the correctness of these reports and if confirmed the election of Hayes is assured by a majority of one in the Electoral College.

The Indianapolis *Journal* explained that Republicans had found hope on November 9, whereas on the eighth they thought there was none: "You could have told a Republican five hundred yards away yesterday morning by the length of his visage." But although things were looking up, Hayes still conceded defeat. The New York *Sun* reported that two days after the election, Hayes said:

I think we are defeated in spite of recent good news. I am of the opinion that the Democrats have carried the country and elected Tilden, as it now seems necessary for the Republicans to carry all the states now set down as doubtful to secure even a majority of one. I don't think encouraging dispatches ought to be given to the public now, because they might mislead enthusiastic friends to bet on the election and lose their money. I do heartily deprecate such dispatches.

On Friday, November 10, the New York *Herald* called the election "Nip and Tuck" and said:

THE BATTLE FOR THE PRESIDENCY
STILL UNDECIDED...THREE STATES
YET ENVELOPED IN THE DUST OF COMBAT

As things began to change, the *World* informed its readers

"Of Course He Wants to Vote the Democratic Ticket!" Democratic "Reformer." "You're as Free as Air, Ain't You? Say Your Are, or I'll Blow Yer Black Head Off!"

The Democratic party's fraud was keeping black voters from voting because the majority of blacks voted Republican.

high, unless he has served an apprentice-ship and can prove that he is capable of doing the work he offers to do...But when you come to our civil service, we serenely fill great numbers of our minor public offices with ignoramuses. We put the vast business of a Custom house in the hands of a flathead who does not know a bill of lading from a transit of Venus, never having heard of either of them before. Under a Treasury appoint-ment we pour oceans of money and accom-panying statistics through the hands and brain of an ignorant villager who never before could wrestle with a two weeks wash bill without getting thrown. Under our con-sular system we send creatures all over the world who speak no language but their own, and even when it comes to that, go wading all their days through floods of moods and tenses and flourishing the scalps of muti-lated parts of speech...We carefully train and educate our naval officers and military men, and we ripen and perfect their capabilities through long services and experience, and keep hold of these excellent servants through a just system of promotion. This is exactly what we hope to do with our civil service under Mr. Hayes. We hope and expect to sever that service utterly from poli-tics and we hope to make it respectable, too. We hope to make worth and capacity the sole requirements of the civil service, in the place of the amount of party dirty work the candidate has done.''

on November 11 that three Southern states—Florida, South Carolina and Louisiana—were in dispute. But the *World* did not anticipate any problems. According to the *World*'s estimates, Tilden had been elected in Florida by 1,500 votes, in Louisiana by 7,000, and in South Carolina by 1,800.

FEAR OF CIVIL UNREST IN THE COUNTRY

The Civil War had ended only eleven years before and the memory of it was still fresh in 1876. So when President Grant sent additional troops to the disputed Southern states, supposedly to "see that the proper and legal boards of canvassers are unmolested in the performance of their duties," visions leapt to the minds of both Northerners and Southerners of another civil war. The Louisville *Courier-Journal* on November 11 warned that:

....The military commanders in Louisiana and Florida are instructed "to be vigilant with the force at their command to preserve peace and good order" and "to insure entire quiet."...This order imposes on the military force of the United States primarily a duty that belongs to it only ultimately in case of extreme emergency....No violence has been

A Lantern Used in the 1876 Presidential Campaign of Governor Samuel J. Tilden

South Carolina—The Dual Legislature—Representative Hamilton of Beaufort, Weeping over the Corruption of His Party

The Democratic Members of the South Carolina Legislature, Presenting Credentials from the Supreme Court, Denied Admittance to the State Capitol on November 28, 1876

"Messers Peck and Jeffries, members of the Legislature...proceeded to the capital where they found all the doors closed and barred, except a side door...They entered there and found the rotunda filled with troops...
They demanded admission and the Corporal stated that they would not be admitted unless by pass from Mr. Jones or General Denis...The members exhibited their certificates of election signed by the clerk of the Supreme Court but were told that they could not pass on it...

"All holders of certificates not issued by the Republican board of Canvassers were refused admission. The Democrats, finding themselves thoroughly duped...met at 7 P.M. in Columbia hall. Sixty-four Democrats and two Republicans participated and were sworn in as Legislators."

Frank Leslie's Popular Monthly Magazine, December 16, 1876

committed, nor has violence been threatened, so that these instructions issued by the President seem to be without warrant.....The President's orders cover the remarkable instructions to..."insure a peaceable count of the ballots actually cast." This is certainly a very extraordinary power to confer, and a very grave responsibility to impose upon a military officer. Such a practice would transfer from the constituted civil authorities to the military authority the entire control of all the machinery for ascertaining the results of an election, and would be the utter destruction of any system devised for reaching the real choice of the people in the selection of their public officers.

Many warned of the renewed possibility of civil strife. The San Francisco *Chronicle* of November 15 warned that:

We have more than once said that we should regard the election of Tilden as a great national calamity, and we are still of that opinion. But it would be a far greater calamity if, owing to any trouble growing out of the election in any of the Southern States, or the subsequent action of Congress thereupon, the people should be impelled by rash and fanatical impulses to resort to the Mexican method of settling political disputes.

SOUTH CAROLINA—SEVEN DISPUTED VOTES

On November 10, three days after the election, the South Carolina Canvassing Board was organized to decide whether the state's electoral votes belonged to Hayes or Tilden. The Board was composed of five members, all of them Republicans; three of the members were actually candidates for local office themselves. On November 19, the Democratic New York *World* reported to its readers on the "fraud" in South Carolina, quoting ex-Governor Theodore F. Randolph of New Jersey, who said:

As is well-known, the board is made up entirely of Republicans; all of its members are State officials and three or four out of the five members sitting are candidates on the Republican State ticket. Thus...the board actually becomes the tribunal by which the election of its own members is decided, as well as the election of the Presidential electors, of the Governor, and of other state officers.

On November 22 the South Carolina Canvassing Board handed down its decision in favor of Hayes. The *World* cried, "The foulest outrage yet," and went on to explain:

The South Carolina Board of Canvassers yesterday stole the electoral vote of that State openly...with the avowed object of offering it to Governor Hayes. The robbery was brazen and shameless. It rests with the American people to decide whether they will surrender the control of their Government into such hands, or maintain their liberties, their self-respect and their prosperity by enforcing the remedies of the law against a lawless conspiracy without parallel in our annals.

The South Carolina Canvassing Board threw out the votes of two counties, thus giving the election to the Republicans. The Board explained that its action was taken because there had been fraud in both Edgefield and Laurens counties. There was, in fact, no registration law in South Carolina, which meant that South Carolinians could vote repeatedly and that nonresidents of the state could also vote. Therefore, there was some basis for the Board's claims of fraud. Despite the decision of the Canvassing Board, Democrats as well as Republicans continued to claim the South Carolina electoral votes. In South Carolina, the gubernatorial race was also hotly contested. Wade Hampton, the first Democrat to run for governor since 1868, opposed the Republican incumbent, Daniel Chamberlain. Chamberlain probably would have won hands down but he made a crucial mistake. After the bloody Hamburg riots of July 1876 in which seven men were killed, Chamberlain called for more federal troops to be sent to South Carolina, evoking in the minds of the voters visions of another Reconstruction. Hampton, a former planter and ex-Confederate soldier who quite properly called himself a "Conservative," assiduously courted the black vote and claimed to be the first Southern white to favor limited Negro suffrage. It so happened that there were 30,000 more black than white voters in South Carolina, so Hampton's views were practical as well as tolerant.

Hampton won the election by 1,100 votes, according to his own estimate, and the South Carolina Supreme Court endorsed him as the victor. But Chamberlain held the State House by force, using the federal troops he had called for and received to help him stay in control. He was also helped by the Canvassing Board, which by disqualifying the votes of two counties gave the Republicans a majority in the state legislature. On November 26 the legislature started its session and the *World* described the scene:

THE CROWNING OUTRAGE
THE STATE-HOUSE AT COLUMBIA, SOUTH CAROLINA SEIZED BY FEDERAL TROOPS. DEMOCRATIC MEMBERS EXCLUDED AT THE POINT OF THE BAYONET—SEPARATE ORGANIZATION OF THE HOUSE.

The Republicans in the state legislature forcibly kept out eight Democratic representatives from the two disputed counties, and the rest of the Democrats walked out and formed a separate legislature.

Wade Hampton—a Democrat Elected Governor of South Carolina in 1876
Hampton, a planter and former Confederate soldier, tried and succeeded in getting much of the black vote. During his campaign he said:

"The only way to bring about prosperity in this state is to bring the two races in friendly relations together. The Democratic Party in South Carolina, of whom I am the exponent, has promised that every citizen of this state is to be the equal of all; he is to have every right given to him by the Constitution of the United States and of this state...And I pledge my faith, and I pledge it for those gentlemen who are on the ticket with me, that if we are elected, as far as in us lies, we will observe, protect, and defend the rights of the colored man as quickly as [of] any man in South Carolina...If there is a white man in this assembly, [who] because he is a democrat, or because he is a white man, believes that when I am elected governor, if I should be, that I will stand between him and the law, or grant him any privilege or immunity that shall not be granted to the colored man, he is mistaken..."

Hampton was re-elected governor in 1878 and later elected senator from South Carolina.

"Voting in the North—New York City—a Characteristic Election Scene—"

"South Carolina—a Rustic Election Scene—Plantation Hands Travelling to the Polls Intending to Vote Democratic—"
Troops had been sent to South Carolina by President Grant before the election, supposedly to guarantee a free vote for all. The Republican *New York Times* defended the President's action:

"...The President said he regretted the necessity which required him to order troops to South Carolina, and in taking this step his purpose was simply to assist the State authorities in enforcing the laws and according to every citizen a full measure of protection...A sufficient force will be sent to the State to insure the public peace and to protect alike Democrats and Republicans against all attempts at intimidation or undue interference...The troops are sent to South Carolina to protect all the people of that State...Democratic newspapers have labored to create the impression that a high state of feeling prevails here in consequence to the President's proclamation..."

South Carolina continued until February 1877 to have two legislatures and two governors. Hampton gradually gained control of the state, not through any one act, but through a gradual erosion of Republican strength.

LOUISIANA: EIGHT ELECTORAL VOTES DISPUTED

On November 16, the Louisiana Returning Board organized to rule on the returns. Louisiana law called for the Board to be composed of five members, one of whom was to be a member of the minority party—in this case the Democrats. But the Board, made up of four Republicans, decided to do without a Democrat, leaving little doubt as to which way the decision would go. The *World* said on Wednesday, November 22:

DISPUTED VOTE SOUTH.
THE LOUISIANA RETURNING BOARD EXCLUDES
DEMOCRATIC ELECTORS FROM THE COUNT.

THE LOUISIANA RETURNING BOARD'S DECISION

On December 5 the Board met and threw out 15,000 of the votes cast, about 13,000 of which were Democratic ballots. This reversed Tilden's majority of between 6,000 and 8,000 votes, and gave the state to Hayes. General opinion is that if there had been no fraud at all in the election, Hayes would probably have carried the state. In Louisiana, as in South Carolina, there was a black majority and most blacks voted Republican. Vice-presidential candidate William Wheeler said:

If the election had been fairly conducted in Louisiana, Mr. Hayes would have carried the state by a majority of fifteen thousand votes.

FLORIDA: FOUR ELECTORAL VOTES IN DISPUTE

Florida's four electoral votes were also claimed by both parties. Only two days after the election, the New York *Herald* spotted fraud in Florida:

There are large Republican gains in the black belt, but they have been made by voting more names than there are resident votes...The democrats will gain in all the white counties....The colored people were emboldened by the presence of the troops to intimidate those desiring to vote the democratic ticket.

Although the *Herald* alluded only to repeat voting by blacks, there was repeat voting by both races in Florida, since voters could legally vote anywhere within the county where they resided.

By November 10 the *Herald* published evidence of Chandler's election-night attempt to alter the Florida voting returns; A. L. Randolph, chairman of one county committee, was quoted in the *Herald* on November 10:

Florida is democratic by 1,500 majority, but Chandler telegraphs...to have returns altered and cheat us out of it.

The *World* on November 30 pointed to "unparalleled frauds in the manipulation of Democratic ballots" in Florida and featured a story on "how the honest vote of Alachua County is being doctored to subserve radical ends." A former New York Attorney General, Francis C. Barlow, who went to Florida as a Republican observer, was sent by William Chandler to look into the Alachua County fraud. Much to Chandler's shock, Barlow said that he saw signs of Republican fraud and thought that the county and the state belonged to the Democrats. Another Republican observer in Florida, General Lew Wallace, usually remembered as the author of *Ben-Hur*, said:

It is terrible to see the extent to which all classes go in their determination to win. Conscience offers no restraint. Nothing is so common as the resort to perjury, unless it is violence—in short, I do not know whom to believe....Money and intimidation can obtain the oath of white men as well as black to any required statement. A ton of affidavits could be carted into the state-house to-morrow, and not a word of truth in them, except the names of the parties swearing, and their ages and places of residence. Now what can come from such a state of things? If we win, our methods are subject to impeachment for possible fraud. If the enemy win, it is the same thing exactly—doubt, suspicion, irritation go with the consequence, whatever it may be.

The two Republicans on the Florida Returning Board gave all the Florida electoral votes to Hayes; the Democratic member of the Canvassing Board issued his own certificates to a slate of Democratic electors. It is generally assumed that if there had been no fraud at all, Florida would have voted for Tilden, giving him the Presidency.

THE CRISIS CONTINUED

After December 6 the country was faced with a serious dilemma. Three Southern states each had two sets of electors. Somehow a decision had to be reached as to which set of election returns the country would recognize. And that decision would determine whether Hayes or Tilden would become President. If the decision of the Republican-controlled returning boards was recognized,

General Lew Wallace
Wallace was sent to Florida (one of the three states in which the electoral votes were disputed) as a Republican observer. He was shocked by the fraud he saw everywhere. His views were confirmed by Samuel Tilden, the Democratic candidate, who claimed that the Florida delegation had offered to sell its votes to him for $200,000. "That seems to be the standard figure," said Tilden.

"The Ballot Box—a National Game That is Played Out," by Thomas Nast

Members of the Electoral Commission which decided the disputed election of 1876 in favor of Hayes. On the Commission were five senators, five congressmen and five Supreme Court Justices.

Thomas F. Bayard

Allen G. Thurman

Eppa Hunton

Stephen J. Field

Hayes would be President. If the original vote totals were accepted, Tilden would be President.

In addition to the controversy over the nineteen electoral votes of the three Southern states, there was one electoral vote in dispute in Oregon. One Republican elector out of three was disqualified because he was a federal-office holder and therefore, under the Constitution, not qualified to serve as an elector. The Democratic governor appointed a Democrat to fill the place of the disqualified Republican elector, but Oregon's Secretary of State gave certificates to all the Republican electors. If the Democratic elector had been recognized, as he was not in the end, Tilden would have been elected President by one vote.

HOW WAS THE DISPUTE TO BE SOLVED?

In December 1876, there was incredible confusion as to how to decide the Hayes-Tilden election. One month had passed since the election and still the country did not know who its next President would be. The Twelfth Amendment to the Constitution provided that "the President of the Senate shall, in the presence of the Senate and the House of Representatives, open all the certificates and the votes shall then be counted." The president of the Senate would have been Vice-President Henry Wilson but he had died. The Senate was Republican and its president was Thomas W. Ferry, a staunch Republican; therefore the Democrats refused to have the Senate arbitrate the dispute. And Republicans did not want the Democratic House of Representatives to determine the fate of the country.

THE ELECTORAL COMMISSION

During January 1877 a House and a Senate committee agreed to create an Electoral Commission to rule on the disputed returns. On Thursday, January 18, the *World* reported:

> THE COMMITTEES AGREE.
> AN ALMOST UNANIMOUS CONCLUSION
> FINALLY REACHED YESTERDAY AFTERNOON.
> THE BOARD TO CONSIST OF FIVE SENATORS,
> FIVE REPRESENTATIVES AND FIVE SUPREME
> COURT JUDGES.

Since the Senate was Republican, there would be three Republican senators and two Democratic senators on the

Commission. For the five House members, the formula would be exactly the reverse, since the House was Democratic. Four Supreme Court Justices were chosen: two Republicans (William Strong and Samuel F. Miller) and two Democrats (Nathan Clifford and Stephen J. Field), and they were to elect the fifth Justice. There was much debate about whether to have an Electoral Commission. Democrats liked the idea better than Republicans, since it was assumed that Judge David Davis, who was generally regarded as an Independent, would be the fifth Justice and would probably vote Democratic. Abram S. Hewitt, the chairman of the Democratic party, later described the debate over the Commission:

> I thought at the time and I still think that the division of parties on this measure was largely controlled by the conviction that Judge Davis would have the casting vote, and that he could be relied upon to see that the will of the people as expressed in the election of Mr. Tilden should not be thwarted.

By January 21 it was still not clear who would be the next President or even by what process the country would decide on a President. The *World* warned:

> For the first time in our history there is cause for serious solicitude growing out of counting votes of the electoral college. Why? Because for the first time the election depends on disputed votes. There has been before this, contested votes, but it was immaterial which way they were counted....

Democrat Abram Hewitt later explained that he supported setting up an Electoral Commission, thinking it would save the country from violence:

> ...I became satisfied that Tilden could not be inaugurated without a resort to arms. After carefully considering the facts, I became satisfied that we could not wage war with any hope of success. I therefore directed my attention to a possible solution, and endeavored to provide a tribunal which would do justice.

Republican Senator George F. Edmunds of Vermont also feared violence if the Commission was not approved; the *World* shared Edmunds' fears. On January 22 the newspaper said:

> When such a man gives voice to prophecies concerning the destruction of the Republic and pictures the possible whelming of our institutions under a sea of anarchy, we do not see how considerate men can any longer question the reality of the danger impending over us.

Fear of chaos rallied votes for the Electoral Commission. But the debate over the Commission dragged on in the

Henry B. Payne

Josiah G. Abbott

George F. Edmunds

George F. Hoar

Nathan Clifford

Frederick T. Frelinghuysen

Joseph P. Bradley

James A. Garfield

Samuel F. Miller

William Strong

Congress until January 25, when the *World* reported that despite the opposition of radical Republicans, the Senate was "pressing to a vote on the Electoral Commission bill."

But that same morning, just as it appeared that the country was fast approaching some sort of solution to the presidential dispute, there appeared in the *World* a hint of more trouble to come. The *World* had been reporting on the Senate race in Illinois, where it looked as if Representative Anderson, the Democratic candidate, would defeat the Republican Logan. But on January 25 the *World* reported that a new candidate had sprung into the lead:

STRIVING TO BE SENATOR— AN IMPENETRABLE MUDDLE IN ILLINOIS— JUDGE DAVID DAVIS AHEAD

On the thirty-ninth ballot (senators were still chosen by the state legislatures) in the Illinois Senate race, Judge David Davis, running as a Democrat, had suddenly shot ahead of the two major candidates, Logan and Anderson. All eyes turned away from the Senate debate on the Commission to the Illinois Senate race. The *World* said:

A good deal more interest was felt today (Jan. 24) in the Senatorial election in Illinois than in anything going on at the Capitol. On both sides of the House it was claimed that the election of Justice Davis to the Senate might make him practically, if not technically, ineligible for the 5th place among the judges of the Electoral Commission.

But David Davis' growing strength in the Illinois Senate race did not stop the U.S. Senate from passing the act creating the Electoral Commission on January 25.

The front page story in the *World* on January 26 was the Senate passage of the Electoral Commission. But on page five the paper reported:

DAVIS SUCCEEDS LOGAN. HE WILL NOT LEAVE THE SUPREME COURT BEFORE MARCH 4.

The story of Davis' election to the Senate (on the same day that the Senate approved the Electoral Commission) is another confusing part of the saga of the election of 1876. Democrats claimed the Republicans had fixed the Illinois Senate election to get Davis off the Commission. Democrat Abram S. Hewitt later recalled:

Whether rightly or wrongly, the conviction was general that a bargain had been made by the Republicans by which Judge Davis, in consideration of his being made Senator, should decline a position upon the Electoral Commission. Certainly if such an agreement were made it was the last move by which, in the long game which had been played between the two parties, the final triumph was assured to the Republican party.

But Hewitt's seemingly plausible theory was thrown into doubt by a letter written by Republican William Henry Smith, one of Hayes's closest confidants. Smith thought that the Democrats had arranged Davis' election, and he wrote in anger:

The hand of Mr. Tilden has been seen in Illinois politics for two weeks past, in urging Democratic members of the Legislature to take up Judge David Davis for Senator. The plan [came] near being successful today and may be entirely so tomorrow....Davis, elected to the Senate by Democratic votes, would feel under obligation, as the fifth Judge, to give the Presidency to Tilden.

During the Illinois balloting, Davis received the votes of every Democrat, but not one Republican voted for him, which seems to indicate that the Republicans were not behind Davis' election contrary to Hewitt's theory. And the Democratic House of Representatives passed the bill approving the Electoral Commission on January 26, after its members were already aware that Davis had been elected senator from Illinois. The only sensible conclusion seems to be that Democrats believed the *World* headline that Davis would not resign from the Court and thought that he would serve on the Commission as he legally could have done. On January 27 the *World* announced:

THE HOUSE AND THE BILL.
IT PASSES BY MORE THAN A TWO-THIRDS VOTE
AFTER A LONG AND SHARP DEBATE.
ALL THAT IS NOW LACKING TO MAKE IT A LAW
IS THE PRESIDENT'S SIGNATURE.

On January 30 the House and Senate elected their representatives to the Electoral Commission. That same day on page one the *World* carried a significant story on the Davis election:

Associate Justice Davis...privately informed some of his friends who desired to have him placed on the Commission as the 5th judicial member that under no circumstances would he accept that position should it be tendered to him by his associates. He considers it indelicate after being elected Senator to take a position which might subject him to criticism and refuses absolutely to reconsider his determination.

The Democrats did not give up hope on Davis. On January 31 the *World* ran a page-one story saying: "Judge Davis certain to be selected if he withdraws his declination

Oliver P. Morton

Judge David Davis
Mary Logan, wife of Davis' opponent in the Illinois Senate race, wrote: "It would be difficult to imagine with what disgust General Logan confronted the situation in the legislature when he found that old farmers, who were supposed to be the soul of honor and integrity, and had been for years enthusiastic supporters of himself, had been changed by some surreptitious influence. While they claimed to be undecided as to whom they would support for the Senate, nothing could induce them to commit themselves to General Logan. Upon investigation later it was found that these men had received from three to five thousand dollars each, with which to lift the mortgages off their farms, from their Granger friends, who had been using the money of ambitious aspirants to the Senate. So trustful was General Logan that it was some time before he could really credit the indubitable evidence that was laid before him of the dishonesty of these old friends. The designing political jugglers had skillfully bought up just enough of the senators and members of the house to prevent General Logan from having a majority in either. The legislature had not long been in session when it was found that a part of the scheme was to defeat General Logan by the election of Hon. David Davis, an Associate Justice of the United States Supreme Court, to prevent him from being chosen on the Electoral Commission."

The Electoral Commission in Session:
February 1877

Justice Joseph P. Bradley
"First a Whig and then a moderate Republican," said the *World* describing Bradley the day he joined the Electoral Commission. It was Bradley's vote which swung the election to the Republican nominee, Governor Rutherford B. Hayes of Ohio.

to serve." But Davis did not change his mind and he refused to be on the Electoral Commission.

ASSOCIATE JUDGE BRADLEY SELECTED AS THE FIFTH JUDGE

Justice Joseph P. Bradley's election to the Commission was announced in the Eastern press on February 1. Bradley, a Republican, had been a practicing lawyer before his appointment to the Supreme Court, and he had been involved in various railroad cases. Many Democrats were not horrified by Bradley's appointment; in fact, the Louisville *Courier-Journal* said that "there does not seem to be any reasonable grounds for supposing that he [Bradley] will succumb to...pressure against his judgment."

ELECTORAL COMMISSION IN SESSION

On February 2 the sessions of the Electoral Commission began. The crucial question the Commission had to decide was whether to "go behind" the returns—whether to merely accept the returns as they were submitted by the state canvassing boards or whether to investigate the actual returns themselves.

THE CONTROVERSIAL DECISION ON THE FLORIDA RETURNS

The first decision that the Commission faced was whether or not to go behind the Florida returns. John G. Stevens, a friend of Justice Bradley's, visited Bradley on the night before the Florida decision was to be handed down; Bradley read Stevens an opinion that favored "counting the vote of the Democratic electors in Florida." But between Stevens' midnight visit and the next morning, something made Bradley change his mind. Whether he was bribed or whether he merely changed his opinion will never be known for sure. But Bradley voted on February 8 with the Republicans, against going behind the Florida returns. This vote was the turning point in the Commission's proceedings because it set the precedent for the way that the Commission would vote on the other disputed states, straight down party lines, 8 to 7 in favor of the Republicans.

Abram S. Hewitt, the Democratic chairman, later recalled his surprise at hearing Bradley read his unexpected opinion:

The history of this opinion forms an important feature in the final outcome of the electoral count...Mr. John G. Stevens was the intimate friend of Judge Bradley. He passed the night previous to the rendition of the judgment in the Florida case at my house. About midnight he returned from a visit to Judge Bradley, and reported...that he had just left Judge Bradley after reading his opinion in favor of counting the vote of the Democratic electors of the State of Florida. Such a judgment insured the election of Tilden to the Presidency with three votes to spare above the necessary majority. We parted, therefore, with the assurance that all further doubt as to the Presidency was at rest. I attended the delivery of the judgment the next day without the slightest intimation from any quarter that Judge Bradley had changed his mind. ...The change was made between midnight and sunrise. Mr. Stevens informed me that it was due to a visit to Judge Bradley by Senator Frelinghuysen [Republican of New Jersey] and Secretary Robeson [Secretary of the Navy and a Republican], made after his departure. Their appeals to Judge Bradley were said to have been reinforced by the persuasion of Mrs. Bradley. Whatever the fact may have been, Judge Bradley himself in a subsequent letter...admitted that he had written a favorable opinion which on subsequent reflection he saw fit to modify.

On February 8, the day that the Florida decision was handed down, Tilden told John Bigelow, his biographer, that one of the Justices on the Commission, whom he did not identify, had been willing to sell his vote to Tilden for $200,000. The implication was that the Justice was Bradley. The New York *Sun* suggested another motive for

Abram S. Hewitt, Chairman of the Democratic National Committee
Hewitt, who helped overthrow the Tweed Ring, was a Democratic Congressman from New York in 1876. Ten years later he became mayor of New York City and was well-known for his reform program.

Tilden and Hendricks Reform Songs for the Centennial Campaign of 1876
Reform was indeed Tilden's song in his campaign, and the song was very appealing to a country exhausted with the scandals of the Grant administration.

"This Will Be a Change"
Chauncey M. Depew, the New York barrister, shared Nast's skeptical view of the change promised by the Democrats. Depew said: "There are some things which in this canvass come directly home to every man in the land. We are in a condition of unparalleled business depression, of stagnation, in all branches of trade, and of want of employment. How shall all this be remedied and times be made good? By the restoration of public confidence....The Democratic Party has succeeded in unsettling everything by its advocacy of inflation, and the confusion it has created in regard to our currency. Nothing is more extraordinary than the Democrat's present love for the greenback....The greenback dollar was a war necessity, and it served its purpose well. When the Government was spending millions of dollars a day, and had not money enough to meet its wants, it did what you or I would do under similar circumstances—issued its paper promise at what it could get for it; and the rate at which the note sold indicated the measure of confidence the world had in our stability and integrity. In 1863 it would buy only thirty-five cents' worth of gold, and the world went only one-third on our stability and integrity. To-day it will buy ninety-one cents in gold, and the world goes seven-eighths on our stability and integrity. And if Hayes and Wheeler are elected, before 1879, it will buy a hundred cents' worth in gold; and the world will go even on our stability and integrity."

Bradley's change of heart—pressure from railroad interests:

During the whole of that night [February 7] Judge Bradley's house in Washington was surrounded by the carriages of visitors who came to see him apparently about the decision of the Electoral Commission...These visitors included leading Republicans as well as persons deeply interested in the Texas Pacific Railroad scheme.

Justice Bradley vigorously denied the story spread by the New York *Sun,* which was a Democratic paper. It is once more impossible to know the truth in this case. Bradley's reply to the *Sun*'s charges was published in the Newark *Daily Advertiser* on September 5, 1877:

The whole thing is a falsehood. Not a single visitor called at my house that evening; and during the whole sitting of the Commission, I had no private discussion whatever on the subjects at issue with any persons interested on the Republican side...Indeed, I sedulously sought to avoid all discussion outside the Commission itself.

Democrats saw the Commission's vote on the Florida returns as evidence of Republican determination to steal the election from Tilden. If the Commission was going to accept the verdict of the returning boards of the three disputed states and ignore all signs of fraud, then Hayes would get the 19 doubtful electoral votes which with the disputed electoral vote of Oregon would make him President. The *World* said in an indignant editorial:

Nothing can be clearer than that it is the duty of the Commission to find out, not who has got the certificates, but who was duly appointed...

If Hayes should be counted in...it will be his misfortune and the fault of his party that he will take into the Presidency a heavier load of infamy than the worst of his predecessors ever carried out.

In line with its decision not to go behind the verdict of the state returning boards, the Commission voted on February 10 to accept the Florida Republican electors and later in the month to accept the Republican electors from South Carolina and Louisiana. All Commission votes were split along party lines, Bradley voting Republican.

THE FILIBUSTER

The Commission's decision not to go behind the election returns in Florida and to accept the Republican electors helped provoke a filibuster by Democratic congressmen. Immediately after the Commission's decision on the Florida returns was announced, House Democrats declared a recess.

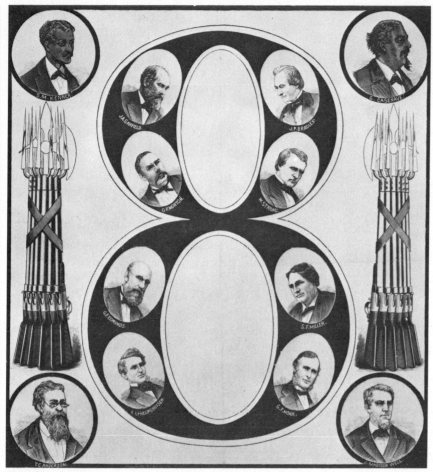

"Ten white men and two negroes who defrauded the American people out of their choice for president in 1876."

A Democratic view of the Election of 1876. The eight men in the center are the Republicans on the Electoral Commission. The four on the outside are the members of the Louisiana Returning Board, who threw out 13,000 Democratic votes, thus giving the state to Hayes.

Sheet music for the campaign song: "Governor Tilden Is Our Man."

BEHIND THE SCENES

On February 17 the Democrats held a meeting to figure out how to beat the Commission's acceptance of the fraudulent election returns by filibustering. But that night it became clear that the Southern Democrats were sticking with the Republicans and standing by the Commission's decisions. Hayes's lieutenants had done their work well. They had won the good will of white Southerners, who were willing to be courted for the simple reason that they were more concerned with arranging for the South to share in the general economic prosperity than with arguing over whether Hayes or Tilden should be President. The Cincinnati *Enquirer* said that the Southerners had obviously made a deal with Hayes:

The Southern disaffection is no longer an illusion. Last night's caucus settled beyond peradventure that their representatives have made

The Inauguration of President Rutherford B. Hayes, March 5, 1877
"President Hayes reached the stand a little before 1 o'clock. His appearance was greeted with successive shouts of applause. For five minutes, at least, deafening cheers rent the air. The new President faced the imposing demonstration with becoming dignity, and returned the compliment with a succession of bows."

Washington *Evening Star,* March 5, 1877

terms. Two cabinet places are claimed and the mess of pottage also includes favors.

A filibuster planned to interrupt the counting of the Louisiana vote was defeated by a vote of 163 to 86 with "all the prominent southern members voting with the Republican Party," reported the Washington *National Republican* on February 21, 1877. More than one theory has been advanced to explain why the Southern Democrats abandoned the filibuster. According to one theory, Southerners cooperated with the Republicans out of eagerness to receive federal subsidies for "internal improvements." Between 1865 and 1873, over $100 million of federal money had been spent on public works, but the South had received less than a tenth of it. But by 1876 Southerners were determined to wait no longer for their share of the plunder, as the St. Louis *Post-Dispatch* explained:

The Southern members of Congress are very wide awake at this session. They have concluded not to wait any longer for outside help, but to help themselves in the matter of internal improvements...They mean to have a Southern railroad across the continent.

Tom Scott, president of the Texas & Pacific Railroad, is thought by some to have helped arrange a deal between Hayes and the Southerners. Scott was particularly eager for federal help to build his railroad. Henry Van Ness

Colonel Thomas A. Scott—the Man Who Fixed the Election?
Tom Scott was granted the charter for the Texas & Pacific Railroad in 1871. Scott, eager to obtain federal subsidies to help him build his railroad, supported Hayes in return for Hayes's support of the Texas & Pacific Railroad. On December 20, 1876, General Boynton wrote to Hayes's close friend, William Henry Smith, "What we want for *practical* success is thirty or thirty-six votes....and *Tom Scott* wants help for the Texas and Pacific Road. These are strong arguments for making that project an exception to the republican policy of opposition to subsidies—provided the aid is within proper bounds & properly secured."

Boynton, who was very close to Hayes, had been working on lining up Scott's support for Hayes since December 1876. Boynton wrote:

He [Scott] can easily see that with Tilden in and a hostile Senate he could do nothing even if T. [Tilden] was friendly; while with Hayes in and friendly, the House under the influences we hope to have prevail would work with H. [Hayes] in such a matter.

During February 1877 there was much talk of a deal between Hayes and the Southerners. The Cincinnati *Enquirer* reported on February 14 the terms of the deal:

First, one or two places in the cabinet; second, the control of their own State Governments; third, a guaranteed policy on the part of the Republicans of liberal appropriations for Southern internal improvements; fourth, the passage of the Texas Pacific Railroad Bill.

When he became President, Hayes did put a Southerner in the Cabinet as promised, and he gave the South control of their state governments by removing the federal troops.

THE WORMLEY AGREEMENTS

The "Wormley Agreements" are also credited by some with helping to end the Democratic filibuster which was threatening to slow up or stop the inauguration of Hayes. The "Wormley Agreements" were worked out in a meeting between Southerners and Northerners at the Wormley Hotel in Washington on February 26, 1877. Governor

The New President, Rutherford B. Hayes
Hayes wrote in his diary, on March 14, 1877, describing his conciliatory policy toward the South:

"My policy is trust—peace, and to put aside the bayonet. I do not think the wise policy is to decide contested elections in the States, by the use of the National army."

Francis T. Nicholls, the Democratic claimant of the governorship of Louisiana, had sent Major E. A. Burke to Washington to seek recognition of the Nicholls government and to get promises from Grant and from Hayes to remove the federal troops from the South. Burke got the desired promises from Grant. He then went on to make his deal with Hayes through John Sherman, who had just agreed to serve as Hayes's Secretary of the Treasury. In exhange for the withdrawal of troops and the recognition of the Nicholls government, Sherman wanted and got the filibuster lifted, guarantees that blacks and Republicans would be treated well by the Nicholls régime, support for James Garfield for Speaker of the House, and agreement that the Louisiana legislature would postpone electing a Democratic senator until after March 10. The official Wormley Conference took place on the evening of February 26. Present besides Burke and Sherman were former Ohio Governor William Dennison, Congressman James Garfield, and Congressmen John Ellis and William Levy of Louisiana, among others.

MARCH 2, 1877: THE COUNT COMPLETED

The "Wormley Agreements," fear of another civil war, and a deal with Tom Scott to give him aid for the Texas & Pacific Railroad, all helped to drain support away from the Democratic filibuster, leaving the way open for the inauguration of Rutherford B. Hayes. Congressman James Garfield, one of Hayes's closest friends, had obviously been correct when he wrote to Hayes on December 12:

The Democratic businessmen of the country are more anxious for quiet than for Tilden; and the leading southern Democrats in Congress, especially those who were old Whigs are saying that they have seen war enough, and don't care to follow the lead of their northern associates who...were invincible in peace and invisible in war.

HAYES INAUGURATED TWICE

Rutherford B. Hayes came to Washington from Ohio on March 2, 1877, on a private railroad car loaned to him for the occasion by Tom Scott of the Texas & Pacific Railroad, who, according to some, had had so much to do with arranging Hayes's election. Fear of chaos still prevailed, and to prevent an interregnum, Hayes was inaugurated secretly on March 3, Saturday. The public inauguration was held on March 5, 1877. The crisis was over.

THE AFTERMATH

As he had promised, Hayes appointed a Southerner, David M. Key of Tennessee as Postmaster General, the Cabinet post with the most lucrative patronage jobs to dispense. Confirmation of Hayes's Cabinet nominations was possible only because of the support he received from Southern senators. Hayes wrote that:

An attempt [by Republicans] to combine with the Democrats to defeat the confirmation of the nominations only failed to be formidable by [reason of] the resolute support of the Southern Senators.

On April 10 Hayes withdrew the troops from South Carolina and on April 24 he removed them from Louisiana, living up to the promises he had made to Southerners. But Hayes did not go along with the bill to aid Tom Scott's Texas & Pacific Railroad. The Cincinnati *Gazette* reported on December 22, 1877, that Hayes was:

...in grave doubt, first whether it would be wise to grant aid to the Texas and Pacific Road at all or not; and secondly if aid was granted, as to the amount of it.

Four months after Election Day, the country at last had a leader. The months had been filled with manipulations of every conceivable kind. Looking back on that period, Democratic Chairman Abram Hewitt wrote:

It is almost impossible to form any adequate idea of the excitement and apprehension which prevailed throughout the country. Business was arrested, the wheels of industry ceased to move, and it seemed as if the terrors of civil war were again to be renewed. Petitions from Chambers of Commerce and from all the centres of trade had deluged Congress in favor of a peaceful settlement of the controversy. Personally I was satisfied that it would be better for the country to have four years of Republican Administration based upon fraudulent returns, than to have four years of civil war.

Hewitt spoke for most Americans, who were eager to get back to business. And he correctly gave much credit to Samuel Tilden, the man who had probably won the election, for yielding to Hayes without a struggle. Many of Tilden's followers had urged him to fight the verdict of the Electoral Commission; J. M. Scovel of Philadelphia wired him: "Counsel resistance. We dare not submit to fraud." But Tilden turned a deaf ear to such pleas and remarked:

I think I can retire to private life with the consciousness that I shall receive from posterity the credit of having been elected to the highest position in the gift of the people without any of the cares and responsibilities of the office.

"Great Acrobatic Feat of Rutherford B. Hayes"
The Atlanta *Constitution* of March 3, 1877, which was less than pleased by the prospect of Hayes's inauguration, wrote: "The farce is over—not merely the work of the electoral commission, for that was too dirty, too villainous to be called a farce—that was a tragedy with eight villains plotting to destroy the republic...in the hundredth anniversary of American independence. That farce is over, and a majority...of the white voters of America has been annihilated. The conspirators will proceed to enjoy the spoils of the high office they have stolen; the receiver of the stolen office is now in Washington prepared to execute his shameful part; and there is nothing left to chronicle except to sum up the result."

THE PLIGHT OF THE POOR
AND THE RISE OF AMERICAN LABOR

In the summer of 1876 the *New York Times* reported that a San Francisco merchant had advertised for a cashier and promptly received 964 applications for the job. The story was a bleak but accurate indication of the desperate lot of working people in the United States in that year. The effects of the great financial panic of 1873 were still widely apparent. There was widespread unemployment, and those lucky enough to hold jobs worked long hours, often in frightful conditions for very little money. Trade unionism was still in a primitive state of development. So severe was the depression that even those workers who had organized fell away rapidly from the infant labor movement.

By 1876, wages were being cut back by up to 50 percent. In New York one out of every four workers was unemployed, and across the country only one out of a hundred was a member of any union. Soup kitchens were crowded with famished vic-

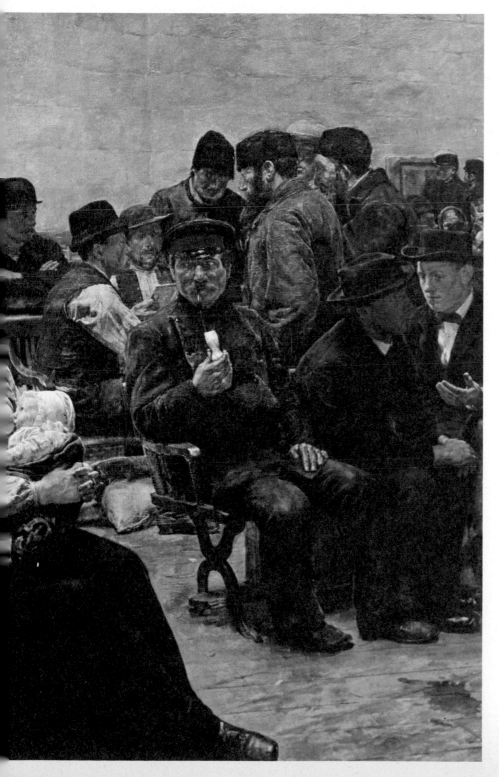

In the Land of Promise: Castle Garden, by Charles F. Ulrich

The immigrant woman nursing her child and sitting on top of her worldly goods was one of seven and a half million immigrants who arrived in America at Castle Garden. Ellis Island became the leading depot for immigrants in 1890. Ulrich, a native New Yorker, completed this painting in 1884. *Harper's Weekly* reproduced the painting and commented:

"Castle Garden, though hallowed by ...memories...is in reality a disgrace....
    "A dungeon door admits the foreigner...Within he finds cheerless and uncomfortable wooden settees...If...he desires to cleanse himself...there is no bath...If hungry...he must confine himself to coarse bread, cheap sausage, and mysterious coffee..."

tims of the slump, and the basements of some police stations had to be thrown open to accommodate homeless vagrants. It has been estimated that over a million tramps roamed the country.

For many of them jail at least offered the promise of food and lodging. In January of 1876 the New York *World* reported the case of George McGowen, who the reporter said was of "cleanly, sober and respectable appearance." McGowen told the judge that he had a job coming up but "I don't want in the meantime to beg or steal and that's the only way in which I could live. Will you for God's sake commit me for eight days?" The judge agreed to do so.

Naturally, amid these terrible conditions and the savage wage cuts, industrial violence rapidly broke out. Middle-class fears of working-class militancy were fueled by the notorious informer McParlan's revelations about the Molly Maguires—Irish laborers in the Pennsylvania coal fields who were said to be murdering their bosses. In 1877 the Great Railroad Strike erupted all over the country, spreading west from Reading, through Baltimore, Pittsburgh, Chicago and St. Louis. The involvement of radical groups produced America's first red scare. By 1878 regroupment began for labor, and the Knights of Labor began a period of rapid growth.

Nowhere were economic hard times more graphically illustrated than in the lot of the new immigrants. News of the great depression had filtered back to Europe, dissuading many from making the crossing. Just under 21,000 immigrants from Great Britain arrived in the United States in 1876, less than half the total for 1875. The bulk of the immigrants still came from northern and western Europe—from Scandinavia, Great Britain and Germany. Only 10 percent came from the "new" areas of southern and eastern Europe. There were the beginnings of more "exotic" immigrations, notably the arrival of a few thousand Chinese on the West Coast. The Chinese were the most despised immigrant group in 1876 and their future in this country was a subject of hot debate. The dislike of the Chinese and other immigrant groups by native American workers stemmed partially from the foreigners' willingness to work long hours for little pay. The immigrants offered industrialists a cheap labor pool, without which American industry could not have taken its enormous strides forward. A writer in *Harper's Weekly* in

Farewell to Fatherland—Emigrants Embarking for America

1876 described the Chinese as "like the mythical laborers in some parts of Europe, who were once described as able to 'work for nothing and live upon less!' He soon drives the white man with his expensive wants off the course. In all departments of servile labor...the Mongolian slowly but firmly pushes the Caucasian out of his path, and leaves thousands of the latter race unemployed and suffering for the actual necessities of life."

Giles and His Friends at the Village Inn
One of the illustrations that accompanied the story "The Immigrant's Progress" in *Scribner's Magazine* when it appeared in 1877.

THE IMMIGRANT'S PROGRESS

A graphic description of an immigrant's voyage to the New World in the mid-seventies was published, anonymously, in *Scribner's Monthly* in 1877. The account described the horrors of the voyage and the internecine hatreds that sprang up among different immigrant groups. It showed, too, the crucial importance of immigrant labor in the development of industrial America. The author proudly boasted that between 1847 and 1870, four million immigrants had come to the United States and had "increased the national wealth by more than five billions of dollars in less than thirty-three years." The story began:

There is scarcely a hamlet in all England which has not been invaded by the emissaries of one of the great steamship lines. Either in the tavern, the reading-room, or the apothecary's shop, a bold red-and-black placard is displayed, bearing the names of half a dozen vessels and the dates of their sailings. Honest Giles, sitting of an evening in his accustomed place by the fire-side of the village inn, has it constantly before him, and makes it the text of many long chats with his neighbors about the wonderful land in the west...The farrier's son is in America, and the glowing accounts he sends to his father of his new home are invariably read aloud to the assembled company. The general opinion of the villagers is favorable to "the States"...

Some of the old villagers who formerly sat around the fire and drowsed away all the evenings of the year are settled in Australia, Canada or the United States. Letters often come to the village from them, with small amounts of money or photographs which represent the writers as brighter-looking and in better dress than they ever appeared at home. The most encouraging accounts of all come from "the States," and when honest Giles is sorely pressed with difficulties, and Mrs. Giles is fading for want of proper nutriment, and her boys are running to waste, after long deliberation and many regrets Giles resolves to sell his little all and embark for New York....

THE DEPARTURE FROM THE OLD WORLD
He selects one of the Liverpool steamers, as they have the best reputation and are the most convenient. His choice is the common one. More than half the whole number of emigrants coming to the United States arrive at New York in vessels from the former port. One morning, then, Giles finds himself surrounded by his numerous family and baggage on the Great Landing-stage at Liverpool. The vast floating pier is crowded with departing emigrants, who are as confused and frightened as a flock of sheep. The majority are English, Irish and Scotch; but there are also bearded Russians and Poles, enveloped in frowzy furs; uncleanly Italians, some of them carrying dingy musical instruments, with a considerable number of Germans...

Mr. Giles is a little dismayed by the appearance of his prospective traveling companions. A good many sinister men and loose women are noticeable...But among the unclean outcasts the sturdy plowman rejoices to find a few who are like himself and his wife—neat in dress and cleanly in person...

The emigrants are taken from the landing-stage by a small steamboat and conveyed to the large vessel anchored in the stream. As they pass up the narrow gangway the tickets are scanned by one officer, while another orders "single men forrad," and "single women aft."...

Each emigrant has a contract ticket which stipulates for his transportation to New York in consideration of four, five or six guineas, according to the current rate of fare. The company engages to provide a full supply of wholesome provisions, cooked and served by its stewards, and the passenger is required to provide himself with bedding and cooking utensils...

The emigrants are berthed by the steerage stewards, and are then marshaled on deck again under the scrutiny of a government inspector who is in search of infectious diseases. Their tickets are also examined again, and some would-be stowaways are sent back to the shore in the little tender.

By and by the cabin passengers are brought on board, and with a full cargo and a thousand souls the great steamer leaves her moorings.

Let us preface all that we have to say against the manner in which Giles and his fellow-voyagers are treated with this frank admission: constant improvements are being made in emigrant passenger vessels...The mortality on vessels bringing emigrants to New York seldom exceeds one and two-thirds percent, and in some instances is no greater than one-eighth percent...The great steamer soon bids good-bye to the Mersey, and rolls on her way through the cross waters of the Irish Sea toward Queenstown...

ACCOMMODATIONS

Giles can scarcely believe that the steerage is intended to be a house for human beings. It is cold, dark, and at the very outset of the voyage—foul-smelling. It extends nearly the whole length of the vessel beneath the saloon deck, and is divided into gloomy compartments. In each compartment there are four tiers of berths or bunks, two on each side. The height of the steerage is about ten feet, which is advertised as unusually lofty by the steamship owners. In each tier there are six berths, eighteen inches wide and six feet long, formed of wooden boards, smelling faintly of chlorate of lime and carbolic acid. One-half of the passengers never had softer or more spacious couches, and accept their lot in good part; but the other half have been used to a comfortable home, and are wretched.

There is no thorough classification of the passengers. The single men and women are separated; but Poles, Germans, English and French are thrown together without discrimination. A cleanly, thrifty English or German woman is berthed next to a filthy Italian woman. Mrs. Giles thinks her bed would be hard enough, even though it were isolated, but her misery is intensified by the presence of a dreadful hag in the next berth....

Some time during the next morning [the vessel] enters the beautiful harbor at Queenstown, and a few hundred weeping, laughing, forlorn Irishmen are introduced into the already overcrowded steerage. At sunset...the ocean voyage has begun.

Giles is probably too much occupied with other grievances for thought about the life-saving equipments of the vessel, and would have no means of satisfying himself were he inclined to inquire...Man has been faithful and fate kind to those old ship-owners at Liverpool. No serious accident has ever happened to their steamers...But what if

Farewell to the Old World

"The emigrants are roughly driven hither and thither, and urged into their places by much hard swearing and abuse. Neither officers nor men consider them worthy of the least respect, and treat them as a drove of cattle. Some of the vagabonds and out-casts submit without complaint: but decent laborers, like Giles, feel indignant and are inclined to resent the savage words."

"The Immigrant's Progress"

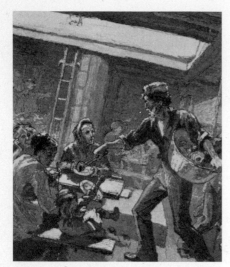

Dinner in the Steerage
"Breakfast, at eight o'clock, consists of oatmeal, porridge and molasses, salt fish, hot bread, and coffee; dinner, at twelve, of soup or broth, boiled meats, potatoes, and bread; and supper, at six, of tea, bread, butter, and molasses."

"The Immigrant's Progress"

Emigrants on shipboard.

disaster should befall? The largest steamers in the trade carry ten open boats, each of which, under favorable circumstances, might accommodate about seventy persons.

During a busy season, some of the larger steamers from Liverpool often bring as many as fifteen hundred emigrants to New York at a time. In some instances seventeen hundred persons, exclusive of the crew, have been packed in the steerage of one vessel. The ten boats will carry seven hundred at the most, and there are not rafts or buoys on board for a hundred more. The consequent loss, in case of fire or wreck in mid-ocean, would include the greater part of both passengers and crew. The truth is, the owners trust to good luck in contemplating the subject, or treat the matter with indifference.

FEEDING TIME
Giles and his friends, who have never been afloat before in their lives, are slow in settling down to the routine of the voyage. They complain to the captain of the narrowness of their quarters, the insolence of the stewards, and the quality of their food; and the captain listens to them, or growls at them, according to the mood he is in. While the weather is fine, their sufferings are not very great. Three meals are served every day, and both in quantity, which is unlimited, and in quality, which is variable, the rations are better than the law demands...But the manner in which the meals are served is careless and uncleanly. The beef, soup, and porridge are placed on the table in great, rusty-looking tins, which need scrubbing; and the passengers scramble for the first choice, often using their dirty fingers instead of their forks, in making a selection. Mrs. Giles finds her appetite gone after watching a filthy rag-picker plunge his hand into a dish of meat for a tender piece. Still, while the sea is calm, Giles can take his family on deck and brace them with the glorious fresh air, which brings roses to pallid cheeks. Indeed, the emigrants are quite merry on deck during a warm summer's day. Some of the squalid Italians are dragged from their suffocating retreat over

the gratings of the engine-room, and induced to give a concert with their harps and violins, to which the cabin passengers liberally subscribe. Card-parties are formed and checkerboards roughly made for the occasion...

It is when a storm comes that the emigrants suffer most. The hatches are battened down, the ports screwed in their places as tightly as possible, and the companionways closed. So long as the sea sweeps the decks, Giles and thirteen hundred others are confined to the steerage. It may be for a day, or two or three...Each hour the atmosphere becomes more close, and in twenty-four hours it is loaded with impurities. The meals are served irregularly, or not at all, and the food is not cooked enough. In the darkness the ignorant and timid lose control of themselves, and pour out imprecations and prayers in shrill chorus. The terror spreads to others, and the bravest quail as the shrieks grow louder. The greater the number of emigrants, the greater the confusion and the worse the atmosphere. We have known of instances in which the sailors have refused to enter the steerage for the purpose of cleaning it after a storm until the captain fortified them with an extra supply of grog.

CONTEMPT OF ENGLISH AND IRISH IMMIGRANTS FOR THE ITALIANS
Giles is pale and feverish when he reaches the open air again, and his wife and children are too weak to stand. The deck is still wet and the wind boisterous; but he cannot endure that "black hole" of steerage. The thought of the filth he has seen and the dread of contamination sicken him. The company is to blame, he thinks, for crowding so many people together, but the habits of some of the emigrants are even more to blame than the overcrowding. The Italians will not wash themselves, and cling to their berths until they are peremptorily ordered out by the captain. They neglect every provision made to insure their personal cleanliness, and they excite little sympathy when they are brought on deck and thoroughly drenched with water from the fire-hose.

"Between Decks on an Emigrant Ship—Feeding Time"
"A dreary sight meets Giles as he comes into the steerage from the open deck...He can dimly see the women and children sitting or lying in their berths, and hear the children's cries. The stewards are fussing about, or making coarse jokes. By and by preparations are made for supper, of which only a few eat, and when the meal is over, the tables are raised to the roof, leaving a clear space in the center of the steerage."

"The Immigrant's Progress"

Inspection at Quarantine

And We Open Our Arms to Them!
An ironic comment on the hostile reception that most Americans in 1876 gave to immigrants.

ARRIVAL IN THE LAND OF PROMISE

In nine or ten days the voyage draws to a close, and hope is revived in Gile's breast. He has very hazy ideas of the country he is approaching, and believes that its characteristic features are Indians, buffaloes, and log-cabins. Very likely he expects to obtain a view of the Rocky Mountains from Chicago, see war-chiefs in their paint on the streets, and hunt for his supper before he eats it. He has heard much about the great cities, the wealth and liberality of the people, the profligacy of municipal government; but it never enters his head that New York has any of the magnificence of London.

His surprise is unbounded when the steamer arrives at Quarantine. The cultivated lands on the heights of Staten Island and on Long Island shore, the tasteful houses, prettier to his eyes than the English villas, the appearance of wealth, comfort, and beauty on each side of the Narrows, astonish him and excite his warmest admiration...That cloud which looms at the head of the bay—that, he is told, is New York, the gate-way to the land of promise, and he points it out to Mrs. Giles and the children to their intense satisfaction.

A little tow-boat brings the doctor on board—the health-officer of the port, who inspects the steerage and the emigrants. As there are no cases of an infectious disease, the steamer is allowed to proceed...The emigrants on deck are looking wistfully toward the city, with its high roofs, spires and towers. Many of them are anxious and sick at heart, almost afraid to enter the new and unfamiliar world now that they are at its portals. Some happy ones...know all about the beneficent offices of Castle Garden, which they explain to others who are not so well informed. By and by the trees and lawns of the Battery Park come into view, with the curious-looking building, in the form of a rotunda, at the water's edge. The steamer's pulse ceases to beat, and several large barges are towed alongside. The baggage is brought from the hold and

transferred with the emigrant passengers to these tenders. There is the same confusion and uproar as at the outset of the voyage. The bewildered people are browbeaten and driven about in the most inconsiderate manner. As soon as the barges are loaded, a steamboat takes them in tow, while the great steamer proceeds to her pier in the North River.

CASTLE GARDEN

Castle Garden has been famous for generations. First it was a fort, and then it was converted into a summer-garden for the sale of chocolate, soda and ices. Afterward it became a concert-hall, in which Jenny Lind and many other celebrated singers made their first appearance in America.

The Board of Commissioners of Emigration was created, in May 1847, and Castle Garden was afterward selected as a convenient and suitable *entrepôt* for immigrants, and such it remains. It was partly destroyed by fire on July 9, 1876, but it has been rebuilt with a few changes which do not materially alter its appearance.

From May, 1847, to March 20, 1876, the laws of the state required the owners or agents of vessels arriving at the port with immigrants to give a bond of $300 for each passenger, conditioned to indemnify every city, town, or county in the state against any charge on account of the relief or care of the passenger during the first five years of his residence in the country. The same law enabled the owners or agents to commute the bond by paying a certain sum known as "head-money" (which varied at different times, the highest being $2.50, and the lowest $1.50) to the Commissioners of Emigration, whose duty it became to pay the expenses incurred by the immigrant in any poor-house or hospital, owing to his infirmity or poverty. The large steamship companies were opposed to the exaction, and on March 20th, 1876, they obtained a decision through the Supreme Court of the United States that the law was unconstitutional and void...

BAGGAGE INSPECTION

The barges are soon moored to the wharf at Castle Garden, where the custom-house officers are in waiting to examine the baggage. Battered old chests, barrels, and great bundles of clothes and bedding are packed together, much against the wishes of their owners, who are in terror of losing all their worldly treasures. The officers then set to work...Some of the bundles are uninviting but they are explored and turned upside down and inside out with a degree of energy and speed highly creditable to the inspectors. Some of the unmarried men have no baggage at all, except a small bundle tied in a handkerchief and slung over a stick...The whole wealth of the Italians consists in their organs, harps, fiddles and the clothes they wear...

VALUE OF IMMIGRANT LABOR

At one time all passengers were questioned at Castle Garden as to the amount of money in their possession; but they scarcely ever gave truthful answers. It is assumed on credible evidence, however, that one hundred dollars, at least, is the average amount in the possession of each person, and that the average quantity of property brought by each is worth fifty dollars more. During 1869, two hundred and fifty-nine thousand immigrants arrived at Castle Garden, and thus the amount added by them to the national wealth was almost equal to thirty-nine

New York City—Health Officers Vaccinating Russian and Polish Emigrants on Board the Steamship Victoria, at Quarantine

The Interior of Castle Garden Crowded with Immigrants

million dollars. Large as this sum is, it becomes trifling in comparison with the capital value of the immigrant's labor. A well-known social economist estimates the capital value of the male laborer at one thousand five hundred dollars, and the capital value of the female at seven hundred and fifty dollars, making the average value of persons of both sexes eleven hundred and twenty-five dollars. Between May, 1847 and January, 1870, four million, two hundred and ninety-seven thousand immigrants were deposited in New York. Adding to the capital value of each immigrant the estimated value of his personal property, we find that immigration increased the national wealth by more than five billions of dollars in less than thirty-three years. The total immigration into the United States for several years previous to 1874 was at the rate of three hundred thousand persons a year, and the country gained nearly four hundred millions of dollars annually from the traffic, or more than one million a day. Less than five percent of the whole number of immigrants are unproductive...

When the baggage has been "passed" by the inspectors, it is checked and sent to a room prepared for its reception. The immigrants are examined by a medical officer who ascertains that no paupers or criminals are among them, and that no persons afflicted with contagious or infectious diseases have escaped the doctor at Quarantine...The immigrants are then ushered into the rotunda, a high-roofed circular building, into which ventilation and light are admitted by a dome seventy-five feet high. The floor is divided into small inclosures containing a post-office, telegraph-office, money exchange, and restaurant. As the crowd files in, each passenger is detained for a moment at the registration desk, where his name, age, nationality, destination, the vessel's name and the date of arrival are carefully recorded and preserved.

The whole number of immigrants landed at Castle Garden during 1873 was 267,000...The whole number arriving in 1874 was 149,584...In 1875 the total number of immigrants was 99,093, and in 1876 the total was 113,979...The railroad companies have agents in the building, and the passengers who wish to leave the city are shown to the ticket offices, while their baggage is rechecked and conveyed to the train or depot without charge. Those who want rest are permitted to remain in the rotunda, where a bowl of coffee, tea or milk and a small loaf of bread are supplied to them for ten cents...

·Attached to Castle Garden there is also a labor bureau, and if Giles had not an opening in view for himself he might present himself as a candidate. During 1873 employment was found for 25,400 emigrants, including 14,400 agricultural or common laborers, 3,500 mechanics, and 7,000 house servants. In 1874 employment was found for 10,148 men and 6,762 women; in 1875, for 7,008 men, and 5,432 women, and in 1876, for 5,394 men, and 4,821 women....

The immigrants are guarded against swindlers by a broker's office in the rotunda, where coin is exchanged for bills at the lowest current rates, and where valuables may be deposited without charge...

The last stage of the immigrant's progress is accomplished by rail, and, as far as the vehicle is concerned, it is the least pleasant. An immigrant train is usually made up of dingy old passenger cars, with few windows or means of ventilation. It runs on special time and is managed by conductors of more than ordinary brutality....

The long, hot, dusty days lapse into long hot and dreary nights. The passengers turn as well as they can in the narrow space of their seats and groan in the vain endeavor to get a wink of refreshing sleep. But after about fifty-six hours of misery Giles arrives at his new home, and with his wife and little ones, stands gazing at a broad expanse of untilled land. His work is before him, and it will not be complete until the waste has been cleared and the earth has yielded a tribute to his industry.

IN 1876 CONGRESS TRIED AND FAILED TO EXTEND TO ALL IMMIGRANTS ARRIVING IN THE UNITED STATES THE SAME HELP THEY WERE GIVEN BY THE STATE OF NEW YORK

Almost two thirds, or six million out of eight million, of the immigrants who came to the United States between 1847 and 1876 arrived in New York. In New York they were cared for:

....under a well-devised but imperfectly administered system of care and protection; they have been forwarded to their places of destination in near or remote parts of the country, have been aided in distress, relieved in sickness, supported in poverty, and sometimes sent back to the land from which they came.

Distributing Food to Italian Emigrants at Castle Garden

The Labor Exchange at Castle Garden—Choosing a Girl

Immigrant's Boarding-house Near the Battery

Some immigrants went to a boarding house, like this one, licensed by the commissioners, which offered food and lodging at the modest price of a dollar or a dollar and a half. The author of "The Immigrant's Progress" hoped:

"...that Giles will not be induced to enter one of these dens. With a few exceptions they are located in an unhealthy neighborhood, frequented by dangerous characters and conducted by reprobate men and women. We pity the immigrant who trusts himself to them. They are defective sanitarily and defective morally..."

"Castle Garden in the Old Days: A Scene Now Past and Gone Forever"
Notice the boat advertising in German the Erie Railroad—"Erie Eisenbahn." Such boats took immigrants from Castle Garden to cities throughout the United States. This particular boat advertised Cleveland, Cincinnati, Louisville, San Francisco, Detroit, St. Louis and Chicago.

In New York, expenses incurred on behalf of the immigrants were paid for out of a common fund created by requiring each immigrant to pay between $1.50 and $2.50 upon landing. An attempt by Congress, in the mid-1870's, to duplicate on the national level the New York levy and system of caring for immigrants failed. Not until 1882 did Congress put a levy of fifty cents upon every immigrant arriving in the United States. The money was put into a fund to be used to aid the immigrants.

MR. FRANK SANBORN, SECRETARY OF THE MASSACHUSETTS STATE BOARD OF CHARITIES, IN HIS REPORT FOR THE YEAR 1876 ADVOCATED ADOPTING THE NEW YORK SYSTEM BECAUSE IT HELPED TO KEEP OUT THE MUCH-FEARED "PAUPERS" AND UNDESIRABLES

The author of *The Immigrant's Progress* pointed out how this country benefited from the influx of immigrants. Others, like Mr. Sanborn, were not so enthusiastic about immigration. Sanborn wanted to keep out what he called "undesirables." He felt that the New York system helped to prevent pauperism among newly arrived immigrants:

It checks pauperism by maintaining such a supervision...that those paupers who are sent over here by persons in their own country in order to escape the burden of supporting them, are in many instances discovered and sent back; while others, who could only be paupers if they remained here, but who could be provided for in their native land, are also returned to the places they came from. This policy of detaining

The New York Harbor
The future site of the Statue of Liberty, Bedloe's Island, lies beyond Castle Garden, which is in the foreground.

A Peep at New York from a Castle Garden Embrasure
"The lower walls [of Castle Garden] are the same that formed the old fort, and the embrasures, through which the cannon peeped, are sometimes selected by the immigrants for smoke and rest, or meditation."

"The Immigrant's Progress,"
Scribner's Monthly Magazine, 1877

and returning paupers (and criminals also, if they can be discovered), when persevered in for a period of years, has the effect to raise very much the standard of immigration, by making it more and more difficult for the unworthy and undesirable elements of the European populations to flow this way and mingle in the ocean-stream of our own industrious, self-reliant people.

The good of the country which receives the immigrant is quite as much to be considered as the good of the individual alien who, for one reason or another, comes to our shores. Immigration is by no means an unmixed blessing...It introduces youth, vigor, poverty and industry, but it also introduces disease, ignorance, crime, pauperism and idleness.

Emigrants Departing for the West
Many emigrants did not remain in New York but went from Castle Garden to other parts of America to make their fortunes. In the West, many of them provided a cheap labor pool to build the railroads.

An Anti-Chinese Riot
The San Francisco *Bulletin* denounced the Chinese: "They fill our prisons, asylums, and hospitals; are a grievous burden to our tax-payers...They will not conform in their habits of life to our sanitary and police regulations. Their diseases are infectious and horrible; their vices are the result of 4,000 years of practice. They buy and sell women for prostitution;...Resolved that the presence of these people in our midst has a tendency to demoralize society...It degrades industrial occupation, drives white labor from the market, multiplies idlers and paupers and is a menace to Christian civilization."

THE CHINESE

Amid the hard times of 1876, the arrival of new immigrants aroused feelings of insecurity and bitterness among the resident work force fearful of being priced out of the labor market. The Chinese immigrants were prime targets for such hostility and consequent racist prejudice.

By 1876 there were 100,000 Chinese in the United States. Rapidly the specter of "hordes" of Chinese entering the United States became the most heated immigration issue. "Asiatics," said the New York *World*, "are cunning, treacherous and vicious, possessing no conception of American civilization." The *World* went on to say that the western states were "degenerating into Chinese colonies" and that any further Chinese immigration would be "disastrous" to the American way of life.

The *World*'s fears for the western states were prompted by the fact that three quarters of the Chinese had settled in California. Their lot there was particularly unhappy since by 1876 the state was in economic disarray. A severe drought resulted in widespread crop failures and catastrophic death of livestock. Output of gold from the mines had declined and land values had slumped. There was already a vast pool of surplus white labor and out of such adverse economic conditions had sprung the Workingmen's Party, opposed to the "rich monopolists" but also to the Chinese who, the Party alleged, were stealing all the available jobs. "Treason," proclaimed its manifesto "is better than to labor beside a Chinese slave."

The Chinese, fearful of such hostility, appealed to the political leaders of San Francisco for tolerance: "large gatherings of the idle and irrepressible elements of the population of this city are nightly addressed...by speakers who use the most violent, inflammatory and incendiary language, threatening in plainest terms to burn and pillage the Chinese quarter and kill our people unless, at their bidding, we leave this 'free Republic'...We appeal to you, the Mayor and Chief Magistrate of this municipality, to protect us to the full extent of your power in all our peaceful, constitutional and treaty rights..."

But the answer to this plea was only more abuse. Frank M. Pixley, representing the municipality of San Francisco before a congressional commission in 1876, said:

"The Chinese are inferior to any race God ever

Along The New York Docks—An Unaristocratic International Restaurant
Note the Chinaman's pigtail being pulled by a worker.

made...Their people have got the perfection of crimes of 4,000 years...The Divine Wisdom has said that He would divide this country and the world as a heritage of five great families; that to the Blacks He would give Africa; to the Red Man He would give America; and Asia He would give to the Yellow races. He inspired us with the determination, not only to have prepared our own inheritance, but to have stolen from the Red Man, America; and it is now settled that the Saxon, American or European groups of families, the White Race, is to have the inheritance of Europe and America, and that the Yellow races are to be confined to what the Almighty originally gave them; and as they are not a favored people, they are not to be permitted to steal from us what we have robbed the American savage of..."

Photograph of Chinese Children in California

"For centuries the poor classes of Chinese have been pupiled...until they are educated down to the miserable perfection of an economy and endurance that is startling... The Chinese have a power with which white labor can by no means cope, for a white man would starve on what John thrives on...Only by degrading white labor to a bestial scale can the two compete..."

Thomas Vivian, *Scribner's Monthly,* December 1876

The Chinese did have some defenders; one was Mark Twain. As a reporter for the San Francisco *Morning Call,* he had first-hand knowledge of the Chinese situation. His story "Disgraceful Persecution of a Boy," published in New York in *The Galaxy* in 1869, was a fierce indictment of the treatment of the Chinese in America.

DISGRACEFUL PERSECUTION OF A BOY, BY MARK TWAIN

In San Francisco, the other day, "A well-dressed boy, on his way to Sunday-school, was arrested and thrown into the city prison for stoning Chinamen."

What a commentary is this upon human justice! What sad prominence it gives to our human disposition to tyrannize over the weak! San Francisco has little right to take credit to herself for her treatment of this poor boy. What had the child's education been? How should he suppose it was wrong to stone a Chinaman? Before we side against him, along with outraged San Francisco, let us give him a chance—let us hear the testimony for the defense.

He was a "well-dressed" boy, and a Sunday-school scholar, and therefore the chances are that his parents were intelligent well-to-do people, with just enough natural villainy in their composition to make them yearn after the daily papers, and enjoy them; and so this boy had opportunities to learn all through the week how to do right, as well as on Sunday.

It was in this way that he found out that the great commonwealth of California imposes an unlawful mining-tax upon John the foreigner, and allows Patrick the foreigner to dig gold for nothing—probably because the degraded Mongol is at no expense for whisky, and the refined Celt cannot exist without it.

It was in this way that he found out that a respectable number of the tax-gatherers—it would be unkind to say all of them—collect the tax twice, instead of once; and that, inasmuch as they do it solely to discourage Chinese immigration into the mines, it is a thing that is much applauded...

It was in this way that he found out that when a white man robs a sluice-box (by the term white man is meant Spaniards, Mexicans, Portugese, Irish, Hondurans, Peruvians, Chileans, etc. etc.), they make him leave the camp; and when a Chinaman does that thing, they hang him.

It was in this way that he found out that in many districts of the vast Pacific coast, so strong is the wild, free love of justice in the hearts of the people, that whenever any secret and mysterious crime is committed, they say, "Let justice be done, though the heavens fall," and go straightway and swing a Chinaman.

It was in this way that he found out that by studying one half of each day's "local items," it would appear that the police of San Francisco were either asleep or dead, and by studying the other half it would seem that the reporters were gone mad with admiration of the energy, the virtue, the high effectiveness, and the dare-devil intrepidity

of that very police—making exultant mention of how "the Argus-eyed officer So-and-so" captured a wretched knave of a Chinaman who was stealing chickens, and brought him gloriously to the city prison; and how "the gallant officer Such-and-such-a-one" quietly kept an eye on the movements of an "unsuspecting, almond-eyed son of Confucius" (your reporter is nothing if not facetious),...and captured him at last in the very act of placing his hands in a suspicious manner upon a paper of tacks, left by the owner in an exposed situation; and how one officer performed this prodigious thing, and another officer that, and another the other—and pretty much every one of these performances having for a dazzling central incident a Chinaman guilty of a shilling's worth of crime, an unfortunate, whose misdemeanor must be hurrahed into something enormous in order to keep the public from noticing how many really important rascals went uncaptured in the mean time, and how overrated those glorified policemen actually are.

It was in this way that the boy found out that the legislature, being aware that the Constitution has made America an asylum for the poor and oppressed of all nations, and that, therefore, the poor and oppressed who fly to our shelter must not be charged a disabling admission fee, made a law that every Chinaman, upon landing, must be *vaccinated* upon the wharf, and pay to the state's appointed officer *ten dollars* for the service, when there are plenty of doctors in San Francisco who would be glad enough to do it for him for fifty cents.

It was in this way that the boy found out that a Chinaman had no rights that any man was bound to respect; that he had no sorrows that any man was bound to pity; that neither his life nor his liberty was worth the purchase of a penny when a white man needed a scapegoat; that nobody loved Chinamen, nobody befriended them, nobody spared them suffering when it was convenient to inflict it; everybody, individuals, communities, the majesty of the state itself, joined in hating, abusing, and persecuting these humble strangers.

The Chinese Agitation in San Francisco— a Meeting of the Workingmen's Party

Mark Twain wrote that he had many memories of the persecution of the Chinese, "but am thinking just at present of one particular one, where the Brannan Street butchers set their dogs on a Chinaman who was quietly passing with a basket of clothes on his head; and while the dogs mutilated his flesh, a butcher increased the hilarity of the occasion by knocking some of the Chinaman's teeth down his throat with half a brick. This incident sticks in my memory with a more malevolent tenacity, perhaps, on account of the fact that I was in the employ of a San Francisco journal at the time, and was not allowed to publish it because it might offend some of the peculiar element that subscribed for the paper."

Mark Twain
In December, 1866, Twain left the West Coast. For over four years he had worked as a journalist in California and Nevada. "Behold, I am prone to boast of having the widest reputation as a local editor, of any man on the Pacific Coast...Everybody knows me, and I fare like a prince wherever I go, be it on this side of the mountain or the other."

And, therefore what *could* have been more natural than for this sunny-hearted boy, tripping along to Sunday-school with his mind teeming with freshly learned incentives to high and virtuous action, to say to himself:

"Ah, there goes a Chinaman! God will not love me if I do not stone him."

And for this he was arrested and put in the city jail.

Everything conspired to teach him that it was a high and holy thing to stone a Chinaman, and yet he no sooner attempts to do his duty than he is punished for it...

Keeping in mind the tuition in the humanities which the entire "Pacific coast" gives its youth, there is a very sublimity of incongruity in the virtuous flourish with which the good city fathers of San Francisco proclaim (as they have lately done) that "The police are positively ordered to arrest all boys, of every description and where-ever found, who engage in assaulting Chinamen."

Still, let us be truly glad they have made the order, notwithstanding its inconsistency; and let us rest perfectly confident the police are glad, too. Because there is no personal peril in arresting boys, provided they be of the small kind, and the reporters will have to laud their performances just as loyally as ever, or go without items.

The new form for local items in San Francisco will now be: "The ever-vigilant and efficient officer So-and-so succeeded, yesterday afternoon, in arresting Master Tommy Jones, after a determined resistance," etc., etc., followed by the customary statistics and final hurrah, with its unconscious sarcasm: "We are happy in being able to state that this is the forty-seventh boy arrested by this gallant officer since the new ordinance went into effect. The most extraordinary activity prevails in the police department. Nothing like it has been seen since we can remember."

A CHINESE WRITER CONFIRMED TWAIN'S DESCRIPTION OF TREATMENT OF CHINESE IN AMERICA AND BEGGED FOR A BETTER FUTURE:

When a man from your country arrives in China, none of our officers or people treat him otherwise than with respect and kindness. When he is defrauded or injured, if the matter is of slight consequence, the offender is fined or beaten; in a grave case, he forfeits his life. Even if there are no witnesses, the officers must thoroughly inquire into the circumstances. In murders and brawls, if the criminal be not discovered, the magistrate is called to account and degraded. When a foreigner commits a deed of violence, a spirit of great leniency and care is manifested upon the trial of the case. This is not because of a lack of power to punish, but we sincerely dread to mar the beautiful idea of gentleness and benignity toward strangers from afar.

Now, why is it that when our people come to your country, instead of being welcomed with respect and kindness, they are, on the contrary, treated with contempt and evil? It happens even that many lose their lives at the hands of lawless wretches. Yet, although there are Chinese witnesses of the crime, their testimony is rejected. The result is our abandonment to be murdered and our business to be ruined...

We go on board ships. We eat little, we grieve much. Our appearance is plain, and our clothing poor. At once when we leave the vessel the boatmen extort heavy prices; all kinds of conveyances require from us more than the usual charges; as we go on our way we are pushed, and kicked, and struck by the drunken and the brutal, but we cannot speak your language, we bear our injuries and pass on. Even when within doors, rude boys throw sand, and bad men stones, after us. Passers by, instead of preventing these provocations, add to them by their laughter. We go up to the mines; there the collectors of licenses make unlawful exactions, and robbers strip, plunder, wound, and even murder some of us. Thus we are plunged into numberless uncommiserated wrongs. But the first root of them all is that very degradation and contempt of the Chinese as a race of which we have spoken, which begins with your honorable nation, and which you communicate to people of other countries, who carry it to greater lengths. Now, what injury have we Chinese done to your honorable people that they should thus turn upon us and make us drink the cup of wrong even to its last poisonous dregs?

BEFORE A COMMITTEE OF THE SENATE OF THE STATE OF CALIFORNIA IN 1876, WITNESSES BEGGED FOR EXCLUSION OF THE CHINESE FROM THE STATE

George W. Duffield, a policeman, testified:

Mr. Haymond: How long have you resided in California?

Mr. Duffield: Twenty-four years in San Francisco.

Q. What has been your occupation?

A. I was connected with the police force...for the last eleven years.

Q. Have your duties called you into the Chinese quarters of this city?

A. Yes, for the last nine years.

Q. Can you give a description of the extent of those quarters? What streets are occupied by them?

A. A great many Chinamen live on Pacific, Jackson, Dupont, and Sacramento Streets. Those are the principal streets.

Q. What is the area occupied, in blocks—about how many blocks of this city?

A. The whole Chinese population is confined to six or seven blocks.

Q. At about what do you estimate that population?

A. From twenty-five thousand to thirty thousand in this city and county. A great many work in factories outside the city...

PROSTITUTION

Mr. Haymond: Do you know anything about the number of Chinese women in this city? Can you approximate?

A. I should think there are from one thousand to one thousand two hundred.

Q. What occupations are they following?

A. Principally prostitution.

Q. How many Chinese women living in the Chinese quarters are not prostitutes?

A. There may be one hundred, but not over that. The balance are prostitutes.

Q. Describe the situation of the houses of prostitution, their general appearance, and the habits of those people?

A. One class of these Chinese women go with white men, and another class go with Chinamen...The Chinese prostitutes who go with Chinamen are of the better class...Where Chinawomen go with Chinamen they will not allow white men at all. I don't think there is any doubt about the women being bought and sold like sheep.

Chinese Sleeping Accomodations

George W. Duffield, a policeman, testified in 1876 before a committee of the California State Senate about the crowded conditions in which the Chinese lived in San Francisco:

Q. Do you know the building called the Globe Hotel?

A. Yes, sir. There are about two hundred and seventy-five or three hundred Chinese living in it.

Q. How is it occupied?

A. The basement and the ground floor...by stores. The upper stories are occupied by rooms of men making collars, tailoring, etc., and sleeping apartments. The sleeping rooms are some twelve by fourteen, some smaller, and fourteen or fifteen feet high. Of such rooms they make two stories out of one, each about six or seven feet high. In some of these little rooms there are only two Chinamen, and in some four or five; in some, more.

Chinese Meat Market, San Francisco
The *New York Times* suggested ironically in April of 1876 that:

"...it cannot be denied that the conduct of the Chinese has provoked and invited public hostility...These alleged men...show a want of manliness as they are not only willing to work...but work with a mean-spirited thoroughness."

Interior of a Chinese Restaurant in San Francisco, c. 1876

Sometimes Chinese women escape and get married, but when they do get away the owners try to get them back, or make the man pay them her value...The women are treated now a great deal better than they used to be. They used to receive very rough treatment. They have not been beaten much lately, because the police watch them and arrest them for beating.

Q. Can you approximate the number of Chinese houses of prostitution in this city?

A. There may be in the neighborhood of forty or fifty.

Q. Are there many Chinese in this city that are married?

A. Very few. Sometimes a Chinaman will get a Chinese woman out of a house of prostitution, go to a Justice's Court, and get married.

Q. Taking the Chinese quarter as a whole, is it as filthy as it can be?

A. Yes, sir. It cannot be much dirtier.

Q. Were you ever in New York City?

A. Yes, sir.

Q. Was there any part of that city, as it existed twenty years ago, that could be compared with the Chinese quarter?

A. No, sir. The Five Points could not be compared with it. The Chinese quarter is dirtier and filthier than the Five Points were.

CRIME

Mr. Haymond: How is this population as to criminal propensities?

A. They are a nation of thieves. I have never seen one that would not steal.

Q. What is the proportion of criminals to the whole number?

A. I call a man who will steal a criminal.

Q. Then nearly all will be criminals?

A. Yes, sir.

Mr. Pierson: What proportion of the convictions in the Police Court are Chinese?

A. I can't exactly tell; but a great many Chinamen are convicted in the Police Court.

Mr. Haymond: What, in your opinion, is the effect of the presence of the Chinese here on the industrial interests of this city?

A. I think it is bad. They are the worst class of people on the face of the earth.

POLICE PAID BY THE CHINESE

Mr. Rogers: Are you a regular officer?

A. I am a special officer.

Mr. Evans: How are the special policemen paid?

A. The same as regular officers.

Q. Who pays them?

A. The Chinese. We draw nothing from the city treasury. We have no regular salary, but we depend on the voluntary contributions from the store-keepers.

Q. How many special policemen are there in the Chinese quarter?

A. Five or six.

Mr. Haymond: Are these special policemen all paid by contributions from the people living on their beats?

A. Yes, sir.

A DOCTOR ACCUSED CHINESE WOMEN OF SPREADING SYPHILIS

Dr. H. H. Toland testified:

Mr. Haymond: Doctor, how long have you practiced medicine in the State?

Dr. Toland: Twenty-three years.

Q. A member of the San Francisco Board of Health?

A. Yes, sir.

Q. It has been stated that these Chinese houses of prostitution are open to small boys, and that a great many have been diseased. Do you know anything about that?

A. I know that is so. I have seen boys eight and ten years old with diseases they told me they contracted on Jackson Street. It is astonishing how soon they commence indulging in that passion. Some of the worst cases of syphilis I have ever seen in my life occur in children not more than ten or twelve years old.

Q. Are these cases of frequent occurrence?

A. Yes, sir. You will find children from twelve to fifteen that are often diseased. In consequence of neglect, they finally become the worst cases we have to treat.

Q. What effect will that have upon the health of the community, in the end?

A. It must have a bad effect, because a great many of these children get secondary syphilis, and it runs until it becomes almost incurable...The disease is hereditary, and will be transmitted...

Q. From your observation, what would you say as to the effect it must have upon this community if these Chinese prostitutes are allowed to remain in the country?

A. It will fill our hospitals with invalids, and I think it would be a very great relief to the younger portion of the community to get rid of them.

A CAPITALIST PRAISED CHINESE LABORERS— EXPLAINED NEED FOR THEM

A. I have employed all kinds of laborers—Scandinavians, French, Irish and Chinese. I prefer to employ white men when I can get them, but they cannot be had, and I am obliged to take Chinese. Were it not for Chinamen, much of my work would be left undone....So far as the labor element is concerned, I think they are an important element in this state. I know in the country, if the Chinese element of labor was taken away from us, it would be a great detriment. In the country there is no competition between Chinamen and white men, but I find this difference: the Chinaman will stay and work, but the white man, as soon as he gets a few dollars, will leave and go elsewhere. Once in a while I get a good white man, and he will work until he gets enough money to buy a farm for himself; then I have to go and get more laborers.

Q. Do the Chinese ever save money and buy farms?

A. No, I don't know that they do, but there is nothing to encourage Chinamen. The unfriendly legislation of this State is such as to discourage them. I believe the laboring man is an advantage to the country, whether Chinese or white men. There is room for all, and there is need for all the labor that can be brought to this country. I believe that if you exclude Chinese you will have to close up every woolen mill on the coast...I prefer white men in my place, but I have come here and tried to get them, but I have failed...They will not go to the country and do what work we want them to...There is not enough labor to carry on the industrial and manufacturing pursuits, so Chinamen are necessary.

" '(Dis) Honors are Easy.' Now Both Parties Have Something To Hang On." Thomas Nast's cynical comment on the Chinese question.

A Cartoon by Thomas Nast on "Chinese Cheap Labor"

"In spite of the murmurs that have arisen concerning the presence of John Chinaman in our land, much can be said in his favor. ...Undoubtedly 'Chinese cheap labor' rather than Chinese bad morals, is at the foundation of the hue and cry that has arisen against the melancholy wearers of the pigtail....

"As carpenters, manufacturers of furniture, and workers in all kinds of wood, the Chinese in San Francisco have crowded out an army of white laborers, who would otherwise be employed at high wages...If there is any branch of mechanical industry in especial demand, the Chinaman is sure to be found at work upon it, and like the mythical laborers in some parts of Europe, who were once described as able to 'work for nothing and live upon less,' he soon drives the white man, with his expensive wants, off the course. In all departments of servile labor—as house servants, cooks, scullions, gardeners, and porters—the Mongolian slowly but firmly pushes the Caucasian out of his path, and leaves thousands of the latter race unemployed and suffering for the actual necessaries of life."

Harper's Weekly, 1876

THE DISTRICT ATTORNEY EXPLAINED CHINESE CRIME AND THE BRUTAL CHINESE METHOD OF JUSTICE–THE MURDER OF AH QUONG

Charles T. Jones testified:

Mr. Haymond: How long have you been District Attorney of this county?

Mr. Jones: A little over two years.

Q. Do you have any difficulty in administering justice, where Chinese are parties?

A. During my term of office I have had considerable to do with Chinese criminals, and always have great difficulty in convicting them of any crime. I remember well the case of Ah Quong...[an] interpreter...honest and capable. The circumstances of the case were these: a Chinaman wanted to marry a woman then in a house of prostitution. She desired to marry him, and he went with two of his friends to the house. She went with them. They drove out of town to get married, when the Chinamen who owned her heard of it, and started some officers after her. She was arrested and surrendered to these Chinamen, with instructions to bring her into Court the next day. I had this man [Ah Quong] to interpret for me, being well satisfied that she would swear that she was not being kidnapped. The next day the owners brought into Court a woman whom the defendants informed me was not the one at all, but another. The attorneys for the other side insisted that it was, believing the statements of their Chinamen to that effect. The case was postponed for two or three days, when it was shown that the woman offered was not the one taken away. This interpreter [Ah Quong] told me they would kill him [if]...these defendants were not convicted...Half an hour afterwards he was brought back, shot in the back, and a hatchet having been used on him, mutilating him terribly. This was in broad daylight, about eleven o'clock in the morning on Third and I Streets, one of the most public places in the City of Sacramento. There were hundreds of Chinese around there at the time, but it was difficult in the prosecution of the case, to get any Chinese testimony at all. It happened that there were a few white men passing at the time, and we were enabled to identify two men, and they were convicted and sent to the State Prison for life, after three trials.

THE CHINESE SYSTEM OF JUSTICE

Mr. Haymond: Do you often find that upon preliminary examinations and before the Grand Jury there is enough testimony to warrant a conviction, but on the trial these same witnesses swear to an exactly opposite state of facts?

A. Very frequently.

Q. To what do you attribute that?

A. I attribute that to the fact that they had tried the case in Chinese Courts, where it had been finally settled. I have records in my office of a Chinese tribunal of that kind, where they tried offenders according to their own rules, [and] meted out what punishment they deemed proper...There was a Chinaman here who opened a wash-house on Second Street, underneath the Orleans Hotel. It appears that he was a member of the Chinese Wash-house Association, and that they had a rule that no wash-house should be opened within ten doors of one already opened. This new house was opened within the proscribed limits, and the association held a meeting. One of the charges was that he was in partnership with a white man—a foreigner, their rules forbidding any such arrangement, and they fined him, I think, thirty dollars. The records recite that the members enter into a solemn compact not to enter into partnership with a foreigner; that this man did so, and the company offers so many round dollars to the man who will kill him. They promise to furnish a man to assist the murderer, and they promise, if he is arrested, they will employ able counsel to defend him. If convicted, he should receive, I think, three dollars for every day he would be confined, and in case he died, certain money would be sent to his relatives.

TESTIMONY BY A CHINAMAN

Mr. Billy Holung did not throw much light on the many accusations leveled against his race. He testified:

Mr. Haymond: How long have you been in California?

Mr. Holung: Since eighteen hundred and forty-eight.

Q. What have you been doing?

A. The first time, mining.

Q. What have you been doing in Sacramento?

A. Worked in a saloon first time for an American man on Front Street...

Q. How do these chinawomen come here—the women that are prostitutes?

A. I don't know.

Q. Do you know anything about Ah Quong being killed?

A. Yes, sir.

Q. Who killed him?

A. I don't know.

Denis Kearney, President, Workingman's Party of California

The Workingman's Party declared in its manifesto on October 16, 1876:

"To an American death is preferable to a life on a par with the Chinaman. What then is left to us? Our votes! ...But this may fail. Congress, as you have seen, has often been manipulated by thieves, speculators, land grabbers, bloated bond-holders, railroad magnates, and shoddy aristocrats—a golden lobby dictating its proceedings. Our own legislature is little better...We declare to them that when the workingmen have shown their will that 'John' should leave our shores, and that will shall be thwarted by fraud or cash, by bribery and corruption, it will be right for them to take their own affairs into their own hands and meet fraud with force...Treason is better than to labor beside a Chinese slave...The people are about to take their own affairs into their own hands and they will not be stayed with by 'Citizen Vigilantes,' state militia, nor United States Troops."

"War of Races in the City of Brotherly Love—Colored Washerwomen Berating Chinese Laundrymen"

"But as a laundry-man is the 'heathen Chinee' peculiarly successful. Although personal cleanliness is not by any means his distinguishing characteristic, he delights to perform miracles in way of purifying the soiled linen of other people. More Chinamen are employed in San Francisco in laundry-work than in any other kind of labor. A system prevails among these Mongolian washer-men whereby the item of shop rent is reduced to the most economical figure. Two firms occupy the same premises and use the same tubs and materials. One works during the daytime, and at dark surrenders the place to the other, who occupies it until morning. By this system there is a great saving in the way of water and fuel. All work is done by hand, the average Chinaman not caring to meddle with the mysteries of machinery."

Harper's Weekly, May 20, 1876

Central Pacific Railroad—Chinese Laborers at Work

Mr. Samuel H. Dwinelle, for twelve years a judge of the Fifteenth District Court in California, was one of the few defenders of the Chinese:

"You can depend upon them attending to their work without watching them. For instance, when I was president of the Napa Valley railroad, I had them in the section gangs, keeping up the roads, without any foreman. When you set them upon doing a piece of work, you can depend upon its being done."

Q. Six years ago...did you not buy a woman and give six hundred dollars for her?
A. Yes, sir; I bought me a wife.
Q. What became of her?
A. I own her.
Q. Are you married to her?
A. Yes, sir.
Q. Why don't you keep her in Sacramento?
A. She quarrels with me.

AN EASTERNER DEFENDED THE CHINESE

An anonymous writer in *Scribner's Monthly* suggested that the charges leveled at the Chinese were very unfair:

It is tossed into the teeth of the Chinaman that he is a heathen, that he is an opium-eater, that he sends his money home, that he does not bring his wife and family with him, but does bring prostitutes, that he is filthy, that the quarters he inhabits are breeders of disease, that he is a gambler, etc....It is a fair question to ask...whether the treatment meted out to this heathen has been such that he sees a marked superiority of Christianity over heathenism...If he smokes opium, who drinks whiskey? If he sends money home, it is precisely what the Irish have been doing in the most filial, brotherly and praiseworthy way...

James Galloway, a lawyer and mine owner, testified before a committee of the Senate of the State of California in 1876 that he disliked the Chinese sticking to their native habits and not becoming Americanized:

"I was for a number of years a practical miner, and for nearly all of the time in the mines, owner and operator. I am acquainted with the Chinese working in the mines, having employed Chinamen to work for me...They wear the Chinese dress, except some of them have our style of soft hats and boots, but many of them still wear the broad Chinese hat made from cane splits and manufactured in China. Nearly all their ware is evidently Chinese manufacture and made in China. They have their own merchants in the mining camps, from whom they buy all their rice and tea, and salt stuffs that are brought from China...

"Many of them in the mining camps smoke opium...They import to nearly all the mining towns or camps lewd women...As a class their character in the mines is that of thieves. They have often been caught robbing sluice-boxes, houses, and stealing chickens, and frequently convicted...[but] their operations in the mines have often been very profitable..."

The prejudice against our heathen brother John in California seems a little unreasonable...We have been in the habit of welcoming all other nationalities. We are strangely insensitive to the importation of thousands of criminals and scamps and scalawags from Europe, and we cannot yet feel sure that the importation of the Chinaman is not a better thing on the whole. He certainly is industrious...He does an honest day's work which is more than can be said of a good many Christian laborers who we have around us...

One observer of the Gilded Age concluded (in the spirit of the age) that anti-Chinese agitation was wrong, not because it was unjust but because it was harmful to business:

Certainly no dispassionate reader of the history of the State can fail to see that the incessant agitation of this question...has retarded the investment of capital and the diversification of industry, prevented, by giving the State a bad name, the immigration of a solid middle class composed of farmers, business men and skilled mechanics, while inviting at the same time the tramp and the turbulent adventurer; and, by giving encouragement to the ignorant and lawless to a degree rare even in pioneer regions, put even conscientious public men at the mercy of the least stable element.

**T. W. Wood, War Episodes:
"The Contraband," 1865**

"It has been said that our history in this
country has been its romance; but it might
have been as truly said, I imagine, that it has
also been its tragedy. The slave ship, the
slave hut and pen, the overseer's whip and
the burning tears of separated husband and
wife, and the equally cruel caste and pro-
scription which has hounded the negro
when free from the cradle to the grave have
mingled in far unequalled proportions the
romantic with the tragic."

Richard T. Greener (a journalist and the first
black to graduate from Harvard)

OUR OWN POOR

The Chinese felt the hostility and passions traditionally
reserved for new and alien immigrants. But if white
Americans were obsessively interested in expelling the
Chinese from this country, they were equally interested in
ignoring the Negro. Too much time and energy had been
spent on Reconstruction in the South, with too few results.
In 1877 the New York *Tribune* announced that Negroes
had been given "ample opportunity to develop their own
latent capacities" and had proven that "as a race they are
idle, ignorant and vicious." By the middle of the decade,
Negroes were, to put it cynically, a losing proposition both
for the North and for the South.

Rutherford B. Hayes became President in 1877 partly
on condition that federal troops be withdrawn from the
South. The ideals of Reconstruction were lost in expedi-
ency, as the blacks were abandoned by their Northern
Republican "benefactors." Excuses and rationalizations
for this abandonment were rapidly found: that whereas
corruption in high places did not disqualify whites from
self-government, far more petty corruption seemed to
disqualify blacks. Conservatives had, by 1876, already
regained control of most Southern states. The writing on
the wall was clear, so far as the blacks were concerned.
Business and electoral exigencies trampled rapidly over
their expectations.

One of the most bitter analysts of this situation was
Albion Tourgée. A veteran of the Union army, he visited
the South after the Civil War, determined to make money
and also to serve humanity—in particular the emancipated
slaves. By 1876 he had served on the North Carolina
Superior Court, battled against the Klan, and had his life
threatened on numerous occasions. In a mood of deep
pessimism he wrote *A Fool's Errand,* finally published in
1879. In the novel, an immense best seller, Tourgée, who
portrayed himself as the Fool, ventilated his despair at the
futility of Reconstruction and at the hollowness and vanity
of liberal expectations. He showed that the war had not
erased the underlying differences between Northerners
and Southerners. The following excerpts from the novel
begin with the Fool's wife writing to her sister in the North.

A FOOL'S ERRAND, BY ALBION TOURGÉE

We miss our friends,—ah! sadly enough,—for we have none here, and somehow can not make any...We are so different, have been reared under such different influences, and have such different thoughts,...I begin to think that we shall always be strangers in the land in which we dwell. I do not see any chance for it to be otherwise. The North and the South are two peoples, utterly dissimilar in all their characteristics; and I am afraid that more than one generation must pass before they will become one.

Tourgée succinctly laid out in a dialogue the dissimilar Northern and Southern postwar views of the Negro:

THE NORTHERN IDEA OF THE SITUATION
The Negroes are free now, and must have a fair chance to make themselves something. What is claimed about their inferiority may be true. But, true or false, they have a right to equality before the law. That is what the War meant, and this must be secured to them.

THE SOUTHERN IDEA OF THE SITUATION
We have lost our slaves, our bank stock, everything, by the War. We have been beaten, and have honestly surrendered. ...The slave is now free, but he is not white. We have no ill will towards the colored man as such and in his place; but he is not our equal, can not be made our equal, and we will not be ruled by him, or admit him as a co-ordinate with the white race in power. We have no objection to his voting, so long as he votes as his old master...advises him; but, when he chooses to vote differently, he must take the consequences.

The newly freed black man did choose to vote differently from his former master; he voted Republican. And during Reconstruction many blacks held political office.

THE NORTHERN IDEA OF THE SOUTHERN IDEA
Now that the Negro is a voter, the Southern people will have to treat him well, because they will need his vote. The Negro will remain true to the government and party which gave him liberty...Enough of the Southern whites will go with them, for the sake of office and power, to enable them to retain permanent control of those States for an indefinite period. The South has no right to complain...if the very weapon by which they held power is turned against them, and is made the means of righting the wrongs which they have themselves created.

Until 1876 the Negro did "remain true to the government and party which gave him liberty." But in 1876 some black leaders like Martin Delany, the abolitionist and journalist, expressed disappointment with the party that had promised so much and delivered so little. Delany backed Democrat Wade Hampton for governor of South Carolina and joined the Democratic party.

Albion W. Tourgée: "Ignorance and Neglect are the Mainsprings of Misrule"
Albion Tourgée, who lived in the post-Civil War South was perhaps describing the folly of his own resistance to the Klan when he wrote of the fight of the former slave, Uncle Jerry, against that secret society:

"Uncle Jerry had been noted for his openly-expressed defiance of the Ku-Klux, his boldness in denouncing them, and the persistency with which he urged the colored men of his vicinity to organize, and resist the aggressions of that body...He had infused into his duller-minded associates the firm conviction which possessed himself,—that it was better to die in resisting such oppression than to live under it. He had an idea that his race must, in a sense, achieve its own liberty, establish its own manhood, by a stubborn resistance to aggression,—an idea which...probably would have been the correct and proper one, had not the odds of ignorance and prejudice been so decidedly against them.

"As matters stood, however, it was the sheerest folly. When experience, wealth, and intelligence combine against ignorance, poverty, and inexperience, resistance is useless. Then the appeal to arms may be heroic; but it is the heroism of folly, the faith—or hope, rather—of the fool."

Thomas Nast's Cartoon of the Hamburg Massacre

On July 8, 1876, in Hamburg, South Carolina, six blacks were murdered in cold blood. The ostensible cause was that on the Fourth of July the all-black militia, celebrating with a parade, refused to move aside to let two white men in a buggy pass through. The Charleston *News and Courier* reported on July 14, 1876, that:

"The feeling among negroes...is that of terrified submission. All the killed had families...and the grief and distress of the women and children were violent and heartrending."

THE SOUTHERN IDEA OF THE NORTHERN IDEA

The Negro is made a voter simply to degrade and disgrace the white people of the South. The North cares nothing about the Negro as a man, but only enfranchises him in order to humiliate and enfeeble us. There are so few colored men there, that there is no fear of one of them being elected to office, going to the Legislature, or sitting on the bench. The whole purpose of the measure is to insult and degrade. But only wait until the States are restored and the "Blue Coats" are out of the way, and we will show them their mistake.

Tourgée commented that "there was just enough of truth in each of these estimates of the other's characteristics to mislead."

THE KU KLUX KLAN

Southerners, who resented the newly freed black man, took the law into their own hands. On July 8, 1876, six unarmed blacks were shot in cold blood by a mob of over two hundred well-armed whites in Hamburg, South Carolina. The offense was the refusal by the blacks to interrupt their military drill on July 4th to let two whites in a buggy pass. Southerners also organized secret societies like the Ku Klux Klan, the Knights of the White Camelia, and the Order of the White Rose in order to persecute the blacks. When Albion Tourgée was a judge on the North Carolina Supreme Court between 1870 and 1876, he had been fearless in attempting to stop the Klan, putting his own life in jeopardy. Tourgée devoted much of *A Fool's Errand* to a description of the Klan. He wrote:

There had been rumors in the air, for some months, of a strangely mysterious organization, said to be spreading over the Southern States...

It was at first regarded as farcical, and the newspapers of the North unwittingly accustomed their readers to regard it as a piece of the broadest and most ridiculous fun. Here and there throughout the South, by a sort of sporadic instinct, bands of ghostly horsemen, in quaint and horrible guise, appeared, and admonished the lazy and trifling of the African race, and threatened the vicious. They claimed to the affrighted Negroes, it was said, to be the ghosts of departed Confederates who had come straight from the confines of hell to regulate affairs about their former homes....

It was in the winter of 1868-69...when it was said that already Reconstruction had been an approved success, the traces of the war been blotted out, and the era of the millennium anticipated,—that a little company of colored men came to the Fool one day; and one of them, who acted as spokesman, said,—

"What's dis we hear, Mars Kunnel, bout de Klux?"

"The what?" he asked.

"De Klux—de Ku-Kluckers dey calls demselves."

"Oh! the Ku-Klux, Ku-Klux-Klan, K.K.K.'s, you mean."

"Yes, dem folks what rides about at night a-pesterin' pore colored people, an' a-pertendin' tu be jes from hell, or some of de battle-fields ob ole Virginny...."

"There is nothing in the world in it,—nothing at all. Probably a parcel of boys now and then take it into their heads to scare a few colored people; but that's all. It is mean and cowardly, but nothing more. You needn't have any trouble about it, boys."

"An' you tink dat's all, Kunnel?"

"All? Of course it is! What else should there be?"

"I dunno, Mars Kunnel," said one.

"You don't think dey's ghostses, nor nothin' ob dat sort?" asked another.

"Think! I know they are not."

"So do I," growled one of their number who had not spoken before, in a tone of such meaning that it drew the eyes of the Fool upon him at once.

"So your mind's made up on that point too, is it, Bob?" he asked laughingly.

"I know dey's not ghosts, Kunnel. I wish ter God dey was!" was the reply.

"Why, what do you mean, Bob?" asked the colonel in surprise.

"Will you jes help me take off my shirt, Jim?" asked Bob meaningly, as he turned to one of those with him.

The speaker was taller than the average of his race, of a peculiarly jetty complexion, broad-shouldered, straight, of compact and powerful build. His countenance, despite its blackness, was sharply cut; his head well shaped; and his whole appearance and demeanor marked him as a superior specimen of his race. Servosse [the Fool] had seen him before, and knew him well as an industrious and thrifty blacksmith,

Robert Smalls, Congressman from South Carolina, 1875–1887
One week after the Hamburg Massacre, Smalls had an eyewitness account of the bloody event read into the *Congressional Record:*

"On the Fourth of July the colored people of the town were engaged in celebrating the day, and part of the celebration consisted in the parade of the colored militia company... The company came to a halt across one of the roads leading out of the town. While resting there two white men drove up in a buggy, and with curses ordered the company to break ranks and let them pass through...The captain of the militia, to avoid difficulty, ordered his men to break ranks and permit the buggy to pass through....

"The next day a colored trial justice issued processes against the officers of the company, based on the complaint of the two white men, citing the officers to appear and answer to a charge of obstructing the public highway. They obeyed the writs, and after a slight examination the justice adjourned the trial until Saturday, the 8th...On that day, at an early hour, the town commenced to fill up with white men, armed to the teeth with repeating rifles and revolvers...

"Late in the afternoon General M. C. Butler, one of the most malignant of the unreconstructed rebels, rode into town, accompanied by a score of well-armed white men, and stated to the leading colored men that he came for the purpose of prosecuting the case on the part of the two white men, and he demanded that the militia company should give up their arms and also surrender their officers...This threat aroused the militia company to a sense of their impending danger, and they at once repaired to a large brick building...used by them as an armory, and there took refuge. They numbered in all about forty men and had a very small quantity of ammunition...The white desperadoes...numbered over fifteen hundred well-armed and ruffianly *(continued on following page)* men...The building where the militia had taken refuge was entirely surrounded and a brisk fire opened upon it...The militia now realized that it was necessary to evacuate the armory at once...By hiding and hard fighting, a portion of the command escaped, but twenty-one were captured by the bush-whackers and taken immediately to a place near the railroad station.

"Here a quasi-drumhead court-martial was organized by the blood-hunters...Not one of the twenty-one colored men had a pistol or gun about them...The orderly sergeant of the militia company was ordered to call the roll, and the first name called out to be shot in cold blood was Allan T. Attaway...He was taken from the sight of his comrades and a file of twelve men fired upon him...He was instantly killed and after he was dead the brutes in human shape struck him over the head with their guns and stabbed him in the face with their bayonets. Three other men were treated in the same brutal manner...

"In another portion of the town the chief of police, a colored man named James Cook, was taken from his house and...brutally murdered. Not satisfied with this, the inhuman fiends beat him over the head with their muskets and cut out his tongue....

"So far as I have been able to learn only one white man was killed. After this holocaust of blood was over, the desperadoes in large bodies entered the houses of most of the prominent colored men of the town and completely gutted them...

Sorting Cotton—St. Helena's Island, South Carolina

"We say to the colored people of the South, though you may be able to obtain employment at home, the time seems to be far distant when you can become owners of the soil, and consequently independent of the will of land-owners. Until you are independent of those who own the land and who can dictate the terms upon which you will be employed, you will be but little better than slaves..."

The New National Era, Washington, D.C., December 12, 1872

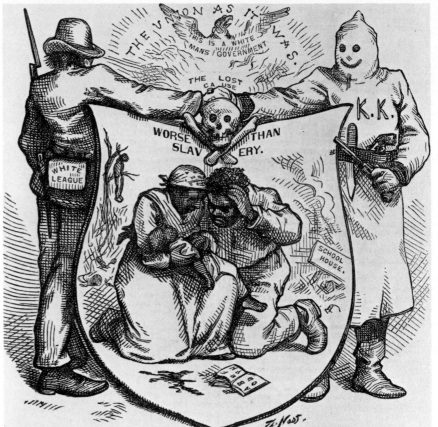

The Union As It Was

"Now that the pistol and bowie knife have begun again their murderous work in Mississippi and Louisiana we may expect again to see the independent press crammed with sensational and unreliable stories about the general uprising of Negroes to exterminate the whites. These outrageous lies in the beginning of each election year are manufactured in order to conceal their murderous outrages..."

"G.W.A.," The People's Advocate, *Alexandria, Virginia, May 27, 1876*

living in a distant part of the country, who was noted as being one of the most independent and self-reliant of his people in all political as well as pecuniary matters,—Bob Martin by name.

When his clothing had been removed, he turned his back towards the Fool, and, glancing over his shoulder, said coolly,—

"What d'ye tink ob dat, Kunnel?"

"My God!" exclaimed the Fool, starting back in surprise and horror. "What does this mean, Bob?"

The sight which presented itself to the Fool's eyes was truly terrible. The broad muscular back, from the nape down to and below the waist, was gashed and marked by repeated blows...The whole back was swollen [and] bruised as if it had been brayed in a mortar. To the eye of the Northern man who gazed at it...unused...to witness the effects of severe whipping, it seemed horrible beyond the power of words to express...He was filled with anger, surprise, and horror.

"What?—Who?—How?—My God! Tell me all about it. Can't I do something for you, my man?"

"Thank ye, Kunnel, nothing," said Bob seriously. "It's been washed in salt an' water. Dat's de bes' ting dere is to take out de soreness. I'se bin a slave goin' on forty-three years, but never hed a lash on my back sence I was a waitin'-boy till las' night."

His face was working with passion, and his eyes had a wicked fire in them, which clearly showed that he did not take this visitation in such a subdued and grateful spirit as his position properly demanded that he should. When his clothing had been resumed, he sat down and poured into the wondering ears of the Fool this story:—

BOB'S EXPERIENCE

Mr. Bob Martin, the victim of a Klan raid, was a former slave, freed by the Civil War, who had set himself up in business as a blacksmith.

"Yer see, I'se a blacksmith at Burke's Cross-Roads. I've been thar ever sence a few days arter I heer ob de surrender. I rented an ole house dar, an' put up a sort of shop, an' got togedder a few tools, an' went to work. It's a right good stan'. Never used ter be ob any count, coz all de big plantations roun' dar hed der own smifs. But now de smifs hez scattered off, an' dey hev ter pay fer der work, dey finds it cheaper ter come ter my shop dan ter hire a blacksmif when dey's only half work fer him to do. So I'se been doin' right well, an' hev bought de house an' lot, an' got it all paid fer, tu. I've allers tended to my own business...I wanted to give de boys an' gals a little eddication, an' let em hev a fa'r start in life wid de rest ob de worl', if I could."

THE CAUSE OF THE KLAN'S ANGER

"Long a while back—p'raps five er six months—I refused ter du some work fer Michael Anson or his boy, 'cause they'd run up quite a score at de shop, an' allers put me off when I wanted pay. I couldn't work jes fer de fun ob scorin' it down: so I quit. It made smart ob talk. Folks said I waz gettin' too smart fer a nigger, an' sech like; but I kep right on; tole em I waz a free man,—not born free, but made free by a miracle,—an' I didn't propose ter do any man's work fer noffin'. Most everybody hed somefin' to say about it; but it didn't seem ter hurt my trade very much. I jes went on gittin' all I could do, an' sometimes moah. I s'pose I acted pretty independent: I felt so, anyhow. When ther come an election, I sed my say, did my own votin', an' tole de other colored people dey waz free, an' hed a right ter du de same. Thet's bad doctrine up in our country. De white folks don't like ter hear it, and 'specially don't like ter hear a nigger say it. Dey don't mind 'bout our getting on ef dey hev a mortgage, so't de 'arnin's goes into ther pockets; nor 'bout our votin', so long ez we votes ez dey tell us. Dat's dare idea uv liberty fer a nigger."

A WARNING

"Well, here a few weeks ago, I foun' a board stuck up on my shop one mornin', wid dese words on to it:—

> BOB MARTIN,—YOU'RE GETTIN' TOO DAM SMART!
> THE WHITE FOLKS ROUND BURKE'S CROSS-ROADS
> DON'T WANT ANY SECH SMART NIGGERS ROUND
> THAR. YOU'D BETTER GIT, ER YOU'LL HEV A CALL
> FROM THE   K.K.K.

"I heard 'bout the Klux...dat dey waz some triflin' boys dat fixed up an' went round jes' ter scare pore ignorant niggers, an' it made me all the madder ter think dey should try dat game on me. So I sed boldly, an' afore everybody, thet ef the Kluckers wanted enny thin' uv Bob Martin, they'd better come an' git it..."

Cotton Is King—A Plantation Scene, Georgia, U.S.A.
J. Stella Martin, a founder of the black paper, *The New National Era*, and also pastor of the Fifteenth Street Colored Presbyterian Church, urged blacks to become landowners:

"We must be owners of the soil; and we need to acquire those habits of economy which will make the nation see our deserts in granting land, and keep us under an ever-present sense of the need to hold it when we get it. Rooted and grounded in the soil, we will be steadied by considerations of our responsibilities; and many of the old traces of oppression will fall from us while truthfulness, honesty, sobriety and industry will take their place..."
The New National Era, Washington, D.C., February 10, 1870

A Black School
Francis E. W. Harper, the black poet, felt that educated black children would not tolerate political inferiority as their parents had:

"The political heavens are getting somewhat overcast. Some of this old rebel element, I think, are in favor of taking away the colored man's vote, and if he loses it now it may be generations before he gets it again.
...Perhaps the loss of his vote would not be a serious grievance to many; but his children differently educated and trained by circumstances might feel political inferiority rather a bitter cup.

"After all whether they encourage or discourage me, I belong to this race, and when it is down I belong to a down race; when it is up I belong to a risen race."

Winslow Homer, "The Carnival," 1877

**Away Down Among "de cotton,"
Louisiana**

In the 1870's, life was difficult for Southern
Blacks. Although they were free legally, the
landowners kept them in a kind of bondage:

"The Southern gentleman rents the land to
his former slave at about the whole value of
the land each year, and thus practically sells
his land each year, recovering it at the end.
This high-toned gentleman, this soul of
honor, does more—he 'furnishes' the people
on his plantation, buys provisions, and sells
to the poor colored man at an advance of 50
to 100 percent, agreeing to wait for his pay
until the crop is picked out and ready for
market. A little judicious exaggeration of the
account usually attends these operations,
and at the end of the year, the colored man
frequently finds that he has nothing due him
for his year's labor..."

The New National Era, Washington, D.C.,
October 3, 1872

The New South Family Circle

Francis E. W. Harper wrote of the importance of family life:

''While I am in favor of Universal Suffrage, yet I know that the colored man needs something more than a vote in his hand; he needs to know the value of a home life; to rightly appreciate and value the marriage relations; to know how to be incited to leave behind him the old shards and shells of slavery; to rise in the scale of character, worth and influence.... A man landless, ignorant and poor may use the vote against his interests; but with intelligence and land he holds in his hand the basis of power and elements of strength.''

Lewis Douglass, the eldest son of Frederick Douglass and an editor of *The New National Era* wrote:

''If a colored child is maltreated, its parents or guardians have the right, in every State of this Union at present, of at least *seeking* a remedy in the courts. But if the mind of the child is poisoned with the knowledge of being proscribed...there is no redress. When we ask for redress, we are told that the progress already attained is so wonderful and unexpected that we ought to be content with what we have, or at least be cautious how we endanger the future by asking too much...''

The New National Era, Washington, D.C., March 24, 1870

Visit of the Ku-Klux

"*Of the slain there were enough to furnish forth a battlefield, and all from those three classes, the negro, the scalawag, and the carpet-bagger,—all killed with deliberation, over-whelmed by numbers, roused from slumber at the murk mid-night, in the hall of public assembly, upon the river-brink, on the lonely woods-road, in simulation of public execution,—shot, stabbed, hanged, drowned, mutilated beyond description, tortured beyond conception.*

"*And almost always by an unknown hand! Only the terribly, mysterious fact of* death *was certain. Accusation by secret denunciation; sentence without hearing; execution without warning, mercy, or appeal. In the deaths alone, terrible beyond utterance; but in the manner of death—the secret, intangible doom from which fate springs—more terrible still: in the treachery which made the neighbor a disguised assassin, most horrible of all the feuds and hates which history portrays.*"

Albion W. Tourgée, A Fool's Errand

THE RAID

"I worked mighty hard an' late yesterday, an' when I went into de house, I was so tired thet I jes' fell down on de trundle-bed dat hed bin pulled out in front ob de souf do'...I nebber woke up till some time in de night. I kinder remember hearin' de dog bark, but I didn't mind it; an', de fust ting I knew, de do' was bust in, an' fell off de hinges ober on de trundle-bed whar I was lyin'. It was no use fer me to struggle...Besides dat, I was feared dey's kill de chillen. So I tole 'em ef dey'd get off, an spar' de chillen, I'd surrender. Dey wouldn't bleve me, dough, till dey'd tied my han's...Dey pulled me out o'do's. Dar was 'bout tirty of 'em standin' dar in de moonlight, all dressed in black gowns thet come down to ther boots, an' some sort of high hat on, dat come down ober der faces, jes' leavin' little holes ter see fru, an' all trimmed wid different colored cloth, but mos'ly white.

"I axed 'em what dey wanted o' me. De sed I was gittin tu dam smart, an' dey'd jes' come roun' ter teach me some little manners. Den dey tied me tu a tree, an' done what you've seen. Dey tuk my wife an' oldes' gal out ob de house, tore de close off 'em, an' abused 'em shockin' afore my eyes. After tarin' tings up a heap in de house, dey rode off, tellin' me dey reckoned I' d larn to be 'spectful to white folks herearter, an' not refuse to work unless I hed pay in advance, an'not be so anxious

'bout radical votes. Den my old woman cut me loose, an we went into de house ter see what devilment dey'd done dar. We called de chillen. Dar's five on 'em...We foun' 'em all but de baby. I don't tink he ebber breaved arter de do' fell on us."

The tears stood in the eyes of the poor man as he finished. The Fool looked at him in...amazement, pity, and shame. He could not help feeling humiliated, that, in his own Christian land, one should be so treated by such a cowardly-seeming combination, simply for having used the liberty which the law had given him to acquire competence and independence by his own labor.

FREEDOM'S BENEFITS DOUBTFUL
There was a moment's silence. Then the colored man asked, "De gov'ment sot us free, an' it 'pears like it oughtn't to let our old masters impose on us in no sech way now. I ain't no coward....I ain't 'feared of no man. I'd be willin' ter fight fer my liberty, er fer de country dat give me liberty. But I don't tink liberty was any favor ef we are to be cut up an' murdered jes' de same as in slave times... Bob'll take keer of himself, an' his wife an' chillen too, ef dey'll only give him a white man's chance. But ef men can come to his house in de middle ob de night, kill his baby, an' beat an' abuse him an' his family ez much ez dey please, jes' by puttin' a little black cloth ober der faces, I may ez well give up, an' be a slave agin."

"If it keeps on, and grows general," responded the Caucasian, "the government will have to interfere."

Cotton Culture—Covering in the Seed —c. 1875
"Last evening I visited one of the plantations, and had an interesting time. Oh, how warm was the welcome! I went out near dark, and between that time and attending my lecture, I was out to supper in two homes. The people are living in the old cabins of slavery; some of them have no windows at all, that I see; in fact, I don't remember of having seen a pane of window-glass in the settlement. But, humble as their homes were, I was kindly treated, and well received....I had quite a little gathering, after less, perhaps, than a day's notice; the minister did not know that I was coming, till he met me in the afternoon. There was no fire in the church, and so they lit fires outside, and we gathered...around the fire. To-night I am going over to Georgia to lecture. In consequence of the low price of cotton, the people may not be able to pay much, and I am giving all my lectures free....

"It is remarkable, however, in spite of circumstances, how some of these people are getting along. Here is a woman who, with her husband, at the surrender, had a single dollar; and now they have a home of their own, and several acres attached—five altogether..."

Frances Ellen Watkins Harper, black poet and writer, on a lecture tour in the South in 1870

Black Leaders: Frederick Douglass
In March 1876 Frederick Douglass, the famous orator and author, spoke to a meeting of blacks in Washington, D.C. "But one thing I know...we must either have all the rights of American citizens, or we must be exterminated, for we can never again be slaves; nor can we cease to trouble the American people while any right enjoyed by others is denied or withheld from us," said Douglass.

President Hayes in 1877 appointed Douglass, Marshal of the District of Columbia. Although many were critical of the appointment as a payoff to the black community for its abandonment by the Republican party, Douglass cheered his own appointment as "an innovation upon long established usage and opposed to the general current of sentiment of the community." There was a bitter fight over Douglass' confirmation in the Senate as many people feared that he would "Africanize the courts."

The First Colored Senator and Representatives in the 41st and 42nd Congress of the United States.
Standing are Congressmen Robert O. De Large of South Carolina and Jefferson Long of Georgia. Seated from left to right are: U.S. Senator H. R. Revels of Mississippi, Congressmen Benjamin S. Turner of Alabama, Josiah T. Walls of Florida, Joseph H. Rainey of South Carolina, and R. Brown Elliott of South Carolina.

MARTIN THREATENED TO TAKE LAW INTO OWN HANDS

The former slave and the Fool agreed that either they would have to take the law into their own hands or leave the South. Tourgée did leave the South in despair, as did many blacks after the 1876 election. Martin explained:

"Ef dere's any mo' Kluckers raidin' roun' Burke's Corners, dar'll be some funerals tu."

"I can't blame you, Bob," said the white man, looking frankly into his face as it worked with agony and rage. "A man has a right to protect himself and his family; and, if our government is too blind or too weak to put down this new rebellion, there are only three courses before us,—you and me, and those who stood with us; the one is to fight the devil with fire,—to kill those who kill,—guard the fords, and, whenever we see a man in disguise, shoot him down; another is to give up every thing for the privilege of living here; and the third is to get away."

"It will come to dat, Kunnel. Ef de gubment won't take keer o' de darkeys y'her, an' gib 'em a white man's chance, dey'll run away, jes' ez dey did in slave times. Dat's my notion," said the freedman, who had fought to save the life of the nation, which would not lift a finger to save his in return.

It was a new and terrible revelation to the Fool. He saw at once how this potent instrumentality might be used so as to effectually destroy the liberty of the newly enfranchised citizen, and establish a serfdom more barbarous and horrible than any on earth, because it would be the creature of lawless insolence.

Heroes of the Colored Race
In the center of the picture are Senator Blanche K. Bruce of Mississippi, Frederick Douglass, and Senator Hiram Revels, of Mississippi. In the bottom corner at the left is Congressman Robert Smalls of South Carolina. In the top left corner is John R. Lynch of Mississippi, who was probably the most influential black congressman of the period. In the top right corner is Congressman Joseph Hayne Rainey of South Carolina, the first Negro congressman.

TOURGÉE'S BLEAK CONCLUSION

Morality took second place to economic growth in America in 1876. Tourgée believed that the country had made all the effort it was willing to make on behalf of the Negro:

The North had yielded, very slowly and unwillingly, to the conviction that slavery was an evil, and the colored man too near akin to white humanity to be rightfully held in bondage, and subjected to another's will. It had slowly and doubtfully been brought to the point of interference therewith on the ground of military necessity in the suppression of rebellion, and, after a grand struggle...had finally settled down to the belief that enfranchisement was all that was required to cure all the ills which hitherto had afflicted, or in the future might assail, the troublesome...African. This had been granted. The conscience of the nation was satisfied, and it highly resolved that thereafter it would have peace, that the Negro *could* have no further ground of complaint, and it would hear no further murmurs. So it stopped its ears, and, when the south wind brought the burden of woe, it shook its head blankly, and said, "I hear nothing, nothing! All is peace."

BLACK POLITICAL LEADERS

Tourgée was correct. In 1876 the nation did indeed turn away from the plight of the blacks, crying, "I hear nothing, nothing!" Between 1869 and 1876 there had been fourteen

Blanche K. Bruce, a black senator from Mississippi, from 1875 to 1881, called for an end to prejudice in a speech in the Senate on March 23, 1876:

"It will not accord with the laws of nature or history to brand colored people a race of cowards. On more than one historic field, beginning in 1776 and coming down to this centennial year of the Republic, they have attested in blood their courage as well as a love of liberty. I ask Senators to believe that no consideration of fear or personal danger has kept us quiet and forbearing under the provocations and wrongs that have sorely tried our souls. But feeling kindly toward our white fellow-citizens, appreciating the good purposes and offices of the better classes, and, above all, abhoring a war of races, we determined to wait until such time as an appeal to the good sense and justice of the American people could be made...I have confidence, not only in my country and her institutions, but in the endurance, capacity, and destiny of my people. We will, as opportunity offers and ability serves, seek our places, sometimes in the field of letters, arts, sciences, and the professions. More frequently mechanical pursuits will attract and elicit our efforts; more still of my people will find employment and livelihood as the cultivators of the soil. The bulk of this people—by surroundings, habits, adaptation, and choice—will continue to find their homes in the South, and constitute the masses of its yeomanry. We will there probably, of our own volition and more abundantly than in the past, produce the great staples that will contribute to the basis of foreign exchange, aid in giving the nation a balance of trade, and minister to the wants and comfort and build up the prosperity of the whole land. Whatever our ultimate position on the composite civilization of the Republic and whatever varying fortunes attend our career, we will not forget our instincts for freedom nor our love of country."

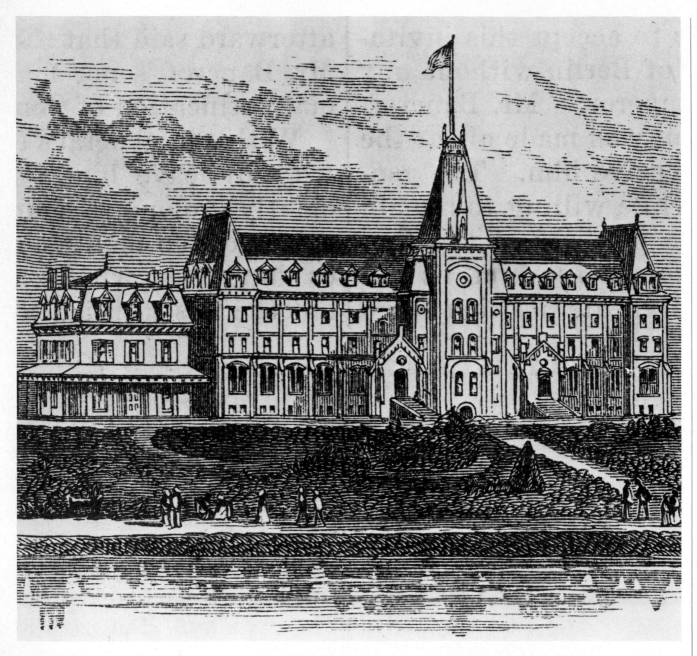

The Hampton Normal and Agricultural Institute

Hampton Institute, located in Hampton, Virginia, was founded in 1868 through the efforts of its first president, General Samuel Chapman Armstrong. Many dedicated white Northerners taught at the Institute, "a rare set of human beings" as Booker T. Washington called them.

black congressmen from the South, and two senators: Hiram Rhoades Revels (1870-71) and Blanche K. Bruce (1875-81). But when Hayes was elected President in 1876, the Republican party more or less abandoned the blacks. Between 1876 and 1901 there were only nine blacks elected to Congress. The make-up of the Congress reflected the nation's change of heart and its preoccupation with economic goals.

Immediately after the Civil War, some black Americans were thrust overnight from the role of slaves into the role of political leaders; Tourgée reflected on this sudden transformation:

Can the African slave of America develop into the self-governing citizen, the co-ordinate of his white brother in power, with less of preparation?...I cannot see how a race can become prepared for absolute autonomy, real freedom, except by the gradual process of serfdom or villenage, or by the scath and tribulation of the sojourn in the wilderness, or its equivalent of isolated self-support, by which individual self-reliance, and collective hardihood and daring, may be nourished and confirmed.

Black Americans had to wait many years to gain the rights which had been promised to them after the Civil War. Tourgée wrote that between the end of the war in 1865 and Hayes's election as President in 1876, blacks "tasted liberty full and complete,...and the loss of that, even by indirection, will add to the natural antipathy of the freedman for the associations and surroundings of his servitude." Tourgée was bitter, too. His hopes for the future of black Americans were not great:

If they were of the same stock as the dominant race, there might be a chance for the line of separation to disappear with the lapse of time. Marked as they are by a different complexion, and one which has long been accounted menial and debased, there is no little of truth in the sad refrain of their universal story, "Niggers never can have a white man's chance here."

As the political power of blacks waned, there was little hope for their participation in the vast economic growth of the decade.

Tourgée predicted that the lot of blacks in the South would not improve until some outside force compelled change. His pessimism was justified. He concluded:

I have given the years of my manhood to the consideration of these questions, and am accounted a fool in consequence....The South will never purge itself of the evils which affect it....The remedy is not from within. The minority knows its power, and the majority realizes its weakness so keenly as to render that impossible.

EDUCATION

When the Fool was asked what the remedy for the black man's plight was, he replied *"The remedy for darkness is light; for ignorance, knowledge; for wrong, righteousness."* Americans in 1876 assuaged any guilt they might have felt over their moral lapse by talking about the importance of education for black Americans. Through all-black institutions, like Hampton Institute, the Negro would supposedly improve himself and also improve his economic position. Tourgée wrote:

The Nation nourished and protected slavery. The fruitage of slavery

"During the whole of the Reconstruction period our people throughout the South looked to the Federal Government for everything, very much as a child looks to its mother. This was not unnatural: the central government gave them freedom, and the whole Nation had been enriched for more than two centuries by the labour of the Negro. Even as a youth, and later in manhood, I had the feeling that it was cruelly wrong in the central government, at the beginning of our freedom, to fail to make some provision for the general education of our people in addition to what the states might do, so that the people would be the better prepared for the duties of citizenship..."
Booker T. Washington

Laura Towne was one of many Northern white women, like the one in this picture, who taught in black schools on the Sea Islands of South Carolina. In April of 1877 she wrote in her diary: "I have been in raging indignation at Hayes...Nobody seems to remember that the South is only half-civilized, and that the Negroes are nearly as well-informed and a great deal more loyal than the whites..."

Hampton Institute: The Printing-Office 1873

"At Hampton it was a standing rule that, while the institution would be responsible for securing some one to pay the tuition for the students, the men and women themselves must provide for their own board, books, clothing, and room wholly by work, or partly by work and partly in cash."

Booker T. Washington

has been the ignorant freedman, the ignorant poor-white man, and the arrogant master....Now, let the Nation undo the evil it has permitted and encouraged. Let it educate those whom it made ignorant, and protect those whom it made weak. It is not a matter of favor to the black, but of safety to the Nation...Let the Nation educate the colored man and the poor-white man *because* the Nation held them in bondage, and is responsible for their education; educate the voter *because* the Nation can not afford that he should be ignorant.

When whites, Northerners and Southerners, spoke of "education" for blacks, they meant not so much education as industrial training. Hampton Institute was founded in 1868 solely to offer industrial training to blacks. Booker T. Washington, who was only twenty years old in 1876 and a schoolteacher in West Virginia, went along with the lowering of expectations for his race, urging his fellow blacks to "perfect themselves in the industries at their doors." Washington wrote:

Though I was but little more than a youth during the period of Reconstruction, I had the feeling that mistakes were being made, and that things could not remain in the condition that they were in then very long. I felt that the Reconstruction policy, so far as it related to my race, was in large measure on a false foundation, was artificial and forced. In many cases it seemed to me that the ignorance of my race was being used as a tool with which to help white men into office, and that there was an element in the North which wanted to punish the Southern white men by forcing the Negro into positions over the heads of the Southern whites. I felt that the Negro would be the one to suffer for this in the end. Besides, the general political agitation drew the attention of our people away from the more fundamental matters of perfecting themselves in the industries at their doors and in securing property.

It would be some twenty years before W. E. Du Bois, who was only eight years old in 1876, challenged Booker T. Washington's policy of accommodation. Du Bois maintained that industrial education was merely another method of continuing the servitude of the blacks. He called for complete social and political equality for blacks, the ideal at the heart of Reconstruction, which had been abandoned by 1876. Such an ideal was a long way off. A black newspaper, *The Colored Citizen*, summed up the bleak situation of blacks in the Centennial Year: "For colored men to expect protection from the government is mere nonsense while Hayes is President, and for them to look for protection from the rebel State governments is foolishness; and for them to attempt to protect themselves by openly resisting or fighting is out of the question."

URBAN POVERTY

Poverty was not limited to the Chinese or the blacks. According to one estimate, there were in 1876 in New York alone some 20,000 to 30,000 "homeless, vagrant youth" and 60,000 persons over age ten who could not even write their names.

"Americans have been accustomed to assume that in a country like our own, whose undeveloped resources are so far in advance of its population, the enigmas of pauperism, as they are propounded in the Old World, can never present themselves," wrote a reporter in *Harper's Weekly* in January 1876. "Yet the unprecedented severity of the weather during the last winter, the stagnation of business throughout the whole year, and the frequent strikes among the laboring classes have entailed upon certain portions of the community an amount of suffering, distress, and poverty hitherto unknown in our prosperous land."

The *Herald* headlined: INCREASING NUMBER OF THE CITY'S DESTITUTE. Some of the poor were tramps, "indolent vagrants, filthy, good-for-nothing creatures." But

Five Points, c. 1876: Probably the Poorest Section of New York

The Streets of New York—Running the Gauntlet of Horrors

Chicago—Interior of the Cincinnati Soup-House, on Peoria Street

many of the poor were honest men who could not find a job. "The number of mechanics in desperate want is assuming an alarming magnitude from day to day," said the *Herald* in December 1876.

A mechanic who was interviewed said, "There is no prospect for work this winter...wages have been reduced, rents have not been; work has not been steady but the costs of the necessities of life has been just the same."

Another worker interviewed on the streets by a *Herald* reporter in December 1876 said, "The city government should give us work...we are treated as if we could live on air. There hasn't been a solitary thing done for the working classes by public officials." All Americans seemed to agree that in the land of progress there should not be poverty. What they could not agree on was its cause. For some, the immigrants remained the prime scapegoat.

The Hearth-Stone of the Poor, *Harper's Weekly, February 1876*

ALIEN PAUPERS

New York State was even in 1876 bearing the tax burden for a disproportionately large number of aliens.

The Eighth Annual Report of the State Board of Charities for the State of New York in 1875 showed that:

By the census of 1870 it will be seen that the foreign-born inhabitants of New York were 1,138,353, or a trifle over one-third of the whole population of the State. But we find that of the paupers supported in poor-houses by taxation for the six years from 1868 to 1873 inclusive, sixty-four percent, or about two-thirds are of foreign birth....

It may be well to inquire how far foreign governments assist their criminal and pauper population to migrate to our country, and also into the extent of their obligation to support their subjects now dependent on the State of New York for maintenance. Regarding those who have become naturalized citizens, there can be no question. These have repudiated their allegiance to the land of their birth, and have assumed the duties, and are entitled to the privileges, of American citizens. For all such we are, of course, bound to provide, if they become poor. But a very large portion of the foreign-born inmates of our poor-houses and insane asylums have never been naturalized, are still aliens. Upon whom then does the obligation to maintain such paupers rest?...A large proportion of the emigrant paupers seem to remain in New York, while the more vigorous and prudent emigrants leave without delay for the western States...

The Irish suffered more than other alien groups in New York. One contemporary report analyzed their plight:

The statistics of the Irish in New York City are worth examining closely, as through them we can best decipher their social and physical condition...According to the census of 1876, the population of New York was 942,292, composed of 523,198, or 55.5 per cent, native Americans; 202,000, or 21.4 per cent, Irish; 151,000, or 16.1 per cent, Germans; and 32,000, or 3 per cent, English, Welsh, and Scotch. The balance comprised all other nationalities.

Of this population there are engaged at common drudgery of the severest and worst-paid kind, 50 per cent of Irish; 20 per cent of native Americans; 16 per cent of Germans; 14 per cent of English, etc.

At the best of times this class of toilers can barely live. A dull season, a severe winter, throws at least one-fourth of them out of employment...

To prove that this degrading servitude and poverty is grinding the life and manhood out of the Irish New Yorker, and that a process of extinction is in active operation, we have only to consult the statistics of the city.

The deaths in New York City for the quarter ending March 31, 1877, were 5,986. Of these, 1,239 were Irish-born, giving an annual death-rate of 24.50 per thousand; and 593 were of German birth, giving an annual death-rate for them of 15.7 per thousand...

The poor food and excessive toil has also its bad effects on the American-born children of Irish parents. For the three months ending March 31, 1877, in New York, 1,218 children were born to Irish fathers,

The catfish woman.

The pepper pot woman

Philadelphia Street Characters
"As things now exist in The States, what is more terrible, more alarming, than the total want of any...fusion and mutuality of love, belief and rapport of interest, between the comparatively few successful rich, and the great masses of the unsuccessful poor?"
Walt Whitman, *Songs for the Centennial*, 1876

Most of the police force was Irish in 1876. Although there was much anti-Irish feeling in America in the 1870's, Philip Baguenal reported that:

"The more modern Americans, however, have accepted facts, and...have turned the Irish population to good advantage. They manipulate Irish nationality, flatter Irish pride, and 'scoop' the Irish vote with the same aptness that they corner wheat in Chicago or 'utilize the margin' on the New York Stock Exchange."

but in the same time there were 1,013 deaths, or 83 per cent of the births, of American children having Irish fathers...so that in New York we find the Irish dying faster than any others, less given to marriage than any others, and more given to hard work and fasting than any others.

As long as 50 per cent of the Irish are poorly paid and ill-fed drudges, so long will they be intemperate, for intemperance is often an effect of poverty as well as a cause. And in proportion as they are intemperate will they be disturbers of law and order. Their poverty will keep them from marrying, and, when combined with severe toil will bring them an early grave.

TENEMENT HOUSE LIFE

The Irish and other urban poor were crowded together in tenement houses. The worst were in New York. On December 3, 1876, the *New York Times* reported:

The truth is that in no city of the civilized world does this terrible evil and cause of disease and crime exist in nearly the same degree as in New York...In the Eleventh Ward, where so large a German population lives, near East Houston Street....there are 196,510 [people] to the square mile, so each person has sixteen and one-tenth square yards for his...space for living...Portions of particular wards are even worse....

And this especially accounts for the mortality as of a pestilence which desolates the juvenile population of our crowded quarters every summer—children dying every July and August at the rate of 1,000 per week...From the nearly 20,000 tenement houses come 93 per cent of the deaths and 90 per cent of the crimes of our population...

CONSEQUENCES OF OVERCROWDING

Overcrowding was thought to be a cause of crime. A *Times* reporter wrote in December of 1876 that:

Inevitably crime grows from such rank soil... The young cannot abide such homes and continually leave them to swell the ranks of homeless children. Even where there is no criminality, no home life is possible in such dens...

Tenement Life in New York
Harper's Weekly *reported in 1876 that "half a million men, women, and children are living in the tenement houses of New York today, many of them in a manner that would almost disgrace heathendom itself. No brush could paint and no pencil describe with all the vividness of the truth itself the utter wretchedness and misery, the vice and crime, that may be found within a stone's throw of our City Hall, and even within an arm's length of many of our churches. A keen observer said recently to a friend, while passing through one of these densely crowded localities, notorious for its crimes as well as for its poverty, 'If you were to cut out one square mile of this territory and hand it over to the devil, no one could dispute his title to the property!'"*

A POSSIBLE REMEDY

The remedy to overcrowding was thought to be "model tenement houses," but the *Times* warned, in the utilitarian spirit of the age: "for a model house to be successful, it must be...profitable, yielding six or seven percent..."

Tenement Life in New York
"Gotham Court," on Cherry Street, [is] the first great tenement-house ever built in this city. Forty years ago it was erected, and that was the beginning of the iniquitous system of making big houses and crowding them from cellar to roof with the unfortunate poor....

"Passing into the nearest hallway on the ground floor, and opening a side door, the visitor gets his first view of a room in the big house. The odor that greets his nose is worse than that of a horse-car on a warm wet morning with a full load of steaming passengers and all the ventilators closed. Ten by fourteen feet is the floor measurement, and barely seven feet the height of the ceiling. Opening out of this is a little side bedroom just as long but only half as wide as the main apartment. The ceiling and walls are as black as the worst of those in "Bottle Alley," and the uncarpeted floor is sadly in need of a thorough scrubbing. There is very little furniture, and that of the meanest kind and very dirty. A stove, a table, a few chairs, a mantel crowded with cheap ornaments, a colored picture or two on the walls, are all that is seen in the outer room. In the inner apartment are two bedsteads, supplied with bedding soiled beyond the possibility of finding out its original colors. How any one can lie down upon it and sleep is a mystery to one who is used to clean, sweet linen and a well-aired mattress. Into these lower rooms the sunlight hardly ever enters, being shut out by the high walls on the opposite side of the narrow court, and at noon on a cloudy day it is as dark as early evening elsewhere."
Harper's Weekly, March 1879

The brutal master punishing the little slave for not earning seventy-five cents during the day with his violin.

Albany Orphan Asylum, Albany, N.Y., c. 1876
This institution had accommodations for about two hundred and fifty children: "The trustees desire to extend the benefits of the Home to as many homeless little ones from 3 to 12 years of age as their accommodations will allow and means permit...These children are received on orders from county and town officials at a very small charge."

The Dining Room—Albany Orphan Asylum
One reformer protested that "...institutions which are founded for the benefit of children become hotbeds for the propagation of disease...there is no classification in the wards, and pneumonia, measles [and] scarlet fever...rage side by side...."

CHILDREN OF THE POOR

The life of the children of the poor was appalling. Many children had no home and no place to sleep. *Harper's Weekly* reported on February 12, 1876:

Everyone who has passed late of a cold winter night through the streets of lower New York must have observed the groups of thinly clad, shivering boys huddled over the sidewalk gratings in front of buildings where steam is used. The writer was passing the *World* office one cold winter morning, just before the hour for going to press, and noticed a little newsboy curled up, fast-asleep, on one of the gratings. A companion was walking up and down, his hands in his pockets, his head shrunk down between his shoulders, and his whole air betokening patient endurance of the biting cold. Just then the Trinity Church clock struck the hour of three. "Wake up, Bill," said the lad who was walking, giving the sleeper a gentle push with his foot; "wake up; it's my turn now." The boy uncurled himself slowly, got up without a word, and began walking back and forth, while his companion, with an expressive "Golly! ain't I cold!" took his place on the grating and was fast asleep in half a minute....

The poor street children, girls and boys together, take comfort at these free hearth-stones—rather cold comfort, think the warmly dressed children who look at them in passing; but the waifs evidently enjoy themselves, and are not disturbed by envious feelings.

Study Room—Albany Orphan Asylum

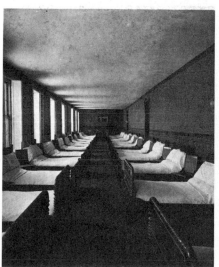

Sleeping Accomodations—Albany Orphan Asylum

Visitors to the Randall's Island Nursery, where conditions were not as good as in the Albany Asylum, described the appalling conditions:

"Found the nurse and prison helpers all away, and a crippled dwarf the sole attendant...The children in one ward had been without any care for several hours, until a Roman Catholic priest notified the matron of the fact....

"...Wards Nos. 4 and 5 of the Nursery Hospital in a deplorable state. Some of the children were ill in bed, and two very ignorant prison women had the care of them. The nurse had gone about a week before....

"...The children are practically in charge of prisoners and pauper women....In the hospitals the ignorance and incapacity of the paid nurses are painfully evident, and in their absence the prison women...are left in sole charge."

One writer observed in 1876 in *Harper's Weekly* that "as a nation we have been profuse in our provision for the relief of suffering humanity, but we have not studied as we ought the means of reaching and eradicating its causes. European literature is rich upon the subject but we do not recall a single systematic treatise on pauperism that has been issued from the American press." The writer did not have long to wait. The following year Richard Dugdale published *The Jukes*, which had a profound influence on the social thinkers of the day. Dugdale wrote:

Pauperism is an indication of weakness at some essential point...It rests chiefly upon disease...and may be called the sociological aspect of physical degeneration. The debility and diseases which enter most largely into the production of pauperism are the result of sexual licentiousness...an hereditary tendency...

Crime, as compared to pauperism, is an indication of vigor...For this reason there is a greater chance for reform in the criminal than there is in the pauper...

Dugdale drew his conclusions from his study of the Juke family, in which 17 out of 29 living males were criminals.

Christmas Dinner for Newsboys

"Mr. James Gordon Bennett, of the *Herald*, did a most kindly and generous act on last Christmas-day, by giving to the newsboys and newsgirls of this city, some twelve hundred in number, without distinction in regard to the journals vended by them, an excellent dinner at Moquin's restaurant, in Ann Street. The urchins were divided into squads of about 200 each, admitted at different hours according to the color of their tickets, and were served with a plentiful meal of roast turkey, potatoes, French rolls, cakes, oranges, and coffee. Twenty waiters... attended to the wants of the juveniles, a street band of Italian harpists and violinists the while enlivening the proceedings with popular melodies. It was in every sense of the word an unceremonious banquet. Immediately upon taking their seats, every boy, as if moved by single impulse, ate the dessert first, pocketed the oranges and apples, and sometimes attempted to lay violent hands on the delicacies of his immediate neighbor. The little people, as may well be imagined, were in high spirits. They cheered the generous provider of the feast, and sang the 'Mulligan Guards,' 'Down in a Coal Mine,' the 'Red, White, and Blue,' and other popular songs, with the expression and feeling peculiar to New York *gamins*."

Harper's Weekly, January 1876

Christmas in a Home for the Poor

The family was not an immigrant family but was descended from early Dutch settlers of this country. Out of 168 women in the family, 84, or 52 percent, had become "harlots." Dugdale concluded from these statistics that:

> It would seem that chastity and profligacy are hereditary characteristics, possible of entailment...In most cases the heredity is also accompanied by an environment which runs parallel to it, the two conditions giving cumulative force to a career of debauch.

CHARITY

It was difficult to change heredity, but if certain environments contributed to making men into paupers and criminals, then it was important to make an attempt to change the environments in question. Dugdale advocated education, early marriage, and industrial training. It was possible for men to accumulate enormous fortunes in 1876; it seemed equally possible to eradicate poverty. For that matter, anything seemed possible in the 1870's. Thus, charity was important not only as a form of *noblesse oblige* but as a means of eradicating poverty and proving that there were no limits to what industrious men could do.

Inmates of the Poor-House on Randall's Island, East River, at New York City, Forming in Line for Dinner

METHODS OF CHARITY

Charity should try to "cure" poverty and help eradicate it if possible. *Harper's Weekly* in 1876 said:

A great amount of suffering exists which it is an imperative duty to alleviate... The relief offered... should be so judiciously administered as not only to ameliorate present suffering, but, as far as possible, reduce the number of those who require aid...Different methods of relieving the poor can be generally divided into two plans. One is to care for them in buildings erected and set apart for the purpose; and the other, furnishing relief to them in their own homes. Both of these systems are a draft upon the productive industry of those members of the community that are able and willing to labor. This draft ought...to be reduced to the smallest amount consistent with the relief of such persons as are really necessitous.

THE DESERVING AND THE UNDESERVING

The undeserving poor were considered to be criminals by this *Harper's Weekly* writer and others of the time:

It is only in times of extraordinary commercial disaster, throwing large numbers out of employment, that healthy men and women can be justified in seeking charity. Persons of sound mind, good health, and virtuous habits are very seldom driven to seek such relief...There is a large class of idle vagabonds who pass from county to county, and during the winter season, or when ill, settle down in those poorhouses which in their travels they find most agreeable and well kept. The policy of the law should be to treat as criminals those who levy upon the public for support while able to earn their own living.

There should also be a sharp distinction made between the treatment of those paupers who have become such by their own criminal choice, and others who are reduced to this level by no fault of their own. The time has arrived when it is imperatively necessary to

Prison Life at "Blackwell's Island"
In the drawing on the top, explained *Harper's Weekly:*

"We see the prisoners...marching to their meals, and taking bread, which is served out to them as they pass, by a convict, from a large basket. In the second sketch they are returning to their cells after the meal. Each prisoner, as the men pass along in single file, deposits his spoon in a receptacle provided for that purpose."

Charles Loring Brace, an authority on poverty in the 1870's, blamed the immigrants for a large amount of the crime in New York. Of 49,923 prisoners in New York jails (in 1872), 32,225 were of foreign birth. If Americans, like Brace, could blame foreigners for crime, they could maintain their own innocence and virtue.

The House of Correction in Detroit, c. 1876

Harper's Weekly reported in 1876 that "...justice is neither swift nor sure in New York, and it is certainly a disgrace to our city that law is to such an extent only a name. During the five years ending December, 1875, there were 281 homicides in the city most of which were murders of an unmistakable character. Only seven of the murderers have suffered death by the law; twenty-four have been imprisoned for life; some have received mild sentences; some have been discharged or have escaped; and more than one-fourth the entire number have never been brought to trial at all, but have escaped without any punishment."

Interior of "the Tombs," a New York Jail

Mark Twain described a cell in "the Tombs": "The cell might be eight feet by ten square, perhaps a little longer. It was of stone, floor and all, and the roof was oven shaped. A narrow slit in the roof admitted sufficient light, and was the only means of ventilation; when the window was open there was nothing to prevent the rain coming in. The only means of heating being from the corridor, when the door was ajar, the cell was chilly and damp. It was whitewashed and clean, but it had a slight jail odor; its only furniture was a narrow iron bedstead, with a tick of straw and some blankets, not too clean."

make the laws more stringent in their application to vagabonds and professional beggars...

CHARITY FOR CHILDREN

Charity for children was considered especially important. It was hoped that removing children from inappropriate environments would teach them industrious habits and prevent them from growing up as criminals or paupers. On January 29, 1876, a writer in *Harper's Weekly* explained:

One of the first objects of intelligent philanthropists...is to prevent hereditary pauperism and crime. It is ascertained that children are born paupers and grow up paupers, with no thought or purpose of following any industry whatever, and that this class is increasing rapidly. Obviously one effective method of dealing with this evil at its source is the removal of children from the society of those who are both idle and criminal, and teaching them to know that he who will not work must starve...

PRISONS

Prisons were as important as any charity; the hope was that criminals might be reformed. Richard Dugdale said that reformatories should be modeled on kindergartens, "for the youth of this class...are moral infants." It was widely believed that criminals should and could be taught industrious habits. Elisha Harris, secretary of the Prison Association of New York, a reformist group, wrote in his introduction to *The Jukes*:

Out of the same social soil from which spring the majority of criminals, there also chiefly grow up the vagrants and the paupers, the ignorant, vicious and incapable classes which annoy and burden the community.

The American prison system should be the best in the world if the country was going to erase poverty. But one reporter complained in February 1876 that the prison system in the United States was not as good as those in Europe:

The investigation into the condition and management of the State prisons and penitentiaries of this State will not begin a moment too soon. Governor Tilden has done well in calling attention to the subject, for a thorough examination will unquestionably reveal evils which should be promptly and radically corrected.

The reporter felt, in the true Gilded Age spirit, that "good" jails like "good" tenement houses should be, if not a profitable business, at least not a losing proposition financially.

FACTORY LIFE

For those lucky enough not to be out of work, factory conditions were far from ideal. Skilled workers, who had earned $3.50 to $5 per day in 1873, in 1876 had their wages reduced to between $1.50 and $2. Unskilled laborers received only $1 per day. Nevertheless, the *New York Times* chided workers for not accepting wage reductions necessitated by the 1873 Panic: why should skilled laborers who "earned liberal wages...sullenly refuse to accept any reduction...It seems almost incredible that men should be capable of such blind folly."

CHILD LABOR

In 1876 Massachusetts passed a child-labor law, but child-labor laws were not enforced and had no effect until many years later. Thus, in 1876, children worked long, hard days and were often involved in very dangerous work. *Harper's Weekly* stated:

Recent legislation in Massachusetts has introduced new regulations for protecting young children from overwork or neglect in factories and workshops. A law which went into operation last March [1876] forbade, under a penalty of from twenty to fifty dollars, the employment in any manufacturing, mechanical, or mercantile establishment of children under ten years of age at all, and of children under fourteen, unless during the preceeding year the child has attended school at least ten consecutive weeks.

"Bell-Time," by Winslow Homer, 1868, shows women, children and men leaving the mills in Lawrence, Massachusetts, at the end of their fourteen-hour day.

John F. Weir, *Forging the Shaft*, 1877
"When a workman was injured in shop, mine, or on the railroad, the claim agent of the employing company would at once present himself with an instrument of agreement for the injured man and his wife, if he had one, to sign," wrote Terence Powderly. "By the terms of this instrument the company would be released from all responsibility in consideration of the payment of a few dollars. Let me tell you of one such case out of the hundreds I witnessed. A coal miner, a neighbor of mine, had his back injured through a fall of rock in the darkness of the mine. The claim agent called to see him; he asked for time to consider and sent for me. He had a wife and children, his means were meager. I advised against signing a release, and here is what he said: 'I am buying this house from the company. If I don't sign this release, I can never get a days' work under that company or any other round here, for if I get well I'll be blacklisted. When my next payment on the house falls due, or the interest is not paid we'll be thrown out on the street. With no work, no money, no friends, what will my wife and my babies do?'..."

A Hat Factory, c. 1876

Putnam Machine Company's Shop, Fitchburg, Massachusetts, c. 1876

LABOR ORGANIZES

We have observed the life of the poor in the country, in the city and in factories. We will now briefly look at some of the attempts by laborers in the 1870's to better their bleak lot. In spite of a drop in the membership of the Cigarmakers' Union to a mere 500 members by the end of 1875, Samuel Gompers persisted in his efforts to organize skilled labor. He wrote in his autobiography:

Despite discouragements, our effort to organize the cigarmakers kept bravely on. We held mass meetings regularly and kept up educational work by means of talks and circulars which we had printed in German, Bohemian, and English. The slogans we raised for the guidance of all were: "Unions for all working people." "Reduce the hours of work." "Bring the worst paid workers to the level of the highest." It was hard work and it was heart-breaking,...for many that belonged to our trade had been out of work from three to twelve months. Hard as that situation was, we knew that the only permanent remedy was organization.

Thomas Nast, "Rules of Trades Unions"
Nast's sympathy lay with the hard-working employer, not with the rising labor movement whose demands are pictured on the wall of the employer's office. A writer in the Atlantic Monthly *explained the labor struggle of the 1870's through the eyes of management:*
"When we consider the enormous shrinkage that has taken place in the value of almost all kinds of property...we see no evidence that labor has suffered disproportionately to other interests...It is divinely ordained that man, in common with other animate beings, shall struggle for existence...the relations of capital and labor must necessarily conform to the divine scheme...."

THE EIGHT-HOUR DAY

The movement for an eight-hour working day was one of the first successful efforts at organization by labor in this country. The eight-hour law, passed by Congress in 1868, called eight hours "a day's work for all laborers, workmen and mechanics...employed by or on behalf of the government of the United States." But the law was never enforced. There was a series of strikes in 1872 to secure enforcement of the law, but the strikes were a failure. By 1880 the law was a dead letter. But Eight Hours Leagues continued to urge acceptance of the eight-hour day; the members of these Leagues were often much more radical than the members of the more conservative Knights of Labor.

The National Eight Hour Law signed into Law by President Grant in 1869: The Law was not Enforced.

Franklin B. Gowen
Gowen, owner of the Reading Coal and Iron Company, and prosecutor at the trial of the Molly Maguires.

Allan Pinkerton
Pinkerton's agency rose to fame after Pinkerton detective McParlan's disclosures; the Pinkerton agency was called in to break many later strikes after its "triumph" in the Molly case.

THE MOLLY MAGUIRES

The Molly Maguires represented another important attempt by labor to organize in the 1870's. The Mollies were Irish workers in the anthracite coal fields of Pennsylvania who were accused of murdering their superiors. After a series of unsolved murders and crimes in the coal fields, Mr. Franklin B. Gowen, president of the Reading Coal and Iron Company, hired the Pinkerton Detective Agency to break up the Mollies. According to Allan Pinkerton's self-serving and biased account, Gowen said:

The coal regions are infested by a most desperate class of men, banded together for the worst purposes—called, by some, the Buckshots, by others, the Molly Maguires—and they are making sad havoc with the country. It is a secret organization, has its meetings in hidden and out-of-the way places, and its members, I have been convinced...are guilty of a majority of all the murders and other deeds of outrage which for many years, have been committed in the neighborhood. I wish you to investigate this mysterious order, find out its interior workings, [and] expose its evil transactions...

Pinkerton did expose the so-called Mollies, by having his agent James McParlan infiltrate their ranks and produce enough evidence to hang twenty supposed members of

After The Explosion
Frank Leslie's Popular Monthly *reported that:*
"There are employed in the anthracite region about 30,000 miners, and the loss of life from accidents incident to the business shows but a very small percentage. It is the terrible nature of the casualties, when they do occur, that awakens such widespread sympathy, and causes the occupation to be looked upon with dread."

the group for killing Gowen's mine supervisors. Whether these men were guilty or not has never been determined. What is certain is that McParlan's success was the foundation on which the future of the Pinkerton Agency was built. The agency's continuing involvement in strikebreaking made its name a household word.

In opposition to Gowen's view, the New York *Tribune* suggested that the Mollies had organized not "for the worst purposes" but to try to alleviate some of the dreadful conditions in the coal fields:

It should be remembered...that the Molly Maguires were originally a band of decent men leagued together for political, partly for beneficiary motives, certainly not for robbery and murder. They belong to a people quick-witted, affectionate, devout. Yet they have sunk into brutes, because no adequate effort has been made to keep them human. Nobody who has seen the coal miner close at hand can wonder that the utter stagnation and misery of his life makes whiskey or crime a relief to it. He lives and breathes in the coal, eats his salt pork, sleeps like the pigs, goes to work in the coal again. A few hardened ruffians thrown out of employment when the war closed found here good material to manipulate. Hence the Mollies and their murders. It is time they were manipulated differently.

A CATHOLIC PRIEST SPOKE IN FAVOR OF HIS IRISH CONSTITUENTS

Father McDermott, who lived in the area of the anthracite coal fields, felt that the Irish had been badly mistreated and were acting out of resentment:

The operators and bosses were mostly anti-Catholic and anti-Irish. They were opposed to giving the Irish-Catholic any alternative except to leave the region or to become a hewer of wood and a drawer of water for others.

THE TRIAL

The first trial of the Mollies was held in May of 1876. Gowen himself was the prosecutor, with his aide, Colonel Albright, standing beside him in full military dress.

Gowen, knowing the Irish dislike of informers, feared—correctly—that Irish women would swear falsely in court to protect their kinsmen. His attempt to stop them from providing false alibis by putting two priests in the courtroom was a failure. Gowen wrote:

We know from our detectives...that arrangements have been made to procure quite a number of people, including many women, to swear to an *alibi* which is of course entirely false...

It has struck me that possibly the presence in court of the parish priests known to these women as their pastors might have some restraining influence upon them...

James McParlan
James McParlan: the infiltrator of the Molly Maguires known as McKenna. McParlan remained a Pinkerton agent for the rest of his life. He became head of the Pinkerton office in Denver. In 1907 Clarence Darrow caught him perjuring himself against "Big Bill Haywood" and the Western Federation of Miners in the Steubenberg case.

James Kerrigan
A Molly who turned state's evidence

McParlan Infiltrates the Mollies

James McParlan, a Pinkerton detective, infiltrated the Molly Maguires under the pseudonym of James McKenna. Here we see his initiation into the Mollies.

House of Molly Leader

The house of the supposed leader of the Molly Maguires, John Kehoe, who was a saloonkeeper. Kehoe, who was also a Democratic high constable, helped defeat Judge Cyrus Pershing for governor in 1875. Pershing, Gowen's candidate, later presided at Kehoe's trial and convicted him.

One of the crimes of which the Mollies were accused: The murder of Gomer James while he was bartending at a picnic near Shenandoah, August 14, 1875.

Gomer James had previously murdered Edward Cosgrove, an Irishman, in 1873. At the trial of the Mollies, F. W. Hughes, Counsel for the Commonwealth, said: "Our desire is to get rid of the Molly Maguires. We regard their organization as the greatest curse that ever fell upon civilized, organized society in this country, and I may, perhaps, be overzealous in the invocation of the influence and forces which all good men should exercise for the purpose of getting rid of this great sin, this moral and social evil."

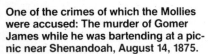

The prosecution said to the jury that the purpose of the Mollies was:

...to get the benefit of and use and enjoy the property of others without owning it, and without paying for it. The purpose was to make the business of mining coal in this country a terror...The purpose was to levy blackmail upon every man engaged in industrial pursuits in this country...

IN REPLY TO GOWEN, THE DEFENSE DENOUNCED McPARLAN, THE INFILTRATOR

Defense attorneys L'Velle and John Ryon claimed that

Murder of Thomas Sanger and William Uren at Raven Run, September 1, 1875:
Sanger was a mine boss and Uren a young miner who lived with the Sangers. A series of murders like this one attributed to the Mollies in the 1860's and 1870's led the Philadelphia *Enquirer* to say in May 1876 that:

"To recite the outrages of which President Gowen's company and its employes were the victims would be to print a volume of murder, plunder, and incendiarism, which for fiendish violence, would read like a romance...Scarce a day passed without its blood-curdling tragedy...Breakers were fired, store houses robbed, workmen butchered, guards shot, and anarchy reigned supreme."

Another Molly Maguire Crime: The Murder of Mine Superintendent John P. Jones, September 3, 1875.
General Albright, Gowen's aide who appeared at the Molly trial in full military dress, said:

"It is almost inconceivable how this bad society has injured...every property-owner in the coal region...you can see how capital, how property, how life, how everything has been imperiled...in consequence the business of this particular community was about being surrendered to lawless and desperate men...."

Another Crime
Attack on "Bully Bill" Thomas, June 28, 1875. Another "attack" of which the Mollies were accused.

McParlan's main aim was to make himself famous, and they implied that he motivated the Mollies to commit outrages so that he could then turn them in and make himself famous. He did, indeed, turn them in and became head of the branch of the Pinkerton Bureau in Denver, Colorado. Defense attorney L'Velle said of McParlan:

He was their leader, their guide, and their general. He was the man who had the cash to supply the whiskey and fire the brain of these poor, susceptible, youthful enthusiasts...From the time that he came into Schuylkill County until he left it, has not crime been increasing?

McParlan Exposed
McParlan discovered: He flees.

The Trial
The trial: McParlan sitting in chair on right waiting to testify.

John Ryon, the other defense attorney, added that he thought McParlan's aim was:

> ...to make himself a great detective...[to do so] he has to make some great and startling disclosures. It could not be done unless some lives were lost, some outrages committed.

MRS. KERRIGAN, THE DEFENSE STAR WITNESS, TESTIFIED AGAINST HER HUSBAND, WHO TURNED "STATE'S EVIDENCE"

Mrs. Kerrigan told the court that on the night of the killing of policeman Yost, her husband went out with a pistol and returned home to tell her that he had killed Yost. Gowen asked her why she had not visited Mr. Kerrigan since his arrest for the crime:

> Mrs. Kerrigan: Because any man that done such a crime as that—that done such a crime that he done, why should I turn around then, and—
> Gowen: And what—go on.
> Mrs. Kerrigan: That is all.

Mrs. Kerrigan did not reveal the true cause of her antipathy—the dislike she and all Irish men and women felt for informers like her husband.

AUGUST 22, 1876: THE MOLLIES FOUND GUILTY

Pat Butler, one of the Mollies, confessed under cross-examination. The jury handed down a verdict of guilty after debating only fifteen minutes. The *Times*, which had no sympathy for the Mollies, condemned workingmen who attended a mass meeting to protest the sentences: "There was no pretense that the convicted men were innocent of the frightful crimes...The plea...was that they had been oppressed by a rich monopoly." The *Times* called the Mollies "monsters" for whom "murder is a trivial proceeding for their own convenience."

TEN MOLLIES HANGED IN ONE DAY: JUNE 21, 1877

Frank Leslie's Illustrated Monthly anticipated the hanging:

The execution of ten murderers, members of the defunct organization of Molly Maguires, in Pennsylvania on Thursday, the 21st of the present month, will be one of the most extraordinary events in the criminal history of the state. Six of the murderers will be hung simultaneously at Pottsville and four at Mauk Church in which places they were tried and convicted...

[James Boyle, James Rairty, Hugh McGehan, James Caroll and Thomas Duffy] were convicted of the murder of Benjamin F. Yost which occurred on the 6th of July 1875. Yost was a police officer...He had given the murderers no provocation except that on one occasion he had arrested Duffy for an infraction of the peace.

Luckily for the cause of justice, it so happened that one of the Mollies named Jimmy Kerrigan was arrested for the murder of John P. Jones whereupon he made a full statement implicating all the accused...

In all [the] cases the secret workings of the Molly Maguire Order were exposed by the testimony of McParlan, the Pinkerton detective...

[Under the name of James McKenna] he was initiated into Shenandoah division of the Molly Maguires and soon became its secretary, and it was in that way that he was enabled almost daily to send transcripts of their secret proceedings to Detective Franklin in Philadelphia.

THE IRISH WORLD EXPRESSED SHOCK AND OUTRAGE

Drive a rat into a corner and he will fight. Drive your serfs to desperation, you grinding monopolists, chain them in enforced idleness half the year and lash them with the whip of hunger to work at semi-starvation wages—semi-starvation for themselves and their little ones...and in their desperation they will some day pounce upon you and destroy you!

The Mollies were hanged, Gowen, Pinkerton and McParlan had triumphed.

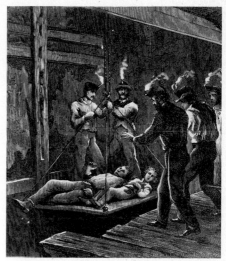

Bodies of Victims of a Mine Disaster
Frank Leslie's Popular Monthly called the Molly Maguires a greater danger to miners than accidents in the mines:

"The danger in the occupation is not so much from accident in the mine as from the wicked combinations of men in the secret order of 'Molly Maguire.'

"According to Detective McParlan, a man of the most wonderful nerve and courage, there has, for long years, existed among the workmen at the mines a regularly organized society or order, numbering, it is said, fully eight hundred members, in which murder and arson were deliberately planned and carried into execution by oathbound members, chosen by lot for the special service.

"The evidence taken in the trial of 'Molly Maguire' murderers at Pottsville, Pa., in May, 1876, exhibited a most alarming state of affairs in the coal regions, and it is believed that the disclosures there made will serve to break up the desperate gangs, and enable the steady and honest miners to pursue their callings without fear of an enemy more dangerous than fire-damp or explosions in the subterranean shafts and galleries."

Peter Cooper: The Greenback Candidate for President in 1876.

Samuel Gompers, the immigrant son of a cigar worker, organized the cigar workers and later became president of the American Federation of Labor.

PETER COOPER FOR PRESIDENT

In the election of 1876, workingmen had their own candidate, Peter Cooper, who ran on the Greenback ticket and received 80,000 votes. Cooper was most certainly not a member of the working force; he was a philanthropist who had made a fortune from iron. "I have always recognized that the object of business is to make money in an honorable manner; I have endeavored to remember that the object of life is to do good," he said.

Samuel Gompers (in his autobiography) described Peter Cooper and the growing Greenback party of 1876, which advocated "soft money," or "greenbacks," as opposed to the resumption of specie payment advocated by Republicans:

The year 1876 found the ranks of the Cigarmaker's Union of New York almost depleted. Our membership had fallen to 1,200 by 1875, and the strike of that year brought the total down to 500. Our wages averaged about twelve dollars a week.

It was this serious industrial situation which gave the greenback its popularity as an issue. The government was trying to get away from cheap money conditions. But wage-earners generally saw in contraction an elimination of money that served our purposes. We could not forget the relations between the Grant Administration and the "gold corner" which have never been satisfactorily explained. We thought the government had entered into an unholy alliance with the goldbugs who to us represented the unscrupulous Wall Street exploiters. In January, 1876, when Congress had about completed legislation which was a step toward the resumption of specie payments, we held in Cooper Union a big protest meeting over which Peter Cooper presided. He was a wonderful old man, the picture of beneficence and humanitarianism. He gave a tremendous presentation of the point of view of the non-banking world and the wage-earners who wanted to pay the national debt in greenbacks and to make treasury notes legal tender convertible into U.S. bonds....

As the labor unions began to lose numbers and power, wage-earners turned to political propaganda.... Peter Cooper was nominated for the presidency on a platform which demanded the repeal of the Specie Payment Act. I cast my second presidential vote for Peter Cooper, as did practically all the wage-earners of New York.

DESPERATE CONDITIONS FOR WORKINGMEN GROW STEADILY WORSE

Gompers described the deteriorating situation:

During the summer of 1876 the unemployment situation grew steadily worse. A feeling of desperation was growing as week after week slipped by and still the unemployed had no dependable means of earning a livelihood...

In the fall of 1876, the seemingly impossible happened. Wages were again reduced and working forces decreased. In December about two-thirds of the shops closed entirely, to remain closed until sometime in January. The others dismissed more than half their men and reduced wages. There were between five and six thousand cigarmakers idle in New York City. Consider for a minute the families dependent on these wage-earners and there develops a picture of misery and want that made the Christmas season of 1876 one that long haunted our memories.

GOMPERS URGED THE WORKERS TO UNITE

All who are present today should be convinced that our condition is growing worse every day and that the future is threatened with danger. Who can deny that reductions are almost daily occurrences because the capitalist's only ambition is profit? The time has come when we must assert our rights as workingmen. Everyone present knows from sad experience that we are powerless in an isolated condition while the capitalists are united.

VIOLENT RAILROAD STRIKES OF 1877

The crash that broke the months of strain [Gompers wrote] came in the revolt of the railroad workers in July, 1877. That was in the pioneer period of railroading...The railway unions were but fledglings. In fierce competitive fights, railroad managements cut passenger and freight rates far below the maintenance level. They were preparing to shift the resulting losses upon their employees by wage cuts. In 1873, wages of railroad workers had been reduced by ten per cent; a similar wage reduction was announced for June 1, 1877. Railroad officials had organized and united upon a uniform policy. They did not even consider consultation with their employees. Although both employment and pay on the railroads were irregular, unemployment was general in all other lines of work, and railroad workers were obliged either to accept conditions, bad as they were, or join the already large ranks of tramps.

The Great Strike—Burning of the Round-House at Pittsburgh
The railroad strikes of 1877 produced America's first Red Scare:

"The fact is clearly manifest that communistic ideas are very widely entertained in America by the workmen employed in mines and factories and by the railroads," said the *National Republican* on July 21, 1877. "This poison was introduced into our social system by European laborers."

The Sixth Regiment Firing Upon a Mob of Workers Striking the Baltimore & Ohio Railroad on July 20, 1877
The railroad strikes of 1877 began in Martinsburg, West Virginia, where ''Peter Zell and the employees of the Baltimore and Ohio Railroad who acted with him...complained of non-employment for two or three days in the week. The nominal wages of firemen and brakemen were, they contended $1.35–$1.50 per day, while the poorer workmen did not average more than 75 or 90 cents per day.''
Frank Leslie's Illustrated Newspaper, August 1877

Made desperate by this accumulation of miseries, without organizations strong enough to conduct a successful strike, the railway workers rebelled...The railroad strike of 1877 was the tocsin that sounded a ringing message of hope to us all.

The railroad rebellion was spontaneous...the only way the workers could secure the attention of employers was through some demonstration of protest in the form of a strike. The strike grew steadily until it surpassed in numbers and importance all previous industrial movements. Strikers and sympathetic workmen crowded into the streets. The New York papers said at the time that so far as the arguments were concerned, the workers had the best of the situation, but that they could not win because of the weakness of the unions...

Long pent-up resentment found vent in destruction. The primitive weapons, fire and violence, were labor's response to arbitrary force.

In New York we were stirred deeply. While we had put our faith in constructive methods, yet the sky of Pittsburgh reddened by fires started by company agents and desperate men denied all other recourse, brought us the message that human aspiration had not been killed or cowed.

KARL MARX SHARED GOMPER'S DELIGHT WITH THE STRIKE

Marx wrote to Friedrich Engels on July 25, 1877:

What do you think of the workers of the United States? This first explosion against the associated oligarchy of capital which has occurred since the Civil War will naturally again be suppressed, but can very well form the point of origin of an earnest workers party...A nice sauce is being stirred over there...

Others did not exhibit the same enthusiasm. The *National Republican* on July 28, 1877, said:

The Great Strike "is nothing less than communism in its worst form...not only unlawful and revolutionary, but anti-American..."

A CALL TO MEET VIOLENCE WITH VIOLENCE

The kindest thing [a journalist wrote in *Harper's Weekly*] which can be done for the great multitudes of untaught men who have been received in these shores, and are daily arriving, and who are torn perhaps even more here than in Europe by wild desires and wilder dreams, is to show them promptly that society as here organized ...is impregnable and can be no more shaken than the order of nature...It would be fatal to private and public credit and security to allow a state of things to subsist in which 8,000 or 9,000 day laborers of the lowest class can suspend, even for a whole day, the traffic and industry of a great nation, merely as a means of extorting ten or twenty cents a day more wages...

President Hayes followed the suggestion, sent troops and quelled the railroad strikes, but not before they had become among the most violent labor disputes in our history.

TERENCE POWDERLY

Terence Powderly was only twenty-seven years old when,

in 1876, he was elected Master Workman of the Knights of Labor. The Knights of Labor became by the end of the 1870's the most important labor organization of its day, and Powderly was its leader from 1879 to 1893. In his autobiography, *The Path I Trod,* Powderly recounted:

A shopmate, in the Cliff Locomotive Works of Scranton, invited me to a "labor lecture" to be given on the evening of September 6, 1876...I...accompanied my friend to the hall and was mystified when we were ushered into a small room and told to wait awhile. Soon after a man wearing a black gown and mask came out to question us. He appeared to be more satisfied with our answers than I was with his appearance, for I had no thought of joining a society of any kind that night.

Local Assembly No. 88 of the Knights of Labor, composed of stationary engineers, was in session. My name had been proposed for membership, acted on favorably, and in the manner described I had been brought forward for initiation...

Local Assembly No. 88 was instituted May 15, 1875, and, being composed of stationary engineers in and around the mines, workmen of other callings were not admitted to membership until the parent body at Philadelphia granted permission to take in miners, laborers, and other classes of workmen in the summer of 1876...Prior to my admission to the Knights of Labor, I had a little time for rest and recreation. After September 6, 1876, I knew no waking hour that I did not devote, in whole or part, to the up-building of the Order....

I never was a reformer and always objected to being called one. If I had the right to give myself a name, I would call it equalizer. The scales didn't tip even, the pendulum didn't swing with steady stroke between capital and labor, between employer and employed. I saw that something was wrong, but didn't realize that long centuries of ownership in men who worked had begotten feelings of caste, pride, intolerance, and even hatred in the breasts of many of the employers of labor in that day...If abuses were to be abolished the workers themselves would have to abolish them. Do it individually they could not. Working shoulder to shoulder in organization, not of one calling but all callings, appeared to me to be the only hope...

"I saw workmen robbed through company stores. I was obliged to submit to being robbed too, and know that I paid exorbitant prices for necessities, in some cases fifty per cent more than I would have paid elsewhere. Injustice in the levying and collection of rents and taxes, filching men's labor through company-store practices, mortgaging the bodies and souls of living men through small pay enforced by the blacklist, and other wrongful acts done the workers by professed Christians without one word of protest against the evils or a word of comfort to the oppressed by Christian ministers or men of influence and standing, convinced me that they who would be free themselves must strike the blow."

Terence Powderly

The 1870's were an era of enormous growth of American enterprise. Railroads spilled out across the country. Steel, coal, oil and other industries expanded rapidly. These industries would be the foundation of the great American fortunes. But this massive capital expansion carried a shadow. In 1879 Henry George posed the question starkly: "So long as all the increased wealth which modern progress brings goes but to build up great fortunes, to increase luxury and make sharper the contrast between the House of Have and the House of Want, progress is not real and cannot be permanent." George indicated the basic problem. Labor challenged the reality of "progress" then, as it has done in every decade since.

THE GREAT FORTUNES
AND THE RISE OF HIGH SOCIETY

There is always a tension between old and new money, but in 1876 this tension was more than usually evident. There were the old American families whose wealth was based on great landholdings and whose style and standards had prevailed until the Civil War. Then there were the very new families, many of them in the Midwest and the West, who were beginning to make their presence felt. Most important were the families that were neither old nor new, who formed a bridge between the traditional style and the raw displays of the newcomers by having access to both the old standards and the new money. This middle group included families like the Astors and the Vanderbilts, not nearly as well established as the Livingstons, the Schuylers or the Van Rensselaers, but rich for three generations and newly mature in social confidence. These families, especially the Astors, would determine the style in which rich Americans would live for the next decade.

**"The William Astor Family,"
by Lucius Rossi, 1878**

The William Astors were in 1876 the top social family in New York. They were painted by Rossi in their very splashy "European" ballroom. All the Astor ladies were dressed for the painting by Worth, the Parisian couturier, and they were sitting on Louis XV furniture.

Caroline Astor is seated with her daughter Carrie on the right, looking far more beautiful than she appeared in real life; William Astor is reading, on the left. Next to him is their daughter Emily, who to her father's great displeasure married James J. Van Alen, on March 14, 1876. (She was given a trust fund of $400,000 at the time of her marriage.) The Van Alens were an old Knickerbocker family, but second-rate in terms of both wealth and social standing. "Damned if I want my family mixed in with the Van Alens," said William Astor. He was more pleased with the marriage of his daughter Helen, pictured standing in the center, to James Roosevelt Roosevelt in November 1878. Helen, too, was given a trust fund of $400,000. Standing on the right behind the couch is young John Jacob Astor IV, who later died on the *Titanic*.

Alexander T. Stewart
The *Times* called A.T. Stewart one of the three richest men in New York City in the mid-1870's, the other two being William B. Astor and Commodore Vanderbilt. Stewart died in April 1876 after a long and successful career.

Commodore Cornelius Vanderbilt
Although John Jacob Astor was dead by 1876, Vanderbilt lived until January 1877.

Business was booming in post–Civil War America, and despite the severe depression which had begun in 1873, the rich and especially the newly rich were accumulating and spending vast fortunes. Gone were the great days of the Livingstons and the Van Rensselaers in New York, the Carrolls in Maryland, and the Byrds in Virginia. These old families had fallen before the spirit of the new age. Describing the scene in Washington which was being repeated in almost every city in the country, John Ellis, in his book *Sights and Secrets of the Nation's Capital* observed, "Fine houses, flashy and showy, sprang up on all sides; the saloons of the city glittered with jewels and rustled with costly fabrics; and magnificent equipages whirled through the streets with a dash that made the 'old citizens' fairly hold their breath. Former social position, good birth, good breeding went for nothing. Money became the standard of social excellence."

In May 1876 the *New York Times* named as "the three great wealthy men of New York": William B. Astor, Alexander T. Stewart and Commodore Cornelius Vanderbilt; of the three, only Vanderbilt still lived. The Astor fortune was based on New York real estate; the urban land passed on by John Jacob Astor to his son, William Backhouse Astor, made the Astor fortune in 1876, according to *Scribner's Monthly Magazine*, "certainly the largest in America, if not in the world." Alexander T. Stewart owned the largest dry-goods store in New York; the *New York Times* of April 11, 1876, said that Stewart had managed by the time of his death in 1876 to amass "the largest fortune ever accumulated within the span of a single life." And Commodore Vanderbilt's enormous fortune, estimated at his death in January 1877 at $100 million, was built largely on railroads. Three fortunes from three distinct new sources of wealth—real estate, commerce and railroads—a perfect paradigm of the new plutocracy.

WILLIAM B. ASTOR

William B. Astor was the main heir to the great properties left by his father, John Jacob Astor, at his death in March 1848. The first Astor's holdings were estimated to be worth about $20 million. John Jacob Astor, a native of Walldorf, Germany, had started life in America in 1784 as the representative of an English manufacturer of musical

"William B. Astor," by Eastman Johnson

Scribner's Monthly *wrote of William B. Astor, who spoke German to his children as his father had to him:*

"Of the late William B. Astor it is said that he used no tobacco and little wine, though when in health...he gave quiet, pleasant dinners. He seldom was out late, did not attend theaters, did not get excited nor indulge in profane adjectives, sported not with dogs and guns, (nor do the two sons who are his principal heirs) never kept a fast horse, never gambled. His whole life was simple and orderly. He could never be induced to 'take the chair' or enter into politics, and had small respect for or confidence in the 'great men' of the period. He minded his own business."

John Jacob Astor I—The Founder of a Dynasty

instruments. By 1785 Astor was already engaged in the fur trade, and in 1809 he had founded the American Fur Company. According to an article published in *Scribner's Magazine* in 1876:

From the time of the establishment of the American Fur Company, Mr. Astor became largely engaged in commerce. His ships freighted with furs for France, England, Germany, and Russia...plowed every sea to receive ..products of the New World, and exchange them for commodities of the Old.

John Jacob Astor was a millionaire by 1830. He made the bulk of his fortune in real estate, not in the fur trade. After the completion of the Erie Canal, New York became the number one city in America, by-passing Philadelphia and Boston. New York City real estate grew enormously in value, and John Jacob Astor took advantage of that growth:

Notwithstanding that magnitude and success of Mr. Astor's business operations, the greatest occasion of his wealth was in the increased value of real estate consequent on the growth of New York City. He never mortgaged, but constantly bought at foreclosure sales. In this mode his wealth was multiplied far beyond the natural accumulation by ordinary interest.

The New York City Residence of William B. Astor, 350 Fifth Avenue, Corner of Thirty-fifth Street and Fifth Avenue

Astor moved into this house in 1872 after the death of his wife when he could not bear to look at the house they had lived in together in Lafayette Place for so many years.

William B. Astor's Country House, Rokeby

Rokeby was the Dutchess County estate of William B. Astor. Originally the family seat of Mrs. William B. Astor, the former Margaret Armstrong, John Jacob Astor bought the house and gave it to the couple as a wedding present. Rokeby was essentially American in style, largely untouched by the kind of European influences that would mark the Vanderbilt Houses of the early 1880's.

James Gordon Bennett called John Jacob Astor, "a self-invented money machine"; the title could equally well have been applied to William Backhouse Astor, who not only managed his father's estate well but also made real estate purchases of his own and increased the Astor fortune so much that by November 1875, when he died, his fortune was estimated at $40 million, double that of his father. A contemporary is supposed to have said that William B. Astor would climb to the top of a hill, look down at New York and exclaim, "This is mine, all mine!" Even if apocryphal, the story is not far from the truth— William B. Astor owned an astonishingly large amount of land in New York. But his personality did not measure up to his wealth; he was described by another, less admiring contemporary as "the richest and least attractive young man of his time." At the time of his death, the newspaper and magazine writers of the day seemed equally disappointed with William Astor. The London-based *Spectator* wrote:

One feels...an extreme disappointment, as if, living in such a country, with such a family history, he ought to have been more original, more splendid, generous, more of a recognized benefactor to his kind...A man is not bound to be lofty, if loftiness is not in him. But there is in the career of Mr. Astor, excellent person that he is always reputed to have been, a want of greatness which power like his would in some natures have called forth.

The New York *Post* expressed disappointment with Astor's bequests to the city where he had made his fortune:

The testator was the representative of an old New York family; the vast estate which he controlled was situated within the city; its growth was dependent upon the growth of the city. It may have been reasonably expected, therefore, that local public institutions would have been remembered liberally in the disposition of his property.

Astor's charitable bequests during his entire lifetime amounted to only $500,000. The man whose income had been $1.3 million in 1865, who had fought the income tax successfully, hoarded his money and left it to his sons.

ALEXANDER T. STEWART

Alexander T. Stewart died in April 1876 after a long and successful career in New York as a merchant. He owned the largest dry-goods store in the city, at the corner of Broadway and Fourth Avenue. Because he was in trade, Stewart was not accepted by Astors and the other social powers, but the *Times* called him:

A moral power in the commercial history of the United States, whose value it would be difficult to over-estimate...His vast business...will be a perpetual example of the great results which can be accomplished by a single mind and will.

Stewart came to this country from Ireland in 1823. By 1824 he was running a small dry-goods store in New York. According to *Frank Leslie's Popular Monthly:*

Mr. Stewart's first store, that of 283 Broadway, is said to have rented at $375 a year. It was a single room, twelve feet front and thirty feet deep. Here Mr. Stewart labored alone for a considerable time in his early experience, making himself acquainted with the business, in which he had engaged, by the most careful study and analysis of which it was susceptible.

When the Civil War came, Stewart, like many others, used it to his financial advantage. According to the London *Spectator,* Stewart:

...bought up at once the materials which he knew that the Northern Government would most need for the clothing and covering of the troops. When at last a large army had to be put into the field, Mr. Stewart was the only man with whom the Government could contract for uniforms, blankets, and other such goods, and what he sold he sold of good quality and at reasonable prices.

By the time of his death in April 1876, Stewart had come a long way—he was a well-known New York figure, enormously rich and successful. The *Times* wrote in 1876:

The North Room, Astor Library, Lafayette Place, New York

This library was the Astors' principal charity. It was founded by John Jacob Astor, who died in 1848, leaving a $400,000 bequest "for the establishment of a public library in the city of New York." The library opened January 9, 1854. William B. Astor, the eldest son of John Jacob, gave the library an additional $250,000 during his lifetime and $200,000 in his will, according to *Frank Leslie's Popular Monthly* in January 1876. The magazine called the Astor Library "as a working library, for students or authors... perhaps, unequaled by any other of its size [then 150,000 volumes] in the world." *Leslie's* gave credit where it felt credit was due, stating the library owed "its existence and its usefulness to the princely Astors."

The Deceased Millionaire, Alexander T. Stewart, in His Store Instructing a Clerk to Avoid Misrepresenting the Quality of Goods

"Mr. Stewart seems to have scorned the usual tricks and dodges of small traders, and to have continued his low estimate of this kind of commercial acumen as his establishment grew larger and his business more extended. Scrupulously neat and exact in his own habits he required the same qualities in those who served him, and rebuked any departure from what he considered orderly conduct with considerable severity. So whenever in his store he perceived any fault or derangement, he made it his personal business to set it right...An old clerk relates that Mr. Stewart never spoke to him but twice, once when he had torn a piece of weak wrapping paper roughly, he was told that people did not 'like to get shiftless looking bundles'; again when the clerk wound a bundle around with an extra turn of string, Mr. Stewart said: 'Never waste even a piece of string; waste is always wrong.' No case of any sale of goods in his establishment accompanied by misrepresentation ever passed his knowledge without rebuke."

Frank Leslie's Popular Monthly, 1876

Mr. Stewart's Wholesale Store, Broadway, Chamber and Reade Streets

This was Stewart's wholesale store, built by him in 1848–49. The *Times* wrote:

"It has been a remarkable feature of Mr. Stewart's business life that he has always been successful in times of great public depression. This has arisen from the fact of his foreseeing financial disturbances and turning them to his own advantage. Thus in the panic of 1873 Mr. Stewart, who was already prosperous and successful, discerned the embarrassing situation which was approaching, and made good use of it. Marking down all his goods to their lowest possible rates, he immediately achieved a reputation for 'selling at cost,' and as everybody was complaining of 'hard times,' his goods at these low rates sold in every direction...

"He...began to establish the system of branch houses, both in Europe and in this country, through which he has been able to create and carry on his magnificent business. These branch houses are at present in Boston, Philadelphia, Paris, Lyons, Manchester, Bradford, Nottingham, Belfast, Glasgow, Berlin, and Chemnitz."

Thousands of spindles ran at his bidding; thousands of employees looked to him, directly or indirectly for bread. He was the centre of great real estate interests, and the parent of comprehensive schemes of supplying homes to the people and lodgings for the poor. He was the largest individual contributor but one to the City Treasury of New York, and by far the largest to the Treasury of the nation. He was the mainstay of more than one bank...and the almost sole employer of manufacturing establishments in both hemispheres.

When he died, in April 1876, Stewart had two thousand employees in his retail store alone, with running expenses in that store of over $1 million per year. According to *Frank Leslie's Popular Monthly* in June 1876:

The sales of the wholesale and retail stores have aggregated as high as $50,000,000 in a single year...The trade transacted by Mr. Stewart became almost fabulous. The sales in the two establishments are said to have amounted to $203,000,000 in three years, and the income of Mr. Stewart has been the largest in the mercantile world. In 1863 his income

A.T. Stewart's House

Just after A.T. Stewart's death in April 1876, Frank Leslie's Popular Monthly *(1876)* *described his house on the corner of Thirty-fourth Street and Fifth Avenue, calling it a:* "*...marble palace...perhaps the handsomest and most costly private residence in the country. This building, elegantly furnished, constructed with lofty and spacious rooms, has been an object of curiosity to sight-seers ever since it was completed. Certainly the most interesting feature of the building, however, is the art gallery in the rear, where are located a large number of important and valuable works, selected by Mr. Stewart during his numerous visits abroad, or by means of his agents, many of them having been purchased in the studios of the artists, or directly ordered from them. Mr. Stewart's collection surpassed in importance and value any other in the country, and is estimated to be worth at least $600,000...The latest and most valuable purchase by Mr. Stewart was a picture by Meissonnier, for...$65,000. It is called '1807,' and represents Napoleon reviewing a troop of cuirassiers.*"

A. T. Stewart's Retail Store at Broadway and Fourth Avenue, Ninth and Tenth Streets, Completed by Him in 1862 at a Cost of $2.7 Million

A. T. Stewart's store made European goods available to Americans who were looking more and more to Europe to find models of "good taste." The *Times* wrote on December 16, 1876:

"The development of an artistic taste in the selections of household decorations is indicated nowhere more truly than in the establishment of A. T. Stewart & Co., at Ninth Street and Broadway. A great change has taken place in the fashion of window draperies, carpetings, and table coverings. The conventional materials and patterns that have so long found undisputed favor with all sorts of people being now set aside to give way to a preference for fabrics in antique French and antique and modern oriental designs wrought in raw silk. Where the head of a house is qualified by culture and rare taste for personally encouraging and assisting the growth of such a taste...the results, as in the case of A. T. Stewart & Co., must be more satisfactory than a haphazard and indiscriminate plunge made by a mere experimentalist...A table-cover is shown, copied especially for this house from a Louis XIV tapestry, in raw silk...the price of which is $30. Persian and oriental draperies in warm, rich colors, at from $3.50 to $6 a yard, are offered to meet a demand for goods that formerly sold at $16 and $18..."

was $1,900,000; in 1864, $4,000,000; in 1865, $1,600,000; in 1866, $600,000—an average of about $2,000,000. When he was nominated for Secretary of the Treasury in 1869, he estimated his annual income at $1,500,000.

The *Times* was pleased to point out to its readers that Stewart made his fortune by "shrewdness, thrift and perserverance" rather than by speculating in stocks:

A. T. Stewart never turned aside from the path of legitimate business to that of daring speculation...His life is a standing proof of the efficacy of honesty, industry, and well-directed intelligence in laying the foundations of vast wealth. The man who has amassed the largest fortune ever accumulated within the span of a single life was simply a hard-working, careful merchant, with a decided talent for organization and a somewhat rare faculty for taking a grasp of petty details as of broad and

1876: Alexander T. Stewart on His Deathbed

Harper's Weekly noted that "Mr. Stewart's bequest of $1,000,000 to his friend Judge Hilton is the largest sum ever given by one man to another, not a relative, either in the United States or in Europe." (It was Hilton who threw Joseph Seligman out of the Grand Union Hotel in Saratoga in 1877.)

The day after Stewart's death on April 10, 1876, the *Times* reported: "A staring crowd remained in the vicinity of the Stewart mansion in Fifth avenue, and continued to gaze into its curtained windows with wistful steadiness that never flagged. At the entrance to the stairway leading to the main door two policemen and two porters kept constant guard, and scrutinized the cards of all visitors with vigilance..."

general principles. There was no gambler's luck in the methods of action which expanded the five thousand dollars of 1822 into the forty or fifty millions of 1876.

Stewart subscribed to the prevalent belief that only the fittest should survive. *Frank Leslie's Popular Monthly* explained:

His dealings with opponents have been characterized as harsh and pitiless, but that was because he looked on commercial competition as a system of warfare in which the longest purse and the best-directed energy were as much entitled to their reward as the most skillful strategy or the most approved weapon of destruction. If the few suffered from such a system, the many were the gainers. Generous impulse would have been set down by Mr. Stewart as an element of weakness in business transactions; exact and unvarying justice as the element of most enduring strength.

A. T. STEWART DIES

Alexander T. Stewart, the great department store magnate, died in April 1876 at the age of seventy-three. The *Times* was disappointed with his lack of bequests:

The prevailing sentiment in regard to the provisions of the will of the late A. T. Stewart will be one of disappointment...It is not more than once in a century that we can expect to see accumulated within the span of a single life so vast a fortune as that which Mr. Stewart possessed at his death. Let it be anywhere from twenty-five to fifty millions of dollars, what boundless opportunities for well-doing presented themselves to the disposer of even a small portion of such a sum? And that not within the limited area of public charities, so much as in the field of social regeneration, of literary or artistic culture, of scientific endowment, and the like...The public will persist in thinking of the noble contribution A. T. Stewart might have made to any or all of these ends...So far as his direct instructions go...nineteen-twentieths of his enormous fortune pass to his widow, without any condition whatever as to its future disposal....

There are many who will compare the work of a man of moderate fortune like Peter Cooper with that of a man of untold resources like A. T. Stewart, and will regret that the great dry goods merchant should not have given the City to which he owed so much, some better reasons than he appears to have done for holding him in lasting honor.

But Stewart was generous to his employees in his will. He directed his wife:

I do desire that you will ascertain the names of all such of my employees who have been with me for a period of ten years and upward. And I request that to each of those who have been in my employment for a period of twenty years, shall be paid $1,000, while to each of those who have been with me for ten years, shall be paid $500.

A. T. STEWART'S FUNERAL

No splendor was spared in Stewart's funeral in St. Mark's Church. The *Times* reported on April 3, 1876:

The display of flowers will be simply superb. The casket is to rest upon an oblong pyramid of flowers seven feet in length by three in width, composed of almost every description of floral treasures...The total cost of the...decorations, which are ordered by the family, will be over $5,000...

The body, which was kept in ice until yesterday, is unchanged, and appears as natural as during life...As the church will only seat 800 persons, great difficulty has been experienced in apportioning the limited number of cards of admission among the thousands of applicants.

Four hundred employes of Mr. Stewart will fill the galleries on both sides of the auditorium, and every seat on the floor, as well as standing room, will be occupied by invited guests. Among the latter will be fifty delegates from the Union League Club and fifty from the New York merchants. Delegations from the principal mercantile bodies will also be present.

Frank Leslie's Popular Monthly reported that crowds surged to see the funeral of the merchant prince:

The funeral cortège moved from Fifth Avenue to St. Mark's Church via Broadway and Ninth Street. Large numbers of people gathered along the route, while crowds occupied the immediate vicinity of the church, clambering upon fences and establishing themselves in all directions at good points of view.

Mr. Stewart Lying in State

"The casket was made of oak, covered with the finest black Lyons velvet, the lid secured with solid gold nails, and extension handles mounted with gold in their proper places. Upon the lid, engraved on a solid silver plate, was the following inscription:

ALEX. T. STEWART
BORN, OCTOBER 12TH, 1803
DIED, APRIL 10TH, 1876"

Frank Leslie's Popular Monthly, June 1876

The Sunken Track of the New Haven & Harlem Railroad, Fourth Avenue, above 126th Street, New York City

Commodore Cornelius Vanderbilt in 1876

Vanderbilt, who began making his money running a ferryboat, went on to become a railroad magnate. He was famed for his remark "What do I care about the law? Hain't I got the power?"

The day after the Commodore died in January 1877, the *New York Herald* wrote of him with unqualified admiration: "His character was that of a most remarkable man...he had nothing but the unconquerable will which in time made him the foremost man of his class. He was born to poverty and effort. It is said of him that he had no vices...As he was nearly seventy...it was supposed he would retire to the enjoyment of his fortune...But he knew himself better. He became the great railway king of the country. Roads which had been the playthings of gamblers...prospered under his hard, cold, daring management...His lesson—courage in the performance of duty—enabled this man to become one of the kings of the earth...It was one honest, sturdy, fearless man against the world and, in the end, the man won."

COMMODORE CORNELIUS VANDERBILT

Commodore Vanderbilt was eighty-two years old in 1876; he died in January 1877, the last of the triumvirate to perish. Vanderbilt died leaving a fortune of about $100 million, which he had accumulated from his railroad and steamship interests. Charles Francis Adams, Jr., the brother of Henry, described Vanderbilt's life:

Vanderbilt...was born in very humble circumstances in the State of New York and...received little education. He began life by ferrying passengers and produce from Staten Island to New York City...He...laid the foundation of his great fortune in the growing steamboat navigation, and...in due course of time, transferred himself to the railroad interest...Vanderbilt was gay and buoyant of temperament...a lover of horses and of the good things of life...It is impossible to regard Vanderbilt's methods or aims without recognizing the magnitude of the man's ideas and conceding his abilities. He involuntarily excites feelings of admiration for himself and alarm for the public. His ambition is a great one. It seems to be nothing less than to make himself master in his own right of the great channels of communication which connect the great city of New York with the interior of the continent and to control them as his private property...Vanderbilt...has sought to make himself a dictator in modern civilization, moving forward to this end step by step with a sort of pitiless energy...As trade now dominates the world, and railways

End of the Line

The Grand Union Depot for the New York Central and Hudson River and New Haven & Harlem railroads, Fourth Avenue, New York. *Frank Leslie's Popular Monthly* reported in 1876 that:

"To the Commodore's grandeur of conception, in magnificent works of practical public utility, is to be attributed the building of that noble structure of masonry, the Fourth Avenue improvement—certainly one of the most extraordinary engineering efforts...in the world; and also that of the Grand Central Depôt, one of the finest buildings of the kind ever erected, comprising within its own area about a mile of track, and offices for the three railroad companies under his control."

The *North Star*

Vanderbilt loaded his family on board—son William Henry and his wife, another son, George Washington, and eight of his daughters and their husbands—and then sailed off to Europe on the *North Star* in 1853. There was even a Baptist minister on the boat. The family visited England, where they were snubbed by royalty, and then went on to Russia, Italy and Constantinople. *Frank Leslie's Popular Monthly* described the voyage in an article in 1876:

"In 1853 Commodore Vanderbilt had built and equipped a magnificent steamer, the *North Star*, and on May 19th he set sail on board of her, accompanied by a portion of his family and friends, on a prolonged tour through the Old World. During his trip he visited all the prominent ports of Europe, being everywhere received with generous hospitality by prominent personages...The entire surroundings of the tour, and the idea of its undertaking in so superb a manner, succeeded in opening the eyes of foreigners to the largeness of the views of this modest and unpretending citizen of the Republic. It should be remembered that on the return of the Commodore, in September of the same year, when his ship rounded Staten Island, he emphasized the regard and affection in which he has always held his mother by saluting her from the guns on board."

dominate trade, his object has been to make himself the virtual master of all by making himself the virtual lord of the railways...Developing his ideas as he advanced, his power and reputation grew, until an end which at first it would have seemed madness to entertain became at last both natural and feasible...First making himself master of the Harlem road, he there learned his early lessons in railroad management, and picked up a fortune by the way...The success of Vanderbilt with the Harlem depended upon his getting rid of the competition of the Hudson River Railroad...Vanderbilt...put an end to competition by buying up the competing line...In his dangerous path of centralization Vanderbilt has taken the latest step in advance. He has combined the natural power of the individual with the...power of the corporation. The famous "L'état, c'est moi" of Louis XIV, represents Vanderbilt's position in regard to his railroads...He has introduced Caesarism into corporate life. He has...pointed out the way which others will tread. The individual will hereafter be engrafted on the corporation, democracy running its course, and resulting in imperialism; and Vanderbilt is but the precursor of a class of men who will wield within the State a power created by the State, but too great for its control. He is the founder of a dynasty.

When Vanderbilt died in January 1877, the New York *Herald* wrote:

It was a giant they buried: the impression made upon the community by both Stewart and Astor was a faint one compared to the deep mark of Vanderbilt.

THE WARS OF ERIE

In 1825 it would have been possible to describe all the large American fortunes. Fifty years later this was no longer true. According to one estimate, in 1883 there were at least 4,000 people in the United States worth at least $1 million each. In every quarter of the country, men were amassing fortunes in the "new" way—by exploiting the natural wealth of the country, the oil, coal, iron and silver, and by organizing the access to this wealth and its distribution by railroads and steamships.

The Americans amassing these immense fortunes did not subscribe to the ethics of the older families. They prospered in a rough climate. Observing the struggle for control of the Erie Railway between Cornelius Vanderbilt on the one hand and Daniel Drew, Jay Gould and Jim Fisk on the other, Charles Francis Adams, Jr., wrote that "it was something new to see a knot of adventurers, men of broken fortune, without character and without credit possess themselves of an artery of commerce more important than was ever the Appian Way, and make levies ...upon it for their own emolument."

Adams was referring to one of the most scandal-sodden episodes of a corrupt age, and one which represented the new way of making money. In the battle over the Erie Railway the combatants bribed whole legislatures, hired gangs of thugs to sabotage their opponents' progress, and duped thousands of investors with bogus stock issues. But the Erie Railway war was not unique—its saga of intricate venality was reproduced in countless enterprises across the country.

To understand the Erie Railroad war is to understand the raw capitalist spirit of that epoch; in the same way that to understand the characters of Drew, Fisk, Gould, Vanderbilt, Morgan and Belmont is to catch a sense of the thousands of other new men who were also fighting for their fortunes.

DANIEL DREW, JIM FISK AND JAY GOULD

By 1876 the struggle for the Erie Railroad was over; Fisk was dead, Drew was bankrupt, and only Gould was still rich and powerful. But the saga of the Erie War and the characters of the combatants were still very much a part of the time, as Charles F. Adams, Jr., explained in his essay *A Chapter of Erie.*

"Ruined," a woodcut from *Harper's Weekly,* symbolizes the plight of Daniel Drew in 1876, who once said: "I have been wonderfully blessed in money making. I got to be a millionaire afore I know'd it hardly." Drew went bankrupt in 1876.

Daniel Drew—The Great Bear

Drew went bankrupt in 1876 and the *Times* reported on March 13, 1876:

"Daniel Drew has gone into voluntary bankruptcy...Financial embarrassment for the last year, consequent upon his heavy losses in Wall street two and three years ago, are the immediate cause of this unexpected proceeding...He dates the beginning of his financial misfortunes, to the loss of a million on a corner in North-western two or three years ago. He next lost on Toledo and Wabash, on which he was 'short,' and on the enterprise of constructing the 'Canada Southern' Railway. He was also a general partner in the firm of King, Cox & Co., brokers...When they failed...they held no property in their own names, and Mr. Drew...was forced to bear the losses. The Quicksilver Mining Company also caused him a heavy loss. Mr. Drew expresses the hope and belief that enough will be realized to meet all the liabilities."

Daniel Drew, who had gambled and mostly won, lost everything in 1876. At the age of seventy-nine, probably the boldest and shrewdest and one of the most corrupt of the independent stock operators of his generation, he was bankrupt, never to recover. His assets totalled $746,459.46; his liabilities were $1,093,524.36. He died in 1879, a broken man living off the charity of his son.

A CHAPTER OF ERIE,
BY CHARLES F. ADAMS, JR.

Call things by their right names, and it would be no difficult task to make the cunning civilization of the nineteenth century appear but as a hypocritical mask spread over the more honest brutality of the twelfth...Pirates are commonly supposed to have been...hung out of existence...yet freebooters are not extinct; they have only transferred their operations to the land.

No better illustration of the fantastic disguises which the worst and most familiar evils of history assume as they meet us in the actual movement of our own day could be afforded than was seen in the events attending what are known as the Erie wars of the year 1868...This strange conflict convulsed the money market, occupied the courts, agitated legislatures, and perplexed the country...The remote political complications and financial disturbances occasioned by it would afford a curious illustration of the close intertwining of interests which now extends throughout the civilized world...No people can afford to glance at these things in the columns of the daily press, and then dismiss them from memory. For Americans they involve many questions;—they touch very nearly the foundation of common truth and honesty without which that healthy public opinion cannot exist which is the life's breath of our whole political system.

Adams began his account of the Erie Wars by describing one of the participants, Daniel Drew, who had survived a poverty-stricken childhood to become one of Wall Street's most famous gamblers.

Mr. Drew is what is known as a self-made man. Born in the year 1797, as a boy he drove cattle down from his native town of Carmel, in Putnam County, to the market of New York City, and, subsequently, was for years proprietor of the Bull's Head Tavern. Like his contemporary, and ally or opponent,—as the case might be,—Cornelius Vanderbilt, he built up his fortunes in the steamboat interest, and subsequently extended his operations over the rapidly developing railroad system. Shrewd, unscrupulous, and very illiterate,—a strange combination of superstition and faithlessness, of daring and timidity,—often good-natured and sometimes generous,—he ever regarded his fiduciary position of director in a railroad as a means of manipulating its stock for his own advantage. For years he had been the leading bear of Wall Street, and his favorite haunts were the secret recesses of Erie...

Those who sought to follow him and those who sought to oppose him, alike found food for sad reflection; until at last he won for himself the expressive *sobriquet* of the Speculative Director. Sometimes, though rarely, he suffered greatly in the complications of Wall Street; more frequently he inflicted severe damage upon others...The outbreak of the Erie war found him the actual possessor of some millions, and the reputed possessor of many more.

In 1866 Drew performed a tricky and profitable stock maneuver. By manipulating Erie stock, he caused the price

Wall Street

The New York Stock Exchange, Built in 1865

The Ticker

to rise by duping most speculators into thinking that there was no more stock available. As treasurer of the corporation he had inside knowledge which allowed him, when the price was right—and he himself was short Erie—to flood the market with shares that only he knew existed. The price of the stock plunged, and Drew swept up his profits. Adams expressed shock at Drew's ruthlessness:

The whole transaction...was in no respect more creditable than any result, supposed to be one of chance or skill, which, in fact, is made to depend upon the sorting of a pack of cards...But the gambler... represents, as a rule, himself alone, and his character is generally so well understood as to be a warning to all the world. The case of the treasurer of a great corporation is different. He occupies a fiduciary position...Vast interests are confided to his care; every shareholder of the corporation is his ward...But passing events, accumulating more thickly with every passing year, have thoroughly corrupted the public morals on this subject. A directorship in certain great corporations has come to be regarded as a situation in which to make a fortune...Our whole system rests upon the sanctity of the fiduciary relations. Whoever betrays them, a director of a railroad no less than a member of Congress or the trustee of an orphan's asylum, is the common enemy of every man, woman, and child who lives under representative government. The unscrupulous director is in fact less entitled to mercy than the gambler, combining as he does the character of the traitor with the acts of the thief. No acute moral sensibility, on this point, however, has for some years troubled Wall Street, nor, indeed, the country at large. As a result of the transaction of 1866, Mr. Drew was looked upon as having effected a surprisingly clever operation and he retired from the field hated, feared, wealthy, and admired.

The Great Race for the Western Stakes: Vanderbilt vs. Fisk

"There is no more singular chapter in all the varied romance of Wall Street than the facts in the remarkable contest now going on between the rival New York Central and Erie Railroads to secure the business of carrying the immense quantities of freight which comes from the West to New York by these two routes. The wealth and importance of the contesting roads; the prominence of the two men who control them and who direct this war; the singularity, not to say the illegality, of the judicial proceedings in the case; the amount of money involved in the quarrel; the numbers of brokers, bankers, and speculators engaged, pecuniarily, in it; the vigor and boldness of the effort to take possession of the Erie road; the...bold manoeuvre of a change of base to New Jersey soil—in short, all the circumstances of the rivalry make it one of the strangest stories of the street."
Harper's Weekly, April 11, 1868

VANDERBILT CHALLENGES DREW

Adams reported that:

The New York Central passed into Vanderbilt's hands in the winter of 1866–7 and he marked the Erie for his own in the succeeding autumn...Three parties were...contending for control of the road.

VANDERBILT DIRECTS HIS HENCHMEN TO "BUY ERIE BUY IT AT THE LOWEST FIGURES YOU CAN, BUT BUY IT"

As an observer of the battle between Drew and Vanderbilt for the Erie Railroad, Adams had less contempt for Vanderbilt, although both men operated from standards alien to his. He saw the conflict between Vanderbilt and Drew as inevitable:

When at last, in 1868, the two came into collision...they were each three score and ten years of age, and both had been successful in the accumulation of millions,—Vanderbilt even more so than Drew. They were probably equally unscrupulous and equally selfish...Drew, in Wall Street is by temperament a bear, while Vanderbilt could hardly be other than a bull. Vanderbilt must be allowed to be by far the superior man of the two. Drew is astute and full of resources, and at all times is a dangerous opponent; but Vanderbilt takes longer, more comprehensive views, and his mind has a vigorous grasp which that of Drew seems to want.

OCTOBER 18, 1867: DEAL BETWEEN VANDERBILT AND DREW

Vanderbilt had Drew in a corner in the fall of 1867. Vanderbilt had made a deal with a group of Boston railway men whereby they, acting in combination with him, had enough votes to oust Drew, who asked for mercy from the Commodore and got it; they pooled their interests. Drew remained in charge of Erie affairs; his henchmen, James Fisk and Jay Gould, were put on the board:

Virtual consolidation in the Vanderbilt interest seemed a foregone conclusion. The reinstalment of Drew was followed by a period of hollow truce. The real conflict was now impending.

THE DEAL FALLS APART: DREW TRICKS VANDERBILT

The deal did not last long. Drew, Fisk and Gould went against the Commodore's wishes and issued more Erie stock. Vanderbilt, in a fury at being outfoxed by the subtle Drew, commanded his henchmen to "Buy every damn share that's offered:"

Vanderbilt...foiled in intrigue...prepared to go out into Wall Street...and to make himself the master of the Erie...The task itself was one of magnitude. The volume of the stock was immense; all of it was upon the street, and the necessary expenditure involved many millions of dollars. The peculiar difficulty of the task...lay in the fact that it had to be undertaken in the face of antagonists so bold, so subtle, so unscrupulous, so thoroughly acquainted with Erie, as well as so familiar with all the devices and tricks...of Wall Street, as were those who now stood ready to take up the gage which the Commodore so arrogantly threw down.

Vanderbilt's problem was that each time he thought he had bought up all the stock there was to buy, Drew, Fisk and Gould would print up more stock—uninterested in any legal technicalities. At last Vanderbilt resorted to the law in his battle with Drew. He got Judge George C. Barnard of the New York State Supreme Court, generally thought to be under Vanderbilt's influence, to enjoin the directors of Erie from issuing any more stock and to order them to return one fourth of the shares they had recently issued plus $3 million worth of convertible bonds issued in 1866:

Manifold and ingenious were the expedients through which the cunning Treasurer furnished himself with Erie, when the exigencies of his position demanded fresh supplies. It was, therefore, very necessary for Vanderbilt that he should, while buying Erie with one hand in Wall Street, with the other close, so far as he could, that apparently inexhaustible spring from which such generous supplies of new stock were wont to flow...

Colonel Jim Fisk: "First in War, First in Peace, and First in the Pockets of His Countrymen."

Jim Fisk was only a ghostly presence in 1876. The partner of Daniel Drew and Jay Gould in the Erie Railroad War, Fisk's career came to an end in January 1872 when he was shot by Edward Stokes, who had been blackmailing Fisk over his mistress, Josie Mansfield. The *Times* described Fisk on October 16, 1869:

"Now there are few men in our city who command so large a share of public notice. He is a man of large wealth, and is the centre of attraction in Wall Street, in theatrical circles, and in the law courts.—Perhaps he has not genius; his education may be deficient; but his practical shrewdness, his almost reckless boldness, and his unparalleled effrontery, make up for the absence of these qualifications. He is known as a man who may be a friend to-day and an enemy to-morrow; as one who comes to his conclusions rapidly, and almost by instinct; and as a man whose hostility can not be provoked with impunity. Having said this, what more could we say as regards his peculiar characteristics?

"James Fisk, Jun., is the son of a Vermont peddler...At twenty-five years of age, he determined to pursue the calling of his father, and returned to his native State of Vermont for that purpose. He commenced his career as a peddler by selling small articles, such as pencils, pens, etc., on the sidewalks of the different towns of the State... Having succeeded...by-and-by he extended his field of operations...until, finally, the gross amount of his sales attracted the attention of a Boston firm from whom he was in the habit of buying goods. In 1860...James Fisk, Jun., became a partner in the firm of Jordan, Marsh, & Co., of Boston. But the firm do not appear to have been so well pleased...for at the end of two years they paid him down the large sum of $64,000 to leave the firm...
(continued on following page)

Obtaining an introduction to Mr. Drew, he managed so to ingratiate himself into the favor of that gentleman that he employed him...Fisk [soon] commenced to operate on his own account...Success...did not attend him on Wall Street as it had done with peddling...and in two years time James Fisk had lost every dollar he had in the world. He had, however, a friend in Mr. Daniel Drew, who in 1865 assisted him to form the firm of Fisk, Belding, & Co., for the purpose of carrying on the business of stock-brokers, and gave them substantial aid by putting business into their hands, and employing them as brokers in many large undertakings.

"In 1867 Mr. Fisk, in connection with Mr. Jay Gould, succeeded in making a large sum of money by operations in Erie stock. They got control over stock to the amount of $10,000,000, and were thus able to depress the general value of Erie stock from 72½ to 35. Mr. Fisk's share of the profits resulting from these operations amounted, it is said, to $1,300,000."

DREW, FISK AND GOULD FIND A WAY TO GET AROUND THE INJUNCTION

It appeared that there was a recently enacted statute of New York which authorized any railroad company to create and issue its own stock in exchange for the stock of any other road under lease to it...Mr. Drew and certain of his brother directors...quietly possessed themselves of a worthless road connecting with the Erie...[and] proceeded to supply themselves with whatever Erie stock they wanted, by leasing their own road to the road of which they were directors, and then creating stock and issuing it to themselves, in exchange...This transaction...affords...a most happy illustration of brilliant railroad financing...The road...cost the purchasers...some $250,000...They then issued in its name bonds for two million dollars.

VANDERBILT GETS A SECOND COURT INJUNCTION:

...restraining the Erie board from any new issue of capital stock, by conversion of bonds or otherwise...Drew...was to be forced...to make Erie scarce by returning into its treasury sixty-eight thousand shares,—one fourth of its whole capital stock...

DREW, GOULD AND FISK FIGHT BACK

The Erie party very freely and openly expressed a decided lack of respect...for the purity of that particular fragment of the judicial ermine which was supposed to adorn the person of Mr. Justice Barnard. They did not pretend to conceal their conviction that this magistrate was a piece of the Vanderbilt property...

DREW & CO. BUY THEIR OWN JUDGE

They betook themselves to their own town of Binghamton...where they duly presented themselves before Mr. Justice Balcom, of the Supreme Court...The injunction was no sooner asked of Judge Balcom than it was granted...and all proceedings in the suits commenced before Judge Barnard were stayed...

During these legal maneuvers, Drew, Fisk and Gould continued to print up stock and flood the Street with shares to keep Vanderbilt from getting control of the Erie—known as "the Scarlet Woman of Wall Street:"

...If Commodore Vanderbilt wanted the stock...they were prepared to let him have all he desired.

"IF THIS PRINTING PRESS DON'T BREAK DOWN, I'LL BE DAMNED IF I DON'T GIVE THE OLD HOG ALL HE WANTS OF ERIE!"–JIM FISK

The market reeled to and fro like a drunken man between these giants, as they hurled about shares by the tens of thousands, and money by the million...

THE ESCAPE

Vanderbilt was finally so enraged by the seemingly endless flow of Erie stock that he got Judge Barnard to order the arrest of the so-called "Erie Guerillas." But on March 11, 1868, the trio, alert to the threatened arrest, fled with $6 million in cash across the river, where they took up residence in a hotel in Jersey City. Adams wrote:

Messrs. Fisk and Gould Escaping to New Jersey

On April 11, 1868, *Harper's Weekly* gave an account of the escape to New Jersey:

"On the night of March 15 Messrs. Fisk and Gould...were dining at Delmonico's, when they heard that warrants had been issued for their arrests. They immediately jumped into a carriage and drove to the foot of Canal Street, where an officer of the steamer *St. John* lowered a boat and, with two deck hands, attempted the passage of the North River in a dense fog. Mr. Fisk directed the men to head up the river, but the fog was so thick that they lost their reckoning and rowed for some time in a circle. They were at one time nearly run down, only saving themselves by the vigorous use of their lungs...Ultimately they determined to endeavor to get some assistance, and for this purpose hailed a Pavonia ferry-boat... They climbed on board, arriving shortly after at Jersey City, safe and sound, ..."

The Erie Railroad Directors' Room at the Taylor Hotel, Jersey City

The *Times* reported in April 1868 that "the Taylor Hotel in Jersey city is used as the quarters of the Drew party, and one of the rooms is now known as the 'Directors Room.'...It is guarded night and day by police...The favored few who pass these portals are received by Mr. Fisk with such...cordiality that it is difficult to imagine that he and his brother directors are in a state of siege."

From this hotel room Fisk sent forth his famous edict to the New York press:

"The Commodore owns New York, the Stock Exchange, the streets, the railroads, and most of the steamships...As ambitious young men, we saw there was no chance for us there to expand, and so we came over here to grow up with the country...Tell Mr. Greeley from us that we're sorry now that we didn't take his advice sooner—about going West."

The Guard Room of the Erie Special Police at Taylor's Hotel

"'The Guard Room' was formerly the ladies' parlor of the hotel. A force of about seventy-five specials are on duty at the hotel during the night, and occupy when off duty this apartment, where they are in waiting to prevent any raid which the 'Vanderbilt party' may attempt to make."

Harper's Weekly, April 11, 1868

Jay Gould: "The Mephistopheles of Wall Street"

Gould was forty years old in 1876. At his death in 1892 he left an estate of $77 million. Charles Francis Adams Jr. described him as "strongly marked by his disposition for silent intrigue...There was a reminiscence of a spider in his nature. He spun huge webs, in corners and in the dark, which were seldom strong enough to resist a serious strain at the critical moment...He was an uncommonly fine and unscrupulous intriguer, skilled in all the processes of stock gambling, and passably indifferent to the praise or censure of society."

Some, like the New York *World,* blamed Gould for the crash of 1873: "There is one man in Wall Street today whom men watch, and whose name, built upon ruins, carries with it a certain whisper of ruin...He is the last of the race of kings...one whose nature is best described by the record of what he has done, and by the burden of hatred and dread that, loaded upon him for two and one-half years, has not turned him one hair from any place that promised him gain and the most bitter ruin for his chance opponents. They that curse him do not do it blindly but as cursing one who massacres after victory."

Jay Gould explained his winning philosophy to a committee of the New York State Legislature in 1873: "In a Republican district, I was a Republican, in a Democratic district, I was a Democrat; in a doubtful district I was doubtful, but I was always for Erie!"

The morning of the 11th...at ten o'clock the astonished police saw a throng of panic-stricken railway directors—looking more like a frightened gang of thieves, disturbed in the division of their plunder, than like the wealthy representatives of a great corporation—rush headlong from the doors of the Erie office, and dash off in the direction of the Jersey ferry...their pockets crammed with assets and securities. One individual bore away with him...six millions of dollars in greenbacks...In Jersey City...free from any apprehension of Judge Barnard's pursuing wrath, [they] proceeded to the transaction of business.

DREW, FISK, GOULD OPERATE FROM NEW JERSEY
The real field of operations had ceased on the morning of the 11th of March to be in the courts of law...Drew was secreted, a standing army was organized from the employees of the road, and a small navy equipped...A garrison of about one hundred and twenty-five men entrenched themselves around the directors in their hotel...The first serious effort of the Erie party was to entrench itself in New Jersey; and here it met with no opposition. A bill making the Erie Railway Company a corporation of New Jersey...was hurried through the legislature in the space of two hours.

THE RING ATTEMPTS TO MOVE BACK TO NEW YORK—JAY GOULD BRIBES THE NEW YORK LEGISLATURE
It was decided that Mr. Jay Gould should brave the terrors of the law, and personally superintend matters at Albany. Neither Mr. Drew nor his associates desired to become permanent residents of Jersey City; nor did they wish to return to New York as criminals on their way to jail. Mr. Gould was to pave the way to a...return by causing a recent issue of convertible bonds to be legalized...Mr. Jay Gould went on his mission, the president of the company having some time previously drawn half a million of dollars out of the overflowing Erie treasury...

This half million dollars was used by Gould to buy enough votes to pass a bill which would allow the Erie Ring to re-enter New York:

The full and true history of this legislative campaign will never be known...[One] individual is reported to have received one hundred thousand dollars from one side, "to influence legislation," and to have subsequently received $70,000 from the other side to disappear with the money; which he accordingly did and thereafter became a gentleman of elegant leisure...Other senators were blessed with a sudden accession of wealth, but in no case was there any jot or title or proof of bribery. Mr. Gould's...checks were numerous and heavy...

GOULD SUCCEEDS
On the 13th of April a bill, which met the approval of the Erie party, and which Judge Barnard subsequently compared not ineptly to a bill legalizing counterfeit money, was taken up in the Senate...and on the 18th was passed.

Gould was pleased with his success and not at all repentant; "I should do what I did again," he said. Adams commented disparagingly on the standards of the American legislative bodies:

Probably no representative bodies were ever more thoroughly venal, more shamelessly corrupt, or more hopelessly beyond the reach of public opinion, than...certain of those bodies which legislate for republican America in this latter half of the nineteenth century. Certainly, none of the developments which marked the Erie conflict in the New York legislature in 1868 would tend to throw doubts on this conclusion...

THE WAR ENDS

In September 1868, in return for immunity from prosecution, the Erie trio agreed to pay Vanderbilt $4.5 million in cash, stocks and bonds. Vanderbilt and Drew ended their battle, and left the Erie to Gould and Fisk:

Mr. Vanderbilt ceased to concern himself with Erie; while Daniel Drew...assumed for a space the novel character of a looker-on in Wall Street.

JULY 1, 1868: GOULD AND FISK TAKE OVER THE ERIE

Two of the combatants were gone, but the struggles over the Erie Railroad continued. Gould and Fisk were in control and they allied themselves with Tammany Hall.

...Messrs. Fisk and Gould found themselves...in absolute control of the Erie Railway...Two new names...appeared in the list of Erie directors, —those of Peter B. Sweeney and William M. Tweed, the two most prominent leaders of that prominent ring which controls...New York City...

ERIE AND TAMMANY WORK TOGETHER

This formidable combination shot out its feelers far and wide; it wielded the influence of a great corporation with a capital of a hundred millions; it controlled the politics of the first city of the New World; it sent its representatives to the Senate of the State, and numbered among its agents the judges of the courts.

THE SAME OLD TRICKS

Gould and Fisk were at the helm but nothing had changed; they issued stock whenever they wanted to. Now it was August Belmont (the agent of the Rothschilds) instead of Vanderbilt who, representing "large foreign holders," filed suit to try to enjoin the Erie directors from issuing all the stock they wanted. Fisk and Gould, of course, filed countersuits and kept on doing exactly what they wanted.

"Public interest" was a term which did not exist. The battle that was fought between the Erie Ring and their opponents was a stock battle; the condition of the railroad, its many accidents and deteriorating rails were matters which did not enter into the struggle.

Russell Sage
Sage was a collaborator of Jay Gould's. Gould had them both elected directors of the Pacific Mail Steamship Company in 1872, from which they soon made $5 million in the next two years in profits. Sage was sixty years old in 1876. When he died some thirty years later he left an estate of $70 million. He is credited with being the originator of "puts" and "calls" in the stock market about 1872. Sage was especially renowned as a moneylender.

Under the Thumb

Thomas Nast's cartoon alludes to Boss Tweed's firm control over the city of New York. Tweed was accused of stealing from the city anywhere from $30 million to $200 million. The Tweed Ring fell in 1871 under attack on all sides, and Tweed was arrested in December 1871. He was convicted in 1873 and sentenced to twelve years in prison. But in 1875 he escaped and fled to Spain; in 1876 Spanish officials shipped him back to America, where he died in jail.

Tweed once said, "This population is too hopelessly split up into races and factions to govern it under universal suffrage, except by the bribery of patronage and corruption."

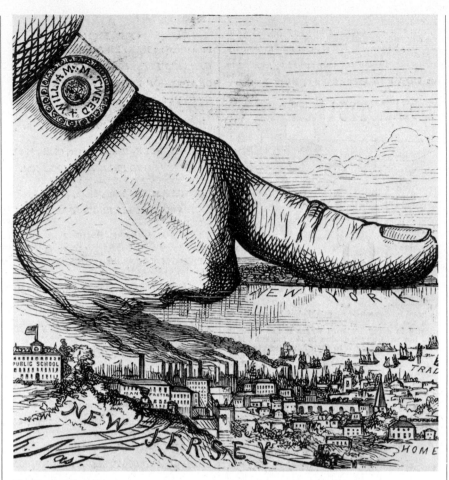

Under the Thumb

ERIE CLASSIFICATION ACT

Gould's ultimate triumph was the passage through the legislature of this act:

...That strange law was enacted which assured these men, elected for one year, a five years' term of power, beyond the control of their stockholders. From that moment all the great resources of the Erie Railway became mere engines with which to work their lawless will...

To Adams, "the end was finally attained" and "a national thoroughfare" rested "in the hands of unscrupulous gamblers."

THE PATRICIAN'S CONCLUSIONS ABOUT THE NEW ORDER:

The facts which have been set forth cannot but have revealed to every observant eye the deep decay which has eaten into out social edifice. No portion of our system was left untested, and no portion showed itself to be sound. The stock exchange revealed itself a haunt of gamblers and a den of thieves; the offices of our great corporations appeared as the secret chambers in which trustees plotted the spoilation of their wards; the law became a ready engine for the furtherance of wrong, and the ermine of the judge did not conceal the eagerness of the partisan; the halls of legislation were transformed into a mart in

American Railroad Scene, by Currier and Ives, 1874

Very Consoling

Ticket Agent (to Hesitating Friend): "Why, you are going by our line surely, Mr. Jones, are you not? We now have an experienced Surgeon and Undertaker on every Train."
A joke on the dangers of railroad travel, since railroad owners like Commodore Vanderbilt concentrated more on profits than on safety.

which the price of votes was haggled over, and laws, made to order, were bought and sold; while under all, and through all, the voice of public opinion was silent or was disregarded.

It is not, however, in connection with the present that all this has its chief significance. It speaks ominously for the future. It may be that our society is only passing through a period of ugly transition, but the present evil has its root deep down in the social organization, and springs from a diseased public opinion. Failure seems to be regarded as the one unpardonable crime, success as the all-redeeming virtue, the acquisition of wealth as the single worthy aim of life. Ten years ago such revelations as these of the Erie Railway would have sent a shudder through the community, and would have placed a stigma on every man who had had to do with them. Now they merely incite others to surpass them by yet bolder outrages and more corrupt combinations....

It is not pleasant to take such views of the future; yet they are irresistibly suggested by the events which have been narrated...The only remedy lies in a renovated public opinion; but no indication of this has as yet been elicited...Even where a real indignation was excited, it led to no sign of any persistent efforts at reform...The danger, however, is day by day increasing, and the period during which the work of regeneration should begin grows always shorter. It is true that evils work their own cure, but the cure for the evils of Roman Civilization was worked out through ten centuries of barbarism.

It remains to be seen whether this people retains that moral vigor which can alone awaken a sleeping public opinion to healthy and persistent activity, or whether to us also will apply these words of the latest and best historian of the Roman republic: "What Demosthenes said of his Athenians was justly applied to the Romans of this period; that people were very zealous for action so long as they stood round the platform and listened to proposals of reform; but, when they went home, no one thought further of what he had heard in the market-place. However those reformers might stir the fire, it was to no purpose for the inflammable material was wanting."

Adams posed the question but left it for Americans in the following century to answer.

OTHER FORTUNES ON THE RISE

THE WORLD OF EASTERN BANKING: A PORTFOLIO OF THE FACES OF SOME ESTABLISHED BANKERS

Wall Street, c. 1876

August Belmont

Jay Cooke: The Once Great

Jay Cooke was probably the most important banker of the Civil War and post–Civil War era. But his great success came to a sharp end on September 18, 1873, when the famous banking house of Jay Cooke and Company had to close its doors, setting off the panic of 1873 and one of the most severe depressions in the history of the United States. Thirty-seven other banking and brokerage houses followed suit that day, the stock exchange closed down, and by the end of 1873 over five thousand commercial businesses had failed. George Templeton Strong described the scene on Wall Street in September 1873 in his diary:

Going into Wall Street, I found crowds standing about and general excitement. The great house of Jay Cooke & Company, with its affiliations and auxiliaries, had hauled down its flag; so had Robinson & Suydam—also Richard Schell. Their example will probably be followed by many others tomorrow, and this may prove preliminary to the general smash that must come before long. One or two gentlemen who looked as if they came from the country and who probably had monies on deposit with these collapsed bankers were walking about in an aimless sort of way and talking loud to nobody in particular about ''d——d infernal swindlers and thieves''...

Jay Cooke played a vital part in financing the Union during the Civil War through the sale of war bonds using clever advertising tactics. But in 1869 he had begun to invest too heartily in the Northern Pacific Railway. Referring to Cooke's Northern Pacific venture, Vanderbilt commented after the collapse: ''Building railroads from nowhere to nowhere is not a legitimate business.''

Not until 1879 would America recover from the depression. Cooke, who had been America's leading banker, recovered enough to pay his debts, but he never regained the influence he had had before 1873.

In 1876 August Belmont, a German Jew who, according to legend, had changed his name from August Schönberg, was sixty years old and well established as a banker and as a member of New York society. Belmont, who had come to America as the agent of the Rothschilds, had been so successful that in 1837 he had opened his own banking house, August Belmont and Company. As the representative of the Rothschilds, he had enormous influence with financiers and politicians eager to gain Rothschild money to finance various projects. Describing Belmont in an article on June 29, 1876, the Times *said:*

He is a banker of good repute, with a very substantial stake in this country. He derives exceptional weight from his connection with the house of Rothschild, and exercises an influence in several directions which only that connection satisfactorily explains. The influence with which it invests him is conceded on all sides.

Belmont is probably remembered more for his social conquest of exclusive New York society (especially exclusive to Jews) than for his banking genius. His success in Eastern society was ensured by his marriage in 1849 to Caroline Slidell Perry, whose family had the social standing that Belmont wanted. From the day of his marriage, Belmont became part of society. The Belmonts gave grand parties, and their house, like that of Julius Beaufort in Edith Wharton's The Age of Innocence, *contained a grand ballroom:*

The Beauforts' house was one of the few in New York that possessed a ballroom...and at a time when it was beginning to be thought ''provincial'' to put a ''crash'' over the drawing room floor and move the furniture upstairs, the possession of a ballroom that was used for no other purpose, and left for 364 days of the year to shuttered darkness, with its gilt chairs stacked in a corner and its chandelier in a bag; this undoubted superiority was felt to compensate for whatever was regrettable in the Beaufort past.

In The Age of Innocence, *Julius Beaufort has many of the traits of August Belmont:*

The question was: who *was* Beaufort? He passed for an Englishman, was agreeable, handsome, ill-tempered, hospitable and witty. He had come to America with letters of recommendation from old Mrs. Manson Mingott's English son-in-law, the banker, and had speedily made himself an important position in the world of affairs; but his habits were dissipated, his tongue was bitter, his antecedents were mysterious...Mr. Beaufort's secret, people agreed, was the way he carried things off. It was all very well to whisper that he had been "helped" to leave England by the international banking-house in which he had been employed; he carried off that rumor as easily as the rest—though New York's business conscience was no less sensitive than its moral standard—he carried everything before him, and all New York into his drawing rooms, and for over twenty years now people had said they were "going to the Beauforts" with the same tone of security as if they had said they were going to Mrs. Manson Mingott's, and with the added satisfaction of knowing they would get hot canvasback ducks and vintage wines, instead of tepid Veuve Clicquot without a year and warmed-up croquettes from Philadelphia.

Belmont became a member of the Union Club, New York's most exclusive men's club, founded the Jerome Park Racetrack with his friend Leonard Jerome (grandfather of Winston Churchill) and built up an impressive art collection including the much discussed and then considered "shocking" nudes of William Bouguereau.
    In 1876 Belmont, a Democrat, attacked the Republican administration of President Grant and supported Tilden for President to the consternation of the Republican Times:

Mr. Belmont...may be supposed to have some voice in determining the degree of credit to which our Government is entitled in the money markets of Europe. The financiers of London, Frankfort, and Amsterdam naturally listen to him as to a trust-worthy exponent of the condition and prospects of the United States...When, therefore, he declares that the party in power, is "leading the country on to ruin"...he expresses an opinion which may produce grave consequences. For if the country is on the high road to ruin, its securities are an undesirable investment. And if the representative of the Rothschilds pronounces judgment against the bonds of the United States, the chance of funding the debt at a lower rate in interest with the help of European capitalists is less than we have supposed it to be.

Mrs. August Belmont, the Former Caroline Slidell Perry, c. 1879

Joseph Seligman said of Belmont: "He is a Jew, yet he goes everywhere, meets everyone, and 'Society' swirls about him." Marriage to Miss Slidell ensured Belmont's social success—her family had the social status he lacked.

Joseph Seligman

Joseph Seligman's business career was a parable of the opportunities available in post–Civil War America to young penniless immigrants. For this was Joseph's status in 1837, when he arrived from Germany. Three years later he was running a store in Selma, Alabama, with two of his brothers, and eight years after that, opened a clothing store in New York. But

his leap to fortune and national prominence really came in the Civil War. The Seligman clothing firm gained lucrative contracts for army uniforms. But better still, Seligman became one of the chief salesmen of Union bonds in Europe. The bonds had been regarded with caution on the other side of the Atlantic. But Joseph Seligman, according to accounts at the time, turned the tide. Writing in 1870, Matthew Hale Smith in his Twenty Years Among the Bulls and Bears *remarked that:*

On the breaking out of the war Mr. Joseph Seligman visited Europe and did more, probably, than any man, in inspiring confidence of capitalists in the ability of the government to meet its liabilities. The Germans made large investments in government securities...They were induced to do this through the agency of Mr. Seligman.

Seligman's investment banking firm, J. & W. Seligman and Co., which he founded in 1864, prospered greatly after the Civil War. Seligman played a crucial role in restructuring the government debt. He also became deeply involved in dealings in railroad bond issues, alternately bemoaning the chancy nature of the business before plunging into it again with renewed zest. In the 1870's the firm of J. & W. Seligman was among the best-known and most influential banking firms in the United States. And Seligman himself was a national figure. He died in 1880, leaving his own banker's epitaph: "Stay liquid. Never invest in property or give a mortgage loan." (He took his own advice. He was once offered the whole of the Upper West Side of Manhattan for $450,000, but turned down the offer as "a bad investment.")

Jesse Seligman

Jesse Seligman, Joseph's younger brother, became head of the firm. By the time of his death in 1894, he had accumulated an estate of $30 million.

"The Hatch Family," by Eastman Johnson

Rufus Hatch, pictured with his family in this painting, was one of the best-known New York stockbrokers. But in 1876, he, like Drew, went bankrupt. At the time of his death in 1893, the Times *explained that the importance of "Uncle Rufus," as he was called, lay in the influence he had wielded on Wall Street in the 1870's:*

"Uncle Rufus" Hatch has been such an odd character in the financial world for more than thirty years, and his personality and affairs have been so much talked about and written of, by himself and others, that he has gained a reputation far wider than can be accounted for on substantial grounds in looking over his very varied career. Because he was such an interesting character and talker, the newspapers have constantly kept him before the public eye.

The Times *said that Hatch's death marked the end of the era of great speculators:*

The death of Mr. Hatch is a more than usually interesting matter of news, for besides meaning that a very widely known character has passed away it suggests that the circle of great speculators who led in Wall Street twenty years ago [in the 1870's], when that thoroughfare was deservedly regarded as the greatest gambling market in the world, has about disappeared...[Mr. Hatch] was one of the boldest of the great operators of that day, a "plunger" who would daily risk a fortune on his judgment.

Hatch, like many of the men who made fortunes in the seventies, started life with nothing. In 1862, after speculating in the grain markets of Chicago, he came to New York with only $2,000 to his name:

With that he plunged into Wall Street speculation. He succeeded, particularly through his handling of Chicago and Northwestern stock...Mr. Hatch became a figure of consequence on the Street...In the panic of 1873 "Uncle Rufus" was very roughly handled, but he managed to keep his head above water...When the panic came, Mr. Hatch was probably worth $1,000,000...He did not fail until 1876, but his failure... was directly due to his great losses in the panic.

Hatch recovered from his 1876 bankruptcy only to lose everything once and for all in 1883, in the downfall of the Northern Pacific Railway ("in which stock he had been a great bull"), which ruined the railroad czar Henry Villard as well. The Times *described Hatch, learning of his downfall, supposedly on a day of glory for the Northern Pacific:*

It was just at the time that the famous ceremony of driving the golden spike to mark the completion of the Northern Pacific Railroad was about to take place. Following Mr. Hatch and his private train was a large party of foreign capitalists whom Henry Villard was taking out to witness the driving of the golden spike in the hope that they would be induced to further invest in the railroad.

It was while these two special trains were moving westward that news was received that there had been a raid on Northern Pacific stock, and it had gone tumbling down. Both Villard and Hatch were financially ruined in that crash, and the foreign capitalists whom they had taken out to interest in future investments laughed at them when they returned.

Hatch never recovered from the 1883 disaster.

THE WORLD OF EASTERN BANKING: YOUNG MEN ON THE WAY UP

John Pierpont Morgan

When Jay Cooke failed, others were waiting to take his place. Among them was J. Pierpont Morgan, thirty-nine years old in 1876, and the son of the international banker Junius Spencer Morgan. Eventually Morgan would become America's leading banker. His first big successful venture had been stopping Gould and Fisk in a furious fight in 1869 for control of the Albany & Susquehanna Railroad. In 1871 Morgan merged with Drexel and Company, the country's second most influential banking house, next to Jay Cooke's; together they formed Drexel, Morgan and Co., which became J. P. Morgan and Co. in 1895. Morgan next gained prominence by marketing New York Central stock for W. H. Vanderbilt in 1879. He went on to many ventures, among them organizing U.S. Steel, the first billion-dollar trust. When he died in 1913 the Times, *estimating his estate at $100 million, said that Morgan was:*

...undoubtedly...the foremost individual banking figure in the world. Surpassing him in resources were the Rothschilds alone and they are and have been for generations a family of whom no single member stood out in a class with Mr. Morgan...In most European Capitals...there are members of the Rothschild family who look after the financial needs of the country, while in the United States, Mr. Morgan stood almost alone, towering above men like...John D. Rockefeller whose wealth is certainly greater.

Morgan had one of the greatest art collections of his day, and its value, at the time of his death, was estimated at $60 million. The Times *pointed out that:*

While Mr. Morgan made vast sums as head of the country's largest banking house, he had also spent money very freely. His benefactions were large and helped swell to a great figure the amount which he spent.

J. P. Morgan in Egypt

In 1876 Morgan was a backer of the Moody and Sankey revival meetings, held in New York from February to April of that year. In June of 1876, Morgan and his family sailed to Europe, where he worked in his father's London office. In

December, Morgan traveled to Egypt. Morgan, the young banker, visited the Temple of Karnak in January 1877. He is pictured wearing a pith helmet and knickers and standing next to his wife with his daughters in front.

he backed the inventor of the process for smelting aluminum in return for a large share of stock in the company which eventually became the Aluminum Company of America. Under Harding, Mellon became Secretary of the Treasury. The Times at the time of Mellon's death in 1937 cited the official estimate of his wealth as $200 million but other estimates have run as high as a billion dollars.

Jacob Schiff

Jacob Schiff was twenty-nine years old in 1876, a member of a wealthy and distinguished German-Jewish family, and an up-and-coming young New York banker. In the previous year Schiff had been made a partner in Kuhn, Loeb and Company and had married Solomon Loeb's eldest daughter, Therese. Solomon Loeb and Abraham Kuhn had founded the banking house of Kuhn, Loeb in February 1867; previously the two had been in trade together in Indiana and Cincinnati, running a merchandising business. By 1885 enterprising young Jacob Schiff had become head of Kuhn, Loeb and Co. He and his firm became famous for financing railroads. One of his best-known feats was the reorganization (with E. H. Harriman) of the Union Pacific when, according to legend, J. P. Morgan had given up on that railroad. One of Schiff's contemporaries remarked, "He carries every railroad in the country, every bit of rolling stock, every foot of track and every man connected with each line—from the president down to the last brakeman—inside his head." At his death in 1906 Schiff left an estate variously estimated between $40 million and $200 million; he was a serious philanthropist who supported many Jewish charities and gave much of his money away during his lifetime.

James Stillman

Stillman was only twenty-six years old in 1876. Like his friend J. P. Morgan, Stillman was born to wealth. But in the world of banking he went on to multiply many times over the sum he had inherited. In 1891 he became president of the National City Bank, which he made the leading bank in New York City as well as in the nation. At the time of his death in 1918 the Times estimated Stillman's wealth at over $100 million.

Andrew W. Mellon

Andrew Mellon was only twenty-one years old in 1876. In 1874 he had entered the private banking house of his father, Judge Thomas Mellon in Pittsburgh, and by 1882 he was the owner of T. Mellon and Sons. He went on to amass one of the largest American fortunes and also one of the finest art collections. He made one of his most important investments in 1889 when

OTHER YOUNG MEN ON THE WAY UP: OIL, STEEL, COKE

Andrew Carnegie, John D. Rockefeller, Henry Clay Frick, E.H. Harriman and Thomas Fortune Ryan were all young men in 1876, and they were all embarked on careers in different, new industries. Each made an enormous fortune in his chosen field—Rockefeller in oil, Frick in coke, Carnegie in steel, Harriman in railroads, and Ryan in street railways. They formed a bridge with the twentieth century, since their careers extended well into it.

The Frick Dollar Bill

During the panic of 1873 when Frick had no money to pay his men, he invented a system of paying them with bills like this which were good at the company store. The custom was continued by Frick even when good times returned and the necessity was removed.

E. H. Harriman

Harriman, age twenty-eight in 1876, was a broker on Wall Street. That year he founded the Tompkins Square Boys Club, the first organization of its kind in this country. In 1870 Harriman, who had begun his Wall Street career as a clerk, purchased a seat for himself on the New York Stock Exchange and opened a brokerage business. August Belmont, who did business with the young Harriman, told him that he was "good to draw on his [Belmont's] credit up to a million dollars." Between 1876 and 1881 Harriman accumulated capital which after 1881 he put into railroad speculation. He rebuilt the Lake Ontario Southern Railroad in 1881 and then sold it at a profit to the Pennsylvania Railroad. In 1883 he became a director of the Illinois Central, of which he became a vice-president and the controlling voice by 1887. Harriman gave up the brokerage business to devote himself to his various railroad enterprises from which he made the bulk of his fortune. He became president of the Union Pacific Railroad in 1903. At the time of his death in 1909 his fortune was estimated at $100 million.

Henry Clay Frick

Frick was the king of coke. Twenty-seven years old in 1876, he would make his first million within three years. It was Andrew Mellon's father, Thomas, who backed Frick from the start. At the age of twenty-one Frick received from Mellon $10,000 for his coke works, H. C. Frick Coke Company, and after the panic of 1873 Frick was saved from bankruptcy by Mellon. Judge Mellon once said of Frick: "He is able, energetic, industrious, resourceful, self-confident. If he continues along his own line as he has begun, he will go far unless he over-reaches. That is his only danger."

Frick fulfilled Mellon's hopes. He made his money from coke (coal put through "beehive" furnaces) which was an essential ingredient in iron and steel production. And Frick became a close friend of Andrew Mellon's; in 1879 they traveled through Europe together. When Frick died in 1919, he left an estate of between $75 million and $100 million, according to the Times; he left his Fifth Avenue mansion and his impressive art collection to the City of New York.

Thomas Fortune Ryan

Thomas Fortune Ryan was another young man in 1876—he was twenty-five years old and working in New York as a stock-

broker, having purchased a seat on the exchange two years earlier. His once prosperous family had been ruined by the Civil War, and Ryan had been orphaned at the age of fourteen. In 1872 he had come to New York and two years later had made his first million. The largest part of his fortune was made later from the New York Street Railways. In 1883, with William C. Whitney and Peter B. Widener, he organized the New York Street Cable Railroad, which came to control almost all the street railways in New York. Whitney called him "the most adroit, suave, and noiseless man" in American finance. By the time of his death in 1928, Ryan had accumulated a fortune of approximately $140 million.

John D. Rockefeller's House in Cleveland

John D. Rockefeller

John D. Rockefeller was thirty-seven years old in 1876, living in Cleveland, and running the largest oil refinery in the world, his Standard Oil Company of Ohio, which had been incorporated in 1870. In 1872 Rockefeller incorporated the South Improvement Company, his initial attempt to monopolize the oil refinery business in Cleveland, but the attempt met with so much opposition that the Pennsylvania legislature finally revoked the charter of the company. He went on to organize the Standard Oil Trust in 1879 and reorganized it in 1882; the trust was made up of forty companies under a single management, which controlled approximately 90 percent of refining and pipe-line capacity in the United States. Reflecting on his success in later years, Rockefeller explained the ruthless philosophy which had helped him accumulate an estate estimated at his death at around $900 million:

The growth of a large corporation is merely a survival of the fittest...The American Beauty Rose can be produced...only by sacrificing the early buds which grow up around it. This is not an evil tendency in business. It is merely the working-out of a law of nature and a law of God.

The Pennsylvania Oil Fields

Oil was discovered in northwestern Pennsylvania in 1859. Oil from fields like these went to John D. Rockefeller's Cleveland refinery. As early as 1865, Rockefeller decided to concentrate all his energies on the oil refinery business. Starting out as one of thirty Cleveland refineries, his was soon the largest in Cleveland, and by 1870 Rockefeller was also the largest shipper of oil in the country.

Andrew Carnegie

In 1876 Andrew Carnegie was forty-one years old and launched on his extraordinary business career that made him $500 million by the time of his death. In 1873 Carnegie, pursuing his famous admonition that the "proper policy was to put all good eggs in one basket and then watch that basket," sold his interests in railroads and sunk his fortune into steel. Like all Carnegie strategies, the move was brilliantly successful. In 1901 he sold Carnegie Steel to J. P. Morgan for $250 million.

Carnegie differed in social outlook from other men of his generation. He wrote that "the amassing of wealth is one of the worst species of idolatry—no idol more debasing than the worship of money." He lived up to his writings by giving away $350 million during his lifetime, $60 million of which went to found libraries in this country and abroad.

Carnegie attributed his success to his "organizing power" and "to the faculty of knowing and choosing others." But perhaps the real secret of his success lay in his comprehension of the capitalistic system; he said that a "man must necessarily occupy a narrow field who is at the beck and call of others. Even if he becomes the President of a great corporation he is hardly his own master, unless he holds control of the stock." He practiced what he preached: "My decision was taken early," said Carnegie. "I would concentrate upon the manufacture of iron and steel and be master in that." And he was.

Edgar Thomson Steel Works, c. 1875

Carnegie and his partners began building the Edgar Thomson Steel Works in 1873—the first plant to produce Bessemer steel on a mass scale in this country. The plant, named after the head of the Pennsylvania Railroad, began operation in 1875. One year later, Carnegie said with pleasure, "In steel rails we have made a wonderful success—every sanguine prediction I have made is more than verified."

Chicago In Ruins—Burning Coal Heaps—1871

Harper's Weekly proclaimed that despite the incredible destruction neither "fire nor flood can quench the indomitable spirit that made Chicago and will remake it greater than before."

Chicago after the Fire

This photograph was taken in 1874, three years after the fire; much of Chicago still lay in ruins. The view is looking south on Wabash Avenue.

Chicago in Ruins—Opening Bank Vaults—Merchants' Savings, Loan, and Trust Company, Corner Lake and Dearborn streets—1871

A Chicago fire-orphan wrote to a friend in Iowa: "Chicago is in ashes. Not one wholesale business left. Such a conflagration was never known on this continent. At present we hardly know the extent of the damage, only that it is terrible."

MIDWESTERN MEN OF FORTUNE

Potter Palmer

In 1871 the city of Chicago was leveled by fire. Potter Palmer, perhaps the most important new man of wealth to come out of Chicago, lost ninety-five buildings in the fire. Legend has it that it was his wife, the former Bertha Honoré, who persuaded Palmer not to abandon the ruined city. The Times *reported that:*

Mr. Palmer felt at first inclined to...leave the work of rebuilding the city to others. During a conversation he had with his wife at that time he made known to her his desire to leave the ruined city. "Mr. Palmer," replied Mrs. Palmer, "it is the duty of every Chicagoan to stay here and devote his fortune and energies to rebuilding this stricken city."

Palmer did remain in Chicago and made a fortune from rebuilding the city. The Times *said that:*

No man contributed so much to the resurrection of the city as did Potter Palmer. As soon as possible after the fire, work on the Palmer House was resumed. It was completed at the cost of $2,000,000, the result being the handsomest and most substantial hotel in the country...He rebuilt many other buildings and his real estate holdings continued to increase in value.

In 1876 Palmer was fifty years old. By the time of his death in 1902, he was worth approximately $25 million, most of it in real estate. Palmer had come to Chicago and opened a dry-goods store on Lake Street in 1852—at the age of twenty-six. Within ten years he had become an affluent man. But like so many other rich men of the seventies, he made his first large amount of money during the Civil War. The Times *explained:*

Mr. Palmer's great fortune came with the Civil War. He foresaw that the impending struggle would interfere with production, and he spent every dollar he had in buying up cotton and woolen goods...His judgment

The Palmer House After the Fire

In 1876 the Potter Palmers were living in the new Palmer House, which Potter Palmer had opened in 1873; it was the second American hotel to be entirely lit by electric lights. In line with the American desire to copy all things European, the dining room was copied from the salon of the Crown Prince of Potsdam and there was an "Egyptian" room. To top things off, the barbershop had 225 silver dollars

proved correct. The war brought the increased prices he had foreseen, and in less than four years he had made over $2,500,000.

In 1865, with a fortune estimated at somewhere between $3 million and $4 million, Palmer chose to retire. He sold his interest in the dry-goods store to Marshall Field and Levi Leiter and then went into real estate, buying $1 million worth of land on State Street. The Times *said:*

He determined to make State Street, then little more than a wide alley, the principal thoroughfare of Chicago...He bought three-quarters of a mile of frontage on that street. He succeeded in having it widened. (by 20 feet)

Palmer succeeded in making State Street the main Chicago business thoroughfare. In the same way, he helped to change the fashionable residential section from Union Park to the lakeside. And following the New York example, Palmer set out to gain social standing for himself and his wife by building her a Gothic castle, (the "damnest mansion ever imagined," according to one contemporary) costing about $700,000, which was finished in 1885. Like its Eastern counterparts, the house contained European furniture. Mrs. Potter Palmer, in the 1880's, would reign not only over her large house, but also over Chicago society. But in 1876 her husband was still accumulating his fortune and getting ready to spend it, along the lines set for him by New York high society.

sunk in the floor. Palmer said that his hotel was "a realization of an era of magnificence." But Rudyard Kipling disagreed and called the hotel "a gilded rabbit-warren...There I found a gilded hall of...marble, crammed with people talking about money and spitting about everywhere." The Palmers lived in the hotel until they moved in 1885 to the elaborate house they built.

Mrs. Potter Palmer

Mrs. Palmer was only twenty-seven years old in 1876. In the 1880's and 1890's she became a famed Chicago hostess, called "The Queen." She was president of the Board of Lady Managers of the Chicago World's Fair in 1893.

OTHER CHICAGO MILLIONAIRES

Marshall Field

In 1876 Marshall Field was forty-two years old and with Levi Leiter the owner of the dry-goods store Field, Leiter and Co. Field had come to Chicago in 1856 and worked as a clerk in a dry-goods store earning a salary of $400 a year and sleeping in the store. He eventually joined Potter Palmer as a junior partner in his large and successful dry-goods store. When Palmer withdrew in 1867, the store was left to Field and Leiter. And in 1881 Leiter, too, withdrew, and the store became Marshall Field and Company. Field also invested successfully in real estate, McCormick reapers, and railroads (the Chicago and Northwestern). When he died in 1906, he left an estate of about $120 million. Summing up Field's career, John Villiers Farwell, a contemporary of Field's, said:

"He had the merchant's instinct. He lived for it, and it only. He never lost it."

Marshall Field's Chicago Mansion, Built in 1876

In 1876 Field built himself a red brick French-style house, designed by the fashionable architect Richard Morris Hunt at a reputed cost of $100,000. The house was on Prairie Avenue in Chicago, known as "the street of the stately few."

Levi Leiter

Leiter, forty-two years old in 1876, was the third partner of Field and Palmer. He became a partner of Field and Palmer in 1865 and served as the credit manager for Field, Leiter and Palmer until he retired in 1881. Like Palmer, Leiter then entered the real estate business. His daughter, Mary, advanced the family socially by marrying Lord Curzon, Viceroy of India. Leiter's motto was: "Cash the rule, credit the exception."

George Pullman

Pullman was forty-five years old in 1876. Only eleven years earlier he had patented the sleeping car, which was the foundation of his fortune. He was not, in fact, the inventor of the sleeping car, but he manufactured and operated the cars on a larger scale then anyone else. In 1881 Pullman moved his base of operations to a town he created south of Chicago called Pullman, which was supposedly a model town for workers, but Pullman had problems with his underpaid and overwatched employees, as evidenced by the bitter Pullman strike of 1894. He died in 1897, leaving a fortune estimated by the Times at between $12 million and $30 million.

Chicago in 1875

The Pullman Car

Accustomed as we are to flying across the country at the rate of from thirty to fifty miles per hour by the mighty power of steam, it seems curious to look back and see what difficulties our forefathers had to contend with when they desired to make even a short journey.
Harper's Weekly, January 1876

Philip Danforth Armour

Philip Armour, who was forty-four years old in 1876, founded Armour and Company in Chicago in 1875. At his death in 1901, the meat-packer's fortune was estimated at $50 million. Armour made his first $2 million during the Civil War when as a Chicago butcher he speculated on pork prices. Other Chicago meat packers who competed ruthlessly with Armour were: Nelson Morris, Gustavus Swift, and the company of Libby, McNeil and Libby. Together these four formed a pool in the 1880's and were known as the "Big Four." They made meat packing the leading Chicago industry. Armour once said, "I like to turn bristles, blood, and the inside and outside of pigs and bullocks into revenue."*

The McCormick Harvester and Wire Binder of 1876

McCormick continually made improvements on his original reaper, such as the addition of the wire binder. By such improvements, McCormick managed to stay ahead of some thirty other rivals.

Cyrus Hall McCormick

Cyrus McCormick, who had patented his reaper in 1834, was sixty-seven years old in 1876. He had already built the factory for his McCormick Harvesting Machine Co. in Chicago and accumulated his fortune in that city. By 1880, fifty thousand McCormick machines were shipped annually from Chicago all over the world. Horace Greeley wrote in the New York Tribune that the reaper was "more beneficial and creditable to the United States than if fifty thousand of her troops had defeated one hundred thousand choice European soldiers." By drastically shortening the process of gathering grain, the reaper made farming on a large scale possible.

THE WEST: MINING KINGS

After 1869, men could travel from the East to California by the transcontinental railroad. The train changed everything; goods could be transported easily to Eastern markets, and machines invented in the East could by shipped to the West, to be used in extracting wealth from the soil. The two major sources of the Western fortunes were railroads and mining.

Adolph Heinrich J. Sutro: First Dirt for the Tunnel, Comstock Lode

Born in Prussia, Sutro first came to America in 1851 and made his home in San Francisco. He drove a tunnel through Mount Davidson from the Carson River to the Comstock Lode, which created a much easier way to move men and supplies to and from the mines. Completed in 1878, the tunnel brought enormous profits to Sutro, who sold it in 1879. Sutro returned to live in San Francisco, made excellent real estate investments and was mayor between 1894 and 1896.

James G. Fair

Fair, forty-five years old in 1876, made his considerable fortune principally from the Consolidated Virginia Mine of the famed Comstock Lode. He also invested in land and railroads. At the time of Fair's death in 1894, his fortune was estimated by the Times *at $40 million. Dan De Quille, who was editor of the Virginia City (Nevada)* Daily Territorial Enterprise *and a friend of Mark Twain's, wrote his* History of the Big Bonanza *in 1876. He said:*

James G. Fair, Esq., one of the principal owners and the superintendent of the Consolidated Virginia and California mines, was born in the north of Ireland. He came to the United States in his youth and settled in Illinois. Upon the discovery of gold in California he determined to try his luck as a miner. He left Illinois in 1849 and reached California in August 1850...In 1860 he...made his way across the Sierras to Virginia City, where he has ever since made his home and where he has constantly been engaged in mining and other enterprises. In 1867 he became the partner of John Mackay in the Hale & Norcross mine, when both he and Mr. Mackay made a snug bit of money.

Since becoming partners, Messrs. Mackay & Fair, and their associates, Messrs. Flood & O'Brien, of San Francisco, who are interested with them in many speculations, have acquired controlling interests in the Gould & Curry, Best & Belcher,

Consolidated Virginia, California, Utah, and Occidental mines...Messrs. Mackay & Fair also have mines in Idaho [and] Montana...

Mr. Fair is a man who never talks when he is acting, and no one knows exactly what Uncle Jimmy,'' as the ''boys'' call him, is up to. You see the hole by which he goes into the ground, but when once he is down out of sight you never know in what direction he is drifting.

John W. Mackay

John Mackay was Fair's partner. Together they exploited the Comstock Lode and accumulated large fortunes. In 1873 they found the ''Big Bonanza,'' the greatest mining strike of the 1870's. In 1876 Mackay was forty-five and worth, by De Quille's estimate, between $50 million and $60 million. De Quille, who dedicated his book to Mackay, described the mining king:

The millionaire miner of the ''big bonanza'' was born in the city of Dublin, Ireland...He came to California soon after the discovery of gold...He had his ups and downs the same as did other miners...Mr. Mackay came to the silver mines of Washoe in the early days and for a time...worked for wages...swinging a pick and shovel as an ordinary miner. It was not long, however, before he began to get ahead financially...He finally obtained a large interest in the Hale and Norcross mine, Virginia City...No man in Nevada more thoroughly understands the Comstock Lode than Mr. Mackay.

John P. Jones

Jones, who was born in Herefordshire, England, made his wealth in mining in Nevada, and then in 1873 became a Republican senator from Nevada. He was another character in De Quille's saga:

The Hon. J. P. Jones, United States senator from Nevada, is a man who had much mining experience in California, previous to his crossing the Sierras and taking up his residence on the Comstock Lode. He has long had control of the Crown Point mine, at Gold Hill, and from its several bonanzas has extracted many millions of dollars. He thoroughly understands the business of silver-mining and is an excellent judge of the ores of the Comstock. He is well acquainted not only with that portion of the great lode which passes through Gold Hill, but also with the mines on all parts of the vein. He owns a controlling interest in the Savage mine, in Virginia City, and still retains the Crown Point mine, which is yielding as largely as ever, though the ore extracted is less rich than that which was being extracted some years since.

The mills of the Nevada Mill Company, nine in number...are owned by Mr. Jones and Hon. William Sharon and are capable of crushing 650 tons of ore per day...Mr. Jones counts his dollars by millions. It is said that he has about five times as many millions as he has fingers and toes.

William Sharon

William Sharon's fortune was estimated by De Quille in 1876 as between $70 million and $80 million, undoubtedly on the rather high side of the truth. In 1874 Sharon became a United States senator from Nevada. He had made his fortune in the Nevada mines; DeQuille described Sharon's activities as the head of the Virginia City branch of the Bank of California:

The Hon. William Sharon, who for many years figured so prominently in the mining...interests of the Comstock Lode as to earn for himself the title of the "King of the Comstock" was born in Jefferson County, Ohio...He was among those who crossed the plains in 1849, and in August of that year reached Sacramento, where he purchased a stock of goods and opened a store. The floods of the winter of 1849–50 swept his stock into the Pacific Ocean...After his store had been swept away by the flood, he went down to San Francisco and opened a real estate office. He continued in this business until 1864...when he began speculating in mining stock...He was sent over the Sierras to Virginia City, Nevada by the Bank of

California to look after certain of the affairs of that institution which required attention...He was shrewd enough to see that he had at last reached the place where all the money on the Pacific Coast was coming from... He at once urged upon the officers of the Bank of California the necessity of opening a branch at Virginia City, which was done and Mr. Sharon was placed at the head of the new institution with unlimited powers. He remained in Virginia City...as the head of the branch bank in that place...

Mr. Sharon is the father of the Virginia and Truckee Railroad, undoubtedly the crookedest railroad in the world, and a wonderful road in many other respects. In building this road, Mr. Sharon secured a subsidy of $500,000 from the people of Washoe in aid of the project, constructed as much of the road as the sum would build, then mortgaged the whole road for the amount of money required for its completion. In this way he built the road without putting his hand into his own pocket for a cent, and he still owns half the road—worth $2,500,000 and bringing him in...$12,000 per day...The road, however, has been of great benefit to the country, and Mr. Sharon was a good man for the country while he was at the head of the Virginia branch of the Bank of California, as he had the nerve to advance money for the development of mines and the building of mills at the time when no outside banking-house would have ventured a cent.

The Palace Hotel, San Francisco

The Palace Hotel in San Francisco, built in 1876, was owned principally by William Sharon. De Quille, author of the well-known history of the Comstock Lode, described the hotel: "The mines of the Comstock give life to the whole Pacific coast and are the mainspring...of all kinds of trades and every kind of business...The army of workmen of all kinds who were employed in the building of the famous Palace Hotel of San Francisco, the largest and most costly structure of the kind in the world, were all paid with money taken out of the mines of the Comstock."

Interior of the Palace Hotel, San Francisco, c. 1876

Three Gentlemen Relaxing in the Palace Hotel, San Francisco, c. 1876

Darius Ogden Mills

Mills made his money in the West but went to spend it in the East, where he had been born. Fifty-one years of age in 1876, Mills had made his fortune in mining stock and banking. He started out in Sacramento as a storekeeper but moved on to start a bank, D. O. Mills and Co., in 1850, and then became president of the

Bank of California between 1864 and 1873. In 1878 Mills went to live in New York, where he bought a large house opposite St. Patrick's Cathedral which he decorated for $450,000. When his daughter married Whitelaw Reid, Mills gave them the Villard mansion as a wedding present, which cost him $400,000. His son married into the socially prominent Livingston family. Mills died in 1910, leaving a fortune estimated at $60 million.

William A. Clark: The Copper King

Clark, thirty-seven years old in 1876, made his fortune in copper mining in Montana. He started out buying and selling tobacco to miners and then went on to establish Montana's first bank in 1870. He next formed the Colorado and Montana Smelting Company. Between 1901 and 1907, Clark was the senator from Montana; Clark's rival in copper mining was Marcus Daly, whom he defeated for the Senate.

George Hearst

George Hearst, age fifty-six in 1876, made his fortune in mining. Born near Sullivan, Missouri, he went west to California by foot in 1850. By 1888 he had been elected senator from California. Eight years earlier he had acquired the San Francisco Examiner, which his only child, William Randolph Hearst, then only a boy of thirteen, inherited.

THE WEST: RAILROAD MAGNATES

Collis P. Huntington

Huntington, like so many men of his generation, went to California in 1849, having heard the news of the gold rush. He began life in California running a hardware store in Sacramento; Mark Hopkins soon joined him and the store became "Huntington and Hopkins." Along with Charles Crocker and Leland Stanford, Hopkins and Huntington eventually formed the Pacific Associates, a group which fought to gain control of the Western railroads; Huntington was the leader of the group in fact if not in title. In 1861 "the quartet," as they became known, won the government charter to build the western half of the transcontinental railroad, the Central Pacific Railroad, which joined the Union Pacific in Utah in 1869. They then moved on to form the Southern Pacific Company (they got the charter for the Southern Pacific Railway in 1868), through which they expanded their railway enterprises into southern California. Huntington stopped at nothing: "If you have to pay money to have the right thing done, it is only just and fair to do it," he once said. One of his contemporaries described Huntington's methods for financing his railroads:

They start out their railway track and survey their line near a thriving village. They go to the most prominent citizens of that village and say, "If you will give us so many thousand dollars we will run through here; if you do not we will run by." And in every instance where the subsidy was not granted this course was taken, and the effect was just as they said, to kill off the little town.

In this manner, the Pacific Associates were able to finance many miles of railway. In the battle between the Pacific Associates, who attempted to expand outside of California, and Tom Scott of the Texas & Pacific Railroad for control of the railways of the Southwest, congressmen were bought and sold. Huntington wrote: "I am fearful this damnation Congress will kill me"; he complained endlessly of the

high cost of fixing things. The Pacific Associates eventually beat Scott, using every available tactic. In 1882 the Texas & Pacific and the Southern Pacific joined at El Paso, Texas, and the battle between the railroad kings came to an end with Huntington triumphant. At Huntington's death in 1900, estimates of his wealth ranged from $50 million to $90 million.

Mark Hopkins' House

The house of one of the Pacific Associates, Mark Hopkins. Hopkins and Huntington began by operating a store in Sacramento, before going on to their profitable railroad schemes. When Hopkins died in 1887 he left an estate, according to the Times, of between $10 million and $15 million.

Leland Stanford, Governor of California and Railroad Magnate

Leland Stanford was a cohort of Huntington's, a member of the Pacific Associates. In 1876 he was fifty-two years old and had been governor of California between 1861 and 1863. Through Stanford, among others, the quartet managed to directly control the political processes of the state. Stanford, while governor, passed four acts helping the Central Pacific Railway, of which he was president. In 1885 he was elected U.S. senator from California. In the annual report of the Board of Directors of the Central Pacific Railway to the stockholders, Stanford said:

There is no foundation in good reason for the attempts made by the General Government and by the State to especially control your affairs. It is a question of might, and it is to your interest to have it determined where the power resides.

Stanford, more than the other Pacific Associates, enjoyed the good life. He owned vineyards in Tehame County and a ranch where he bred race horses. It was Stanford who asked Eadweard Muybridge to photograph one of his horses, Occident, in motion, thus leading to the famous Muybridge studies of motion. Stanford's estate, at his death in 1893, was estimated by the Times at between $40 million and $60 million. He founded Stanford University in 1885 as a memorial to his son, who had died young.

The Residence of Governor Leland Stanford

Residence of Charles Crocker, San Francisco

Crocker's mansion cost him $1.5 million to build and furnish.

Mr. and Mrs. Charles Crocker in 1876 in San Francisco

Crocker, who weighed in at 265 pounds, was a partner of Huntington, Stanford, and Hopkins in the Central Pacific Railway and their other railway ventures. It was Crocker who supervised the construction of the Central Pacific, actually living in camps on the construction sites. As a result of his watchfulness, the Central Pacific was completed seven years earlier than required: "for four years, without pause, three thousand Irishmen and ten thousand Chinese coolies toiled away through desert heat and mountain cold or snow," building the western end of the transcontinental railroad.

Crocker's famed threat against Los Angeles, made in 1876, was typical of the ruthless methods used by him and his partners to build their railroads and make the maximum profit for themselves. Harris Newmark, a resident of Los Angeles in 1876, recalled that after the completion of the Southern Pacific, "the people of Los Angeles became very much dissatisfied with the Company's method of handling their business, and especially with the...freight rates...This dissatisfaction on the part of an enterprising community accustomed to some liberality found in

(continued on following page)

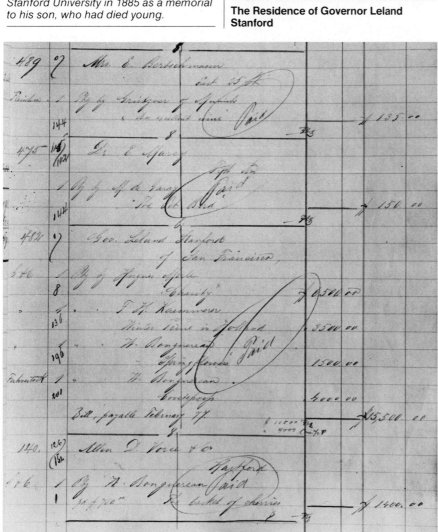

Stanford's Painting Purchases

In December of 1876 M. Knoedler & Co. entered in their stockbook paintings purchased by Leland Stanford amounting to $15,000. Two of the paintings were by the fashionable artist Bouguereau; a painting of a nude by Bouguereau, belonging to the banker August Belmont, was the talk of New York in the 1870's.

time such an open expression that Charles F. Crocker, one of the original promoters of the Central, and one of the owners of the Southern Pacific...came down to confer with the City Council at a public meeting."

After much discussion, most of it unsympathetic to his cause, Crocker said, "If this be the spirit in which Los Angeles proposes to deal with the railroad upon which the town's very vitality must depend, I will make grass to grow in the streets of your city." Newmark commented that "considering the fate that has befallen more than one community which coldly regarded the proposals of these same California railroads, Crocker's warning was not without significance."

When Crocker died in 1888, he left an estate of about $20 million.

James J. Hill

James J. Hill was the famous railroad magnate of the northwest, with a kingdom which eventually extended from the Great Lakes to Oregon. Although Hill began life with no financial resources, he ended up at his death in 1916 worth $53 million. In 1878 he was part of a syndicate that purchased the bankrupt St. Paul & Pacific Railroad and renamed it the St. Paul, Minneapolis & Manitoba Railway. Hill went on to build the Great Northern Railway Company (created in 1890). He proposed to build west to Puget Sound from St. Paul, a radical idea since his railway did not enjoy the enormous land grants that the Union Pacific and the Central Pacific had received. (The Northern Pacific, Hill's rival, had also received a big land grant.) Called "the Empire Builder" and "the man who made the Northwest," Hill triumphed; he reached Puget Sound in 1893 and eventually bought out most of the stock of Henry Villard's Northern Pacific Railway. Hill once explained his success by saying that "intelligent management of railroads must be based on exact knowledge of facts. Guesswork will not do." Hill was only thirty-eight years old in 1876 and at the beginning of his long and magnificent career as a railroad czar in the Northwest.

THE SOUTH

In 1787 there was not one man in New York worth a million dollars. At that time Charles Carroll of Maryland, with his 80,000 acres of land, was richer than any New Yorker. But by 1876 everything had changed. Wealth was by then concentrated in the North, the Midwest, and the West and came not from land but from industrial pursuits. The South was still recovering from the damages inflicted by the Civil War. But the image of a totally ruined South is not correct. There was in the 1870's some regional wealth in the South, although nothing on a scale comparable to the fortunes being amassed in the North. The war had obliterated the fortunes of most of the Southern plantation aristocracy. Then came Reconstruction with its restrictive land laws and political chaos. But with the election of 1876, a new era was at hand. It is generally believed that Rutherford B. Hayes promised Southern congressmen federal aid for their states—aid for Tom Scott's Texas & Pacific Railroad, a Southerner in the Cabinet, and the removal of federal troops—in return for an end to the filibuster by Southern congressmen which was blocking his accession to the Presidency. Whatever the deal was, it was clearly an attempt by a newly emerging group of Southern businessmen to help themselves. As journalist Henry Grady said a few years later, the South had clearly put "business above politics."

In the year 1876 came another important change: a stringent federal Land Act of 1866 was repealed and for the first time since the war, thousands of acres of Southern land were available to speculators. Men rushed in to take advantage of the situation. The Illinois Central ran special trains from Chicago to Louisiana and Mississippi to accommodate the eager speculators. One congressman alone bought 111,188 acres of Louisiana land in 1876. And during the next ten years, over five and a half million acres of federal land alone were sold.

While the North was convulsed by violent railroad strikes in 1877, one Southerner boasted that "money invested here is as safe from the rude hand of mob violence as it is in the best United States bond." And the Philadelphia *Ledger* pointed out to its readers that in the South, "land, labor, fuel, water power, and building facilities are cheap. The way to clear and large profits is open." Northern capital took this advice and moved into the South, stripped its forests, helped build its railroads and bought much of its land. Foreigners joined in these undertakings; in the early 1880's one English syndicate purchased two million acres of Florida land, and a Philadelphia newspaper reported that "foreign capital is pouring in at an unprecedented rate."

The economic development of the South took place largely *after* 1876, but by 1876 the industries that would later flourish in the South—cotton, tobacco, cottonseed oil, iron and steel—were getting under way.

Among the men involved in the beginning of the industrial development of the South was John Inman, thirty-three in 1876 and the son of a plantation owner. Cotton was certainly not a new business in the South, but Inman approached it in a new way, going north to organize the New York Cotton Exchange. He used his own capital and any capital he could raise to invest in the industrial development of the South.

Another Southerner who helped to mobilize the growth of the South was Henry Fairchild De Bardeleen, known as "the king of the Southern iron world." De Bardeleen married the daughter of the wealthiest man in Birmingham and inherited his father-in-law's company in 1873, the Red Mountain Iron and Coal Company. By the end of the next decade his company, then known as De Bardeleen Coal and Iron, was capitalized at $10 million and De Bardeleen, the owner of coal and ore mines as well as coke ovens and railroads, would boast that "I wanted to eat up all the crawfish I could—swallow up all the little fellows and I did."

Another important figure in the industrial development of the South was Milton Hannibal Smith, president for forty years of the Louisville & Nashville Railroad. That railroad owned about half a million acres of Alabama land, and Smith invested about $30 million in extracting minerals and pig iron from the land.

Tobacco was responsible for other Southern fortunes. In the seventies, Virginia was the leading state in tobacco production, but the men who came to control the tobacco industry in the eighties were for the most part North Carolinians—Julian S. Carr, R. J. Reynolds and the Dukes. James B. Duke, who was just starting his career in the seventies, was one Southerner who made a truly significant fortune on the national scale.

James B. Duke

James B. Duke, only twenty years old in 1876, was a young Southerner who made an immense fortune from tobacco. Duke grew up on a farm in North Carolina. Immediately after the end of the Civil War, he and his brother, Benjamin, and his father, a farmer named Washington Duke, began packaging tobacco on their farm and selling it in nearby villages. In 1873 the trio opened a factory in Durham, North Carolina, where they packaged their tobacco. Before long the small factory grew into W. Duke and Sons (1878), with the aid of a $14,000 investment by an outsider. By 1885 the company was an enormous success, doing $600,000 a year in business and producing over a billion cigarettes each year.

In the 1870's, the cigarette was still a novelty. Part of Duke's success in popularizing cigarettes was due to his brilliant advertising techniques—lovely ladies began to adorn the packages of Duke cigarettes. A New York merchant, Asa Lemlein, described Duke's brilliant selling techniques: "Billboards began to flare out with Duke ads and newspapers, too. I got circulars offering camp chairs and clocks and crayon drawings if I'd order so many thousand Duke cigarettes. Customers started asking for the cigarettes by name."

Duke ruled the retail trade in tobacco as president of the American Tobacco Company until his death in 1925. Duke once said, "If John D. Rockefeller can do what he is doing for oil, why should I not do it in tobacco?" And he did; the American Tobacco Company was his creation.

Edith Wharton in 1876

Describing her childhood in New York in the 1870's, Wharton wrote:

"My parents' guests ate well, and drank good wine with discernment; but a more fastidious taste had shortened the enormous repasts and deep bumpers of colonial days, and in twenty minutes the whiskered gentlemen had joined the flounced ladies on the purple settees for another half hour of amiable chat, accompanied by the cup of tea which always rounded off the evening... Small parochial concerns...formed the staple of the talk. Art and music and literature were rather timorously avoided (unless Trollope's last novel were touched upon, or a discreet allusion made to Mr. William Astor's audacious acquisition of a Bouguereau Venus) and the topics dwelt upon were personal: the thoughtful discussion of food, wine, horses ('high steppers' were beginning to be much sought after), the laying out and planting of country-seats, the selection of 'specimen' copper beeches and fern-leaved maples for lawns, just beginning to be shorn smooth by the new hand-mowers, and those plans of European travel which filled so large a space in the thought of old New Yorkers."

HOW THEY SPENT IT

In 1876 the taste of the rich was at a turning point. In matters of style, Americans had always looked to Europe. But in the past, efforts to imitate or adapt European styles had always been balanced by fear of un-republican ostentation. Mrs. Pennilow in *The Age of Innocence* bought her dresses from Worth, the famous Paris fashion house, but refused to wear them new. Her caution was reflected in the prudence of many Americans who brought to the style they imported from Europe a matter-of-fact quality, not ashamed to appear provincial.

Such a sense of caution was swiftly abandoned. The heirs of the vast new fortunes found these signs of sturdy provincialism embarrassing and sought to leap-frog over the old gentry to create a new, princely caste. What style were they to adopt? In 1876 they had many options. If the architect Louis Sullivan had had his way, the rich would have chosen a style American in essence but modern in spirit and adventurous in tone. Sullivan did not have his way, and by 1883 it became clear what had happened. In that year Alva Vanderbilt gave her famous costume ball, and the form the festivities took clearly displayed the direction society had taken, reactionary in style, feebly cosmopolitan and imitative of Europe. It was a distressing failure of nerve. Old Commodore Vanderbilt had needed no models in putting together the New York Central. But when his descendants began to spend the money he had accumulated, they lacked his brash self-confidence, meekly searched for precedents and found them in Europe. Their choice had far-reaching effects. The Vanderbilts copied Europe and in their turn were duly copied by the newly rich in the Midwest and West of America. Thus were lost the possibilities that Louis Sullivan dreamed of.

NEW YORK SOCIETY

Edith Wharton was fourteen years old in 1876. She would later become the social chronicler of the 1870's. In *The Age of Innocence*, set in the 1870's, she brilliantly described the tension between the older, provincial style and the emerging cosmopolitan one:

The New York of Newland Archer's day was a small and slippery pyramid, in which as yet, hardly a fissure had been made or a foothold gained. At its base was a firm foundation of what Mrs. Archer called "plain people"; an honorable but obscure majority of respectable families who...had been raised above their level by marriage with one of the ruling clans. People, Mrs. Archer always said, were not as particular as they used to be; and with old Catherine Spicer ruling one end of Fifth Avenue; and Julius Beaufort the other, you couldn't expect the old traditions to last much longer.

Firmly narrowing upward from this wealthy but inconspicuous substratum was the compact and dominant group which the Mingotts, Newlands, Chiverses and Mansons so actively represented. Most people imagined them to be the very apex of the pyramid; but they themselves...were aware that, in the eyes of the professional genealogist, only a still smaller number of families could lay claim to that eminence....

Mrs. Archer and her son and daughter, like everyone else in New York, knew who these privileged beings were: the Dagonets in Washington Square, who came of an old English county family...the Lannings...and van der Luydens, direct descendants of the first Dutch governor of Manhattan, and related by pre-Revolutionary marriages to several members of the French and British aristocracy... The van der Luydens, who stood above all of them, had faded into a kind of super-terrestrial twilight, from which only two figures impressively emerged; those of Mr. and Mrs. Henry van der Luyden.

Caroline Astor—Mrs. William Astor—the Queen of New York Society in 1876. *The event of the New York social season was the ball which she gave every year on the third Monday in January.*

CAROLINE ASTOR: QUEEN OF NEW YORK SOCIETY

The position occupied by Mr. and Mrs. van der Luyden in *The Age of Innocence* was occupied in New York in the seventies by Mr. and Mrs. William Astor. William Astor was the younger of the two sons of William Backhouse Astor; his wife, Caroline, a member of one of the "old" families, the Schermerhorns, was the queen of New York society. Her husband spent most of his time at his country estate, Ferncliff, in Dutchess County on the banks of the Hudson, about a hundred miles north of the city.

WARD McALLISTER

Samuel Ward McAllister was by profession a lawyer. In partnership with his father and brother in San Francisco in the early 1850's, McAllister made enough money to satisfy himself and then moved to New York, where he and Mrs. William Astor became the social arbiters of the 1870's. They ruled over New York society with the same iron hand with which Drew, Fisk and Gould had ruled over the Erie Railway. Of course, McAllister and *the* Mrs. Astor, as she became known (to distinguish her from her sister-in-law, Augusta), did not associate with the likes of Drew, Fisk or Gould. For that matter, they did not associate with the Vanderbilts who did not as yet have the social clout of the

Ward McAllister

McAllister said that in the United States "four generations of gentlemen make as good and true a gentleman as forty."

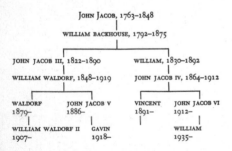

The House of Astor

DESCENT IN THE MALE LINE

JOHN JACOB, 1763–1848
|
WILLIAM BACKHOUSE, 1792–1875

| JOHN JACOB III, 1822–1890 | WILLIAM, 1830–1892 |
| WILLIAM WALDORF, 1848–1919 | JOHN JACOB IV, 1864–1912 |

| WALDORF 1879– | JOHN JACOB V 1886– | VINCENT 1891– | JOHN JACOB VI 1912– |

| WILLIAM WALDORF II 1907– | GAVIN 1918– | WILLIAM 1935– |

John Jacob Astor and His Children

JOHN JACOB ASTOR, 1763–1848, m. SARAH TODD, ca. 1762–1834
1. MAGDALEN, 1788–1832, m. { ADRIAN BENTZON / JOHN BRISTED
2. SARAH, 1790, d. young
3. JOHN JACOB II, 1791–ca. 1869
4. WILLIAM BACKHOUSE, 1792–1875, m. MARGARET REBECCA ARM-
   [STRONG, 1798–9?–1872
5. DOROTHEA, 1795–1853, m. WALTER LANGDON
6. HENRY, 1797–1799
7. ELIZA, 1801–1838, m. COUNT VINCENT RUMPFF
8. BOY, 1802, d. unchristened

The Astor Family Tree

Astors. McAllister, in his memoirs, *Society as I Have Found It*, described the changing New York social scene and attributed the change largely to the new money created by the industrial revolution.

SOCIETY AS I HAVE FOUND IT, BY WARD McALLISTER

New York society turned over a new leaf. Up to this time, for one to be worth a million of dollars was to be rated a man of fortune, but now, bygones must be bygones. New York's ideas as to values, when fortune was named, leaped boldly up to ten millions, fifty millions, one hundred millions, and the necessities and luxuries followed suit. One was no longer content with a dinner of a dozen or more, to be served by a couple of servants. Fashion demanded that you be received in the hall of the house in which you were to dine, by from five to six servants, who, with the butler, were to serve the repast. The butler, on such occasions, [was] to do alone the head-work, and under him he had these men in livery to serve the dinner, he to guide and direct them. Soft strains of music were introduced between the courses, and in some houses gold replaced silver in the way of plate, and everything that skill and art could suggest was added to make the dinners not a vulgar display, but a great gastronomic effort, evidencing the possession by the host of both money and taste.

CAROLINE ASTOR: THE MYSTIC ROSE

Mrs. Winthrop Chanler (an Astor by marriage), in her memoirs, *Roman Spring*, described Caroline Astor:

New York society was still a closed circle to which one did or did not belong. Mrs. William B. Astor was the acknowledged leader. She always sat on the right of the host when she went to dinner parties; she wore a black wig and a great many jewels; she had pleasant, cordial manners and unaffectedly enjoyed her undisputed position. She gave very grand dinners and the great Astor Ball was the social event of the season.

Caroline Astor easily overwhelmed the other Mrs. Astor, Augusta, the wife of John Jacob Astor III, who was by rights *the* Mrs. Astor, since she was married to the older of the two brothers. But Caroline, with Ward McAllister by her side, prevailed. She first met McAllister in the winter of 1872–3; he described her as:

[A] great personage [representing a silent power that had always been recognized and felt in this community, so long as I can remember, by not only fashionable people, but by the solid old quiet element as well.]...I...for the first time, was brought in contact with this *grande dame*, and at once recognized her ability, and felt that she would become society's leader, and that she was admirably qualified for the position.

In her later years, Mrs. William Astor received her guests standing under this painting of herself by Carolus Duran. The only authorized portrait of Mrs. Astor, it was completed in 1890.

William Astor, c. 1876
William Astor spent most of his time away from New York yachting and going to Ferncliff, his Dutchess County estate, leaving his wife to reign over New York society.

Caroline Astor and her husband, William, lived in this brownstone, built in 1873. The house was located at Fifth Avenue and Thirty-fourth Street, then in the heart of the fashionable district. Most wealthy New Yorkers in the 1870's lived in brownstones whose "uniform hue coated New York like a chocolate sauce," wrote Edith Wharton. She recalled that: "One of the most depressing impressions of my childhood...is my recollection of the intolerable ugliness of New York, of its untended streets and the narrow houses, so lacking in external dignity, so crammed with smug and suffocating upholstery. How could I understand that people who had seen Rome and Seville, Paris and London, could come back to live contentedly between Washington Square and Central Park?"

It was not long before circumstances forced her to assume the leadership, which she did, and which she has held with marked ability ever since, having all the qualities necessary,—good judgment and a great power of analysis of men and women, a thorough knowledge of all their surroundings, a just appreciation of the rights of others, and, coming herself from an old Colonial family, a good appreciation of the value of ancestry; always keeping it near her, and bringing it in, in all social matters, but also understanding the importance and power of the new element; recognizing it, and fairly and generously awarding to it a prominent place.

Caroline Astor gave her husband entreé into old New York families like her own—the Schermerhorns. He gave her access to an enormous fortune, far larger than anything the Schermerhorns or Livingstons ever knew.

Mr. and Mrs. John Jacob Astor III

John Jacob Astor III inherited two thirds of his father's fortune when William B. Astor died in November 1875. Charlotte Augusta Gibbes Astor (Mrs. John Jacob Astor III), originally of Philadelphia, was automatically considered the leader of New York Society by virtue of her marriage to the older of the two Astor brothers. But she was soon eclipsed by her more ambitious sister-in-law, Caroline Astor. When John Jacob Astor III died in 1887, Caroline Astor was left to rule, completely without a rival. William Waldorf Astor, the son and only child of John Jacob Astor III, tried to get his wife to battle Caroline Astor for the privilege of being known as "The Mrs. Astor" but there was no contest. William Waldorf Astor left for England, where he purchased a title and founded the English branch of the family.

THE UNACCEPTABLES

Beyond the world of Caroline Astor lay "the almost unmapped quarter inhabited by artists, musicians, and people who wrote!" Newland Archer in *The Age of Innocence* knew that:

There were societies where painters and poets and novelists and men of science, and even great actors, were as sought after as Dukes; he had often pictured to himself what it would have been to live in the intimacy of drawing rooms dominated by the talk of Merimée...of Thackeray, Browning, or William Morris. But such things were impossible in New York.

In her memoirs, Mrs. Winthrop Chanler confirmed Archer's point:

Society was based on a sort of untitled but long-established social hierarchy, from which all random elements were rigorously excluded. It held many attractive people, good-looking, agreeable, well-dressed women and men, but as a society it seemed flat and arid, a Sahara without lions or lion hunters. The Four Hundred would have fled in a body from a poet, a painter, a musician, or a clever Frenchman.

The Four Hundred was the term coined by Ward McAllister to describe the "acceptables" in New York society. "Why," he said, "there are only about 400 people in fashionable New York society."

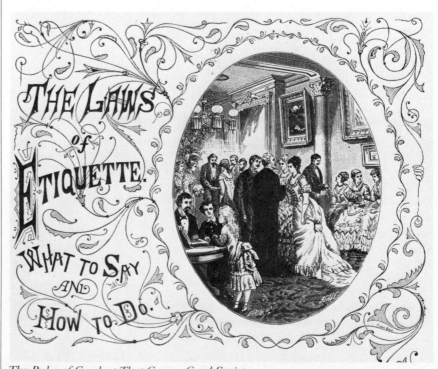

The Rules of Conduct That Govern Good Society

This etiquette book explained that: "To be happy, we strive for the acquisition of wealth, for position and place, for social and political distinction."

THE LIFE OF A GENTLEMAN

A gentleman, as described by Edith Wharton, "stayed at home and abstained" from the life of action. He did not enter politics as his aristocratic forbears had done before the Civil War. Politics had become an occupation for men who were willing and able to work with immigrants:

Everyone in polite circles knew that in America "a gentleman couldn't go into politics."...Everyone knew the melancholy fate of the few gentlemen who had risked their clean linen in municipal or state politics in New York. The day was passed when that sort of thing was possible: the country was in the possession of the bosses and the emigrant, and decent people had to fall back on sport or culture.

MONDAY NIGHT: THE OPERA

The rich fell back on culture and sport. On Monday nights they attended the Opera at the Academy of Music on Fourteenth Street. Caroline Astor usually appeared at nine, weighed down by her jewels. One of the great appeals of the Academy of Music was that there was no room for newcomers. It had only eighteen boxes. William H. Vanderbilt offered the Governors of the Academy $30,000 in 1880 for a season box, but he was refused. Vanderbilt, along with Jay Gould and others excluded from the Academy of Music, went on to organize the Metropolitan Opera, where there would be room for them. The Metropolitan Opera House opened its doors on April 28, 1880, at the corner of Thirty-ninth Street and Broadway on land that had cost $600,000. *The Age of Innocence* offers a description of a typical Monday night in the seventies at the Academy of Music:

On a January evening of the early seventies, Christine Nilsson was singing in *Faust* at the Academy of Music in New York.

Though there was already talk of the erection, in remote metropolitan distances "above the Forties," of a new Opera House which should compete in costliness and splendor with those of the great European capitals, the world of fashion was still content to reassemble every winter in the shabby red and gold boxes of the sociable old Academy. Conservatives cherished it for being small and inconvenient, and thus keeping out the "new people" whom New York was beginning to dread and yet be drawn to...

It was Madame Nilsson's first appearance that winter, and what the daily press had already learned to describe as "an exceptionally brilliant audience" had gathered to hear her, transported through the slippery, snowy streets in private broughams, in the spacious family landau, or in the humbler but more convenient "Brown *coupé*." To come to the Opera in a Brown *coupé* was almost as honorable a way of arriving as in one's own carriage; and departure by the same means had the immense advantage of enabling one (with a playful allusion to

"Newland Archer, leaning against the wall at the back of the club box, turned his eyes from the stage and scanned the opposite side of the house. Directly facing him was the box of old Mrs. Manson Mingott, whose monstrous obesity had long since made it impossible for her to attend the Opera, but who was always represented on fashionable nights by some of the younger members of the family. On this occasion, the front of the box was filled by her daughter-in-law, Mrs. Lovell Mingott, and her daughter, Mrs. Welland."

Edith Wharton, *The Age of Innocence*

Position for Round Dancing

In describing round dancing, William B. DeGarmo wrote (in 1879):

"The present style of round dancing is of a gliding character—different from the old style of solid stepping and high hopping—retaining, however, the attendant springs—the bendings and risings or actions of the knees—...The position is of the utmost importance. Preparatory to commencing, the lady takes position on the gentleman's right, as in Quadrille dancing. The gentleman places his right arm round the lady's waist, supporting her firmly, yet gently...The lady's left hand rests lightly upon the gentleman's right arm...the fingers together and curved, and not grasping or bearing down upon the gentleman's arm.

"The gentleman holds the lady's right hand with his left. The lady turns the palm of her right hand downward. The gentleman places the inner side of the fingers of his left hand against the inner side of the fingers of the lady's right, his thumb being alongside and touching his finger, so that her fingers do not project beyond his, and thus lightly clasps the hand...It is inelegant to place these hands against the gentleman's side or hip—they should be kept clear of the body..."

Going to the Pantomime Matinee

The pantomime was another favorite enjoyment of the rich: "This scene can be witnessed almost every Saturday afternoon when the weather is fine, during the entire winter season of the New York theaters," reported the magazine Happy Home *on March 3, 1874. "The pantomime, like the circus, possesses an attraction for most people, and especially the young folk, entirely distinct from the legitimate drama."*

democratic principles) to scramble into the first Brown conveyance in the line, instead of waiting till the cold-and-gin congested nose of one's own coachman gleamed under the portico of the Academy. It was one of the great livery-stableman's most masterly intuitions to have discovered that Americans want to get away from amusement even more quickly than they want to get to it.

AFTER THE OPERA: THE PATRIARCH BALL

After Mrs. William Astor's appearance at the Opera, she usually went to a subscription dance—either the Patriarchs Ball or the Assembly Ball. Ward McAllister organized the Patriarchs Balls, which he hoped would determine by their guest lists "whom society shall let in and whom society shall shut out." In were the Astors, two Livingstons, one Van Rensselaer, a Jones, one King and one Schermerhorn. A committee of twenty-five men (Patriarchs) were each allowed to invite nine guests. McAllister described, in glowing terms, the success of the Patriarchs in mixing the old families with some of the new men of wealth:

The object we had in view was to make these balls thoroughly representative: to embrace the old Colonial New Yorkers: our adopted citizens, and men whose ability and integrity had won the esteem of the

The Position in Quadrille

"*The dance of society, as at present practiced...consisting of movements at once easy, natural, modest and graceful, affords an exercise sufficiently agreeable to render it conducive to health and pleasure...Exercise may be considered as one of the necessaries of life, and there is no exercise at once so innocent, pleasurable, healthful, universally popular, and appropriately adapted to the joyous intermingling of ladies, gentlemen and children, as the dance...*"

William B. DeGarmo, The Dance of Society, *1879*

Ward McAllister

The founder of the Patriarch Balls and the mentor of Caroline Astor, McAllister consulted with Mrs. Astor on the dances:

"Whenever we required advice and assistance...we went to her, and always found ourselves rewarded in so doing by receiving suggestions that were invaluable. [She was] quick to criticise any defect of lighting or ornamentation, or arrangement..."

community, and who formed an important element in society. We wanted the money power, but not in any way to be controlled by it...We knew then, and we know now, that the whole secret of the success of these Patriarch Balls lay in making them select; in making them the most brilliant balls of each winter; in making it extremely difficult to obtain an invitation to them, and to make such invitations of great value; to make them the stepping-stone to the best New York society, that one might be sure that any one repeatedly invited to them had a secure social position. The Patriarchs, from their very birth, became a great social feature...

THE PATRIARCH BALLS HELP TO CHANGE AND TO "EUROPEANIZE" NEW YORK:

Applications to be made Patriarchs poured in from all sides; every influence was brought to bear to secure a place in this little band, and the pressure was so great that we feared the struggle would be too fierce and engender too much rancor and bad feeling, and that this might of itself destroy them. The argument against them, the one most strongly urged, was that they were overturning all old customs; that New Yorkers had been in the habit of taking an active part in society only when they had daughters to bring out, *lancée-ing* their daughters, and they themselves taking a back seat. But that here in this new association, the married women took a more prominent place than the young girls; *they* were the belles of the balls, and not the young girls. This was Europeanizing New York too rapidly.

Mrs. William Astor in Ball-dress, c. 1875

The New Home of Delmonico's in 1876—"Uptown" at Twenty-sixth Street and Fifth Avenue

The new Delmonico's at Madison Square had a dining room and a café on the ground floor; upstairs there was a ballroom and some private dining rooms. The *Tribune* described the restaurant:

"The three members of the Delmonico family of restauranteurs—Lorenzo, Siro, and Charles—were found at their new rendez-vous of gastronomes on Fifth Avenue...A steady stream of celebrities—social, pluto-cratic, artistic, journalistic, legal and every other shade of professional gentlemen... poured through the door of the café, a salon of almost saracenic splendor, and sauntered in and out...all over the beautiful build-ing...The recent great increase of American travel in Europe, and familiarity with the most famous restaurants of the old civilization, have taught our citizens to appreciate their debt to the Delmonico family...There is now no restaurant in Paris, or London or Vienna which can compete with our Delmonico's in the excellence and variety of its fare..."

DELMONICO'S

Delmonico's was *the* place to entertain. There the Patriarch, the Family Circle, and Assembly Balls were held. In 1876 Delmonico's moved "uptown" to Fifth Avenue and twenty-sixth Street. "Lower" Fifth Avenue at this point ceased to be *the* fashionable place. In 1873 Mr. Edward Lukemeyer, a shipowner and importer, spent $10,000 on a gala at Delmonico's. McAllister reported the wondrous results:

A banquet was given of such beauty and magnificence, that even New Yorkers, accustomed as they were to every species of novel expenditure, were astonished at its lavishness....The banquet was given at Delmonico's...There were seventy-two guests in the large ball-room, looking on Fifth Avenue. The table covered the whole length and breadth of the room, only leaving a passageway for the waiters to pass around it. It was a long extended oval table, and every inch of it was covered with flowers, excepting a space in the centre, left for a lake, and a border around the table for the plates. The lake was indeed a work of art; it was an oval pond, thirty feet in length, by nearly the width of the table, inclosed by a delicate golden wire network, reaching from table to ceiling, making the whole one grand cage; four superb swans, brought from Prospect Park, swam in it, surrounded by high banks of flowers of every species and variety, which prevented them from splashing the water on the table...All around the inclosure, and in fact above the entire table, hung little golden cages, with fine songsters, who filled the room with their melody...It seemed like the abode of fairies; and when surrounding this fairyland with lovely young American womanhood, you had indeed an unequaled scene of enchantment... Such a feast as the gods should enjoy, was done, and so well done that all present felt, in the way of feasting, that man could do no more!

"DECENT PEOPLE HAD TO FALL BACK ON SPORT OR CULTURE"– THE METROPOLITAN MUSEUM

It was a long way from P. T. Barnum's American Museum—the most popular museum in New York in the forties and fifties—to the Metropolitan Museum, which was incorporated in 1870. In 1880, when the Museum moved uptown to its present home, its youngest trustee, Joseph H. Choate, hoped that the Museum would provide:

The diffusion of a knowledge of art in its higher forms of beauty [which] would tend directly to humanize, to educate and refine a practical and laborious people.

The Museum would bring European refinements to America; it would also have practical benefits. It would serve:

...not only for the instruction and entertainment of the people but...also show to the students and artisans of every branch of industry...what the past has accomplished for them to imitate and excel.

The observation of the past would be useful and profitable; Choate justified the Museum to a businesslike nation:

Every nation that has tried it has found that every wise investment in the development of art pays more than compound interest.

Choate urged newly rich men to:

convert pork into porcelain, grain and produce into priceless pottery...railroad and mining stocks—things which perish without the using, and which in the next financial panic shall surely shrivel like parched scrolls—into glorified canvas of the world's masters, that shall adorn these walls for centuries...Convert your useless gold into things of living beauty that shall be a joy to a whole people for a thousand years.

Many wealthy Americans, among them Henry Clay Frick, John Pierpont Morgan and William H. Vanderbilt, followed Choate's advice and formed first-rate art collections. By 1876 a few men, like August Belmont and Alexander T. Stewart, already had large art collections.

Americans like William Cullen Bryant, editor of the New York *Post* and one of the original founders of the Metropolitan Museum, also hoped that the Museum would help keep up the old standards, which were being swept away by the new age. Bryant said:

Lorenzo Delmonico

Lorenzo Delmonico's restaurant was the favorite place in the 1870's of every celebrity. Mark Twain, William Dean Howells, August Belmont and many others ate in Delmonico's dining room and danced in the ballroom. Lorenzo Delmonico came to America in 1832 to work for his uncles, Peter and John, who had founded the original Delmonico's in 1827. Lorenzo persuaded his uncles to build a restaurant on South William Street, which became the celebrated "downtown" Delmonico's. As business grew, he next moved north to Fourteenth Street and Fifth Avenue; in 1876, Delmonico followed the tide uptown to Madison Square.

Metropolitan Museum Before Its Move Uptown

The Museum was located on Fourteenth Street between 1873 and 1879 before it moved "uptown." The Metropolitan was originally located for one year at 681 Fifth Avenue. On February 24, 1876, the *Times* reported on a reception at this Metropolitan Museum:

"Yesterday evening one of the most brilliant receptions of the season took place at the Metropolitan Museum of Art. By 9 o'clock the spacious rooms and galleries were filled. Many new additions have been made to the loan collection; among them may be mentioned the Chinese and Japanese objects, the property of Prof. Pumpelly. In one case may be found many curious agates, jades, jaspers, and crystals. As every day swells the bulk of the loan collection, it would be impossible to give in full the details. Many judicious changes have been made in the decorations of the rooms, and the former somewhat crowded character of the collection has been avoided."

The Present Fashion in Visiting Cards

McAllister included this illustration in his book to show Americans how to use visiting cards in the European way.

Mark Twain, in *The Gilded Age,* also wrote about the importance of visiting cards in America: "...when a lady of any prominence comes to one of our cities and takes up her residence, all the ladies of her grade favor her in turn with an initial call, giving their cards to the servant at the door by way of introduction. They come singly, sometimes; sometimes in couples;—and always in elaborate full dress. They talk two minutes and a quarter and then go. If the lady receiving the call desires a further acquaintance, she must return the visit within two weeks; to neglect it beyond that time means 'let the matter drop.' But if she does return the visit within two weeks, it then becomes the other party's privilege to continue the acquaintance or drop it. She signifies her willingness to continue it by calling again any time within *(continued on following page)*

Metropolitan Museum Before Its Move Uptown

It is important that we should encounter the temptations to vice in this great and too rapidly growing capital by attractive entertainments of an innocent and improving character.

In *The Age of Innocence*, the Museum served as a meeting place for the lovers, Newland Archer and Countess Olenska. When Archer announced that he must meet with her somewhere alone, the Countess replied: "In New York? But there are no churches...no monuments." To this charge, Archer patriotically replied:

"There's the Art Museum—in the Park," he explained, as she looked puzzled. "At half-past two. I shall be at the door..."

Avoiding the popular "Wolfe collection," whose anecdotic canvases filled one of the main galleries of the queer wilderness of cast-iron and encaustic tiles known as the Metropolitan Museum, they had wandered down a passage to the room where the "Cesnola antiquities" mouldered in unvisited loneliness.

They had this melancholy retreat to themselves, and seated on the divan enclosing the central steam-radiator, they were staring silently at the glass cabinets mounted in ebonized wood which contained the recovered fragments of Ilium.

"It's odd," Madame Olenska said, "I never came here before."

"Ah, well—, Some day, I suppose, it will be a great Museum."

"Yes," she assented absently.

The *New York Times* noted on January 9, 1876, that the Metropolitan Museum was not as popular as it should have been:

The custodians of the Metropolitan Museum of Art, which seems to be strangely neglected by those who might find both amusement and

The New Home of the Metropolitan Museum, Fifth Avenue at Eighty-second Street

instruction in the varied and interesting collections of statues, pictures, arms, [and] coins...have recently placed on view a number of curious and valuable articles, and have rearranged or are rearranging others so that they can be seen to greater advantage than formerly. Among the pictures not heretofore noticed are a very fine example of Schreyer, "Crossing the Ford,"...H. J. Duwee's "Alone in the .World," "The Conspiracy" by Valies, and a fancy portrait by Madrazo...

Among the statuary is the late Mr. Rinehart's "Latona"...the bust of Sir Walter Scott, by Westmacott...At the present moment the museum is rather deficient in statuary...

Among the curiosities contained in the museum, which a casual visitor would be likely to overlook, a few may be mentioned. There is an antique hock glass with a curious map of the Rhine cut upon its crystal surface, backed up by an ancient Danish drinking cup...As companion pieces, we find a Norwegian tankard and silver cup, the latter decorated with small shell-like pieces of metal, which, hanging loose, tinkle against the sides as the cup is raised to the drinker's lips...A curious Dutch wardrobe, ornamented with small saucers...is worthy of notice...Among the smaller curiosities are specimens of the French assignats, issued in the third year of the Republic, some old Italian paper money, a Washington cent, a number of ancient keys and some very old watches...

Of arms there are several good collections, one of which belonged to the Sultan of Turkey...

The Cesnola Collection is to be removed downstairs to the first floor, and Mr. Prime's collection of ancient and modern pottery is to take its place...The gallery of old masters and the hall of statuary from Cyprus remain unchanged, with the old Kings and warriors frowning or smirking and smiling from their niches just as they did when fresh from the sculptor's hands 3,000 years ago.

The museum is now open daily from 10 to 5. On Mondays no admission fee is charged.

twelve months; after that, if the parties go on calling upon each other once a year, in our large cities, that is sufficient, and the acquaintanceship holds good. The thing goes along smoothly, now. The annual visits are made and returned with peaceful regularity and bland satisfaction, although it is not necessary that the two ladies shall actually *see* each other oftener than once every few years. Their cards preserve the intimacy and keep the acquaintanceship intact."

Menu for First Dinner of the Coaching Club, 1875.

Lawn Tennis—a New and Popular Sport

Here Junius Spencer Morgan and his son-in-law play lawn tennis at Morgan's house, "Dover House," in England in 1876. When the Wellands in *The Age of Innocence* visited Florida "they were planning to lay out a lawn tennis court...but no one but Kate and May had racquets, and most people had not even heard of the game."

"The Music Lesson," by John George Brown, 1870
Another "cultural" activity of the rich.

Americans were very sensitive to the charge that they had no culture. In the 1870's they were determined to create an American culture and the Metropolitan Museum was part of their self-conscious, often awkward effort. By the end of the seventies, the Museum's success seemed assured. In their annual report for 1876 the trustees reported that:

The Museum today is not surpassed as an educational power among the people by any university, college, or seminary of learning in the metropolis.

SPORTS OF THE RICH

The American rich looked to Europe for their sports as well as for their architecture. Polo, horse racing, lawn tennis and coaching all became popular society sports in America in the seventies. In 1876 James Gordon Bennett introduced polo to America. He had learned the game in England, where it was very popular; the English had learned the sport in India. Bennett and his friends formed polo teams in New York and played their first match in Jerome Park. With August Belmont's help, Bennett formed the Westchester Polo Club. *Harper's Weekly* reported in July 1876 that:

The Game of Polo, Played on the Polo Club Grounds at Jerome Park, June 10, 1876—the Year the Game Was Introduced to America by James Gordon Bennett, Jr.

The exhilarating and healthful game of polo has already become quite popular among New Yorkers, and a large number of invited spectators gathered at the grounds of the Westchester Polo Club, at Jerome Park, on the afternoon of June 6, to witness the first of the series of match games to be played for the Challenge Cup presented to the club by its president, J. G. Bennett, Esq. The game was commenced about half past six, after the races. The club grounds were in fine order, and the playing was very spirited...

Polo is a modification of a game which the officers of the British army learned in India...The English officers, finding the Indian climate unfavorable to scampering on foot after a ball, discovered that they could mount a pony and play the game equally well, and with less fatigue to themselves...

THE COACHING CLUB

The Coaching Club was formed in 1875. "The object of the club," reported the *Times* on January 17, 1876, was "to encourage coaching and other out-door sports, such as polo, [and] lawn tennis...Considering the taste, wealth, and spirit of the gentlemen who have organized it there can be no question of its success." Coaching was a popular sport in England with noblemen acting as coachmen on runs between London and Dorking. In their mania to be more English than the English, rich New Yorkers imported their first coaches from England. On January 17, 1876, the *Times* predicted that the Coaching Club would be a great success:

SUMMER ARRANGEMENT.

On and after July 5th the 1876.

NEW ROCHELLE AND PELHAM COACH

will make a single trip daily (Sundays excepted) between New York and New Rochelle. Leaving the NEPTUNE HOUSE, New Rochelle, every Monday, Wednesday and Friday at 7.30 A.M., will arrive at the Hotel Brunswick, N.Y., at 9.30 A.M.; and leaving the Brunswick every Tuesday, Thursday and Saturday at 4.45 P.M., will arrive at the Neptune, N.R., at 6.45 P.M.

TIME TABLE and FARES.

Fares.	DOWN.	Time.	Fares.	UP.	Time.
	LEAVING	A.M.		LEAVING	P.M.
	Neptune House	7.30		Hotel Brunswick	4.45
	WILL ARRIVE AT			WILL ARRIVE AT	
25 cts	Bolton Priory	7 37	50 cts	Harlem	5.22
	Bartow (Hotel.)	7 50		Mott Haven (W. Park Hotel.)	5.30
50 cts.	*Pelham Bridge (Capt. Delany and Arcularius Hotels.)	7.55	75 cts	Fox Corners	5.45
			$1 00	Union Port (Hotel.)	6.5
75 cts.	Westchester (Osseo Hotel.)	8.7		Westchester (Osseo Hotel.)	6.8
"	*Union Port (Hotel.)	8.10	1.50	Pelham Bridge (Arcularius and Capt. Delany Hotels.)	6.20
$1.00	Fox Corners	8.30			
1.25	*Mott Haven (Wallack Hotel.)	8.45	1 75	Bartow (Hotel.)	6.25
1.50	Harlem	8 53		Bolton Priory	6.37
2 00	New York (Hotel Brunswick.)	9 30	2.00	Neptune House (New Rochelle.)	6.45
	*Change Horses.			*Change Horses.	

BOX SEAT, 50 CENTS EXTRA EACH WAY.

Passengers by this Coach will find most excellent accommodation at Neptune House Those wishing to return to N.Y. same evening, can do so by train. This Coach stops to pick up and set down passengers wherever hailed except between Hotel Brunswick and 59th Street. Passengers' baggage, up to 50 lbs., free. Parcels at moderate rates, and delivered with care and despatch anywhere on the road. Passengers caution is to be on time.

Col. DeLancey Kane's Schedule for His New York–New Rochelle Trip during the Summer of 1876

The notice said: "This coach stops to pick up and set down passengers wherever hailed except between Hotel Brunswick and 59th Street. Passengers' baggage, up to 50 lbs., free."

James Gordon Bennett

Frederic Bronson

William P. Douglas

Original Members of the Coaching Club

Harper's Weekly in 1876 described the Coaching Club:

"A club of wealthy gentlemen in New York, who have for some time been organizing plans for introducing the driving of English coaches as an out-of-door amusement, lately united in an exhibitory trip, which *(continued on following page)*

Leaving the Brunswick Hotel. Col. DeLancey Kane, Coachman
In 1876 DeLancey Kane took paying passengers for his own amusement on "pleasure drives in the English style." The Brunswick Hotel was the departure point. The Times *described the first extraordinary trip:*
"Col. Kane's coach is the exact reproduction of the English coach, and in its management the rules and customs of England are rigidly observed. The top of the coach yesterday was occupied exclusively by personal friends of Col. Kane, who had engaged their seats a fortnight ago. Miss Astor had the box seat...The inside of the coach was occupied by the representatives of the Sun *and* Times...*From the hotel Col. Kane drove straight up Fifth Avenue, and the coach created the greatest possible stir all along the way. The windows of the residences were filled with ladies who waved their handkerchiefs and nodded their heads with enthusiasm as the coach rolled swiftly by. Rows of young men bowed in unison from the curbstones, where they had been waiting for at least half an hour to pay their respects to the turnout and its passengers...The fascination of the coach and four-in-hand was even greater than the fascination of the May morning, and from the stoops of houses littered with all manner of household furniture, men, women, and teamsters, for the once on terms of democratic equality, looked down with curious interest."*

The Coaching Club of this City bids fair to be a brilliant success. Since the Autumn races, when the first muster was held, and the appearance of five coaches in line to Jerome Park made such a decided sensation, the organization of the club has been completed and several enthusiastic meetings have been held; and now at least twelve coaches are counted upon as sure to make their appearance in the Spring parade. Among the rules adopted is one providing for two parades in each year...These will be similar to the parades of the four-in-hand clubs in London. On these occasions the club is expected to turn out in full force, and every coach is required to appear in perfect regulation trim.

The course will be from Madison Square up Fifth Avenue, (pavement permitting,) round Central Park, and back again to Madison Square...No one can be a member who is not owner or part owner of a drag and able to drive four horses.

THE COACHING CLUB PARADE

The first of the two annual Coaching Club parades was held on Saturday, April 22, 1876. The *Times* reported the affair at some length:

Col. DeLancey Kane's Coach, "Tally-Ho," on Its Daily Run
The aim of the Coaching Club was to encourage four-in-hand driving in America. Dress rules required tall white silk hats for spring, black hats for autumn, and uniforms consisting of bottle-green coats with white waistcoats and gold buttons with the C-C insignia.

A clear sky, roads free from dust, and air warm enough to make driving delightful, combined to render the first meeting this season of the Coaching Club a complete success. The start of seven fours-in-hand was to have been made from Madison square at 4 o'clock yesterday afternoon...It was twenty minutes after the stated hour when the coaches, six in number, actually started...The east side of Madison square was crowded with lookers-on, and the number increased each moment until the police had difficulty in keeping a double carriage-way open in the middle of Madison avenue...Dashing in all directions were scores of carriages, dog-carts, and T-carts, in which were seated persons well-known in fashionable society, who bowed greetings to dozens of gentlemen on horseback and to their friends on the drags of the Coaching Club. Nor were these all: grocers' and butchers' boys, truck-drivers and cabmen increased the crowd...When the start was made, Mr. William Jay led with his English coach...driven by two bays, a brown, and a chestnut horse...On each coach were seated several guests and two grooms...

DeLANCEY KANE OPERATES NEW ROCHELLE-PELHAM COACH LINE

DeLancey Kane, whom *Harper's* called "one of the more enthusiastic and benevolent members" of the Coaching Club, took to driving paying riders on "pleasure drives in the English style." The rides commenced daily from the Hotel Brunswick on Madison Square. The *Times* covered Kane's first trip in May of 1876:

A fine airy day, a lively company, a delightful ride, with plenty of pleasing incidents, and no untimely happening, attended the intro-

William Jay

Leonard W. Jerome

DeLancey A. Kane

attracted much attention. Seven coaches, each driving four-in-hand, composed the cavalcade. The start was from Madison Square, and was witnessed by immense crowds of sight-seers. On each coach were seated, besides the proprietor, driving, several guests and two grooms. The route lay up Fifth Avenue and through Central Park, and the ride was highly enjoyed."
(continued on following page)

Original Members of the Coaching Club

S. Nicholson Kane

Thomas Newbold

A. Thorndike Rice

duction yesterday of... DeLancey Kane's New Rochelle and Pelham Four-in-Hand Coach Line. The purpose of the line...is not pecuniary profit, for under the most favorable circumstances, with every seat full every day of the season, the coach cannot pay its expenses. Col. Kane will drive his coach mainly for his own amusement, with, perhaps, the secondary idea of affording the pleasure of novel rides through an interesting and picturesque country, with a sojourn of four hours on the shore of Long Island Sound at Pelham Bridge, between going and returning. Viewed in this light the New Rochelle and Pelham coach...probably gives the best possible excursion out of New York, and it is sure of meeting the appreciation and patronage it deserves. It is a public coach in the fullest sense of the word. For the next week the seats are all engaged, mostly by friends of Col. Kane, but there has been no unjust discrimination. The coach-book is kept at the Hotel Brunswick, and seats are engaged by those who come first. The coach leaves the Hotel Brunswick at 10:30 every morning, and...reaches Pelham Bridge at precisely 12 o'clock. Returning, it leaves Pelham Bridge at 4 o'clock, and reaches the Hotel Brunswick at 5:30 o'clock...The tariff is low, being fifty cents to Harlem, seventy-five cents to Fox Corners, $1 to West Chester, and Middletown, and $1.50 to Pelham Bridge, with fifty cents extra for the box seat each way. The coach is after the regular four-in-hand pattern. It was built in England and is perfect in every detail. It has a canary colored body and carriage...

DeLancey Kane continued his extraordinary pursuit during the summer of 1876. On December 2 the *Times* reported on the last trip of Colonel Kane's coach for the 1876 season. Despite the cold weather, passengers went with Kane to Pelham:

The last load of passengers who were regularly "booked" for the Pelham Coach was carried on Thursday...The coach left the Hotel Brunswick at 11 o'clock. A keen north-west wind was blowing, and the "outsiders" were wrapped thickly in blankets to protect them from the cold. A short halt was made at Pelham, which "outsiders" and "insiders" improved in restoring the circulation to their chilled bodies, and in discussing an abundant dinner.

Col. Kane has scarcely missed a trip during the entire season, and has become so accustomed to "tipping" his hat repeatedly and to everybody that rode with him, that he frequently greets his friends in coachman fashion even when he is not on duty upon the box.

The expense of running the coach for seven months exceeded the receipts by nearly eight hundred dollars, so that the pleasure of maintaining the establishment has cost Col. Kane about five dollars a day......Col. Kane expresses no regret at the loss he has sustained. He has had an abundance of outdoor exercise in good company, and has helped to stimulate the love of coaching in the City.

THE IDEA BEHIND COACHING

In a long analysis of coaching which appeared in the *Times* on December 5, 1876, the reporter suggested that coaching was an attempt by men of the Industrial Age to turn back the clock to simpler days:

Every one, of course, fully understands the motive of amateur coaching. It is an effort to revive the romance of pre-railway travel, and to roll back the prosaic progress which has swept coaches and sedan-chairs...out of existence. While Col. Kane's efforts to "materialize" the ghost of the banished stage-coach have been earnest, and, to a certain extent, successful, he must be aware that in some important respects he has failed to reproduce the true spirit of ancient coaching....Whatever a man could do to reproduce with pre-Raphaelite fidelity the coach of the eighteenth century Col. Kane has done, but he could not reproduce the inns, the inn-keepers, and the highwaymen of the period, and hence his coaching performances were a well-meaning anachronism.

Why lovers of pre-railway simplicity should confine their efforts to the revival of coaching does not appear. If railways have driven out coaches, have not steamboats superseded the passenger sloops of the North River and the fast packets of the Erie Canal? Why should not some aquatic Kane give us back the sloops and canal-boats of our forefathers? A line of tri-weekly sloops running between this City and Albany would doubtless command the enthusiastic patronage of the same class of persons who love to ride in Col. Kane's coach...

And yet, do what we will, we can only play at coaching or canal-boating or "slooping." Railroads and steam-boats are ugly facts which cannot be ignored except by a determined effort at "making believe." The romance of the land and of the water has been hopelessly slain, and its dim ghost can be only faintly materialized, no matter how earnestly we yearn after it...The coach and the passenger sloop and the canal packet are as out of place in the year 1876 as would be the galliot of the *Flying Dutchman.*

Col. William Jay, President & Founder of the Coaching Club

On February 20, 1876, the *Times* reported that:

"Yesterday was an excellent day for driving, because there was a lovely and spring-like atmosphere, and the roads were hard and good for cattle. Fifth Avenue and Central Park and the great driving avenues beyond were crowded with vehicles of every kind, and two of the four-in-hands were among the throng. There were the old Dorking coach, owned by the Knickerbocker Club, driven by Col. Jay, and the drag of Mr. James Gordon Bennett, driven by himself. The coaches were crowded, many ladies being seated among the gentlemen on the top. The servants and grooms were inside, according to the custom...Both vehicles remained on view for about an hour...to the admiration of the numerous pedestrians who thronged the fashionable thoroughfare [Fifth Avenue]."

The New York Yacht Club at Newport, 1872

Ward McAllister had a farm at Newport and entertained lavishly there. In his memoirs he wrote of Newport:

"The most charming people of the country had formed a select little community there; the society was small, and all were included in the gaieties and festivities. Those were the days that made Newport what it was then and is now, the most enjoyable and luxurious little island in America...The charm of the place then was the simple way of entertaining; there were no large balls; all the dancing and dining was done by daylight, and in the country. I did not hesitate to ask the very *crème de la crème* of New York society to lunch and dine at my farm, or to a fishing party on the rocks."

"Long Branch, New Jersey," by Winslow Homer, 1869

Long Branch was a popular resort in the 1870's, although the *New York Times* said on July 9, 1876, that:

"Long Branch affords mainly large and expensive hotels, and rather monotonous scenery, though with a grand ocean view."

FASHIONABLE RESORTS: NEWPORT

Caroline Astor spent her summers at Newport. The resort was becoming popular with fashionable society in the seventies and would eventually eclipse all other "watering-places," but in 1876 the Vanderbilts had yet to build their great mansions. In June 1876 the *Times* featured an article on "The Beauties of Newport" boasting that:

Now that the foreigners have discovered the existence of the Great Exhibition at Philadelphia, and are beginning to come over in large numbers, we may expect a series of severe criticisms upon our manners and customs, and our summer resorts surely will not escape. Probably in our own eyes Newport is the least open to censure or to harsh judgment. It is a fair specimen of American growth, because it has arrived at the highest development, and is as good as it can be made...

LONG BRANCH, NEW JERSEY, ANOTHER FASHIONABLE RESORT, COMPARED UNFAVORABLY WITH NEWPORT BY THE *TIMES:*

At Long Branch they are just planting trees; here they have planted them for fifty years and more, and consequently the small avenues are shady paths with great maple and horse chestnuts on both sides; and from the universal lawns come the strong perfumes of the flower shrubs, which are at their highest beauty...There is no long line of rolling breakers coming onward with the fierceness of charging cavalry, as at Long Branch, but the blue water rushes swellingly upward to the shore like a fond mother to her babe, and the white foam rolls over the rocks as if inviting caresses and gambolings.

NEWPORT: THE TOWN OF ROMANCE

The *Times* reporter said:

I am not surprised that match-making mamas are fond of Newport, and invariably propose to papa to take a cottage at this place when they want to settle Jane or Lillie in the holy estate of matrimony. There is that in the air and earth, in the trees, and lawns, and spreading wealth of flowering shrubs which acts upon the nerves like an anodyne, and upon the senses like a caress. The young men like Newport because the fishing is so good, and the girls think so, too—especially the husband-fishing.

NEWPORT: THE LAND OF TASTE AND WEALTH

The *Times* recommended Newport:

Wealth is everywhere, but presented in its most pleasing applications, and guided by refined and delicate taste. All that one sees makes one sympathize with the millionaires who created these lovely scenes which can be enjoyed by any one with eyes as much as by the proprietor.

NEWPORT REAL ESTATE VALUABLE

The *Times* reported the high price one summer cottage in Newport rented for in 1876:

Real estate is as valuable in this place as it ever was, though the rental of cottages has gone down very considerably...The King cottage, opposite to the Ocean House, which has very spacious lawns, and which has rented for more than $5,000, was leased this year by Mr. John Townsend for $3,000.

Henry James, who went to live in England in 1876, described Newport in the first part of *An International Episode*, published in 1879. In the story, set in 1874, two young Englishmen are sent to Newport by a fictional New York businessman, Mr. Westgate:

AN INTERNATIONAL EPISODE, BY HENRY JAMES

It isn't a town," said Mr. Westgate, laughing, "it's a—well, what shall I call it? It's a watering-place. In short, it's Newport. You'll see what it is. It's cool; that's the principal thing...You will be expected at Newport. We have a house there; half the people of New York go there for the summer..."

MRS. WESTGATE EXTENDS AMERICAN HOSPITALITY TO THE VISITING ENGLISHMEN

"We hope you will stay a long time. Newport's a very nice place when you come really to know it—when you know plenty of people. Of course you and Mr. Beaumont will have no difficulty about that. Englishmen are very well received here; there are almost always two or three of them about. I think they always like it, and I must say I should think they would. They receive ever so much attention. I must say I think they sometimes get spoiled..."

Newport from the Bay, c. 1874

"It is impossible to chronicle the leaders of fashion, or even those composing the smart set of Newport, from 1850 to the present time. The suns rise and set rapidly, so the persons with their feet on the lowest rung of the social ladder of one season have mounted to the top within a few months. Those who have but lately scaled the heights are always most scornful of the climbers below them, totally ignoring their own struggles."

Mrs. King Van Rensselaer, *Newport, Our Social Capital*

Watts Sherman House

This Newport house, designed by H. H. Richardson and Stanford White in 1874, was under construction in 1876. The *Times* observed in June of 1876 that Americans were modeling their vacation houses after English houses:

"Building still continues at Newport, though, of course, the impetus of construction has been greatly lessened by the hard times. During the past months Mr. Will Sherman, who married Miss Wetmore, the great heiress, has built a very charming cottage... It is in the style of the British buildings at Fairmont Park, and the English mind feels flattered at the passionate admiration which is felt for their structures all over the land by everyone of aesthetic tendencies...Now the architects have greedily adopted the Elizabethan half-timber style, or modifications of it. Mr. Sherman's villa is a genuine half-timbered Elizabethan house."

The Drive

"The regular afternoon diversion at Newport was a drive. Everyday all the elderly ladies, leaning back in a victoria or barouche, or the new-fangled vis-à-vis, a four seated carriage with a rumble for the footman, drove down the whole length of Bellevue Avenue, where the most fashionable villas then stood, and around the newly laid out 'Ocean Drive,' which skirted for several miles the wild rocky region between Narrangansett Bay and the Atlantic. For this drive it was customary to dress as elegantly as for a race-meeting at Auteuil."

Edith Wharton, A Backward Glance

MRS. WESTGATE COMPARES AMERICA AND ENGLAND

"You must take us as we come—with all our imperfections on our heads. Of course we haven't your country life, and your old ruins, and your great estates, and your leisure class, and all that. But if we haven't, I should think you might find it a pleasant change—I think any country is pleasant where they have pleasant manners...I admit our drawbacks. But I must confess I think Newport is an ideal place. I don't know anything like it anywhere...It's entirely different from most watering-places; it's a most charming life. I must say I think that when one goes to a foreign country one ought to enjoy the differences. Of course there are differences, otherwise what did one come abroad for? Look for your pleasure in the differences, Lord Lambeth; that's the way to do it; and then I am sure you will find American society—at least, Newport society—most charming and interesting. I wish very much my husband were here; but he's dreadfully confined to New York, I suppose you think that is very strange—for a gentleman..But you see we haven't any leisure class."

LORD LAMBETH DRIVES THROUGH NEWPORT

Lord Lambeth got into a little basket-phaeton with Bessie Alden [Mrs. Westgate's sister] and she drove him down the long avenue, whose extent he had measured on foot a couple of hours before, into the ancient town, as it was called in that part of the world, of Newport. The ancient town was a curious affair—a collection of fresh-looking little wooden houses, painted white, scattered over a hill-side and clustered about a long, straight street, paved with enormous cobblestones. There were plenty of shops, a large proportion of which appeared to be those of fruit venders, with piles of huge watermelons and pumpkins stacked in front of them; and, drawn up before the shops, or bumping about on the cobble-stones, were innumerable other basket-phaetons freighted with ladies of high fashion, who greeted each other from vehicle to vehicle, and conversed on the edge of the pavement in a manner that struck Lord Lambeth as demonstrative, with a great many "oh, my dears," and little, quick exclamations and caresses. His companion went into seventeen shops—he amused himself with counting them—and accumulated at the bottom of the phaeton a pile of bundles that hardly left the young Englishman a place for his feet. As she had no groom nor footman, he sat in the phaeton to hold the ponies, where, although he was not a particularly acute observer, he saw much to entertain him—especially the ladies just mentioned, who wandered up and down with the appearance of a kind of aimless intentness, as if they were looking for something to buy, and who, tripping in and out of their vehicles, displayed remarkably pretty feet. It all seemed to Lord Lambeth very odd and bright and gay...

The young Englishmen spent the whole of that day and the whole of many successive days in what the French call the *intimité* of their new friends. They agreed that it was extremely jolly, that they had never known anything more agreeable. It was not proposed to narrate minutely the incidents of their sojourn on this charming shore, though...I might present a record of impressions none the less delectable that they were not exhaustively analyzed. Many of them still linger in the minds of our travellers, attended by a train of harmonious images—images of brilliant mornings on lawns and piazzas that overlooked the sea; of innumerable pretty girls; of infinite lounging and talking and laughing and flirting and lunching and dining; of universal friendliness and frankness; of occasions on which they knew everyone and everything, and had an extraordinary sense of ease; of drives and rides in the late afternoon over gleaming beaches, on long sea-roads beneath a sky lighted up by marvelous sunsets; of suppers, on the return, informal, irregular, agreeable; of evenings at open windows or on the perpetual verandas, in the summer starlight, above the warm Atlantic. The young Englishmen were introduced to everybody, entertained by everybody, intimate with everybody.

Henry James returned to travel in America in 1904 and 1905. One of the places he revisited was Newport. In his story "The Sense of Newport," published in *Harper's Monthly Magazine* in August 1906, James mourned the passing of the established gentleman who had been as at ease with his European learning as with his American upbringing. After all, Americans had not discovered Europe in the 1870's—wealthy American gentlemen in both the eighteenth and nineteenth centuries had traveled to Europe as part of their education. But in the 1870's, Americans changed their attitude to Europe, and the new men of wealth, more cosmopolitan but strangely less confident than their predecessors, turned their efforts toward imitating their European counterparts.

The Walk on the Cliff at Newport, c. 1872
Mark Twain took a dim view of Newport; in *The Guilded Age* he wrote:

"Newport is damp, and cold, and windy and excessively disagreeable, but it is very select."

The Cliff House, Newport, c. 1873
Newport was a town exclusively for the rich, as the *Times* observed on July 9, 1876:

"Newport in itself is certainly unsurpassed either in America or Europe; but its great enjoyments are for the cottage and boarding-house population. The hotels are usually placed quite away from the characteristic scenery, the only exceptions being the Bateman Hotel and the Cliff House, both expensive houses. But, through all the lovely sites of this unequaled watering-place, there is not an inn or quiet, cheap hotel placed where a gentleman would place his cottage; scarcely a garden overlooking the blue sea where the passing strangers could refresh themselves; no café or humble inn by the sea-cliffs, such as on so many Swiss lakes, or near the Rhine and the Danube, give such endless enjoyment to the multitude of common folk."

Residences of the Late Mr. G. Griswold Gray, and the Late Miss Cushman

Henry James in *An International Episode* described Newport villas like this one:

"And so the two inquiring Englishmen... descended from the veranda of the big hotel and took their way...along a large, straight road, past a series of fresh-looking villas embosomed in shrubs and flowers, and enclosed in an ingenious variety of wooden palings. The morning was brilliant and cool, the villas were smart and snug, and the walk of the young travellers was very entertaining. Everything looked as if it had received a coat of fresh paint the day before—the red roofs, the green shutters, the clean, bright browns and buffs of the house fronts. The flower beds on the little lawns seemed to sparkle in the radiant air, and the gravel in the short carriage sweeps to flash and twinkle. Along the road came a hundred little basket-phaetons, in which, almost always, a couple of ladies were sitting—ladies in white dresses and long white gloves, holding the reins and looking at the two Englishmen—whose nationality was not elusive—through the thick blue veils tied tightly about their faces, as if to guard their complexions."

THE SENSE OF NEWPORT, BY HENRY JAMES

Do I grossly exaggerate in saying that this company, candidly, quite excitedly self-conscious, as all companies not commercial, in America, may be pleasantly noted as being formed for the time of its persistence, an almost unprecedented small body—unprecedented in American conditions; a collection of the detached, the slightly disenchanted and casually disqualified, and yet of the resigned and contented, of the socially orthodox; a handful of mild, oh delightfully mild, cosmopolites, united by three common circumstances, that of their having for the most part more or less lived in Europe, that of their sacrificing openly to the ivory idol whose name is leisure, and that, not least, of a formed critical habit. These things had been felt as making them excrescences on the American surface, where nobody ever criticised, especially, after the grand tour, and where the great black ebony god of business was the only one recognized. So I see them, at all events, in fond memory, lasting as long as they could and finding no successors...I understand how it was this that made them ask what would have become of them, and where in the world, the hard American world, they *could* have hibernated, how they could even, in the Season, have bowed their economic heads and lurked, if it hadn't been for Newport.

James denounced the new men of wealth who had come to Newport and turned it into a land of huge fake castles which looked to James wrong for the spot:

The white elephants, as one may best call them, all cry and no wool, all house and no garden, make now, for three or four miles, a barely interrupted chain...They look queer and conscious and lumpish—some of them, as with an air of the brandished proboscis, really grotesque—while their averted owners, roused from a witless dream, wonder what in the world is to be done with them. The answer to which, I think, can only be that there is absolutely nothing to be done; nothing but to let them stand there always, vast and blank, for reminder to those concerned of the prohibited degrees of witlessness, and of the peculiarly awkward vengeances of affronted proportion and discretion.

McALLISTER: A DIFFERENT VIEW OF NEWPORT

Ward McAllister enjoyed the side of Newport which James despised. He thought of the resort as a passport to New York Society. In his memoirs, McAllister wrote that in Newport:

You formed lifetime intimacies with the most cultivated and charming men and women of this country.

These little parties were then and are now, the stepping-stones to our best New York society. People who have been for years in mourning and thus lost sight of, or who having passed their lives abroad and were forgotten, were again seen, admired, and liked, and at once brought into society's fold. Now, do not for a moment imagine that all were indiscriminately asked to these little fetes. On the contrary, if you were not of the inner circle, and were a new-comer, it took the combined efforts of all your friends' backing and pushing to procure an

Saratoga—Scene on the Veranda of a Fashionable Hotel
"The fountains of Saratoga will ever be the resort of wealth, intelligence, and fashion. As a political observatory no place can be more fitly selected. Gentlemen are continually coming from and going to every section of the country; information from all quarters is received daily; and it is the best of all places for politicians to congregate."
Harper's Monthly Magazine, *1876*

Fashionable Ladies at Saratoga, c. 1876

invitation for you. For years, whole families sat on the stool of probation, awaiting trial and acceptance, and many were then rejected. But, once received, you were put on an intimate footing with all. To acquire such intimacy in a great city like New York would have taken you a lifetime...

SARATOGA—ANOTHER FASHIONABLE RESORT

The *Times* on June 24, 1876, declared that there was only one "watering-place" for foreigners, and that was Saratoga:

It is certain that to foreigners all that is gay, sparkling, brilliant, fashionable and entrancing is summed up in the word Saratoga. For the Transatlantic visitors to this land, America means New York, the Centennial Exhibition, the Falls of Niagara, the springs of Saratoga, and the big trees of the Yosemite Valley...There are really more foreign guests in Saratoga at this minute than native...

The *Times* writer went on to explain the many reasons for the popularity of Saratoga:

The prestige of Saratoga, which is bringing these foreigners to the gay village in such numbers, is, of course, due primarily to the excellence of the mineral springs, but secondarily to the reputation of the unrivalled hotels. I am satisfied that at no time in the past, not even in the days when Southern chivalry knelt before Northern beauty, were there such hotels as exist in this place to-day. Yet...there are but two hotels which fully represent the ideas of their owners...the Clarendon and the Grand Union. The former is a quiet, refined, aristocratic summer home; the latter is a superb, artistic, brilliant palace. It astonishes even

Clarendon House
In June 1876, the *Times* reported that:
"There have been very few arrivals at any house save the Clarendon. Here the arrivals were exceedingly numerous from the very date of the opening...The majority of the guests were undoubtedly Americans, leading families of New York and Albany, with some choice specimens of the blue blood of Boston."
     In contrast to the Grand Union, the Clarendon House was decorated in good, simple American taste:
     "The whole place, from the front portico to the western wing, is painted in pure white, with the relief of green shutters and the green foliage of the pine trees by which the house is surrounded on every side...In the rooms, neither large nor small, there is the same preference for white, and furniture of the most solid character is often supplemented by cane chairs and sofas. The effect of this style is wonderfully calming and soothing to irritated nerves. There is an atmosphere of quiet everywhere, and the great capitalists who come here regularly sit themselves down in the great wooden chairs on the shady piazza with a prolonged ah! of satisfaction, which testifies loudly to their appreciation of the style of things."

The Grand Union Hotel

The Grand Union Hotel was owned by A. T. Stewart until his death, when it passed into the hands of Stewart's friend, Judge Henry Hilton.

The United States Hotel, c. 1876

Built in 1824, the hotel was frequented by "the rich, mercantile class." *Harper's Monthly Magazine* boasted in 1876 that: "The hotels at Saratoga are of world- wide reputation. They afford the means of judging of the manners and forming some estimate of the diversified character of our countrymen from the various parts of the extended Union, and enable us to catch a glimpse of the prevailing follies and fashions of the day."

the foreigners who are accustomed to the glitter of the Cafe du Grand Balcon, and the Grand Hotel du Louvre of Paris, and the splendid structures of Baden-Baden...

The *Times* in June 1876 explained that A. T. Stewart, who had owned the Grand Union until his death in April of 1876 (whereupon it passed into the hands of Stewart's best friend Col. Hilton), had for the hotel "an affection as ardent as the late Sultan Abdul Aziz ever felt for the palaces which he built." The *Times* said:

Year after year additions have been made, increasing its beauties, its accomodations, its internal arrangements, until to-day...it stands the confessed masterpiece of American hotels. When Dom Pedro came here the other week, he scrutinized it in his free fashion, wandering off unattended into the kitchens and offices, evidently taking mental notes of all he saw. He explored the whole structure in his business-like way and when asked...what he thought of it, he replied: "Eet ees magnificent. I have seen se Palace Hotel at San Francisco, and ze hotels of New York, but zis truly surpasses zem all."...

The decoration of the Grand Union was very extravagant, very foreign, and therefore very admirable, according to the *Times*:

The second leading thought is the splendor of decoration due entirely to A. T. Stewart...In decorating this superb, this palatial, structure, he passed the happiest days of his declining life. With the ardor of a lover he pondered over the colors to be used in painting the walls, the style of the frescoing for the ceilings, the wall papers, the carpeting, the furniture, even to the windows. The Grand Union was the child of his old age, and he lavished gifts upon it. He would have nothing mean or commonplace about it...All the rooms were papered with the imitation of stamped Venetian leather, rich in colors of vermilion, olive green, and dull gold. Every window was supplied with huge panes of plate glass, every mirror was of French plate, and furniture of the most solid kind and of the most ample size was placed in each chamber...In fact, Mr. Stewart labored to perfect this hotel as no agent or friend, however faithful, could have done, and he has made it a thing of wonderful beauty.

The *Times*, ever worried about what foreigners might think of America, felt that the Grand Union and Clarendon were up to any foreign standard:

Taking these both together [the Clarendon and the Grand Union] as two perfect specimens of different types of American hotel-keeping, they cannot but awaken the admiration of intelligent foreigners, and compel contemplation of the nature of a race that has in so short a time developed so high a standard of hotel life.

Saratoga's race track, favored by Pierre Lorillard among others, continued to keep Saratoga in favor in the later part of the century when the spa was succeeded in brilliance by Newport.

Inside the cartoon:

Seligman "JEW"

Hilton "HEBREW"

GRAND UNION

"Father forgive them for they know not what they do."

"Vhere, oh, vhere is my summer home?"

"I get square on'm, you bet, who vill buy his voollen goods?"

Unobjectionable Gentiles in SARATOGA

"A sure device to keep them out."

"A neat device to gain admission."

J. Keppler

NO JEWS ADMITTED: SELIGMAN EXCLUDED FROM THE GRAND UNION AT SARATOGA BY JUDGE HILTON

In June 1877 Joseph Seligman, the friend of former President Grant and a well-known German-Jewish financier, was excluded from the Grand Union Hotel in Saratoga by Judge Henry Hilton, a New York politician, a friend of A. T. Stewart, and a supporter of the Tweed Ring. A great uproar followed the exclusion. The story commanded three columns in the *New York Times* on June 19, and the entire first and second page the following day. It continued to make headlines for a week. Hilton explained that Christians did not like to be around Jews; guests, "particularly female, do not wish to meet this class of Jews." The expulsion of Seligman from the Grand Union has been called the first widely publicized anti-Semitic incident in America. The *Times* gave this account of the scene:

On Wednesday last Joseph Seligman, the well-known banker of this City...visited Saratoga with his wife and family. For 10 years past he has spent the summer at the Grand Union Hotel. His family entered the parlors, and Mr. Seligman went to the manager to make arrangements for the rooms. That gentlemen seemed somewhat confused, and said:

Puck, the leading humor magazine of the day, featured this cartoon in June 1877 about the widely publicized expulsion of Jewish financier Joseph Seligman from the Grand Union Hotel at Saratoga. In the middle of the cartoon is Christ, with Seligman on his left and Judge Henry Hilton, who expelled Seligman from the Grand Union, on the right. Seligman asks himself, "Vhere, oh vhere is my summer home?"

"Taking the Waters" at Saratoga

"That Ebrew Jew," by Bret Harte

Bret Harte wrote a poem about Seligman being banned from the Grand Union. The "tradesman" in the poem was A. T. Stewart, who owned the Grand Union Hotel in Saratoga until his death, in April 1876, when Judge Hilton (who was Stewart's best friend and inherited a million dollars from him) took over the Grand Union and Stewart's New York store.

There was once a tradesman renowned as a screw
Who sold pins and needles and calicoes too,
Till he built up a fortune—the which as it grew
Just ruined small traders the whole city through—
    Yet one thing he knew,
    Between me and you,
    There was a distinction
    'Twixt Christian and Jew.

Till he died in his mansion—a great millionaire—
The owner of thousands; but nothing to spare
For the needy and poor who from hunger might drop,
And only a pittance to clerks in his shop.
    But left it all to
    A Lawyer, who knew
    A subtile distinction
    'Twixt Ebrew and Jew.

This man was no trader, but simply a friend
Of this Gent who kept shop and who, nearing his end,
Handed over a million—'twas only his due,
Who discovered this contrast 'twixt Ebrew and Jew.
    For he said, "If you view
    This case as I do,
    There *is* a distinction
    'Twixt Ebrew and Jew.

"For the Jew is a man who will make money through
His skill, his *finesse,* and his capital too,
And an Ebrew's a man that we Gentiles can 'do,'
So you see there's a contrast 'twixt Ebrew and Jew."
Then he kept a hotel—here his trouble began—
In a fashion unknown to his primitive plan;
For the rule of this house to his manager ran,
"Don't give entertainment to Israelite man."
    Yet the manager knew,
    Between me and you,
    No other distinction
    'Twixt Ebrew and Jew.

"You may give to John Morissey supper and wine,
And Madame N. N. to your care I'll resign;
You'll see that those Jenkins from Missouri Flat
Are properly cared for; but recollect
    Never a Jew
    Who's not an Ebrew
    Shall take up his lodgings
    Here at the Grand U.
"You'll allow Miss McFlimsey her diamonds to wear;
You'll permit the Van Dams at the waiters to swear;

Christmas in Florida, 1876

Some families went to Southern resorts in the winter. The Illustrated London News *offered its readers in December 1876 this vision of a Southern Christmas.*

    The Wellands in The Age of Innocence *spent their holidays in the South: "In obedience to a long-established habit, the Wellands had left the previous week for St. Augustine, where, out of regard for the supposed susceptibility of Mr. Welland's bronchial tubes, they always spent the latter part of the winter."*

"Mr. Seligman, I am required to inform you that Mr. Hilton has given instructions that no Israelites shall be permitted in future to stop at this hotel."

Mr. Seligman was so astonished that for some time he could make no reply. Then he said: "Do you mean to tell me that you will not entertain Jewish people!" "That is our order, Sir," was the reply.

Before leaving the banker asked the reason why Jews were thus persecuted. Said he, "are they dirty, do they misbehave themselves, or have they refused to pay their bills?"

"Oh, no," replied the manager, "there is no fault to be found in that respect. The reason is simply this: business at the hotel was not good last season, and we had a large number of Jews here. Mr. Hilton came to the conclusion that Christians did not like their company, and for that reason shunned the hotel. He resolved to run the Union on a different principle this season, and gave us instructions to admit no Jew! Personally he (the manager) was very sorry, inasmuch as Mr. Seligman had patronized the hotel for so many years but the order was imperative."

The background of the incident was that Seligman had been a member of the "Committee of Seventy," which had helped bring about the downfall of Boss Tweed, who had been a friend and ally of Judge Hilton's. Hilton had always disliked Seligman and many people suspected that the Saratoga incident was Hilton's revenge.

THE JEWS FIGHT BACK

Joseph Seligman returned to New York "feeling outraged," according to the *Times*. "In a very indignant state of mind he...penned a letter to Mr. Hilton, couched in very bitter and sarcastic terms." A meeting of Seligman's friends was held to consider the best course of action. They decided to boycott A. T. Stewart and Company, the store Hilton had inherited from Stewart.

After some time passed, Judge Hilton tried to halt the boycott with a pledge of $1,000 to Jewish charities. But the Jews refused to be bought. *Puck*, a leading humor magazine, in 1878 ran an editorial titled "Alas! Poor Hilton," calling Hilton the ultimate loser in his battle with Seligman:

It is to be regretted that Mr. Hilton is as unsuccessful a drygoods man and a hotel-keeper as he notoriously was as a jurist. ...He took it upon himself to insult a portion of our people whose noses had more of the curvilinear form of beauty than his own pug and he rode his high-hobby horse of purse-proud self-sufficiency until he woke up one day to find that the drygoods business was waning...Then Mr. Hilton arouses himself...He has remembered that he has insulted the Jews. Aha! we'll conciliate them. So out of the coffers that A. T. Stewart filled he gropes among the millions and orders the trustees of a few Hebrew charities to bend the pregnant hinges of their knees at his door and receive a few hundred dollars. But in this country the Jew is not ostracized. He stands equal before the law and before society...And the Jew has stood up like a Man and refused to condone the gross and uncalled for insults of this haphazard millionaire, merely because he flings the offer of a thousand dollars in their faces. All honor to the Jews for their manly stand in this instance.

Despite *Puck*'s conclusion, exclusion of Jews from resort hotels continued and became an accepted practice in the 1880's.

You'll allow Miss Décolleté to flirt on the stair;
But as to an Israelite—pray have a care;
    For, between me and you,
    Though the doctrine is new,
    There's a business distinction
    'Twixt Ebrew and Jew.'

Now, how shall we know? Prophet, tell us, pray do,
Where the line of the Hebrew fades into the Jew?
Shall we keep out Disraeili and take Roths-child in?
Or snub Meyerbeer and think Verdi a sin?
    What shall we do?
    O, give us a few
    Points to distinguish
    'Twixt Ebrew and Jew.

There was One—Heaven help us!—who died in man's place,
With thorns on his forehead, but Love in his face:
And when "foxes had holes" and birds in the air
Had their nests in the trees, there was no spot to spare
    For this "King of the Jews."
    Did the Romans refuse
    This right to the Ebrews
    Or only to Jews?

Camping in Portland, Maine c. 1875
Aside from Newport and Saratoga there were other popular resorts—Long Branch, New Jersey, the Thousand Islands, and Florida in the winter. Newland Archer in *The Age of Innocence* wanted to go to Maine for the summer instead of Newport:

"Archer had tried to persuade May to spend the summer on a remote island off the coast of Maine (called, appropriately enough, Mount Desert), where a few hardy Boston-ians and Philadelphians were camping in 'native' cottages, and whence came reports of enchanting scenery and a wild, almost trapper-like existence amid woods and waters.

"But the Wellands always went to New-port, where they owned one of the square boxes on the cliffs, and their son-in-law could adduce no good reason why he and May should not join them there. As Mrs. Wel-land rather tartly pointed out, it was hardly worthwhile for May to have worn herself out trying on summer clothes in Paris if she was not allowed to wear them...''

Mary Mason Jones's House on the Corner of Fifty-seventh Street and Fifth Avenue

The house, pictured on the left, was built in 1871 by Mary Mason Jones in the ''Parisian style.'' The house was a radical change from the brownstones that were popular at the time, and its location ''uptown'' at Fifty-seventh Street was another departure from established tradition.

CHANGES IN NEW YORK—MARY MASON JONES

Mrs. Mary Mason Jones, age seventy and a widow, chose in 1871 to build a row of residences on the east side of Fifth Avenue between Fifty-seventh and Fifty-eighth streets, with a very grand house for herself on the corner of Fifth Avenue and Fifty-seventh Street. Mrs. Jones, Edith Wharton's aunt and member of a patrician family, had previously lived on Broadway and Waverly Place. To move to Fifty-seventh Street in the 1870's was unheard of, so Mrs. Jones' move "uptown" caused considerable talk. Her house was a sign of the many changes that were taking place in New York. Edith Wharton modeled Mrs. Manson Mingott in *The Age of Innocence* on Mrs. Mason Jones; Mrs. Mingott recalled the reaction to her move uptown:

"When I bought this house you'd have thought I was moving to California! Nobody ever had built above Fortieth Street...No, no; not one of them wants to be different; they're scared of it as the smallpox."

Mrs. Jones did not build a brownstone: she built a house in

the Parisian style. Edith Wharton described Mrs. Manson Mingott's house:

Whatever man dared (within Fifth Avenue's limits)...old Mrs. Manson Mingott...would dare...The high and mighty old lady...put the crowning touch to her audacities by building a large house of pale cream-colored stone (when brown sandstone seemed as much the only wear as a frock-coat in the afternoon) in an inaccessible wilderness near the Central Park...But the cream-colored house (supposed to be modelled on the private hotels of the Parisian aristocracy) was there as a visible proof of her mortal courage; and she throned in it...as placidly as if there was nothing peculiar in living above Thirty-fourth Street, or in having French windows that opened like doors instead of sashes that pushed up.

Although she favored architectural changes, Mrs. Jones did not favor social changes. Mrs. Paran Stevens was one of the "new" people; her husband had made millions of dollars in the hotel business in Boston. Mrs. Stevens had come to New York determined to capture a place in society; Mrs. Jones was equally determined to keep Mrs. Stevens from succeeding. She said:

"There is one house that Mrs. Stevens will never enter. I am old enough to please myself, and I do not care to extend my sufficiently large circle of acquaintances."

Mrs. Jones succeeded in keeping Mrs. Stevens out of her house when she was alive but after her death her house was bought by Mrs. Stevens. A lady like Mrs. Stevens (called Mrs. Lemuel Struthers—wife of a shoe-polish manufacturer) appears in *The Age of Innocence;* Mrs. Struthers, like her real-life counterpart, gave Sunday-night parties, defying New York tradition, and gained partial social acceptance:

It was thus, Archer reflected, that New York managed its transitions: conspiring to ignore them till they were well over, and then, in all good faith, imagining that they had taken place in a preceeding age. There was always a traitor in the citadel; and after he (or generally she) had surrendered the keys, what was the use of pretending that it was impregnable? Once people had tasted of Mrs. Struther's easy Sunday hospitality they were not likely to sit at home remembering that her champagne was transmuted Shoe-Polish.

Change was in the air in the 1870's in New York. In *The Age of Innocence*, Newland Archer's mother remarked that:

She was able...to trace each new crack in its surface, and all the strange weeds pushing up between the ordered rows of social vegetables...New York had changed; and Newland Archer, in the winter of the second year of his marriage, was himself obliged to admit that if it had not actually changed it was certainly changing.

Hair Styles in 1876 Featured in *Harper's Bazar*

Charles Frederick Worth

From Charles Frederick Worth, the famed Parisian couturier, wealthy and fashionable American women purchased their clothes in the 1870's. Isabella Stewart Gardner traveled to Paris to purchase Worth clothes—among them a black velvet afternoon dress with a hat and muff made of Russian sable. Hoops were still the style in Boston in 1868 when Mrs. Gardner returned with her clinging and hoopless Worth dresses, which became the talk of the town.

Ladies' Evening Dresses Pictured in *Harper's Bazar* **in 1876**

"It is advisable for ladies who go out a great deal in the evening to have two handsome black dresses—one of velvet and the other of silk. It is also necessary to have black and white laces which are readily employed for almost any toilet; with these and some skill in selecting the proper accessories, a great deal can be accomplished with dresses that are not perfectly new...

"The baby-dress is at the height of its popularity...but few low-necked dresses have been seen as yet...

"It is possible that white will be eclipsed by yellow for evening wear this winter. Blondes, to whom this color is exceedingly unbecoming, will wear it notwithstanding."

The *New York Times*, January 9, 1876

A CHANGE IN FASHION MARKS THE CHANGE IN SOCIETY—FLASH BECOMES ACCEPTABLE

Ladies were no longer putting their gowns made by Worth—the leading Paris couturier of the day—into storage before wearing them. In *The Age of Innocence,* a Miss Jackson remarked that the change in fashion was especially noticeable on the first night of the opera season:

"Jane Merry's dress was the only one I recognized from last year; and even that had had the front panel changed. Yet I know she got it from Worth only two years ago..."

"Ah, Jane Merry is one of *us*," said Mrs. Archer sighing, as if it were not such an enviable thing to be in an age when ladies were beginning to flaunt abroad their Paris dresses as soon as they were out of the Custom House, instead of letting them mellow under lock and key, in the manner of Mrs. Archer's contemporaries...

"In my youth," Miss Jackson rejoined, "it was considered vulgar to dress in the newest fashions; and Amy Sillerton has always told me that in Boston the rule was to put away one's Paris dresses for two years..."

"Ah, well, Boston is more conservative than New York; but I always think it's a safe rule for a lady to lay aside her French dresses for one season," Mrs. Archer conceded.

"It was Beaufort who started the new fashion by making his wife clap her new clothes on her back as soon as they arrived: I must say at times it takes all Regina's distinction not to look like...like..."

THE VANDERBILTS

The Vanderbilts altered both the architectural and the social landscape of New York. In 1873 the family of William H. Vanderbilt was living fairly simply in an unpretentious brownstone at Fifth Avenue and Forty-second Street. But their life changed when, on January 4, 1877, at the age of eighty-three, Commodore Vanderbilt died in his house at 10 Washington Place, leaving an estate of about $100 million. Most of the Commodore's vast estate went to his son, William Henry, who had been his father's chief aide. Like William B. Astor (the second-generation Astor), William H. Vanderbilt doubled his father's fortune. In the early 1880's, by then president of the New York Central, he declared:

"I am the richest man in the world. I am worth one hundred and ninety-four million dollars...I would not walk across the street to make a million dollars."

And with the possible exception of the Duke of Westminster, Vanderbilt was indeed the richest man in the world.

At his death in 1885, William H. Vanderbilt left an estate estimated at more than $200 million.

Street Toilette—*Harper's Bazar*, 1876

"Major Amberson had 'made a fortune' in 1873, when other people were losing fortunes, and the magnificence of the Ambersons began then. Magnificence, like the size of a fortune, is always comparative...and the Ambersons were magnificent in their day and place. Their splendour lasted throughout all the years that saw their Midland town spread and darken into a city...In that town, in those days, all the women who wore silk or velvet knew all the other women who wore silk or velvet...

"During the earlier years of this period, elegance of personal appearance was believed to rest more upon the texture of garments than upon their shaping. A silk dress needed no remodelling when it was a year or so old; it remained distinguished by merely remaining silk.

"Shifting fashion of shape replaced aristocracy of texture; dressmakers, shoemakers, hatmakers, and tailors, increasing in cunning and power, found means to make new clothes old...Surely no more is needed to prove that so short a time ago we were living in another age!"

Booth Tarkington, *The Magnificent Ambersons*

"The William H. Vanderbilt Family in 1873," by Seymour J. Guy

Here the family is pictured inside their brownstone living fairly simply before they had started to spend the Commodore's millions. At the left is William H. Vanderbilt, with his wife, Maria, next to him. They are surrounded by their eight children and two servants (seen in the background). The lady standing in the center is Margaret Shepard, the eldest daughter. William Kissam Vanderbilt, who would live much more ostentatiously than his father, is pictured standing in the rear with his sister Florence.

A room in the grand house that Cornelius Vanderbilt later built for himself on Fifth Avenue. The room was designed by Louis Tiffany.

William H. Vanderbilt

Although he got into the family business late, William H. Vanderbilt (son of the Commodore) made up for lost time. In 1882, at Michigan City, Indiana, while discussing the rate wars he was fighting with the Pennsylvania Railroad, Vanderbilt was asked by a naïve journalist: "But you don't run it [the train] for the public benefit?" Vanderbilt made his famous reply: "The public be damned! I am working for my stockholders. If the public want the train, why don't they support it?"

Vanderbilt's hobby was horses—trotters and carriage horses. His Manhattan stables, which cost him $600,000 were located at Madison Avenue and Fifty-second Street. His most famous trotter was Maud S., bought by Vanderbilt in 1878 for $20,000.

The Japanese Room of the William H. Vanderbilt House

What was foreign was fashionable, as is evident at a glance at this room in William H. Vanderbilt's mansion; antiques were piled one on top of another in this so-called Japanese Room.

"Three Magnificent Dwellings in One—Doors of Bronze, Pavements of Mosaic and Columns of Marble"—The New York Times, *1881*

In 1879 William H. Vanderbilt, determined not to be outdone by his son, William Kissam, commissioned Christian Herter and his brother to design a palace for him on Fifth Avenue, between Fifty-first and Fifty-second streets. He spent $3 million on his house, which was, of course, modeled after European mansions. Six to seven hundred men worked on the mansion; Vanderbilt even imported sixty sculptors from Europe to decorate the interior of his house, which was finished in the autumn of 1881. The Times *reported that:*

"The great Vanderbilt palace on Fifth Avenue approaches completion. For three years it has been the course of erection, and it is now so nearly finished that its owner expects to occupy it before Christmas. In size, in elegance, in costliness, there is no house like it. A few princes and emperors of the Old World may have had more pretentious palaces, but it has been reserved for an American sovereign to eclipse them in the construction of an edifice which, while it contains all that can be desired in architecture and in art, is also replete with everything that contributes to the comfort of a real home."

THE VANDERBILT STYLE

It was the children of William H. Vanderbilt, the third generation of Vanderbilts, who (like the third-generation Astors) would spend the money accumulated by the first two generations and create a life style which would become the model for men of wealth. Cornelius Vanderbilt II and his younger brother, William Kissam Vanderbilt, both sons of William H. Vanderbilt, remained in New York and gained the social acceptance that the first two generations of Vanderbilts had not achieved. The moving force was the wife of the younger Vanderbilt brother, William Kissam. An executive in the family railroad business, William K. Vanderbilt married Alva Erskine Smith, a member of a distinguished Southern family, on April 20, 1875. The *Times* wrote:

Miss Alva Smith was born in Mobile, Alabama, on January 17, 1853.

She was the daughter of a cotton planter, Murray Forbes Smith...Her education was received in private schools in France. Even in her girlhood, her likes and dislikes were pronounced. Although her marriage to Mr. Vanderbilt brought her a notable place in New York society, she captured its leadership five years later.

THE WILLIAM K. VANDERBILT MANSION

In 1878 Alva and William K. Vanderbilt made their first big move: they hired Richard Morris Hunt to build a palace for them at 660 Fifth Avenue, at Fifty-second Street. The house would make Caroline Astor's brownstone look dingy; it would have a two-story paneled dining room and a two-story gymnasium, as well as stained-glass windows. The exterior would be Caen stone. When it was finished, the *Times* heaped praise on the William Kissam Vanderbilt house and its European furnishings:

[There was] a noble room on the front of the house in the style of François Premier, 25 feet in width by 40 in length, wainscotted richly and heavily in carved French walnut and hung in dark red plush. Vast carved cabinets and an immense, deep fire-place give an air of antique grandeur to this room...[Then there was] a bright and charming *salon* of the style of Louis XV, 30 feet in width by 35 in length, wainscotted in oak and enriched with carved work and gilding. The whole wainscotting on this beautiful apartment was brought from a chateau in France. On the walls hang three French Gobelin tapestries a century old...The furniture is of the bright and gracious style of that age of airy arrogance and perfumed coquetry which preceded the tragedy of the great Revolution.

Immediately upon the completion of the William K. Vanderbilt mansion in 1881, Ward McAllister, sharing in the general enthusiasm, allowed the Vanderbilts to attend the exclusive Patriarch Balls. Although almost everyone felt that Alva Vanderbilt's Gothic house was a great success, architect Louis Sullivan dared to differ:

Must I show you this *French château*, this little Château de Blois, on the street corner, here, in New York, and still you do not laugh?...Must you wait until you see a *gentleman* in a silk hat come out of it before you laugh? Have you no sense of humor, no sense of pathos? Must I then tell you that while the man may live in the house physically (for a man may live in any kind of house, physically), that he cannot possibly live in it morally, mentally, or spiritually, that he and his home are a paradox, a contradiction, an absurdity, a characteristically New York absurdity; that he is no part of the house, and his house no part of him?

But Sullivan's view would not prevail for many years. For the moment, Richard Morris Hunt and William Kissam Vanderbilt's house were both widely applauded. The Vanderbilts had changed American taste in architecture.

William Kissam Vanderbilt
William K. Vanderbilt, the second son of William H. Vanderbilt, was only twenty-seven years old in 1876 and newly married to Alva Smith of Mobile, Alabama. In 1877 Willie K., as he was known, was made second vice-president of the New York Central. And in 1878 he and his wife decided to build the first of the Vanderbilt mansions.

The Mansion of William Kissam Vanderbilt — Far from the Traditional Brownstone
It has been said that William K. Vanderbilt's splashy Fifth Avenue house with its limestone exterior looked somewhat like an American version of the Château of Blois. Architect Richard Morris Hunt was certainly greatly influenced by the architecture of French châteaux.

Miss Carrie Astor

For her daughter Carrie, Caroline Astor lowered her pride and called on Alva Vanderbilt to get an invitation to Mrs. Vanderbilt's costume ball. At the ball Mrs. Astor organized one of the quadrilles and the *Times* reported on March 27, 1883, that:

"Another striking quadrille was the 'Star Quadrille,' organized by Mrs. William Astor. In this quadrille appeared Mrs. Lloyd Bryce, Miss Astor, Miss Beckwith, Miss Carroll, Miss Hoffman, Miss Marie, Miss Warren, and Miss McAllister. These ladies were arrayed as twin stars in four different colors—yellow, blue, mauve, and white."

Costumed Guests at Alva Vanderbilt's Ball—Mr. and Mrs. Reginald Francklyn

ALVA VANDERBILT TO GIVE A COSTUME BALL

Alva Vanderbilt's new house may have gained admission for her and her husband to the Patriarch Balls, but it had not succeeded in getting the young Vanderbilts admitted to Mrs. Astor's annual ball. So when Alva Vanderbilt decided to give a costume ball, a house-warming party for her new house on March 26, 1883, she invited all of New York society except the William Astors, since, she said, Mrs. Astor had never called on her. The *Times* reported that:

"Everyone of importance" acknowledged her sway, save only the Astors. Mrs. Vanderbilt issued invitations to a function at her home...and the names of the Astors were not included on the list. Emissaries inquired why the admitted leaders of the "Four Hundred" had been left out, and it was explained by Mrs. Vanderbilt that she could not ask persons who had never called on her. The Astors called on the forceful young matron, and the belated invitations were hurriedly dispatched.

Alva Vanderbilt had gained social recognition of the Vanderbilts by the Astors, the most important achievement of her ball.

PREPARATIONS FOR THE BALL

According to the *Times*, the question of what to wear to the Vanderbilt ball:

...disturbed the sleep and occupied the waking hours of social butterflies both male and female, for over six weeks...

William K. Vanderbilt's Fifth Avenue house had provided rich Americans with a model of a pseudo-French house. Mrs. Vanderbilt's ball gave Americans—eager to create in America an aristocracy like the aristocracies of the Old World—a chance to dress up as European kings and queens.

THE VANDERBILT COSTUME BALL—MARCH 26, 1883

The *Times* reported that:

The fancy ball given by Mr. and Mrs. W. K. Vanderbilt in their new and elegant house at the corner of Fifth Avenue and Fifty-second Street on the evening of March 26th, was, perhaps, the most brilliant and picturesque entertainment of the kind ever given in the metropolis...The grand house was in a blaze of light, and beautiful as a garden in its profuse decorations of flowers.

And *Frank Leslie's Illustrated Newspaper* gave an ecstatic description of the ball:

The guests began to arrive about half-past ten o'clock, and a little after

Alva Vanderbilt's Costume Ball, March 26, 1883
A drawing from Frank Leslie's Illustrated Newspaper. *April 7, 1883.*
The Times *anticipated the ball which was:*

"The first event of the season, in importance as well as in the order of occurrence...The long-talked-of fancy-dress ball of Mrs. William K. Vanderbilt...will take place to-morrow evening at her husband's new residence, at Fifty-second street and Fifth avenue. To borrow a common society phrase, "everybody who amounts to anything," that is, in the eyes of society itself, will be present, as over 1,000 invitations have been issued, and it is not likely that anybody who has been invited will fail to go....

"What costumes will be worn, and who will wear them, form now the all absorbing topic of conversation, but, on the other hand, great care is being taken by each prospective guest to conceal from the others what his or her costume will be...It is said that the Empress of China, Queen Elizabeth, Marie Stuart, Marie Antoinette, the Maid of Orleans, Helen of Troy, Cleopatra...Pocahontas...[and] Minerva...are each to be personated by ladies...Some of the historical costumes have been copied, it is said, from paintings in the Hampton Court Palace and the British Museum, while that of Queen Elizabeth is taken from a picture in the gallery of Mr. August Belmont, of this City...

"Miss Kate Bulkley will congeal into ice; Miss Turnure will be transformed into an Egyptian Princess...Miss Belle Wilson will endeavor to justify the application of her Christian name...Mrs. Richard Irwin, as Mary will show that she is quite contrary; Miss Marion Langdon will soar as a golden butterfly, while one of her ardent admirers will pursue her as an entomologist."

Alva Vanderbilt's Costume

"Mrs. Vanderbilt's irreproachable taste was seen to perfection in her costume as a Venetian Princess taken from a picture by Cabanel. The underskirt was of white and yellow brocade, shading from the deepest orange to the lightest canary, only the highlights being white. The figures of flowers and leaves were outlined in gold, white and iridescent beads; light blue satin train embroidered magnificently in gold and lined with Roman red. Almost the entire length of the train was caught up at one side, forming a large puff. The waist was of blue satin covered with gold embroidery—the dress was cut square in the neck, and the flowing sleeves were of transparent gold tissue. She wore a Venetian cap, covered with magnificent jewels, the most noticeable of these being a superb peacock in many colored gems..."
The *New York Times,* March 27, 1883

eleven, to the strains of Gilmore's Band, the six quadrilles, comprising in all nearly a hundred ladies and gentlemen, were formed in order in the gymnasium and began to move in a glittering processional pageant down the grand stairway and through the hall. The ball was opened by the "Hobby-Horse Quadrille"...The workmen had been two months in finishing the horses. They were of life-size, covered with genuine hides, and had large, bright eyes and flowing manes and tails, but were light enough to be easily and comfortably attached to the waists of the wearers, whose feet were concealed by richly embroidered hangings. False legs were represented on the outside of the blankets. The costumes were red hunting-coats, white satin vests, yellow satin knee-breeches, white satin stockings. The ladies wore red hunting-coats and white satin skirts, elegantly embroidered. All the dresses were in the style of Louis XIV.

When this wonderful quadrille had been danced, the "Mother Goose Quadrille" came on,...Another striking quadrille was the "Star Quadrille," organized by Mrs. William Astor...Supper was served in the gymnasium soon after one o'clock, and the entertainment as a

"Mrs. Cornelius Vanderbilt appeared as the 'Electric Light,' in white satin trimmed with diamonds, and with a magnificent diamond headdress. Mrs. Cornelius Vanderbilt was accompanied by her children daintily apparelled, one as a rose, in pink tulle, with a satin overdress of green leaves, a waist of green satin and a headdress of white satin, fashioned like a bouquet-holder; another as Sinbad the Sailor, in white satin breeches, a white chemisette, a flying jacket, embroidered in gold, and Turkish shoes, and a third as a little courtier, in a light-blue satin hand-embroidered coat, with waistcoat and breeches of white satin, and embroidered in roses and daisies."

The *New York Times*, March 27, 1883

whole constituted an event which will long be remembered in fashionable circles.

The *Times* singled out certain costumes for special mention:

Among the hundreds of striking and unique costumes but a few can possibly be noted. These, however, will convey some idea of the scene as it presented itself at midnight, when the hall, the grand stairway, and the spacious apartments were all thronged with animated groups enjoying the double pleasure of seeing and of being seen...

Mr. W. K. Vanderbilt appeared as the Duke de Guise, wearing yellow silk tights, yellow and black trunks, a yellow doublet and a black velvet cloak embroidered in gold, with the order of St. Michael suspended on a black ribbon, and with a white wig, black velvet shoes and buckles.

Mr. Cornelius Vanderbilt appeared as Louis XVI, in a *habit de cour* and breeches of fawn-colored brocade, trimmed with silver point d'Espagne...

Mrs. Pierre Lorillard as a Phoenix, wore a magnificent dress—a Worth creation—which had a front of gray silk bordered by an irregular band of flame-colored satin.

Among the guests attending the ball, mentioned by the *Times*, were:

Gen. and Mrs. Grant, Mr. and Mrs. Hamilton Fish,....Mr. and Mrs. August Belmont, Mr. and Mrs. John Jacob Astor, Mrs. William Astor, Miss Astor,....Mr. and Mrs. J. R. Roosevelt,....Mr. and Mrs. D. Ogden Mills, Mr. and Mrs. Maturin Livingston,....Mr. and Mrs. William C. Schermerhorn,....Mr. and Mrs. Stuyvesant Fish,....Col. and Mrs. DeLancey Kane, Mr. and Mrs. Robert Goelet,....Mr. and Mrs. Pierre Lorillard,....Mr. and Mrs. R. T. Wilson,... Stanley Mortimer, Ward McAllister,...

Alva Vanderbilt had arrived and as the *Times* put it, she had "successfully stormed the innermost social citadels of New York." And the direction of American Society, undecided in 1876, had been chosen. The *Herald* was certain that the ball was up to the highest European standards:

The shifting gleams of gorgeous color and of quaint and curious outlines in a thousand costumes flitting through the rooms—themselves a study fit for an artist—made up a scene probably never rivalled in Republican America and never outdone by the gayest court of Europe.

The cost to achieve the brilliant effects of the ball was enormous. One dressmaker, Lanouette, who made over one hundred and fifty costumes for the ball, told the *World* that:

"I had one hundred and forty dressmakers and seamstresses at work night and day for the past five weeks. Many of my dresses...cost between five and seven hundred dollars. I don't see how you can make a full estimate of the cost of all the costumes, for to my knowledge, many ladies had their gowns made at home either by their own seamstresses or by dressmakers hired for the occasion. At any rate, thirty thousand dollars for the dresses made by me is rather below than above the mark."

The banker Henry Clews, summed up the most important result of Alva Vanderbilt's efforts:

The ball seemed to have the effect of...placing the Vanderbilts at the top of the heap in what is recognized as good society in New York.

The ball was a signal triumph for Alva Vanderbilt, and beyond that, a climax and a symbol of a whole decade of social striving. In a generation of strivers, Alva Vanderbilt was the ultimate striver, and the tenacity with which she achieved her purpose was typical of the spirit of the newly rich throughout the country. But Mrs. Vanderbilt's success in New York was not enough to satisfy her. She went on to conquer Newport the same way she had conquered New York, by first building a lavish house and then giving an extravagant ball. The *Times* described her "Marble House" at Newport:

Its magnificence was her challenge to Newport society after she had successfully stormed the innermost social citadels of New York. Her Newport house was the sensation of the day. It cost $2,000,000 to build and $7,000,000 more was spent on the furniture and decoration...The house was designed by Richard M. Hunt, then a well-known architect, and was completed in 1892...In due course it was opened with a ball of the utmost splendor. For the first three years, it was the center of a social clique as impregnable as the stone of which it was built. Extravagance and ostentation marked every social gathering. The jewels worn at balls were valued at millions of dollars. Then in 1895...the 24-year-old Duke of Marlborough arrived, and his engagement to Mrs. Vanderbilt's daughter, Consuelo, then seventeen years old, resulted...

The marriage of Alva Vanderbilt's daughter, Consuelo, to the Duke of Marlborough was the crowning achievement of Alva's social career. And it was also the ultimate symbol of the movement of American society toward the creation of a princely class on the European model.

Alva Vanderbilt had realized all her ambitions, but in the end she was more interested in the process of striving than in any particular goal. And so, the architect of the new American aristocracy began to unravel what she had created. She did the unthinkable by divorcing William K. Vanderbilt, marrying O. P. Belmont, and becoming fervently interested in women's rights. In the end she testified to help get her daughter's marriage annulled, thus helping to undo what had been her greatest social achievement.

Julian H. Kean posed as a squire in the Mother Goose quadrille at the Vanderbilt ball.
    The *World* estimated the total cost of the ball—costumes, flowers, music and food—at $250,000. The favorite florist of the rich, Klunder, said: "I have decorated the houses of princes and ambassadors but never have I seen floral embellishments on a scale of such regal grandeur. Mr. Vanderbilt gave me *carte blanche.*"

P. T. BARNUM
THE GREATEST SHOWMAN ON EARTH

One of the great attractions of New York City in 1876 was the Centennial Show put on by P. T. Barnum. Crowds flocked to the American Institute Building to see the Japanese jugglers and the "World Renowned Carlos" in his acrobatic feats.

Barnum should really have put himself in a display case to be viewed by the admiring populace, for no one was more colorfully symbolic of the possibilities available to industrious men in post-Civil War America. "Barnum is not an ordinary showman," said John Delaware Lewis, a contemporary of Barnum's. "He is not one who will be handed down to posterity only on the strength of the objects which he has exhibited....He stands alone. I should say that Barnum is a representative man. He represents the enterprise and energy of his countrymen in the 19th century, as Washington represented their resistance to oppression in the century preceding."

The Aquarium

"Having made up my mind to capture and transport to my Museum at least two living whales, I prepared in the basement of the building a brick and cement tank, forty feet long, and eighteen feet wide for their reception. This done, I started upon my whaling expedition.

"...The excitement was intense, and, when at last these marine monsters arrived and were swimming in the tank that had been prepared for them, anxious thousands literally rushed to see the strangest curiosities ever exhibited in New York...I did not know how to feed or to take care of the monsters, and, moreover, they were in fresh water, and this, with the bad air in the basement, may have hastened their death, which occurred a few days after their arrival, but not before thousands of people had seen them. Not at all discouraged, I resolved to try again. My plan now was to connect the water of New York bay with the basement of the Museum by means of iron pipes under the street, and a steam engine on the dock to pump the water. This I actually did at a cost of several thousand dollars ...I constructed another tank in the second floor of the building. This tank was built of slate and French glass plates six feet long, five feet broad, and one inch thick, imported expressly for the purpose, and the tank, when completed, was twenty-four feet square, and cost $4,000. It was kept constantly supplied with what would be called, Hibernically, "fresh" salt water, and inside of it I soon had two white whales, caught, as the first had been, hundreds of miles below Quebec....

"...Having a stream of salt water at my command at every high tide, I was enabled to make splendid additions to the beautiful aquarium, which I was the first to introduce into this country. I procured living sharks, porpoises, sea-horses, and many rare fish from the sea in the vicinity of New York...."

P.T. Barnum

P. T. Barnum: ''There's a Sucker Born Every Minute''

Barnum developed advertising and publicity in a way undreamed of before. He was the true originator and inventor of hype. Charles Godfrey Leland, a contemporary of Barnum's, explained that when Barnum had "concocted some monstrous cock-and-bull curiosity [he] was wont to advertise that 'it is with great reluctance that he presented this unprecedented marvel to the world, as doubts had been expressed as to its genuineness—all that we ask of an enlightened and honest public is, that it will pass a fair verdict and decide whether it be a humbug or not... Barnum abode by their decision and then sent it to another city to be again decided on." Year after year he came up with new prodigies, new marvels, and new inducements for his customers to part with their money.

Barnum was born in 1810 in Bethel, Connecticut. A childhood of poverty graduated into a succession of petty business ventures—grocery stores, boarding houses and the like. His first coup was to exhibit a woman he claimed to be not only over a hundred years old but also the nurse of George Washington. He never looked back. From George Washington's nurse he moved on to Tom Thumb, Jenny Lind, and other attractions which made him a national celebrity. Barnum's fame spread overseas when he took his show to Europe, displaying Tom Thumb in England and France.

Disasters as colorful as his personality dogged him. His houses and museums were consumed by fire. At the age of forty-seven he plunged into bankruptcy, only to recover magnificently and press forward once more.

He died at the age of eighty-one. The day after Barnum's death the *New York Times* wrote: "There is hardly an American now in the vigor of life who can remember when the name of Barnum was not familiar to him, and there are very few Americans who do not feel that they owe him a certain debt of gratitude for brightening their lives or the lives of their children. It is really wonderful and unexampled, the career that closed yesterday. Since the beginnings of history there has been no showman to be compared to the showman whose long connection with the show business is now broken... No child of ripe or unripe years ever left his show...without... having been amused to the value of the charge for admission. To real children he was a great benefactor, and how many generations of children has he benefited!"

STRUGGLES AND TRIUMPHS OF P. T. BARNUM TOLD BY HIMSELF

I was born in the town of Bethel, in the State of Connecticut, 5 July, 1810....My father, Philo Barnum, was a tailor, a farmer, and sometimes a tavern-keeper, and my advantages and disadvantages were such as fall to the general run of farmers' boys...

On 17 September, 1825, my father...died. My mother was left with five children, of whom I, at fifteen years of age, was the eldest, while the youngest was but seven. It was soon apparent that my father had provided nothing for the support of his family: his estate was insolvent, and did not pay fifty cents on the dollar. My mother, by economy, industry, and perseverance, succeeded in a few years afterwards in redeeming the homestead and becoming its sole possessor; but, at the date of the death of my father, the world looked gloomy indeed.

I literally began the world with nothing and was barefooted at that.

I went to Grassy Plain, a mile north-west of Bethel, and secured a situation as clerk in a store at six dollars a month...I soon gained the confidence and esteem of my employers; they afforded me many facilities for making money on my own account, and I soon entered upon sundry speculations, and succeeded in getting a small sum of money ahead.

EARLY BUSINESS ENTERPRISES

Mr. Oliver Taylor...kept a grocery store...In the fall of 1826, he offered me a situation as clerk in his Brooklyn store, which I accepted, and before long was entrusted with the purchasing of all goods for his store...

...Well treated as I was by my employer, who manifested great interest in me, still I was dissatisfied. A salary was not sufficient for me. My disposition was of that speculative character which refused to be satisfied unless I was engaged in some business where my profits might be enhanced, or, at least, made to depend upon my energy, perseverance, attention to business, tact and calculation.

...In February 1828 I returned to Bethel, and opened a retail fruit and confectionary store in a part of my grandfather's carriage-house...This beginning of business on my own account was an eventful era in my life. My total capital was one hundred and twenty dollars, fifty of which I had expended in fitting up the store, and the remaining seventy dollars purchased my stock-in-trade...I decided to open my establishment on the first Monday in May...when I closed at night I had the satisfaction of reckoning up sixty-three dollars as my day's receipts.

...There was nothing more for me to do in Bethel; and in the winter of 1834-5 I removed my family to New York...I had no pecuniary resources...I went to the Metropolis literally to seek my fortune...In the spring I...opened a small private boarding-house at No. 52, Frankfort Street. We soon had a very good run of custom from our Connecticut acquaintances who had occasion to visit New York, and as this business did not sufficiently occupy my time, I bought an interest with Mr. John Moody in a grocery store, No. 156, South Street.

Poster for Barnum's American Museum
Barnum's brilliant publicity was not the only key to his success, according to Robert Sherwood: "It must not be assumed...that the battle is won for a circus by skillful publicity alone. Countless sinews and nerves must be constantly strained to make good every public boast of the press agent. And the chief of these public boasts...is expressed in the simple phrase: 'Will positively appear.' Barnum taught the circus world that lesson and it's still a law to-day with showmen. The circus must go on..."

In the 1870's, ladies started charming snakes.

Siamese Twins
Siamese twins have always been great crowd pleasers. At his museum, Barnum exhibited Chang and Eng, Siamese twins. Chang, an inch shorter than Eng, wore special shoes to make himself the same height as Eng. They married separately and spent three days with one wife and three with the other.

SHOW BUSINESS

The least deserving of all my efforts in the show line was the one which introduced me to the business; a scheme in no sense of my own devising; one which had been some time before the public and which had so many vouchers for its genuineness that at the time of taking possession of it I honestly believed it to be genuine.

In the summer of 1835, Mr. Coley Bartram, of Reading, Connecticut, informed me that he had owned an interest in a remarkable Negro woman whom he believed to be one hundred and sixty-one years old, and whom he believed to have been the nurse of General Washington...Joyce Heth was certainly a remarkable curiosity, and she looked as if she might have been far older than her age as advertised. She was apparently in good health and spirits but from age or disease or both was unable to change her position...Nevertheless, she was pert and sociable, and would talk as long as people would converse with her. She was quite garrulous about her *protégé*, "dear little George," at whose birth she declared she was present...Everything seemed so straightforward that I was anxious to become the proprietor of this novel exhibition, which was offered to me at one thousand dollars, though the price first demanded was three thousand. I had five hundred dollars, borrowed five hundred dollars more, sold out my interest in the grocery business to my partner, and began life as a showman. At the outset of my career I saw that everything depended on getting the people to think, and talk, and become curious and excited over and about the "rare spectacle." Accordingly, posters, transparencies, advertisements, newspaper paragraphs—all calculated to extort attention—were employed, regardless of expense. My exhibition rooms in New York, Boston, Philadelphia, Albany, and in other large and small cities, were continually thronged, and much money was made. In the following February Joyce Heth died, literally of old age, and her remains received a respectable burial in the town of Bethel.

At a post-mortem examination of Joyce Heth...it was thought that the absence of ossification indicated considerably less age than had been assumed for her; but the doctors disagreed, and this "dark subject" will probably always continue to be shrouded in mystery.

I had at last found my true vocation.

BARNUM'S FIRST CIRCUS

In April 1836, I connected myself with Aaron Turner's travelling circus as ticket-seller, secretary and treasurer, at thirty dollars a month and one-fifth of the entire profits...

THE AMERICAN MUSEUM

In 1841 Barnum bought the American Museum in New York. It was as the owner of this museum, not as a circus owner, that Barnum rose to fame. With its new owner, the museum's income immediately tripled. There were banners outside, lights on the roof, and a band playing music on the balcony: "I took pains to select and maintain the poorest band I could find—one whose discordant notes would drive the crowd into the Museum, out of earshot of my outside orchestra." Barnum thought of everything and boasted that his "puffing was more persistent, my posters

The American Museum

Museum Posters

"The transient attractions of the Museum were constantly diversified, and educated dogs, industrious fleas, automatons, jugglers, ventriloquists, living statuary, tableaux, gipsies, Albinos, fat boys, giants, dwarfs, rope-dancers, live 'Yankees,' pantomime, instrumental music, singing and dancing in great variety, dioramas, panoramas, models of Niagara, Dublin, Paris and Jerusalem; Hanington's dioramas of the Creation, the Deluge, Fairy Grotto, Storm at Sea; the first English Punch and Judy in this country, Italian Fantoccini, mechanical figures, fancy glass-blowing, knitting machines and other triumphs in the mechanical arts; dissolving views; American Indians, who enacted their warlike and religious ceremonies on the stage—these, among others, were all exceedingly successful."

P.T. Barnum

more exaggerated, [and] my flags more patriotic..."

The American Museum was the ladder by which I rose to fortune...I had casually learned that the collection of curiosities comprising Scudder's American Museum, at the corner of Broadway and Ann Street, was for sale....I thought I saw that energy, tact and liberality were only needed to make it a paying institution, and I determined to purchase it if possible.

"You buy the American Museum!" said a friend, who knew the state of my funds; "what do you intend buying it with?"

"Brass," I replied, "for silver and gold have I none."

...I...bought...the American Museum.

I was still in the show business, but in a settled, substantial phase of it, that invited industry and enterprise, and called for ever earnest and ever heroic endeavour. Whether I should sink or swim depended wholly upon my own energy. ...I meant to make it my own; and brains, hands and every effort were devoted to the interests of the Museum.

...The Museum was always open at sunrise, and this was so well known throughout the country that strangers coming to the city would often take a tour through my halls before going to breakfast or to their hotels. I do not believe there was ever a more truly popular place of amusement...Nor do I believe that any man or manager ever laboured more industriously to please his patrons.

...At first my attractions and inducements were merely the collection of curiosities by day, and an evening entertainment, consisting of such variety performances as were current in ordinary shows. Then...the popularity of the Museum grew so rapidly that I presently found it expedient and profitable to open the great Lecture Room every afternoon, as well as every evening, on every week-day in the year...Of course I made the most of the holidays, advertising extensively and presenting extra inducements.

...I confess that I liked the Museum mainly for the opportunities it

BARNUM'S AMERICAN MUSEUM

Every Day and Evening this Week
COMMENCING MONDAY, AUGUST 19th, 1861.

THE GREAT MAMMOTH

BEAR SAMSON
The largest BEAR ever captured alive, weighing near 2,000 pounds.

THE GREAT SEA LION
The only animal of the kind ever captured alive.

WHAT IS IT ? or MAN MONKEY

SUMMER SEASON OF DRAMATIC NOVELTY.

CONCENTRATION OF DRAMATIC AND MUSICAL TALENT

PETITE DRAMAS, VAUDEVILLES, BURLETTAS and FARCES

MISS DAWRON, THE DOUBLE VOICED SINGER
AFTERNOON AND EVENING.

RE-ENGAGEMENT FOR SIX NIGHTS ONLY OF

MLLE. MATILDA E. TOEDT
THE TALENTED YOUNG VIOLINIST.

Entire Change of Performance

Friday and Saturday, Aug. 23 & 24,
AFTERNOON AT 3, EVENING AT 7½.

A HARD STRUGGLE

MISS DORA DAWRON
In her Double Voiced Entertainment.

MLLE. MATILDA E. TOEDT
In her great Solo Performance on the Violin.

ARTFUL DODGE

Museum Posters

After Barnum's death, the *New York Times* admitted that "...there was a flavor of humbug about many of Barnum's announcements, especially in his early and struggling years. Those who remember 'Joyce Heth,' the Woolly Horse, the Mermaid, and the 'What Is It' will agree that, in respect of these things, the show did not entirely come up to the bills, and that there were elements of doubt about these curiosities. Indeed, Barnum himself confessed the unreality of some of these attractions in his autobiographies with a frankness that leaves nothing to be desired and that quite disarms criticism. After an attraction had served his turn, he had not further interest in maintaining its genuineness. But it would be a great mistake to assume on this account that his show was ever mostly or largely composed of objects that were other than they were represented to be. The child in years or the child in intellectual development was never heard to complain that he had been deceived. Even if he had been lured into the show for the sake of seeing something that was not altogether what his artful temper had represented it to be, he always found enough to repay his curiosity."

afforded for rapidly making money. Before I bought it, I weighed the matter well in my mind, and was convinced that I could present to the American public such a variety, quantity and quality of amusement, blended with instruction, "all for twenty-five cents, children half-price," that my attractions would be irresistible, and my fortune certain. I myself relished a higher grade of amusement, and I was a frequent attendant at the opera, first-class concerts, lectures, and the like; but I worked for the million, and I knew the only way to make a million from my patrons was to give them abundant and wholesome attractions for a small sum of money.

AN UNUSUAL WAY OF ADVERTISING

I thoroughly understood the art of advertising, not merely by means of printer's ink, which I have always used freely, and to which I confess myself so much indebted for my success, but by turning every possible circumstance to my account.

As an illustration: one morning, a stout, hearty-looking man came into my ticket-office and begged some money. I asked him why he did not work and earn his living? He replied that he could get nothing to do, and that he would be glad of any job at a dollar a day. I...told him...I would employ him, at light labour, at a dollar and a half a day. When he returned, I gave him five common bricks.

"Now," said I, "go and lay a brick on the sidewalk, at the corner of Broadway and Ann Street; another close by the Museum; a third diagonally across the way...; put down the fourth on the sidewalk, in front of St. Paul's Church; then, with the fifth brick in hand, take up a rapid march from one point to the other, making the circuit, exchanging your brick at every point, and say nothing to anyone."

"What is the object of this?" inquired the man.

"No matter," I replied; "all you need to know is that it brings you fifteen cents wages per hour. It is a bit of my fun, and to assist me properly you must seem to be as deaf as a post; wear a serious countenance; answer no questions; pay no attention to anyone; but attend faithfully to the work, and at the end of every hour...show this ticket at the Museum door; enter, walking solemnly through every hall in the building; pass out, and resume your work."

The man placed his bricks, and began his round. Half an hour afterwards, at least five hundred people were watching his movements. He had assumed a military step and bearing, and, looking as sober as a judge, he made no response whatever to the constant inquiries as to the object of his singular conduct. At the end of the first hour, the sidewalks in the vicinity were packed with people, all anxious to solve the mystery. The man, as directed, then went into the Museum, devoting fifteen minutes to a solemn survey of the halls, and afterwards returning to his round. This was repeated every hour till sundown, and whenever the man went into the Museum a dozen or more persons would buy tickets and follow him, hoping to gratify their curiosity in regard to the purpose of his movements. This was continued for several days—the curious people who followed the man into the Museum considerably more than paying his wages—till finally, the policeman, to whom I had imparted my object, complained that the obstruction of the sidewalk by crowds had become so serious that I must call in my "brickman"...This trivial incident excited considerable talk and amusement; it advertised me; and it materially advanced my purpose of making a lively corner near the museum.

TOM THUMB

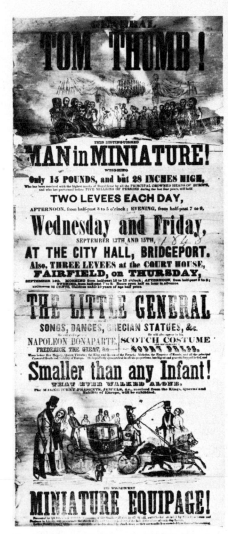

One Of Barnum's Advertisements for General Tom Thumb

Barnum's major contribution, wrote Robert Sherwood, "was modern publicity methods...Mr. Barnum came into his own as the first really modern press agent..."

When Charles Stratton met Barnum in November, 1842, he was a four-year-old midget from Bridgeport, Connecticut, two feet one inch tall, weighing 15 pounds. With his promotional genius, Barnum changed the midget's name to General Tom Thumb, his age to eleven years, and his birthplace to England, to make the tiny creature more interesting to audiences. Knowing the love of royalty for dwarfs, Barnum went to Europe with Tom Thumb, where the General was a hit with Queen Victoria. In France on Longchamps Day, Tom's tiny carriage caused a great stir. According to Barnum, who was not famous for the art of understatement, "thousands upon thousands rent the air with cheers for 'General Tom Pouce'!" As was so often the case with Barnum's attractions, Tom Thumb's success was in large part due to Barnum's brilliant use of advertising techniques; biographies of the General were printed and widely circulated, as were lithographs.

General Tom Thumb—As He Appeared Before Queen Victoria

" 'General,' continued the Queen, 'this is the Prince of Wales.'

" 'How are you, Prince?' said the General, shaking him by the hand; and then, standing beside the Prince, he remarked, 'The Prince is taller than I am, but I feel as big as anybody': upon which he strutted up and down the room as proud as a peacock, amid the shouts of laughter from all present."

P. T. Barnum

In November 1842, I was at Bridgeport, Connecticut, where I heard of a remarkably small child, and at my request, my brother, Philo F. Barnum, brought him to the hotel. He was not two feet high; he weighed less than sixteen pounds, and was the smallest child I ever saw that could walk alone; but he was a perfectly formed, bright-eyed little fellow, with light hair and ruddy cheeks, and he enjoyed the best of health. He was exceedingly bashful, but after some coaxing he was induced to talk with me, and he told me...that his name was Charles S. Stratton. After seeing him and talking with him, I...determined to secure his services from his parents and to exhibit him in public.

I engaged him for four weeks, at three dollars a week, with all travelling and boarding expenses for himself and his mother at my expense. They came to New York on Thanksgiving Day,...1842, and I announced the dwarf on my museum bills as "General Tom Thumb."

I took the greatest pains to educate and train my diminutive prodigy, devoting many hours to the task by day and by night, and I was very successful, for he was an apt pupil, with a great deal of native talent and a keen sense of the ludicrous.

TOM THUMB AND BARNUM SWEEP EUROPE BY STORM

I proposed to test the curiosity of men and women on the other side of the Atlantic...On Thursday, 18 January, 1844, I went on board the new and fine sailing *Yorkshire*...bound for Liverpool. Our party included General Tom Thumb, his parents, his tutor, and Professor Guillaudeu, the French naturalist.

Immediately after our arrival in London, the General came out at the Princess's Theatre, and made so decided a "hit" that it was difficult to decide who was best pleased, the spectators, the manager, or myself. I was offered far higher terms for re-engagement, but my purpose had been already answered; the news was spread everywhere that General Tom Thumb, an unparalleled curiosity, was in the city; and it only remained for me to bring him before the public, on my own account, and in my own time and way.

I took a furnished mansion in Grafton Street, Bond Street, West End, in the very centre of the most fashionable locality...From this magnificent mansion, I sent letters of invitation to the editors and several of the nobility, to visit the General. Most of them called, and were highly gratified.

QUEEN VICTORIA INVITES TOM TO THE PALACE

Determined to make the most of the occasion, I put a placard on the door of the Egyptian Hall: "Closed this evening, General Tom Thumb being at Buckingham Palace by command of Her Majesty."...

...We were conducted through a long corridor to a broad flight of marble steps, which led to the Queen's magnificent picture gallery, where Her Majesty and Prince Albert, the Duchess of Kent, and twenty or thirty of the nobility were awaiting our arrival. They were standing at the farther end of the room when the doors were thrown open, and the General walked in, looking like a wax doll gifted with the power of locomotion. Surprise and pleasure were depicted on the countenances of the royal circle at beholding this remarkable specimen of humanity so much smaller than they had evidently expected to find him.

The General advanced with a firm step, and, as he came within hailing distance made a very graceful bow, and exclaimed, "Good-evening, ladies and gentlemen!"

A burst of laughter followed this salutation. The Queen took him by the hand, led him about the gallery, and asked him many questions, the answers to which kept the party in an uninterrupted strain of merriment. The General familiarly informed the Queen that her picture gallery was "first-rate," and told her he should like to see the Prince of Wales. The Queen replied that the Prince had retired to rest, but that he should see him on some future occasion. The General gave them his songs, dances, and imitations...

The *Court Journal* of the ensuing day gave an account of our appearance at Court, which was published in all the London daily journals.

This notice of my visit to the Queen wonderfully increased the attraction of my exhibition, and compelled me to obtain a more commodious hall for my exhibition...

...I ought to add that after each of...three visits to Buckingham Palace, a very handsome sum was sent to me...This, however, was the smallest part of the advantage derived from these interviews, as will be at once apparent to all who consider the force of Court example in England.

The British public was now fairly excited. Not to have seen General Tom Thumb was decidedly unfashionable, and from 20th March until 20th July, the levées of the little General, at the Egyptian Hall, were continually crowded, the receipts averaging during the whole period about five hundred dollars per day...At the fashionable hour, sixty carriages of the nobility have been counted, at one time, standing in front of our exhibition rooms in Piccadilly.

Portraits of the little General were published in all the pictorial papers of the time. Polkas and quadrilles were named after him, and songs were sung in his praise. He was an almost constant theme for the London *Punch,* which served up the General and myself so daintily that it no doubt added vastly to our receipts.

HOME TO AMERICA

We had visited nearly every city and town in France and Belgium, all the principal places in England and Scotland, besides going to Belfast and Dublin, in Ireland...Thus closing a truly triumphant tour, we set sail for New York, arriving in February 1847.

On my return, I promptly made use of General Tom Thumb's European reputation. He immediately appeared in the American Museum, and for four weeks drew such crowds of visitors as had never been seen there before.

LAVINIA WARREN

In 1862 I heard of an extraordinary dwarf girl, named Lavinia Warren...I found her to be a most intelligent and refined young lady, well educated, and an accomplished, beautiful and perfectly developed woman in miniature. I succeeded in making an engagement with her for several years.

I purchased a very splendid wardrobe for Miss Warren, including scores of the richest dresses that could be procured, costly jewels, and in fact everything that could add to the charms of her naturally charming little person. She was then placed on exhibition at the Museum, and from the day of her debut was an extraordinary success.

...In the autumn of 1862, when Lavinia Warren was on exhibition at the Museum, Tom Thumb...called...on me, while Lavinia was holding

Tom Thumb

A friend of Barnum's wrote: "Tom Thumb was one of the most interesting of all circus people. His brain was developed to a degree far ahead of his body. If he had not been handicapped by his diminutive size, he might have become a Napoleon of finance. And even in spite of his handicap, Tom put over some shrewd business deals...Tom Thumb was not the smallest, but he was the smartest dwarf ever placed on exhibition. Under Barnum's able guidance he became the most famous freak of his time and made a fortune for himself and Barnum."

Tom Thumb's Wedding Bed—A Present from Mr. Barnum

Tom Thumb's wedding occurred in Grace Church on February 10, 1863. Among the guests were Mrs. John Jacob Astor and Mrs. Wm. H. Vanderbilt. The best man was Commodore Nutt, another dwarf, who was a rejected suitor of Lavinia's.

On their honeymoon Lavinia and the General visited President and Mrs. Lincoln at the White House. Barnum happily reaped the profits from the wedding publicity.

Tom Thumb's Wedding: 1863

one of her levées. Here he now saw her for the first time, and very naturally made her acquaintance. He had a short interview with her, after which he came directly to my private office and desired to see me alone.

He then said, with great frankness, and with no least earnestness: "Mr. Barnum, that is the most charming little lady I ever saw, and I believe she was created on purpose to be my wife!...I have got plenty of money, and I want to marry and settle down in life, and I really feel as if I must marry that young lady."

...He had been...very fond of his country home in Bridgeport, where he spent his intervals of rest with his horses, and especially with his yacht, for his fondness for the water was his great passion. But now he was constantly having occasion to visit the city, and horses and yachts were strangely neglected.

...In the course of several weeks the General found numerous opportunities to talk with Lavinia...

TOM PROPOSES

..."I hope you are not offended," replied the General, "for I was never more in earnest in my life, and I hope you will consent. The first moment I saw you I felt that you were created to be my wife."

"I think I love you well enough to consent, but I have always said I would never marry without my mother's consent."

Ten minutes afterwards Tom Thumb came rushing into my room and, closing the door, he caught hold of my hand in a high state of excitement and whispered:

"We are engaged, Mr. Barnum! we are engaged! we are engaged!" and he jumped up and down in the greatest glee.

A PROFITABLE ENGAGEMENT

The approaching wedding was announced. It created immense excitement. Lavinia's levées at the Museum were crowded to suffocation, and her photographic pictures were in great demand. For several weeks she sold more than three hundred dollars' worth of her *cartes de visite* each day. And the daily receipts at the Museum were frequently over three thousand dollars. I engaged the General to exhibit, and to assist her in the sale of pictures, to which his own photograph, of course, was added. I could afford to give them a fine wedding, and I did so.

...I did not hesitate to seek continued advantage from the notoriety of the prospective marriage. Accordingly, I offered the General and Lavinia fifteen thousand dollars if they would postpone the wedding for a month and continue their exhibitions at the Museum.

"Not for fifty thousand dollars," said the General, excitedly.

They both laughed heartily at what they considered my discomfiture; and such, looked at from a business point of view, it certainly was. The wedding day approached and the public excitement grew.

It was suggested to me that a small fortune in itself could be easily made out of the excitement. "Let the ceremony take place in the Academy of Music, charge a big price for admission, and the citizens will come in crowds." I have no manner of doubt that in this way twenty-five thousand dollars could easily have been obtained. But I had no such thought. I had promised to give the couple a genteel and graceful wedding, and I kept my word.

THE WEDDING

The day arrived, Tuesday, 10 February, 1863. The ceremony was to take place in Grace Church, New York.

I know not what better I could have done had the wedding of a prince been in contemplation. The church was comfortably filled by a highly select audience of ladies and gentlemen, none being admitted except those having cards of invitation. Among them were governors of several of the States, to whom I had sent cards, and such of those as could not be present in person were represented by friends, to whom they had given their cards. Members of Congress were present, also generals of the army, and many other prominent public men. Numerous applications were made from wealthy and distinguished persons for tickets to witness the ceremony, and as high as sixty dollars was offered for a single admission. But not a ticket was sold: and Tom Thumb and Lavinia Warren were pronounced "man and wife" before witnesses.

IRANISTAN

In visiting Brighton, in England, I had been greatly pleased with the Pavilion erected by George IV. It was the only specimen of Oriental architecture in England, and the style had not been introduced into America. I concluded to adopt it and engaged a London architect to furnish me a set of drawings after the general plan of the Pavilion,

Tom and Lavinia Thumb and Their Baby
"The bigger the humbug, the better the people will like it," Barnum once said. In line with this theory, he announced a few years after Tom Thumb's wedding that Tom and Lavinia had given birth to a baby girl. In fact, it was impossible for the Thumbs to have children. So Barnum borrowed a baby and had the trio photographed together. The public enthusiastically received Barnum's hoax.

The Pavillion In Brighton which inspired Barnum to build his house, Iranistan.

differing sufficiently to be adapted to the spot of ground selected for my homestead. On my second return visit to the United States, I brought these drawings with me, and engaged a competent architect and builder, giving him instructions to proceed with the work,...and to spare neither time nor expense in erecting a comfortable, convenient, and tasteful residence.

...My new home at Bridgeport, Connecticut...was the well-known Iranistan. More than two years [were] employed in building this beautiful residence.

...Elegant and appropriate furniture was made expressly for every room in the house. I erected expensive waterworks to supply the premises. The stables, conservatories, and out-buildings were perfect in their kind. There was a profusion of trees set out on the grounds. The whole was built and established literally "regardless of expense," for I had no desire even to ascertain the entire cost.

The whole was finally completed to my satisfaction. My family removed into the premises, and, on 14 November, 1848, nearly one thousand invited guests, including the poor and the rich, helped us in the old-fashioned custom of "house-warming."

...I was staying at the Astor House, in New York, when, on the morning of 18 December, 1857, I received a telegram from my brother...informing me that Iranistan was burned to the ground that morning...My beautiful Iranistan was gone! This was not only a serious loss to my estate, for it had probably cost $150,000, but it was generally regarded as a public calamity. It was the only building in its peculiar style of architecture of any pretension in America, and many persons visited Bridgeport every year expressly to see Iranistan. The insurance on the mansion had usually been about $62,000, but I had let some of the policies expire without renewing them.

Iranistan, near Bridgeport, Connecticut

Jenny Lind, who was paid $1,000 a performance by Barnum, was a sensation in America. The public fought for tickets. At her first Boston concert, Mr. Ossias E. Dodge paid $625 for one ticket. Barnum made almost a quarter of a million dollars from Jenny Lind's concert series.

Welcome to Jenny Lind

Barnum described Jenny Lind's arrival in New York "...Thousands of persons covered the shipping and piers, and other thousands had congregated on the wharf at Canal Street, to see her. The wildest enthusiasm prevailed as the steamer approached the dock. A bower of green trees, decorated with beautiful flags, was discovered on the wharf, together with two triumphal arches, on one of which was inscribed 'Welcome, Jenny Lind!' The second was surmounted by the American eagle, and bore the inscription, 'Welcome to America!' These decorations were not produced by magic, and I do not know that I can reasonably find fault with those who suspected I had a hand in their erection.''

JENNY LIND: THE SWEDISH NIGHTINGALE

And now I come to speak of an undertaking which all will admit was bold in its conception, complete in its development, and astounding in its success...

It was in October 1849 that I conceived the idea of bringing Jenny Lind to this country. I had never heard her sing...Her reputation, however, was sufficient for me...

...I then began to prepare the public mind, through the newspapers, for the reception of the great songstress. How effectually this was done, is still within the remembrance of the American public.

...Jenny Lind's first concert was fixed to come off at Castle Garden, on Wednesday evening, 11th September [1850]...

The reception of Jenny Lind on her first appearance, in point of enthusiasm, was probably never before equalled....The entire audience rose to their feet, and welcomed her with three cheers, accompanied by the waving of thousands of hats and handkerchiefs.

...The Rubicon was passed. The successful issue of the Jenny Lind enterprise was established. The amount of money received for tickets to the first concert was $17,864.05.

...The first great assembly at Castle Garden was not gathered by Jenny Lind's musical genius and powers alone. She was effectually

P. T. Barnum: "Every Sham Shows There Is a Reality"

Barnum often visited his shows incognito. Once he overheard a country farmer speaking to his wife: "...I tell you, Jane, nobody under Heaven but Barnum could ever get up such a wonderful show. Derned ef I wouldn't give more to see Barnum himself than this hull show, wonderful as 'tis."

"I was tempted to gratify my friend, and was just about to speak to him when one of my best riders came dashing into the arena riding four horses, standing on their backs while they were at the top of their speed. He was a young athlete, finely formed, and as sprightly as a deer. Presently, while the horses were running like greyhounds, he turned a somersault and stood upon his head on the back of one of the horses. His feet were high in the air, and the horse kept up his rapid gallop round the ring. The audience was half wild with excitement, and gave vent to deafening hurrahs. At this moment my farmer friend, with his eyes almost starting from their sockets, jumped upon his feet, and swinging his old hat over his head, he screamed at the top of his voice, 'By thunder! I'll bet five dollars that is Barnum!' My country friend had got his money's worth. He had seen Barnum, as he supposed, and I felt it a pity to disabuse his mind. I said nothing. He probably still thinks I am about twenty-four years old, and the best rider living."

introduced to the public before they had seen or heard her. She appeared in the presence of a jury already excited to enthusiasm in her behalf. She more than met their expectations, and all the means I had adopted to prepare the way were thus abundantly justified.

As a manager, I worked by setting others to work. Biographies of the Swedish Nightingale were largely circulated, and "printer's ink" was invoked in every possible form to put and keep Jenny Lind before the people. I am happy to say that the press generally echoed the voice of her praise from first to last.

BANKRUPT

At the age of forty-six, Barnum faced total bankruptcy. In attempting to build a new city in Bridgeport, Barnum had agreed to lend his name as security for $110,000 to the Jerome Clock Company if that company would move to Bridgeport. The company never moved and Barnum discovered that:

...I had endorsed for the clock company to the extent of more than half a million dollars, and most of the notes had been exchanged for old Jerome Company notes due to the banks and other creditors. My agent who made these startling discoveries came back to me with the refreshing intelligence that I was a ruined man!

In his memoirs he took a very staunch attitude toward the bankruptcy, calling it:

...one of the most remarkable experiences of my life—an experience which brought me much pain and many trials; which humbled my pride and threatened me with hopeless financial ruin: and yet, nevertheless, put new blood in my veins, fresh vigour in my action, warding off all temptation to rust in the repose which affluence induces, and developed, I trust, new and better elements of manliness in my character.

...At the age of forty-six, after the acquisition and the loss of a handsome fortune, I was once more nearly at the bottom of the ladder, and was about to begin the world again. The situation was disheartening, but I had energy, experience, health and hope.

OUT OF DEBT

In 1855, before his bankruptcy, Barnum had sold the American Museum to John Greenwood, Jr. and Henry D. Butler. In 1860, out of debt at last, Barnum was able to repurchase the museum from these gentlemen.

...This fact was thoroughly circulated, and it was everywhere announced in blazing posters, placards and advertisements, which were headed, "Barnum on his feet again"...At nearly fifty years of age, I was now once more before the public with the promise to put on a full head of steam, to "rush things," to give double or treble the amount of attractions ever before offered at the Museum, and to devote all my own time and services to the enterprise...The daily number of visitors at once more than doubled, and my exertions to gratify them with rapid changes and novelties never tired.

Burning of Barnum's Museum, 1865:
The Animals During the Fire

THE MUSEUM BURNS JULY 13, 1865

On 13 July, 1865, I was speaking in the Connecticut Legislature, in session at Hartford...when a telegram was handed to me stating that the American Museum was in flames, and that its total destruction was certain...My first impulse, after reckoning up my losses, was to retire from active life and from all business occupation beyond what my large real estate interests in Bridgeport and my property in New York would compel...But two considerations moved me to pause: first, one hundred and fifty employees, many of whom depended upon their exertions for their daily bread, were thrown out of work at a season when it would be difficult for them to get engagements elsewhere. Second, I felt that a large city like New York needed a good Museum, and that my experience of a quarter of a century in that direction afforded extraordinary facilities for founding another establishment of the kind, and so I took a few days for reflection.

A SECOND MUSEUM: NOVEMBER 13, 1865

...The thirteenth day of November saw the opening of "Barnum's New American Museum," which was also subsequently destroyed by fire.

THREE YEARS LATER: SECOND MUSEUM BURNS

On Tuesday morning, 3 March, 1868, it was bitterly cold. A heavy body

The New York *Herald* on July 14, 1865, headlined the destruction of Barnum's museum by fire. Fires were to haunt Barnum throughout his career.

Four Giants and Two Dwarfs

Robert Sherwood, the clown, who knew Barnum well, explained: "...the freak show held a thrill equal to that of the circus performance itself...*and* genuine freaks are few and far between. There usually is some foundation of truth in what the posters and ballyhoo men state, but it is elaborately embroidered. We like to attend, however, even when we know we're being bunked. That is the universal trait of human nature that makes the side shows prosper.

"As Mr. P. T. Barnum once remarked: 'The American people love to be humbugged'."

of snow was on the ground, and, as I sat at the breakfast-table with my wife...I read aloud the general news from the morning papers. Leisurely turning to the local columns, I said, "Hallo! Barnum's Museum is burned."

...The papers of the following morning contained full accounts of the fire; and editorial writers, while manifesting much sympathy for the proprietors, also expressed profound regret that so magnificent a collection, especially in the zoological department, should be lost to the city.

RETIREMENT

After the destruction by fire of my Museum, 3 March, 1868, I retired from business, not knowing how utterly fruitless it is to attempt to chain down energies peculiar to my nature...Having "nothing to do," I thought at first was very pleasant, as it was to me an entirely new sensation...But nature will assert herself...lectures, concerts, operas, and dinner-parties are well enough in their way; but to a robust, healthy man of forty years' active business life, something else is needed to satisfy.

BACK IN BUSINESS: 1871

In the fall of 1870, W. C. Coup went to work with Barnum on organizing P. T. Barnum's Museum, Menagerie, and Circus. In the spring of 1871 the show opened in Brooklyn and was a great success. Coup was an old-timer in the circus business; he had organized Dan Costello's Circus with Costello which had toured the Midwest.

...In the autumn of 1870...I began to prepare a great show enterprise, comprising a Museum, Menagerie, Caravan, Hippodrome and Circus, of such proportions as to require five hundred men and horses to transport it through the country. On 10 April, 1871, the vast tents, covering nearly three acres of ground, were opened in Brooklyn, and filled with ten thousand delighted spectators, thousands more being unable to obtain entrance. The success which marked the inauguration of this, my greatest show, attended it the whole season, during which time it visited the Eastern, Middle and Western States from Maine to Kansas.

At the close of a brilliant season, I recalled the show to New York, secured the Empire Rink, and opened in that building on 13 November, 1871, being welcomed by an enthusiastic audience of ten thousand people. The exhibitions were continued daily, with unvarying popularity and patronage, until the close of the holidays, when necessary preparations for the spring campaign compelled me to close.

The success of Barnum's 1872 show was in large part due to his putting the show on rails. The use of the railroad was largely Coup's idea, although Barnum gave him no credit in his autobiography. Coup persuaded the public to come to the circus through his widespread use of posters and excursion trains with cut rates. Traveling by rail, the circus could reach many more people. Barnum wrote:

During the winter of 1871 and 1872 I worked unremittingly, reorganizing and reinforcing my great travelling show.

I so augmented the already innumerable attractions that it was shown beyond doubt that we could not travel at a less expense than five thousand dollars per day, but, undaunted, I still expended thousands of dollars, and ship after ship brought me rare and valuable animals and works of art.

Perceiving that my great combination was assuming such proportions that it would be impossible to move it by horse-power, I negotiated with all the railway companies...for the transportation by rail, of my whole show, requiring sixty to seventy freight cars, six passenger cars, and three engines. This is the first time a tent show ever travelled by rail in any country.

The result is well remembered. The great show visited the States of New Jersey, Delaware, Maryland, Pennsylvania, District of Columbia, Virginia, Ohio, Indiana, Kentucky, Illinois, Missouri, Kansas, Iowa, Minnesota, Wisconsin, and Michigan, often travelling one hundred miles in a single night to hit good sized towns every day, arriving in time to give three exhibitions, and the usual street pageant at eight o'clock

A visitor to Barnum's American Museum asked, "Is it real or is it humbug?" Mr. Barnum replied, "That's just the question: persons who pay their money at the door have a right to form their own opinions after they have got up stairs!"

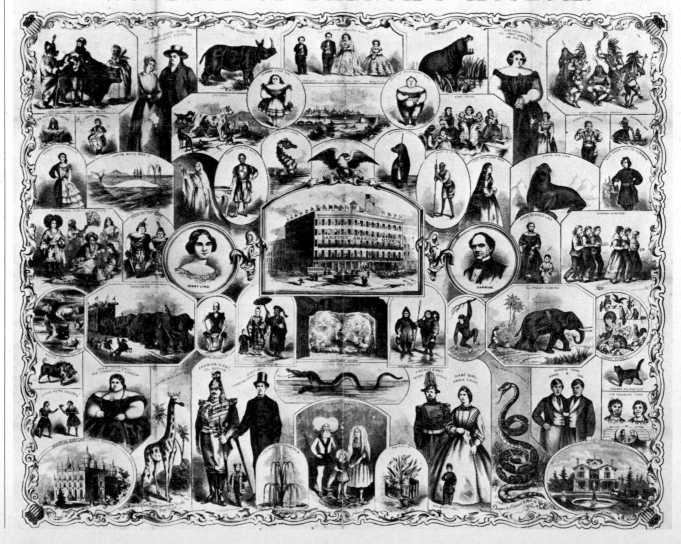

WONDERS OF BARNUM'S MUSEUM.

The Grand Lay-out

This lithograph, done in 1874 by Gibson & Company, shows Barnum's great traveling circus. There were three performances a day; admission was fifty cents for adults and twenty-five cents for children. After Barnum's death in 1891, the *New York Times* commented: "It was his pride and boast from the beginning of his career until the end of it, that he gave the people who went to see his various and diverse shows 'the worth of their money.' The boast was justified and so was the pride."

The Lion Tamer

Barnum's lion tamer, George Conklin, wrote: "My act with the animals was one of the principal parts of the show. For a man to appear in a cage with loose lions was a comparatively new thing.... The act was made as impressive as possible. When its turn came the big performing cage with the lions and myself in it was slowly pushed into the ring by an elephant.... When all was ready I opened the act by holding out my leg and having the lions jump over it.... I would lie across the three, with my head...resting on the head of one of the lions.... I would go up to him....open his mouth as wide as possible and put my head in it as far as it would go.....This never failed to make the crowd hold its breath but it was not so risky as it seemed, for with my hold on the lion's nose and jowl I could detect the slightest movement of his muscles and govern my actions accordingly."

a.m. By means of cheap excursion trains, thousands of strangers attended daily, coming fifty, seventy-five, and a hundred miles. Thousands more came in wagons and on horseback, frequently arriving in the night and "camping out."

With wonderful unanimity the public press acknowledged that I exhibited much more than I advertised, and that no combination of exhibitions that ever travelled had shown a tithe of the instructive and amusing novelties that I had gathered together. This universal commendation is, to me, the most gratifying feature of the campaign, for, not being compelled to do business merely for the sake of profit, my highest enjoyment is to delight my patrons. The entire six months' receipts of the Great Travelling World's Fair amounted to nearly one million dollars.

ANOTHER LOSS TO FIRE: THE HIPPOTHEATRON: 1872

In August, I purchased the building and lease on Fourteenth Street, New York, known as the Hippotheatron, purposing to open a Museum, Menagerie, Hippodrome and Circus...I enlarged and remodelled the building, almost beyond recognition, at an expense of $60,000, installed in it my valuable collection of animals, automatons and living curiosities, and on Monday evening, 18th November, the grand opening took place. It was a beautiful sight: the huge building, with a seating capacity of 2,800, filled from pit to dome with a brilliant audience, the dazzling new lights, the sweet music and gorgeous ornamentation completing the charm. The papers next morning contained loud and eulogistic editorials.

Four weeks after this inauguration I visited New Orleans. While there, the following telegram was handed to me:

New York, 24 December, 1872

To P. T. Barnum, New Orleans,
    About 4 a.m. fire discovered in boiler-room of circus building; everything destroyed except 2 elephants, 1 camel.

S. H. Hurd, Treasurer

THE SHOW GOES ON: 1873

Calling for writing materials, I then and there cabled my European agents to send duplicates of all animals lost, with positive instructions to have everything shipped in time to reach New York by the middle of March. I directed them further to procure, at any cost, specimens never seen in America; and through sub-agents to purchase and forward curiosities—animate and inanimate—from all parts of the globe.

By the first week in April, 1873—but three months after the fire—I placed upon the road a combination of curiosities and marvellous performances, that by far surpassed any attempt ever made with a travelling exhibition in any country. Indeed so wonderfully immense was "Barnum's Travelling World's Fair" in 1873, that my friends almost unanimously declared that it would "break" me. I suppose there is a limit beyond which it would be fatal to go, in catering for public instruction and amusement, but I have never yet found that limit. My experience is that the more and the better a manager will provide for the public, the more liberally they will respond. The season of 1873 was far from being an exception to this experience. My tents covered double the space of ground that I had ever required before, and yet they were never so closely crowded with visitors. Where thousands attended my show in 1872, numbers of thousands came in 1873.

Circus Clowns—Woodcut 1870

Robert Sherwood, once the chief clown of Barnum's circus, wrote: "...In my day the clown was the hub from which radiated the entire circus...Clown humor has a curious kinship with the psychology of dreams, for in dreams we are always escaping from preposterous situations in preposterous ways... The clown is...the embodiment and dramatization, burlesqued if you will, of the introvert, the lonely soul, the John-o'-Dreams...Of the eight or nine clowns with the Barnum show...all were silent, and it was a rule with the management of that concern that as soon as a man opened his mouth, he was handed his salary and dismissed."

BARNUM'S HIPPODROME: 1874

[The Hippodrome was] bounded by Fourth and Madison Avenues and Twenty-sixth and Twenty-seventh Streets, containing several acres, for the purpose of carrying out my long-cherished plan of exhibiting a Roman Hippodrome, Zoological Institute, Aquaria, and Museum of unsurpassable extent and magnificence.

The show at the Hippodrome opened nightly with a:

...truly stupendous and superb spectacle...an allegorical representation of a "Congress of Nations," a grand procession of gilded chariots and triumphal cars, conveying the Kings, Queens, Emperors, and other potentates of the civilized world, costumed with historical correctness...The correctness and completeness of this historical representation required nearly one thousand persons and several hundred horses, besides elephants, camels, llamas, ostriches, etc....Never before since the days of the Caesars had there been so grand and so interesting a public spectacle.

Following the superb historical introduction were all kinds of races by high-bred horses...wonderful performances of...Japanese athletes, [and] thrilling wire-walking exploits.

...Although the Hippodrome could accomodate ten thousand spectators, for weeks in succession all the best seats were engaged days in advance, and it is literally true that at every evening performance thousands were turned away...

Exterior View of the Hippodrome

Banner Act—Lithograph, 1875
On September 25, 1876, a writer in *Harper's Weekly* observed: "Circus-riding, when kept within moderate limits, is often very elegant. ...The...rider, standing on the horse, may leap up and down in various ways, and jump over bars and shawls, or through hoops or casks, and yet alight upon the horse again although in a gallop. This is because the rider partakes of the forward motion of the horse, and is really moving on when he seems to be only jumping up. But oh! the falls, bruises, disasters, that have to be encountered before the smiling, berouged, tinselled performers are fitted to make their bow or courtesy to the public! An 'Ella' or an 'Elise' or an 'Angelique' has to pass through a wearisome, long-continued, prosaic discipline before she can appear as a fascinating *equestrianne*, jumping through hoops of fire, or dancing in a *pas de deux* with a male performer on two horses. How many broken limbs occur during the apprenticeship the public never knows: the 'profession' does not talk of those things..."

P. T. Barnum's Grand Roman Hippodrome
The Hippodrome, built in 1874, covered the entire block between Fourth and Madison Avenues from Twenty-sixth to Twenty-seventh streets. There Barnum exhibited his circus and menagerie.

Ad for Barnum's Centennial Show

On January 21, 1876, *The New York Times* wrote: "With the advent of the Centennial year, the great showman, P. T. Barnum, announces his intention to organize and exhibit the most colossal show ever collected...He is about to produce the culminating show combination of his lifetime, and will exhibit them in the Centennial year to the greatest multitude of citizens and strangers that has ever upon any one great occasion or celebration been drawn together in the world's history. It will comprise many departments, among which will be the museum, a menagerie, a circus, and a hippodrome combined."

In 1874 Barnum announced that daily balloon ascensions would be a feature of the hippodrome show. He promised to send a balloonist across the Atlantic at some future time; he never did, but he received much publicity from the announcement.

The New York Times *reported on May 2, 1874, that Barnum said that even if the balloon should burst, "the people will have had their money's worth in having witnessed the rest of the show."*

THE GREAT CENTENNIAL SHOW

In 1876 Barnum organized his Great Centennial Show. The New York *Tribune* reported on April 28, the day after the opening of the show, that "the crowds which gathered about the entrance of the American Institute Building gave warning at an early hour that the veteran showman was remembered in New York. When the doors were opened hundreds of people thronged into the hall...The hall was brilliantly illuminated, and lines of flags and streamers waved over the multitude of spectators...The show was opened by a grand oriental cavalcade, and a long train of animals followed...The whole program occupied about three hours. During the entertainment Mr. Barnum...made a brief speech, in which he disclaimed all pretense of being 'in the ring'...but said that he had concluded to throw in the 'old showman' for the season, in order that his audiences might be sure to get the worth of their money."Barnum was alluding to his resignation as Mayor of Bridgeport in the spring of 1876 in order that he might devote all his energy and ingenuity to show business. Barnum wrote:

My great travelling show is by far the most expensive and marvellous combination of the world's wonders ever brought together for a similar purpose. It is the result and culmination of my experience in that line for nearly half a century. *I own every railway car*—nearly one hundred in number—on which this "army with banners" is transported through the country from April to November, travelling each season about twelve thousand miles, and exhibiting in one hundred and forty different towns and cities, reaching from Nova Scotia to California. It is preceded a fortnight in advance by my Magnificent Advertising Car, carrying press agents, the "paste brigade," numbering twenty, and tons of immense coloured bills, programmes, lithographs, photographs, electrotype cuts, etc., to arouse the entire country for fifty miles around each place of exhibition to the fact that "P. T. Barnum's New and Greatest Show on Earth," with its acres of tents and pavilions, could be reached by cheap excursion trains on certain days specified in the bills and advertisements. I frequently visited the show during its summer progress, my presence on these special occasions being announced, with the statement that I would address my patrons from the arena.

JUMBO

"Jumbo," the largest elephant ever seen, either wild or in captivity, had been for many years one of the chief attractions of the Royal Zoological Gardens, London. I had often looked wistfully on Jumbo, but with no hope of ever getting possession of him, as I knew him to be a great favourite of Queen Victoria, whose children and grandchildren are among the tens of thousands of British juveniles whom Jumbo has carried on his back...I did not suppose he would ever be sold. But one

The Miracle of Mortal Marvels: Tattooed from Head to Foot!

On October 7, 1876, the *New York Times* reported on Barnum's latest curiosity, Captain Georges Costentenus, a man tattooed from head to toe: "The representatives of the daily newspapers were yesterday afforded an opportunity of inspecting Mr. P. T. Barnum's latest and most wonderful addition to his living curiosities. In one of the parlors of the Astor house, Capt. George Costentenus exhibited his body, which is completely tattooed from head to foot, with the exception of the nose, ears, and the soles of his feet. On the surface of the body are reproduced no less than 386 figures, comprising fishes, animals, birds, mummies, and hieroglyphics. A number of physicians examined the Captain thoroughly and pronounced him in perfect health, and one of the most extraordinary specimens of genuine tattooing they had ever seen. The figures are artistically executed in blue and red, and their intricacy could only be understood by a personal examination. The history of Costentenus, as gleaned from his attendant, Mr Conklin, is as follows: In 1862, he, together with a Spaniard and an American, engaged in a conspiracy against the Greek government in Chinese Tartary and was captured. The conspirators were offered the alternative of being beheaded or tattooed from head to foot, and all chose the latter. The two others died while undergoing the process, but Costentenus, owing to his extraordinary physical strength, survived. The operation consumed some five or six hours a day for three months, and was so terribly painful that the prisoner frequently begged to be put out of his misery. He is now forty-four years of age and has exhibited in various places in Europe...."

Jumbo

Barnum's last great coup was his purchase from the London Zoological Garden of Jumbo. To Barnum's great delight, a huge controversy arose. The English public tried to stop Jumbo's departure; Americans eagerly awaited the large elephant's arrival. Barnum's favorite clown would later write: "But for the inspiration of a press agent, in the person of P. T. Barnum, Jumbo would have been just another elephant instead of the greatest of his kind."

Describing Jumbo's departure from England, Barnum wrote: "Jumbo was dragged miles to the steamship *Assyrian Monarch* where quarters had been prepared for him by cutting away one of the decks. The Society for the Prevention of Cruelty to Animals hovered over Jumbo to the last, and titled ladies and little children brought to the ship baskets of dainties for Jumbo's consumption during the voyage. After a rough passage he arrived in New York, in good condition, Sunday morning, April 9, 1882, and the next day was placed on exhibition in the menagerie department of our great show, where he created such a sensation that in the next two weeks the receipts *in excess of the usual amounts* more than repaid us the $30,000 his purchase and removal had cost us."

Barnum Meets Bailey

James A. Bailey and his partner, James Cooper, bought Howes Great London Circus and Sanger's Royal British Menagerie. For the first time Barnum had a rival and he admitted that he had met his match. Late in 1880 Barnum, Bailey and James L. Hutchinson, Bailey's friend, combined. By this time Cooper had sold out to Bailey; Hutchinson would soon drop out, and the famous combination of Barnum and Bailey would dominate the circus world.

of my agents...ventured to ask my friend, Mr. Barlett, Superintendent of the Zoological Gardens, if he would sell Jumbo...Further conversation led my agent to think that possibly an offer of $10,000 might be entertained. He cabled me to that effect, to which I replied: "I will give ten thousand dollars for Jumbo, but the Zoo will never sell him." Two days afterwards my agent cabled me that my offer of $10,000 for Jumbo was accepted.

...From that time an excitement prevailed and increased throughout Great Britain which, for a cause so comparatively trivial, has never had a parallel in any civilized country. The Council and Directors of the Royal Zoo were denounced in strong terms for having sold Jumbo to the famous Yankee showman, Barnum. The newspapers, from the London *Times* down, daily thundered anathemas against the sale...These facts stirred up the excitement in the United States, and scores of letters sent to me daily, urged me not to give up Jumbo.

...After much trouble...[Jumbo] was shipped...in charge of his old keeper...After a rough passage he arrived in New York, in good condition, Sunday morning, 9th April. On landing, Sunday evening,...his cage was placed on its original wheels, and drawn up Broadway by sixteen heavy draught horses, assisted by our two largest elephants. On Monday, 10 April, 1882, Jumbo was placed on exhibition in the Menagerie Department of our Great Show, where he created an immense sensation, and augmented our receipts during two weeks to such an extent as to considerably more than repay us for his purchase and subsequent expenses, amounting in all to nearly 30,000 dollars.

BARNUM MERGES WITH BAILEY

Late in 1880, no travelling show in the world bore any comparison with my justly called "Greatest Show on Earth." Other show-managers boasted of owning shows equalling mine, and some bought off the printers large coloured show-bills pictorially representing my marvellous curiosities, although these managers had no performances or curiosities of the kinds which they represented. The cost of one of their shows was from twenty thousand to fifty thousand dollars, while mine cost millions of dollars...The public soon discovered the difference between the sham and the reality...

My strongest competitors were the so-called "Great London Circus, Sanger's Royal British Menagerie and Grand International Allied Shows." Its managers, Cooper, Bailey and Hutchinson, had adopted my manner of dealing with the public, and consequently their great show grew in popularity!

...We decided to join our two shows in one mammoth combination, and...to exhibit them for, at least, one season for one price of admission. The public were astonished at our audacity, and old showmen declared that we could never take in enough money to cover our expenses, which would be fully forty-five hundred dollars per day. My new partners, James A. Bailey and James L. Hutchinson, sagacious and practical managers, agreed with me that the experiment involved great risk.

...The Barnum and London Circus opened in New York, 28 March, 1881.

Phineas Taylor Barnum—The Later Years

"Phineas Taylor Barnum, in my estimation, was the greatest genius that ever conducted an amusement enterprise in this country," wrote Robert Sherwood. "He was a man of superlative imagination, indomitable pluck, and real artistic temperament. I knew him intimately for nearly twenty years, and never once did I see him falter in anything he set out to do. As I remember him best, he was a good, kindly old man, perfectly satisfied to have the public call him humbug and charlatan in return for the revenues he reaped from his ventures in amusement enterprises.

"People liked him and followed him, even when they knew he was humbugging them. I grant that many of his freak offerings were humbugs, but they were always harmless... The greater the fake, the more people laughed, the better the advertisement."

Scenes From a Long and Busy Life

(far right)

"It may seem odd, but we believe it to be true, that what distinguished Barnum from other public entertainers of equal or nearly equal conspicuousness was really the absence of humbug," wrote the *New York Times* on April 9, 1891. "Barnum was never under any illusion, nor did he ever encourage any illusions, about the nature of his function. He did not pretend to be an evangelist or an artist, but simply a showman. He might not have been willing to make oath to all his advertisements, but he never disguised the fact that he was in 'the show business,' and that he meant to give the public what it wanted. If in any instance he failed, he did not blame the public for its failure to appreciate the moral or aesthetic lesson he had endeavored to inculcate. He simply dropped the unsuccessful feature, and substituted something else that was likely to prove more attractive. This is not, perhaps, a very lofty vocation, and it has no pretense of being a 'mission,' but there is nothing dishonest or offensive about it. It is only when a man who is in fact a showman pretends to be an evangelist or an artist, and blames his public for his failure to entertain it, that he becomes a real and thorough humbug..."

ANOTHER ADVERTISING TECHNIQUE

We brought, in drawing-room cars, from Washington, D.C., and Boston, and all the principal cities on those routes, the editors of all the leading papers. The gentlemen, nearly one hundred in number, witnessed the torchlight procession on Saturday night, and our opening performance at the Madison Square Garden, Monday night, 28th March. They were lodged at hotels at our expense, and by us returned to their homes on Tuesday; a very costly piece of advertising, which yet yielded us a magnificent return in the enthusiastic editorial endorsements of so many papers of good standing, whose representatives had seen our show, and exclaimed as did the Queen of Sheba to King Solomon, "The half was not told me."

Very early in the travelling season of 1881 we enlarged our already immense tents three different times, and yet so great was the multitude that attended our exhibitions—many coming on excursion trains twenty, thirty, and even fifty miles—that at half the towns we visited we were unable to accommodate all who came, and we turned away thousands for want of room. In every town we were patronized by the elite, and frequently the public and private schools, as well as manufactories, were closed on "Barnum Day," school committees and teachers recognizing that children would learn more of natural history by one visit to our menagerie than they could acquire by months of reading.

AGE OF PROGRESS AND PROFIT

This is decidedly an age of progress. Every person must continually make improvements in his business and his manner of conducting it, or he will inevitably be left behind in the race. I have never felt inclined to give an inferior exhibition and as a matter of mere policy, if I had no higher motive, I know I cannot *afford* to exhibit anything except *the very best,* without a moment's consideration of its cost.

On this principle I always conduct my business. Consequently each season my "Greatest Show on Earth" grows larger and larger, and better and better.

AMERICA IN
1876

TOM SAWYER
THE PUBLICATION OF A CLASSIC

Aunt Polly and Tom

Tom Sawyer lived with his Aunt Polly in the town of St. Petersburg, a small imaginary town located on the banks of the Mississippi River. Tom "was not the model boy of the village," wrote Twain. "He knew the model boy very well though—and loathed him." At the opening of the novel Tom was, as usual, up to mischief, this time eating his aunt's special jam. Aunt Polly said:

"'Forty times I've said if you didn't let that jam alone I'd skin you. Hand me that switch.'

"The switch hovered in the air—the peril was desperate—

"'My! Look behind you, Aunt!'

"The old lady whirled around, and snatched her skirts out of danger. The lad fled, on the instant, scrambled up the high board fence, and disappeared over it."

To punish Tom, Aunt Polly made him whitewash her fence. But Tom converted the punishment into wealth. By pretending to enjoy the work, he managed to tempt the other boys into trading him their treasures in exchange for a chance to whitewash: "Boys happened along every little while; they came to jeer, but remained to whitewash....And

(continued on following page)

December 1876 saw the publication of the first American edition of Mark Twain's *The Adventures of Tom Sawyer.* (*Tom Sawyer* was published for the first time in England in June 1876.) At the time Twain's novel appeared, America was fast becoming an industrialized society; railroads were spreading across the country, oil refineries were springing up along with steel and coke mills, and cities were becoming crowded with immigrants who supplied the cheap labor for industry. Twain offered Americans the reverse image: a myth in the form of *Tom Sawyer,* a saga of pre–Civil War life which allowed readers the chance to step back into a lost simplicity.

The Adventures of Tom Sawyer was at once well received by critics. Among the first reviews was one by Twain's friend William Dean Howells which appeared in the *Atlantic* in May 1876. Twain sent him the manuscript before the American edition came out, and Howells wrote to Twain saying that he considered *The Adventures of Tom Sawyer* "the best boy's story I ever read."

WILLIAM DEAN HOWELLS REVIEWS *TOM SAWYER*

Mr. Clemens...has taken the boy of the Southwest for the hero of his new book, and has presented him with a fidelity to circumstance which loses no charm by being realistic in the highest degree, and which gives incomparably the best picture of life in that region as yet known to fiction. The town where Tom Sawyer was born and brought up is some such idle, shabby little Mississippi River town...Tom belongs to the better sort of people in it, and has been bred to fear God and dread the Sunday-school according to the strictest rite of the faiths that have characterized all the respectability of the West. His subjection in these respects does not so deeply affect his inherent tendencies but that he makes himself a beloved burden to the poor, tender-hearted old aunt who brings him up...and struggles vainly with his manifold sins, actual and imaginary. The limitations of his transgressions are nicely and artistically traced. He is mischievous, but not vicious; he is ready for almost any depradation that involves the danger and honor of adventure...he resorts to any strategem to keep out of school, but he is not a downright liar...He is cruel, as all children are, but chiefly because he is ignorant: he is not mean, but there are very definite bounds to his generosity...In a word, he is a boy, and merely and exactly an ordinary boy on the moral side. What makes him delightful to the reader is that on the imaginative side he is very much more, and though every boy has wild and fantastic dreams, this boy cannot rest till he has somehow realized them. Till he has actually run off with two other boys in the character of buccaneer, and lived for a week on an island in the Mississippi, he has lived in vain; and this passage is but the prelude to more thrilling adventures, in which he finds hidden treasures, traces the bandits to their cave, and is himself lost in its recesses. The local material and the incidents with which his career is worked up are excellent, and throughout there is scrupulous regard for the boy's point of view in reference to his surroundings and himself, which shows how rapidly Mr. Clemens has grown as an artist...The story is a wonderful study of the boy-mind, which inhabits a world quite distinct from that in which he is bodily present with his elders, and in this lies its great charm and its universality, for boy-nature, however human nature varies, is the same everywhere...The whole little town lives in the reader's sense, with its religiousness, its lawlessness, its droll social distinctions, its civilization qualified by slave-holding, and its traditions of the wilder West which has passed away.

"Part of my plan," wrote Twain in the preface to *Tom Sawyer*, "has been to try to pleasantly remind adults of what they once were themselves, and of how they felt and thought and talked..." Twain did not just remind his adult readers of what it had been like to be young. He also reminded them what it had been like to live, before the Civil War, before the triumph of industrialization, in a young country.

Tom Sawyer Finds Injun Joe

when the middle of the afternoon came, from being a poor poverty-stricken boy in the morning, Tom was literally rolling in wealth... He had discovered a great law of human action...namely, that in order to make a man or a boy covet a thing, it is only necessary to make the thing difficult to attain."

Tom Sawyer and Huck Finn Find Treasure in a Cave

"It was the treasure-box, sure enough...."

The two boys found $12,000. Tom was comfortable with his new wealth, but Huck was not. He said, " 'It ain't for me; I ain't used to it...Looky here, Tom, being rich ain't what it's cracked up to be. It's just worry and worry, sweat and sweat, and a-wishing you was dead all the time.' "

Tom Sawyer Finds Injun Joe

Twain did not present his readers with a totally unmarred vision. While the village of St. Petersburg "lay drowsing in the sun," Injun Joe, the "murderin' half-breed," committed a murder under the eyes of Tom Sawyer and Huck Finn. Injun Joe ultimately perished in the cave in which Tom once got lost with Becky. Twain commented that Injun Joe's death "stopped the further growth of one thing—the petition to the Governor for Injun Joe's pardon. The petition had been largely signed; many tearful and eloquent meetings had been held, and a committee of sappy women been appointed to go into deep mourning and wail around the Governor, and implore him to be a merciful ass and trample duty under foot. Injun Joe was believed to have killed five citizens of the village, but what of that? If he had been Satan himself there would have been plenty of weaklings ready to scribble their names to a pardon petition, and drip a tear on it from their permanently impaired and leaky waterworks."

BIBLIOGRAPHY

I THE EXHIBITION OF 1876

BOOKS

Hale, Lucretia P., *The Complete Peterkin Papers*. Boston: Houghton Mifflin, 1960. (Seventh printing.)

McCabe, James D., *The Illustrated History of the Centennial Exhibition*. Philadelphia: National Publishing Company, 1876.

Twain, Mark, *Mark Twain's Notebook*, Albert Bigelow Paine, ed. New York: Harper & Brothers, 1935.

Whitman, Walt, *Two Rivulets*. Camden, N.J.: By the Author, 1876.

PERIODICALS

Harper's Weekly (Vol. XX for the year 1876).

Howells, William Dean, "A Sennight of the Centennial." *Atlantic Monthly* (July 1876).

MISCELLANEOUS

Appleton's Annual Cyclopaedia and Register of Important Events. New York: Appleton, 1876.

Frank Leslie's Illustrated Historical Register of the United States Centennial Exposition—1876, Frank Henry Norton, ed. New York: Frank Leslie Publisher, 1877.

II THE WESTERN EMPIRE

BOOKS

Brown, Dee, *Bury My Heart at Wounded Knee*. New York: Holt, Rinehart & Winston, 1970.

Catlin, George. *Illustrations of the Manners, Customs and Condition of the North American Indians*. Vols. I and II. London: Chatto & Windus, 1876.

Cushing, Frank Hamilton. *Zuni Breadstuff*. New York: Museum of the American Indian, 1974.

Custer, Elizabeth B., *"Boots and Saddles" or, Life in Dakota with General Custer*. Norman: University of Oklahoma Press, 1961.

Custer, Gen. George Armstrong, *Wild Life on the Plains and the Horrors of Indian Warfare*. St. Louis: Sun Publishing, 1883.

de Quille, Dan. *The Big Bonanza*. New York: Knopf, 1967.

Ewers, John C., *Artists of the Old West*. Garden City, N.Y.: Doubleday, 1973.

Harte, Bret, *The Letters of Bret Harte*. Assembled and edited by Geoffrey Bret Harte. New York: Houghton Mifflin, 1926.

——, *The Luck of Roaring Camp and Other Sketches*. Boston: Fields, Osgood, 1870.

Hendricks, Gordon, *Albert Bierstadt, Painter of the American West*. New York: Harry Abrams in association with the Amon Carter Museum of Western Art, 1974.

Jackson, Helen Hunt, *A Century of Dishonor*, Andrew F. Rolle, ed. New York: Harper & Row, The University Library, 1965.

King, Clarence, *Mountaineering in the Sierra Nevada*. Boston: J. R. Osgood, 1872.

Miller, David Humphreys, *Custer's Fall*. New York: Bantam Books, 1972.

Monaghan, Jay, *The Life of General George Armstrong Custer*. Boston: Little, Brown, 1959.

Naef, Weston J., in collaboration with James N. Wood, *Era of Exploration*. Boston: Albright- Knox Art Gallery and The Metropolitan Museum of Art, 1975. (Distributed by New York Graphic Society.)

Nordhoff, Charles, *California: For Health, Pleasure, and Residence. A Book for Travellers and Settlers*. New York: Harper & Brothers, 1873.

Rideing, William Henry, *A Saddle in the Wild West*. New York: Appleton, 1879.

Stevenson, Robert Louis, *The Amateur Emigrant Across the Plains: The Silverado Squatters*. New York: Scribner, 1895.

——, *From Scotland to Silverado*, James D. Hart, ed. Cambridge: Belknap Press of Harvard University Press, 1966.

Taft, Robert, *Artists & Illustrators of the Old West 1850–1900*. New York: Crown, Bonanza Books, 1951.

Van de Water, Frederic F., *Glory-Hunter*. Indianapolis: Bobbs-Merrill, 1934.

Washburn, Wilcomb E., *The American Indian and the United States*. Vol. I. New York: Random House, 1973.

——, *The Indian in America*. New York: Harper & Row, 1975.

MISCELLANEOUS

Annual Report Upon the Geographical Survey West of the One Hundredth Meridian in California, Nevada, Utah, Colorado, Wyoming, New Mexico, Arizona, and Montana by George M. Wheeler, First Lieutenant of Engineers, U.S.A., Being Appendix JJ of the Annual Report of the Chief of Engineers for 1876. Washington, D.C.: Government Printing Office, 1876.

Williams' Illustrated Transcontinental Guide of Travel. The Pacific Tourist. New York: Henry T. Williams, Publisher, 1876.

III WASHINGTON

BOOKS

Adams, Henry Brooks, *Democracy*. New York: Airmont, 1968. (Originally published in 1880.)

Ames, Mary Clemmer, *Ten Years in Washington: Life and Scenes in the National Capital, as a Woman Sees Them*. Hartford, Conn.: H. D. Worthington, 1877.

Buel, J. W., *Mysteries and Miseries of America's Great Cities, Embracing New York, Washington City, San Francisco, Salt Lake City, and New Orleans*. Cincinnati: Cincinnati Publishing Co., 1883.

Ellis, John B., *The Sights and Secrets of the National Capital: A Work Descriptive of Washington City in all its Various Phases*. New York: United States Publishing Company, 1869.

Green, Constance McLaughlin, *The Secret City: A History of Race Relations in the Nation's Capital*. Princeton: Princeton University Press, 1967.

Washington: Village and Capital, 1800–1878. Princeton: Princeton University Press, 1962.

Hutchins, Stilson, and Moore, Joseph West, *The National Capital Past and Present: Its Historical Objects, Public Buildings, Memorial Statuary and Beautiful Homes*. Washington, D.C.: Post Publishing Co., 1885.

Keim, de B. Randolph, ed., *Washington its Public and Private Edifices, Interiors, Monuments and Works of Art: A Collection of Superior Engravings on Wood, by Eminent Artists*. Washington, D.C.: 1881.

Moore, Joseph West, *Picturesque Washington: Pen and Pencil Sketches*. Providence, R.I.: J. A. & R. A. Reid, 1884.

Roberts, Chalmers M., *Washington Past and Present: A Pictorial History*. Washington, D.C.: Public Affairs Press, 1949–1950.

Twain, Mark, and Warner, Charles Dudley, *The Gilded Age: A Tale of To-Day*, Bryant Morey French, ed. Indianapolis: Bobbs-Merrill, 1972.

MISCELLANEOUS

Keim's Illustrated Hand-Book. Washington and Its Environs: A Descriptive and Historical Hand-Book of the Capital of the United States of America. Washington City: The Compiler, 1884.

Morrisons' Stranger's Guide and Etiquette, for Washington City and its Vicinity. Washington, D.C.: W. H. & O. H. Morrison, 1862.

Roose's Companion and Guide to Washington and Vicinity. Washington, D.C.: Gibson Brothers, Printers, 1882.

Roose's Illustrated Washington. Washington, D.C.: Gibson Brothers, Printers, 1876.

IV THE STOLEN ELECTION OF 1876

BOOKS

Anthony, Susan B., and Stanton, Elizabeth Cady, eds., *History of Women's Suffrage*. New York: Published by Anthony and Matilda Joslyn Gage, 1886.

Bigelow, John, ed., *Letters and Literary Memorials of Samuel J. Tilden*. Port Washington, N.Y.: Kennikat Press, 1971: (Reprint of 1908 edition.)

Bradley, Charles, ed., *Miscellaneous Writings of the Late Honorable Joseph P. Bradley*. Newark, N.J.: L. J. Hardham, 1902.

Eckenrode, H. J., *Rutherford B. Hayes: Statesman of Reunion*. Port Washington, N.Y.: Kennikat Press, 1963.

Flick, Alexander Clarence, *Samuel Jones Tilden: A Study in Political Sagacity*. New York: Dodd, Mead, 1939.

Jarrell, Hampton M., *Wade Hampton and the Negro: The Road Not Taken*. Columbia: University of South Carolina Press, 1950.

Logan, Mary, *Reminiscences of the Civil War and Reconstruction*, George Worthington Adams, ed. Carbondale & Edwardsville: Southern Illinois University Press, 1970.

Nevins, Allan, *Abram S. Hewitt with some Account of Peter Cooper*. New York: Harper & Brothers, 1935.

Parker, Gail, ed. and intro., *The Oven Birds: American Women on Womanhood 1820–1920.*Garden City, N.Y.: Doubleday, Anchor books, 1972.

Polikoff, Keith Ian, *The Politics of Inertia*. Baton Rouge: Louisiana State University Press, 2973.

Stanton, Elizabeth Cady, *Eighty Years & More: Reminiscences, 1815–1897*. Intro. by Gail Parker. New York: Schocken Books, 1971.

Swanberg, W. A., *Sickles the Incredible*. New York: Scribner, 1956.

Wall, Joseph Frazier, *Henry Watterston: Reconstructed Rebel*. New York: Oxford University Press, 1956.

Wallace, Lew, *An Autobiography*: Vol. II. New York: Garrett Press, 1969. (Photographic reprint of 1906 edition.)

Williams, T. Harry, ed., *Hayes: The Diary of a President, 1875–1881*. New York: David McKay, 1964.

Woodward, C. Vann, *Origins of the New South 1877–1913*. Baton Rouge: Louisiana State University Press, 1971.

Reunion and Reaction: The Compromise of 1877 and the End of Reconstruction. Boston: Little, Brown, 1966.

——, *The Burden of Southern History*. New York: Random House, Vintage Books, 1961.

PERIODICALS

Sternstein, Jerome L., "The Sickles Memorandum: Another Look at the Hayes-Tilden Election-Night Conspiracy." *Journal of Southern History*, Vol. XXXII (August 1966).

MISCELLANEOUS

The Declaration of Women's Rights, 1876.

Wade Hampton, Free Men, Free Ballots, Free Schools—The Pledges of General Wade Hampton, Democratic Candidate for Governor to the Colored People.

Schatten, Samuel Jay, *The Election of 1876 and the Compromise of 1877: A Different Viewpoint*. Unpublished M.S. senior thesis. Department of History, Princeton University.

V THE PLIGHT OF THE POOR

BOOKS

Baguenal, Philip, *The American Irish and Their Influence on Irish Politics*. London and Boston: Roberts Brothers, 1882.

Brace, C. L., *The Dangerous Classes of New York and Twenty Years Work Among Them*. New York: Wynkoop & Hallenbeck, 1872.

Bremner, Robert, *From the Depths: The Discovery of Poverty in the United States*. New York: New York University Press, 1956.

Broehl, Wayne G., Jr., *The Molly Maguires*. Boston: Harvard University Press, 1964.

Cable, George W., *The Negro Question*. Garden City, N.Y.: Doubleday, 1958.

Clemens, Samuel, *The Writings of Mark Twain*. New York: G. Wells & Co., 1922–25.

Coolidge, Mary R., *Chinese Immigration*. New York: Holt, 1909.

Dann, Martin E., ed., *The Black Press 1827–1890*. New York: Putnam, 1971.

Delaney, Martin R., *The Beginnings of Black Nationalism*. Boston: Beacon Press, 1970.

Dewees, F. A., *The Molly Maguires: The Origin, Growth, and Character of the Organization*. Philadelphia: Lippincott, 1877.

Dugdale, Richard, *The Jukes*. New York: Putnam, 1877.

Eggleston, Edward, *The Hoosier Schoolmaster*. New York: O. Judd, 1871.

Foner, Philip S., ed., *The Life and Writings of Frederick Douglass*. Vols. I–IV. New York: International Publishers, 1950-55.

George, Henry, *Progress and Poverty*. New York: Robert Schalkenbach Foundation, 1963.

Gompers, Samuel, *Seventy Years of Life and Labor*. Vol. I. New York: Augustus Kelley, 1967.

Harlan, Louis R., *The Negro in American History*. Washington, D.C.: American Historical Association, 1965.

Harris, Middleton, et al., *The Black Book*. New York: Random House, 1973.

Harte, Bret, *The Writings of Bret Harte*. 19 vols. Boston: Houghton Mifflin, 1896–1903.

Hofstadter, Richard, *Great Issues in American Thought*. Vols. I and II. New York: Knopf, Vintage Books, 1958.

Holland, R. W., ed., *Letters and Diary of Laura M. Towne 1862–1884, Written from the Sea & Shards of South Carolina*. Cambridge: Riverside Press, 1912.

Hughes, Langston, et al., *A Pictorial History of Black Americans*. New York: Crown, 1973.

Jones, Maldwyn Allen, *American Immigration*. Chicago: University of Chicago Press, 1960.

Pinkerton, Allan, *The Molly Maguires and the Detectives*. New York: Dover, 1973.

Powderly, Terence V., *The Path I Trod*. New York: Columbia University Press, 1940.

Schnapper, M. B., *American Labor: A Pictorial Social History*. Washington, D.C.: Public Affairs Press, 1972.

Seward, George F., *Chinese Immigration: Its Economical & Social Aspects*. New York: Scribner, 1882.

Smith, Matthew Hale, *Sunshine and Shadow in New York*: Hartford, Conn.: Q. B. Burr, 1869.

Tourgée, Albion, *A Fool's Errand*. New York: Fords, Howard and Hulbert, 1879.

Twain, Mark, *Life as I Find It*. Garden City, N.Y.: Hanover House, 1961.

——, *The Gilded Age*. Hartford, Conn.: American Publishing Co., 1873.

Washington, Booker T., *Up From Slavery*. New York: Doubleday, Page, 1901.

Whitman, Walt, *Two Rivulets*. Camden, N.J.: By the Author, 1876.

William, George W., *History of the Negro Race in America from 1619–1880*. Vol. II. New York: Putnam, 1882.

PERIODICALS

"Three Typical Workingmen." *Atlantic Monthly* (December 1878).

"The Southern Question." *North American Review* (November 1873).

"The Immigrant's Progress." *Scribner's Monthly*, Vol. XIV (September 1877), pp. 577–88.

Frank Leslie's Popular Monthly Magazine

Harper's Weekly (1876)

MISCELLANEOUS

Andersen, M. B., "Alien Paupers." *The Eighth Annual Report of the State Board of Charities of the State of New York, 1875*, pp. 132–39. Albany: Weed, Parsons & Co., 1875, for New York State Government.

California Senate Memorial to Congress, 1876.

Chinese Immigration: Testimony Before a Committee of the Senate of the State of California, 1876.

Report by Frank B. Sanborn, Secretary of the Massachusetts State Board of Charities for the National Conference of Charities and Correction. Proceedings, 1876. Boston, 1876.

Testimony Before a Committee of the Senate of the State of California, Appointed April 3, 1876. Sacramento: State Printing Office, 1876.

The Congressional Record, 1876. Robert Smalls' Speech on the 44th Congress, 1st Session. Hamburg Riots. Vol. IV, part 5, 4641–4642.

Transactions of the American Medical Association. Vol. XXVII, 1876, pp. 106–7.

"Workingmen's Party Anti-Chinese Platform, California, 1876." *Workingmen's Party of California: An Epitome of Its Rise & Progress.* San Francisco, 1878.

VI   THE GREAT AMERICAN FORTUNES

BOOKS

Adams, Charles F., Jr., and Adams, Henry, *Chapters of Erie and Other Essays (1871).* New York: Augustus Kelley, 1967. (Originally published in 1871.)

Adler, Cyrus, *Jacob H. Schiff, His Life and Letters.* 2 vols. Garden City, N.Y.: Doubleday, Doran, 1929.

Andrews, Wayne, *The Vanderbilt Legend.* New York: Harcourt, Brace, 1941.

Auchincloss, Louis, *Edith Wharton: A Woman in Her Time.* New York: Viking, 1971.

Birmingham, Stephen, *The Grandees: America's Sephardic Elite.* New York: Harper & Row, 1971.

——.*"Our Crowd": The Great Jewish Families of New York.* New York: Harper & Row, 1967.

Blay, John S., *After the Civil War: A Pictorial Profile of America from 1865 to 1900.* New York: Crown, Bonanza Books, 1960.

Blum, Stella, ed. and intro., *Victorian Fashions & Costumes from Harper's Bazar: 1867–1898.* New York: Dover, 1974.

Brown, Dee, *The Year of the Century: 1876.* New York: Scribner, 1966.

Canfield, Cass, *The Incredible Pierpont Morgan: Financier and Art Collector.* New York: Harper & Row, 1974.

Carnegie, Andrew, *Autobiography of Andrew Carnegie.* Boston: Houghton Mifflin—Riverside Press, Cambridge, 1920.

Chanler, Mrs. Winthrop, *Roman Spring.* Boston: Little, Brown, 1934.

De Garmo, Wm. B., *The Dance of Society: A Critical Analysis of all the Standard Quadrilles, Round Dances, 102 Figures of Le Cotillon ("The German,"), Etc.* New York: By the Author, 1879.

DePew, Chauncey, *My Memories of 80 Years.* New York: Scribner, 1922.

De Quille, Dan, *The Big Bonanza,* Oscar Lewis and Robert Glass Cleland, eds. New York: Knopf, 1967. (Originally published in 1876.)

Downing, Antoinette F., and Scully, Vincent J., Jr., *The Architectural Heritage of Newport, Rhode Island: 1640–1915.* Cambridge: Harvard University Press, 1952.

Eliot, Elizabeth, *Heiresses and Coronets: The Story of Lovely Ladies and Noble Men.* New York: McDowell, Obolensky, 1959.

Elliott, Maud Howe, *This Was My Newport.* Cambridge: The Mythology Company—A. Marshall Jones, 1944.

Eskew, G. L., *Willard's of Washington: The Epic of a Capital Caravansary.* New York: Coward-McCann, 1954.

Gaston, Paul M., *The New South Creed: A Study in Southern Mythmaking.* New York: Random House, Vintage Books, 1973.

Harte, Bret, *The Writings of Bret Harte.* 19 vols. Boston: Houghton Mifflin, 1896–1903.

Harvey, George, *Henry Clay Frick, The Man.* New York: Scribner, 1928.

Holbrook, Stewart H., *The Age of the Moguls,* Lewis Gannett, ed. Garden City, N.Y.: Doubleday, 1953.

Hoyt, Edwin P., Jr., *The House of Morgan.* New York: Dodd, Mead, 1966.

James, Henry, *An International Episode.* London: Macmillan, 1879.

James, Theodore, Jr., *Fifth Avenue.* Photographs by Elizabeth Baker. New York: Walker, 1971.

Josephson, Matthew, *The Robber Barons.* New York: Har-

court, Brace & World, 1962.

Kavaler, Lucy, *The Astors: A Family Chronicle of Pomp and Power.* New York: Dodd, Mead, 1966.

Kennan, George, *E. H. Harriman: A Biography.* 2 vols. Boston: Houghton Mifflin—Riverside Press, Cambridge, 1922.

Kogan, Herman, and Wendt, Lloyd, *Give the Lady What She Wants!: The Story of Marshall Field & Company.* Chicago: Rand McNally, 1952.

Lewis, R. W. B., *Edith Wharton—A Biography.* New York: Harper & Row, 1975.

Lynes, Russell, *The Taste-Makers.* New York: Harper & Brothers, 1955.

McAllister, Ward, *Society as I Have Found It.* New York: Cassell, 1890.

McCormick, Cyrus, *The Century of the Reaper.* Boston: Houghton Mifflin—Riverside Press, Cambridge, 1931.

Minnegerode, Meade, *Certain Rich Men.* New York: Putnam, 1927.

Morris, Lloyd, *Incredible New York (1850–1950).* New York: Random House, 1957.

Nevins, Allan, *Study in Power: John D. Rockefeller, Industrialist and Philanthropist.* 2 vols. New York: Scribner, 1953.

Nevins, Allan, and Thomas, Milton Halsey, eds., *The Diary of George Templeton Strong, 1835–1875.* 4 vols. New York: Macmillan, 1952.

Newmark, Harris, *Sixty Years in Southern California: 1853–1913.* Maurice H. and Marco R. Newmark, eds. Los Angeles: Zeitlin & Verbrugge, 1970.

O'Connor, Harvey, *The Astors.* New York: Knopf, 1941.

——, *Mellon's Millions.* New York: John Day, 1933.

Rives, Reginald W., *The Coaching Club: Its History, Records and Activities.* New York: Derrydale Press, 1935.

Saarinen, Aline B., *The Proud Possessors: The Lives, Times and Tastes of Some Adventurous American Art Collectors.* New York: Random House, 1958.

Satterlee, Herbert L., *J. Pierpont Morgan: An Intimate Portrait.* New York: Macmillan, 1939.

Saunders, Edith, *The Age of Worth: Couturier to the Empress Eugénie.* Bloomington: Indiana University Press, 1955.

Scully, Vincent J., Jr., *The Shingle Style and the Stick Style: Architectural Theory and Design from Downing to the Origins of Wright.* Rev. ed. New Haven: Yale University Press, 1971.

Smith, Matthew Hale, *20 Years Among the Bulls & Bears of Wall Street.* Hartford, Conn.: J. B. Burr, 1870.

Swanberg, W. A., *Jim Fisk: The Career of an Improbable Rascal.* New York: Scribner, 1959.

Tarkington, Booth, *The Magnificent Ambersons.* New York: Avon Books, 1969.

Thomas, Lately, *A Pride of Lion: The Astor Orphans—The Chanler Chronicle.* New York: Morrow, 1971.

Tomkins, Calvin, *Merchants and Masterpieces: The Story of the Metropolitan Museum of Art.* New York: Dutton, 1970.

Twain, Mark, *The Gilded Age.* Hartford, Conn.: American Publishing Co., 1873.

Van Rensselaer, Mrs., King, *Newport, Our Social Capital.* Philadelphia: Lippincott, 1905.

Wall, Joseph Frazier, *Andrew Carnegie.* New York: Oxford University Press, 1970.

Wecter, Dixon, *The Saga of American Society: A Record of Social Aspiration 1607–1937.* New York: Scribner, 1970.

Wharton, Edith, *The Age of Innocence.* New York: Scribner, 1920.

——, *A Backward Glance.* New York: Scribner, 1933

Winkler, John K., *Tobacco Tycoon: The Story of James Buchanan Duke.* New York: Random House, 1942.

Woodward, C. Vann, *Origins of the New South, 1877–1913.* Volume IX, Wendell Holmes Stephenson and E. Merton Coulter, eds. Louisiana State University Press—The Littlefield Fund for Southern History of the University of Texas, 1951.

PERIODICALS

James, Henry, "The Sense of Newport." *Harper's Monthly Magazine* (August 1906).

"Saratoga Springs." *Harper's New Monthly Magazine*, Vol. 53 (June–November 1876), p. 385.

VII   P. T. BARNUM

BOOKS

Barnum, P. T., *Struggles and Triumphs of P. T. Barnum Told by Himself,* John G. O'Leary, ed. The Fitzroy Edition. London: MacGibbon & Kee, 1967. (First published in 1882.)

Conklin, George, *Ways of the Circus.* New York: Harper & Brothers, 1921.

Durant, Alice, and Durant, John, *Pictorial History of the American Circus.* New York: Barnes, 1957.

Fenner, Mildred Sandison, and Fenner, Wolcott, compilers and eds., *The Circus: Lure and Legend.* Englewood

Cliffs, N.J.: Prentice-Hall, 1970.

Harris, Neil, *Humbug: The Art of P. T. Barnum.* Boston: Little, Brown, 1973.

Leland, Charles Godfrey, *Memoirs.* New York: Appleton, 1893.

May, Earl Chapin, *The Circus from Rome to Ringling.* New York: Dover, 1932 and 1963.

Rourke, Constance Mayfield, *Trumpets of Jubilee.* New York: Harcourt, Brace, 1927.

Sherwood, Robert Edmund, *Here We Are Again.* Indianapolis: Bobbs-Merrill, 1926.

——.*Hold Yer Hosses!* New York: Macmillan, 1932.

VIII   TOM SAWYER

BOOKS

Anderson, Frederick, ed., with the assistance of Kenneth M. Sanderson, *Mark Twain: The Critical Heritage.* New York: Barnes & Noble, 1971.

Kaplan, Justin, *Mr. Clemens and Mark Twain: A Biography.* New York: Simon & Schuster, 1966.

Lynn, S. Kenneth, *The Dream of Success: A Study of the Modern American Imagination.* Boston: Little, Brown, in association with the Atlantic Monthly Press, 1955.

Meltzer, Milton, *Mark Twain Himself: A Pictorial Biography.* New York: Crown, Bonanza Books, 1960.

Paine, Albert Bigelow, commentary, *Letters of Mark Twain.* London: Chatto & Windus, 1920.

——, commentary, *Mark Twain's Letters.* 2 vols. New York: Harper & Brothers, 1917.

——, intro., *Mark Twain's Speeches.* New York: Harper & Brothers, 1923.

Twain, Mark, *Tom Sawyer in the Family Mark Twain.* New York: Harper & Row, 1972.

PERIODICALS

Howells, William Dean. Unsigned review of *Tom Sawyer. Atlantic,* Vol. XXXVII (May 1876), pp. 621–22.